FRENCH LEGITIMISTS

Robert R. Locke

FRENCH LEGITIMISTS
and the
POLITICS OF MORAL ORDER
in the
EARLY THIRD REPUBLIC

PRINCETON UNIVERSITY PRESS

PRINCETON, NEW JERSEY

Library of Congress Cataloging in Publication Data will
be found on the last printed page of this book

Publication of this book has been aided by the
Andrew W. Mellon Foundation

This book has been composed in Times Roman

Printed in the United States of America
by Princeton University Press, Princeton, New Jersey

To PATSY

CONTENTS

ACKNOWLEDGMENTS

When I first arrived in France in order to conduct research on legitimists, I was completely ignorant about private manuscript sources. Inasmuch as legitimists belonged to prominent French families, I decided to look for their descendants, hoping that they might direct me to manuscript collections. I consulted the *Bottin mondain* and *Who's Who in France*, selected scores of names that were the same or similar to those of the men who interested me, and sent out letters of inquiry. The response was gratifying. People who were not related to the legitimists (despite their names) but who knew of the family in question often passed my letter on to the proper person or gave me his address. Addressees who came from a family's collateral branch frequently gave me the address of the family head. Sometimes, of course, people did not cooperate and never bothered to reply. One fellow, who was not related to the legitimist, mistook my request for a practical joke and responded in kind. But the number of letters that I received expressing interest in my project and offering aid greatly exceeded expectations.

Usually, the correspondent informed me either that the family's archives did not exist (because they had been lost when the family moved from its ancestral home or because they had been destroyed by the Germans, but never the allies, during World War II) or that they contained nothing about the legitimist. But in the same letter or package that brought this disappointing news, I often received newspaper clippings, death notices, biographical sketches, brochures, pamphlets, and even books written about or by the member of the family in whom I was interested. A number of people, moreover, answered that they possessed papers which I could consult. As a result, I spent several months working in private manuscript sources, in municipal libraries, and in departmental archives located in almost every region of France. This reception from the descendants of the legitimists made research not only profitable in terms of scholarship but also a rich and memorable personal experience for both my wife and myself.

I should like therefore, to express my gratitude toward the many people who responded so graciously to my requests. In particular, I want to thank the following descendants of the royalists for their hospitality when we visited their homes: Messieurs et Mesdames Bleynie (of Limoges), Benoist d'Azy (of St-Benin d'Azy, the Nièvre), de La Boisse (of Toulon), Chaurand (of Paysac, Ardèche), de Cornulier-Lucinière (of Rennes), Costa de Beauregard (of Douvaine, Haute-Savoie), Gontaut-Biron (of the Château de Navailles, Basses-Pyrénées), Fresneau (of Bourg-des-Comptes, Ille-et-Vilaine), de La Guiche (of St. Bonnet-de-Joux, Saône-et-Loire), Malartre (of Dunières, Haute-Loire), d'Iribarne (of St-Jean-le-Vieux, Basses-Pyrénées), de Lordat (of St-Chaptes, Gard), de Sugny (of Paris), and Viennet (of Béziers, Hérault). Without their cooperation this book could not have been written.

I should also like to thank the staffs of the Bibliothèque nationale, the Archives nationales, and of the numerous departmental archives and municipal libraries for their labors on my behalf. I am deeply indebted to Eugene N. Anderson, Emeritus Professor of the University of California, Los Angeles, for his constant encouragement and invaluable criticism, and to Richard H. Levensky, Hans Medick, and Douglas Wagner whose incisive but friendly comments have helped to focus my ideas. Charles J. Zekus III drew the maps. Fellowships from the University of California at Los Angeles partially defrayed the cost of a two-year stay in France. A grant from the Fordham University Research Council helped pay for clerical costs. Last of all, I must thank my wife whose tireless effort, endless patience, and good humor have made the writing of this book bearable.

R. R. L.

FRENCH LEGITIMISTS

Systems of religion, of general politics, morality, of public instruction are nothing else than applications of a system of ideas, or if one prefers, it is the system of thought considered under different aspects.

Henri de Saint-Simon
Mémoire sur la science de l'homme

INTRODUCTION

The terms royalist or monarchist can be applied to anybody who believes in a monarchical form of government. That of legitimist refers specifically to people who support hereditary monarchy. Legitimists are royalists and monarchists, royalists and monarchists can be legitimists, but not necessarily. In nineteenth-century French political parlance, legitimist is used to identify those who favor the restoration of the elder branch of the Bourbon monarchy, and this is the sense in which it is employed here. Technically, legitimists existed as a viable, if unstable, group during the short time span from 1830 to 1883. The first date marks the fall of Charles X, the elevation of Louis Philippe, and consequently the creation of a deep schism between the supporters of the elder and the cadet branch of the royal family. This division ended formally in 1883 when, with the death of the childless Comte de Chambord (grandson of Charles X), his cousin, the Comte de Paris (grandson of Louis Philippe), became the legitimate heir to the throne. There were inveterate anti-Orleanists in Chambord's entourage who, rather than recognize an Orleanist as the legitimate pretender, threw their support to the Spanish Bourbons, but they were few in number. After Chambord's death, legitimacy devolved to the Orleanist line. When all royalists, with the exception of the Bonapartists, supported the hereditary monarchy they were technically legitimists, but there was no reason to refer to them as such because the terms royalist and legitimist were interchangeable. Only when the supporters of the hereditary monarchy constituted a group among other monarchists did legitimist have a special meaning, and this was the case while Chambord lived. Still this is just a clarification of the term. The question of who could be called a legitimist during the historical period under consideration is a complicated one, and will be handled later.

Between 1830 and 1883 the political fortunes of legitimism varied considerably. Less than two years after the Revolution of 1830, the Duchesse de Berry, Chambord's mother, appeared in

France and raised the standards of revolt in favor of her son, but the venture collapsed without posing much of a threat to the July Monarchy. Indeed, it degenerated into farce when the queen mother embarrassed the monarchy's supporters by giving birth to a bastard child—the result of an affair with an Italian noble-man—while in the act of upholding the sacred principle of legiti-macy. Thereafter an occasional prolegitimist demonstration oc-curred inside and outside of France but they troubled the Orleanist regime even less than the Duchess's escapade. The Revolution of 1848 brought a brief recrudescence in legitimist activity because of the monarchist victory in the legislative elec-tions of 1849, but while Orleanists bickered with legitimists over a possible restoration, Louis Napoleon executed the *coup d'état* that silenced all opposition. Then ensued a long twilight during the Second Empire when Chambord and his adherents suffered a political eclipse—to be followed, however, after the Empire's col-lapse and the election of a National Assembly, by a sudden re-versal of fortune and the most sustained and serious attempt to restore the old monarchy since 1830. For the first few years of the Third Republic, legitimists in France carried on an active cam-paign among all monarchists on Chambord's behalf, but they failed when the pretender refused to make the concessions crucial for gaining broad conservative support. There the matter ended. The occasion lost, there were no more occasions.

This brief narrative, of course, does not do justice to the inter-esting and sometimes exciting intrigues among the various mon-archist groups and the negotiations between them and Chambord that formed the chain of events constituting the attempts to restore the monarchy. But these events, which have been described in an abundant historical literature, are not what inspired this study of legitimism.[1] It was the phenomenon of legitimism itself considered

---

[1] For narratives of the polemics among monarchists see, among others, relative sections in Marvin L. Brown, Jr., *The Comte de Chambord, The Third Republic's Uncompromising King* (Durham, North Carolina, 1967); Emmanuel Beau de Loménie, *La restauration manquée: L'affaire du drapeau blanc* (Paris, 1932); Gabriel-Adrien Robinet de Cléry, *Les deux fusions, 1800–1873* (Paris, 1908); Claude-Noël Desjoyeaux, *La fusion monarchique, 1848–1873* (Paris, 1913); and Arthur Loth, *L'échec de la restauration monarchique en 1873* (Paris, 1910). Innumerable memoirs also touch on the subject. See M. L. Brown's bibliography and in particular, Charles Chesnelong, *Un témoignage sur un point d'histoire: La campagne monar-chique d'octobre 1873* (Paris, 1895); Marquis Henri-Scipion-Claude de

against the long-term process of social, economic, and political change in nineteenth-century France that drew my attention. When I first discovered the legitimists, while studying the origins of the Third Republic, it was surprising to find, in a France profoundly affected by the French and Industrial Revolutions, so many legitimists, especially those in a position of national prominence, for I had conceived of legitimists as some sort of historical freaks, men who existed without any contact with or idea about the world. It was as if time had stopped for them in 1789 and they had not been touched by their environment. If this were true, then the mentality of the men and their political influence could be explained only as a historical anachronism. On the other hand, it seemed equally incredible and unhistorical that this could be the case. Every generation lives in a specific environment. It might be possible to long for a golden age in the past or yearn for a paradise in the future, but each could be conceived of only in terms of the present. If this is true, legitimists could not be anachronisms, but very much of their time. These considerations prompted me to ignore political events, in order to concentrate on an analysis of the effects that socioeconomic change (and the tensions it produced in French society) had on the socioeconomic position of legitimists, the legitimists' own criticism of the historical period in which they found themselves, and how a desire to restore the monarchy reflected their reaction to this changing environment. This decision was not determined by personal interest alone. The more I studied legitimists, the more convinced I became that to them politics was rooted in socioeconomic events and that a sociopsychological study of men within a specific historical context would add a dimension to understanding legitimism absent from political and intellectual histories because this approach was, in fact, their own.

Yet if the overall aim is to shed light on legitimism through a socioeconomic study of political psychology, the means for accomplishing this end are restricted. Historians are forced to base their reflections on extensive documentation and since research is time-consuming and often fruitless the number of historical figures subject to examination is limited. This is especially true for

---

Dreux-Brézé, *Notes et souvenirs pour servir à l'histoire du parti royaliste, 1872–1883* (Paris, 1902); and Duc d'Audiffret-Pasquier, *La Maison de France et l'Assemblée nationale. Souvenirs, 1871–1873* (Paris, 1938).

a study that purports to determine not only what a man's political convictions were but also why he held them and what they meant to him. To answer such questions, details about experience and thought are required that can only be furnished by extensive documentation. Moreover, the problem of documentation is compounded by the necessity to find subjects for analysis who will permit the historian to acquire the most information according to the analytical methods employed and aims sought. Thus, it was necessary to choose which legitimists should and could be studied, in order to gain the maximum insight into legitimism, and I chose to concentrate mainly on the legitimist deputies in the National Assembly of 1871.

Parliaments are debating societies where members express their opinions about the multitude of problems that beset a society. These viewpoints are duly recorded and preserved for public inspection. It scarcely needs to be stressed that parliamentary debates, minutes of committee hearings, legislative bills, and parliamentary investigations provide a great amount of information on what legitimist deputies thought of their world—information that cannot be duplicated for nonparliamentarians. Since members of elected assemblies, moreover, are people about whom biographical data is systematically collected, parliamentarians are more easily identifiable than others in society. This does not mean that the task of studying parliamentarians is simple. Even when working with elected representatives, the problem of finding information can be exasperating. Some men wrote memoirs, made speeches, spoke frequently in committee meetings, and corresponded with their friends and family who saved their letters for future historians. Some men's presence in a legislature is revealed only by the perfume of their votes, and for others only very brief and not completely reliable biographical information is extant. In one case, the standard biographical dictionary (A. Robert, Bourlotin, and Cougny, *Dictionnaire des parlementaires français*) confused two legitimists with the result that there is no information on the man who actually served in the legislature and a biographical notice on the one who never did.[2] Yet the very difficulties involved in study-

---

[2] The biographical note given was for a Fleuriot de Langle. He was a candidate in 1871 (in Paris) but he lost. The deputy elected from Loire-Inférieure was Jacques Fleuriot de La Fleurière not Fleuriot de Langle. For biographical information on the deputy, see René Kerviler, *et al.*, *Répertoire général de bio-bibliographie bretonne* (Rennes, 1902), xiv, 90.

6

ing deputies is a justification for selecting them because the absence of information on men who did not sit in a legislature is all the greater.

Just as the lives of parliamentarians are easier to reconstruct than those of nonparliamentarians, so too are those of the members of some parliaments as opposed to others. Legitimists were especially numerous in the Legislative Assembly of 1849 and the National Assembly of 1871. Newspapers, parliamentary, and biographical sources are more complete for the latter assembly than for the former. The holdings for the National Assembly are very extensive and include the minutes of legislative committee hearings, while those for the Legislative Assembly are nonexistent. Because of the availability of source material for the former, the legitimists of this period were more suitable subjects for analysis.

Besides these men merit attention for more important reasons than practical research considerations. They were not typical legitimists, if for no other reason than that they were deputies. They were spokesmen for the legitimist community in France, formulators as well as reflectors of opinion, an elite among a group of notables who believed in elites. Who they were and what they thought were of more consequence than similar information about just any two hundred men. From the point of view adopted in this study, they were surely more significant than the pretender himself. Except for his childhood and a brief visit to France at the beginning of the Third Republic, Chambord lived in exile, most of the time in the tiny Austrian village of Frohsdorf where he occupied the château and in Venice where he kept a winter residence. While living abroad, he did not have much contact with France, not even regarding the politics of restoration. During the Second Empire, he formally communicated with supporters by corresponding with royalist committees set up in Paris and the provinces. But his agents inspired so little fear among the imperial police that they let his couriers travel freely though well aware of their identity. Even Chambord tacitly admitted his weakness when in 1870 he discontinued his courier service and corresponded with his moribund royalist committees through the regular mail.[3] Neither he nor his immediate entourage nor his committees had brought about the royalist political victories of royalists in 1871. They

[3] For a witty but revealing discussion of the ineffectuality of Chambord's organization and royalist activities, see Marquis de Belleval, *Souvenirs de ma jeunesse* (Paris, 1895). Belleval was one of Chambord's couriers.

7

sprang from the peculiar circumstances engendered by the Franco-Prussian War. Chambord's only impact on the restoration, although significant, was negative, for when the initiative came from his followers he, to their horror, spurned their advances. Since the politics of restoration were inextricable from the internal political situation, an investigation of the deputies who participated in the events, who were affected by them, and who in this capacity were agents of Chambord's restoration goes further in explaining the conjuncture of events and the part legitimists played in them than a study of any other group of men at this crucial moment in monarchist history.

The deputies, moreover, did not just pop out of the ground in 1871; their average age was fifty-two; many remembered the Restoration and July Monarchies; most had vivid recollections of the Revolution of 1848 and the June Days; and all had witnessed the rapid economic development of the Second Empire with its accompanying social dislocations, the Commune, and, as deputies, had seen the culmination of the sociopolitical process that led to the democratization of France under the Third Republic. In addition, the special circumstances under which the deputies took office compelled them to think more carefully than others before them about the complexities of the long-term economic, social, and political transformations that they had experienced. Because of the collapse of the Second Empire, the National Assembly was a constituent body. While the deputies fought over the restoration, they also struggled with reorganizing the army; reforming local and central government, state administration, and the magistracy; and with other vital matters including, of course, the causes of social discontent that had been so vividly expressed during the Commune. The special legislative situation that forced the deputies to record their attitudes about fundamental issues in great detail, and their participation in electoral conflicts, as well as their other experiences, make them particularly suitable subjects for analysis.

Throughout the research and writing of this book, I was constantly aware of certain historical problems. Social scientists and historians (to a much lesser extent) have developed teleological frameworks of historical analysis in which political, economic, and social factors are closely intertwined. In the context of recent French history, the transformations of society, brought about by industrialization, have formed the basis for analyzing the evolution of political strife. Indeed, politics in France during the last quarter of the nineteenth century has been conceived of not only as a reflection of underlying social and economic conditions but also as a key to the peculiar dynamics of industrialism. These ideas have special significance for a study of legitimists because they have been seen as the political representatives of socioeconomic groups who were being destroyed in the industrial process, whereas their opponents have been viewed as representatives of the political forces created by the social effects of the Industrial Revolution. The precise content given to the theoretical conceptions of the interrelatedness of political, economic, and social life raises problems that are frequently discussed here in connection with the place the legitimist deputies and their opponents occupied in their changing environment. These are old problems but important ones. In fact, most important problems are old ones because they present theoretical and practical complexities that are difficult to solve. But they are worth the effort. Therefore, it is hoped that this study of legitimists in France at the beginning of the Third Republic will make a contribution to the collective historical enterprise that seeks to clarify the social, political, and economic bases of the recent ideological struggles among Frenchmen for an appropriate social order and proper set of social values.

Chapter One

THE LEGITIMISTS IN 1871:
A PROBLEM IN IDENTIFICATION

The history of the election of February 8, 1871, which chose the deputies on whom this study is based, begins with the reanimation of French political life during the last few years of the Second Empire. After antagonizing much of the Right by his Italian and his trade policies, Napoleon III sought to rebuild the foundation of his dynasty on a popular basis by progressively liberalizing his regime. The powers of the Legislative Corps were increased vis-à-vis the executive. The Legislative Corps was authorized to elect its own officers, to debate the "discourse from the throne," to initiate laws, to vote the budget by chapter; and each member was permitted to question the government in the Chamber. At the same time, elections to the Legislative Corps were gradually freed from some of the worst abuses of Napoleonic authoritarianism. The radical republican exiles were allowed to return to France (1862); the government's close surveillance over the press was relaxed (1868); and the electorate was granted much freer rights of public assembly (1868). In addition, the imperial government sought the support of the industrial workers whose ranks had been rapidly augmented as a result of the unprecedented industrial expansion after 1851. Before 1864 disgruntled workers had been fairly well silenced by the heavy penalties that they incurred if they attempted to organize "a concerted cessation of work." In that year, however, the Emperor signed a law that granted the worker the right to strike. Although its terms were menacingly ambiguous (a strike could only be legal if it did not "infringe upon the free exercise of industry and the right to work,"[1]), the working classes seemed, for the first time, to have a government that would not invariably take the position of the employer in a labor dispute.

If Louis Napoleon sincerely hoped to induce liberals to rally to his Empire and to pacify the workers he was to be profoundly

---

[1] The text quoted from is given in Jean Montreuil, *Histoire du mouvement ouvrier en France des origines à nos jours* (Paris, 1946), p. 127.

disappointed. A few liberal republicans accepted the Empire, but radicals of Gambetta's stripe and the nineteenth century equivalent of the *sans culottes*—Blanquists, Proudhonists, and Marxists—remained irreconcilably republican. As for the workers, they seized on their new found freedoms to express their dissatisfaction. The liberalization of the regime, therefore, unleashed forces of popular discontent that had been pent up for more than a decade. During the years that preceded the Empire's collapse, strikes and radical political agitation became a normal part of the national scene, and the tempo of these disturbances augmented as the regime neared its unsuspected end. The year 1868 brought the great strikes at Roubaix and Decazeville, the summer and fall of 1869 the strikes of the miners in Rive-de-Gier and Carmaux, of the textile workers at Pellusin, Elboeuf, and Rouen, and of the carpenters in Vienne. In January 1870 a strike began in Le Creusot that dragged on intermittently into spring, spread to the neighboring ironworks in Fourchambault, and had repercussions in the industrial basin of St-Etienne. In March of the same year the textile workers in Le Havre, Sotteville, and Saint-Etienne-du-Rouvray went out on strike. In effect, just three weeks before the outbreak of the Franco-Prussian War the industrial world was in full ferment. As one anxious journalist wrote, "it was a tidal wave: for the single day June 24 there were strikes of various trades in Marseilles, Rouen, Fourchambault, Vienne, Lyons, Givors, Saint-Etienne, Rive-de-Gier [not to mention the most seriously affected area of all, Haut-Rhin]."[2] Concurrently, in the legislative elections of May 1869, the nation experienced the impact of a democratic electoral campaign, replete with the broad dissemination of electoral literature and the holding of mass electoral meetings. César Berthelon in St-Etienne and Raspail in Paris, both of whom had been exiled in 1852, made their reentry into political life. The young radical journalist Rochefort announced his candidacy in the capital. At Belleville Gambetta stated his famous manifesto that stood as a byword for French radicalism for more than a quarter of a century: complete freedom of assembly and the press; separation of Church and state; free, obligatory, lay, primary education; the election of all public officials; and "economic reforms

---

[2] Fernand L'Huillier, *La lutte ouvrière à la fin du Second Empire* (Paris, 1957), p. 59. L'Huillier gives a good description of this industrial strife. Also see, Pierre Ponsot, *Les grèves de 1870 et la Commune de 1871 au Creusot* (Paris, 1957).

which touch on the social problem, whose solution . . . must be constantly studied and sought after in the name of the principles of justice and social equality."[3] The feverish excitement which the radical campaign generated in the popular quarters of Paris and other big cities, the election of Adolphe Crémieux, Raspail, and Gambetta, and Rochefort's narrow loss in the Latin Quarter (to a republican) demonstrated conclusively that the revolutionary Left had reemerged as a major factor in French politics. Leftist political activities, moreover, did not stop after the legislative elections of 1869. Success at the polls and the realization that the industrial world was in turmoil spurred social democrats and radical republicans into a relentless campaign against the regime. The months that followed the May elections were trying ones for the Empire's supporters. The political agitation in the big cities and the industrial strikes reached such an intensity in the winter of 1869–1870 that they produced what one prominent historian has called a "climate of revolution" in the country.[4]

Thus France went to war in July 1870 against this background of political agitation and social unrest. This might have been of little immediate importance had the imperial armies won but they suffered irremediable reverses which, in turn, brought the Revolution of September 4 and the proclamation of the Republic. The heroic but tragic history of the period of national defense will not be recounted, but it is important to stress the connection between war and domestic politics. Although most Frenchmen responded to the call to national defense with patriotic enthusiasm, their patriotism was too often interpreted in terms of narrow partisanship. Most of the militant urban Left, the social democrats, would have seconded the opinion of a prominent member of the International who said, on September 4, that the "two great duties" of the revolutionaries were "the surveillance of the forces of reaction, within, and the defense of Paris against the enemy, without."[5] And radical republicans, if not interested in the social ideas of Blanquists, Proudhonists, Bakuninites, or Marxists, were no less partisan about the war. In the best Jacobin

---

[3] The quotation is taken from the Belleville manifesto in J. Rougerie, "Belleville," in Louis Girard, ed., *Les élections de 1869*, Bibliothèque de la Révolution de 1848, xxi (1960), 13.

[4] Marcel Blanchard, *Le Second Empire* (Paris, 1964), p. 191.

[5] Quoted in Edward S. Mason, *The Paris Commune* (New York, 1930), p. 65.

tradition, they believed that the conflict could be won only if it were waged "revolutionarily," that is, by a *levée en masse* carried out under their leadership. They would not have admitted that they subordinated the interests of national defense to their own political goals, yet they never separated the national from the political question. Partisanship and national interests merged in their minds.

As a result, the radical republican minority in the new government sought to impose its solution on the problems raised by national defense. Gambetta, as minister of the interior in the provisional government, installed "proven republicans" in his administration and dissolved, as centers "of every Bonapartist conspiracy," the monarchist-dominated general and municipal councils that had been chosen during the Second Empire.[6] The radicals consistently opposed armistice negotiations and general elections, for they feared that the ballots of the conservative peasantry would swamp the urban republican vote (as they had in 1849, 1869, and 1870) and undo the Revolution of September 4. In most large cities, moreover, social democratic clubs met on a regular basis to debate the conduct of the war, and in some they managed, during the confusion that accompanied the fall of the Empire, to gain control of the municipal government. This was true in Lyons, where the local social democrats established a committee of public safety and declared a commune (symbolically the red flag flew over the *Lyonnais Hôtel de ville* from September 4 until the end of the war); in Marseilles, where a civic guard "composed primarily of workers who were members of the International" had chased imperial civil and departmental authorities from office on September 5; and in Toulouse, where Jacobin extremists took over the municipal government as well as the government of the department of Haute-Garonne.[7] In Paris, as early as September 4, the Federal Council of the International decided to establish "a committee with members in every district [of the capital] whose function would be to supervise, or at least

---

[6] The quotation "of every Bonapartist conspiracy" is cited in Jacques Gouault, *Comment la France est devenue républicaine* (Paris, 1954), p. 33. For a list of Gambetta's prefectual appointments, see Pierre-Henry, *Histoire des préfets* (Paris, 1950). Also see J. P. T. Bury, *Gambetta and the National Defense* (London, 1936).

[7] For a discussion of leftist activities in Lyons and Toulouse, see Bury. For Marseilles see Antoine Olivesi, *La Commune de 1871 à Marseille et ses origines* (Paris, 1950), pp. 67–130.

investigate, the actions of government officials."[8] The International's organizational efforts were by no means exceptional, for other groups, professing a similar distrust of the "reactionaries," established watchdog committees of their own in various districts in the city. Indeed they soon amalgamated so that by September 11 the social democrats, like their counterparts in Russia in 1917, had created executive committees representing the various districts of Paris that constituted a rudimentary government within the capital independent of the regular communal administration.

In the chaos of revolution and invasion, radical republicans and social democrats served notice that they intended to combine patriotism with partisan politics. The period of national defense was punctuated by a number of revolutionary "days" that take their place in the rhetoric of French revolutionary history. Most of the disturbances occurred after news of military defeat aroused the suspicion that the "reactionaries" were selling out the nation in order to crush the revolution at home. After Bazaine's surrender at Metz (October 30), for example, units of the revolutionary National Guard in Paris, whose leaders demanded a radicalization of the government's policies, besieged *Hôtel de ville*, and almost toppled the shaky provisional government. Similar disturbances occurred in St-Etienne, where a "mob" succeeded in temporarily raising the red flag over city hall, and in Marseilles, where the revolutionary-minded civic guard, after deposing the government's officials, proclaimed a commune that reigned for three days over France's second city before Gambetta's talented *commissaire extraordinaire* Alphonse Gent could reestablish the government's control over the situation. These revolutionary "days" were only the more spectacular manifestation of the persistent discontent that emanated from the working class quarters of the bigger cities between September 1870 and February 1871. Throughout the war, as one of Gambetta's men in Lyons anxiously noted, "we lived in constant alarm. We were on the brink of a disturbance everyday."[9] The war therefore did not bring a respite in the left-wing political and social agitation that emerged at the end of the Second Empire. Radical republicans and social democrats, who had fought the Empire, continued to struggle after September 4, to make sure that the Republic assumed the political and social form they desired. Their efforts also continued

---

[8] Quoted in Mason, *The Paris Commune*, p. 65.
[9] Bury, *Gambetta and the National Defense*, p. 228.

after the armistice. In effect, the Commune was the dénouement of the revolutionary drama that had begun months before the outbreak of the conflict. It, not the war, was the real dividing point in the domestic history of France.

If democratic discontent was a dominant theme in domestic French history during these turbulent months, anxiety about this discontent was its counterpart. Perhaps the intensity of the fear was best expressed by a legitimist deputy at Versailles who wrote at the height of the Commune, "there are those who totally fail to see that social war is declared that the antagonism between those who possess and those who have nothing is ever growing, that it is our lives, our families, our possessions which are menaced as they have never been before."[10] But if fear of social revolution had been most pronounced during this civil war, it was not a feeling that was born with the outbreak of the insurrection. Radical political agitation and labor strife had convinced a large number of social conservatives of all political nuances at the end of the Empire that, in the words of the ultramontane Catholic deputy Charles Chesnelong, they should try "to regroup a nexus of social energies, of conservative forces, around the Empire in order to combat, by this league of public good, the coalitions of passions, hates, and revolutionary designs [in the country]."[11] The Empire's demise, therefore, was hardly greeted with enthusiasm by men of order. The Revolution of September 4, Gambetta's appointment as minister of the interior, his installation of "proven" republicans in his administration, and, above all, the popular disturbances in the cities throughout the conflict deepened their concern with the threat of social revolution. Many believed that the radical republican plan to wage a popular war threatened to destroy society more than the invading Germans, for they felt that an indiscriminate arming of the restless urban "mobs" would lead, as one anxious conservative put it, to the "moral" disintegration of

[10] Ltr., Pierre Soury-Lavergne to unknown, May 10, 1871. The letters of Soury-Lavergne are located in the family home in Rochechouart, the Haute-Vienne. They are not classified. Hereafter cited as *Soury-Lavergne MSS.*

[11] Ltr., Charles Chesnelong to Charles Kolb-Bernard, Oct. 23, 1869, Archives départementales (Basses-Pyrénées), *Chesnelong MSS*, Correspondance 1860–1876. Not classified. Hereafter cited as *Chesnelong MSS*. References to Archives départementales will be cited as A. D. (department's name). Chesnelong sat in the Legislative Corps, 1863–1870, and in the National Assembly of 1871.

15

the army and to "civil war."[12] However, this emphasis on counter-revolution was more concealed during the war than in other periods of domestic turmoil (as in 1848–1849 for example), for the war itself became the overriding issue in the fall and winter of 1870–1871. Yet the concern with anarchy and revolution that gripped conservatives determined to a very large extent their attitudes toward the war. They were outraged at the prospect of a dismemberment of the nation, and, in addition, many were reluctant to yield in what they considered a life and death struggle between Protestant Prussia and Catholic France. But as the war ground hopelessly on toward defeat, and as the country, in their eyes, seemed increasingly subject to revolutionary anarchy, more and more conservatives began to identify peace with their cause. "Peace will be hard," one monarchist noted in a typical statement, "but as an alternative there exists what has been called the red specter which for me is not a *spectre de théâtre* but a very real enemy, well armed, a great deal better organized than is supposed, and which is preparing for a veritable *jacquerie*."[13] Thus the Commune confirmed the darkest foreboding that social conservatives had felt in France since 1869. Their hysterical reaction to events in Paris formed a set piece with their uneasiness about labor strife and political discord at the end of the Empire and their alarm about domestic events during the war.

It was against this background of fairly rigid polarized revolutionary and counterrevolutionary opinion that Frenchmen engaged in electoral affairs in 1871. Elections were crucial contests because many Frenchmen believed that this elemental struggle would be decided on their outcome. The electoral confrontation, moreover, did not reflect the "normal" political divisions in France, for conservatives of all nuances tended to form a "party of order" against radical republicans and social democrats. There was nothing unprecedented about such electoral behavior. After the June Days of 1848, the apparition of the red specter had led to a

[12] Ltr., Charles Kolb-Bernard to Charles Chesnelong, Jan. 23, 1871, *Chesnelong MSS*. There are numerous letters from Kolb-Bernard to Chesnelong in the *Chesnelong MSS*. Kolb-Bernard represented the Nord in the Legislative Assembly of 1849, the Legislative Corps (1859–1870), the National Assembly of 1871, and the Senate (1876–1888).
[13] Ltr., Denys Benoist d'Azy to Charles Benoist d'Azy, Oct. 3, 1870, Archives of the Benoist d'Azy family: Correspondance, Comte Denys Benoist d'Azy, Château du Vieil Azy, St-Benin d'Azy (Nièvre). Hereafter cited as *Benoist d'Azy MSS*.

suspension of political antagonisms among conservatives, as, in the words of the manifesto issued by the central conservative committee, men of all parties "united in a common defense of a menaced society."[14] Moreover, the reawakening of fears of the revolutionary Left prevented anti-Bonapartist conservatives from pressing their attacks against the government's candidates in the legislative elections of 1869. There had been a plan for republicans, liberal monarchists, and legitimists to cooperate in the event of runoff elections but the success of the radicals on the first balloting, "carried out in the glittering arena of Paris and the other big cities," so frightened the monarchists that they quickly forgot any ideas they might have entertained about allying with republicans, even moderate ones. When forced to choose between a republican or a Bonapartist "the liberal conservatives and above all the legitimists voted for the official candidate [the Bonapartist] or abstained."[15] This tendency to subordinate dynastic convictions to a common fear of revolution was reinforced during the May plebiscite. The presence of active and noisy revolutionaries and the prevalence of industrial strikes contributed once again to the consolidation of a counterrevolutionary party. Republicans stayed in opposition, but legitimists, liberal monarchists, and nondynastic Catholics voted overwhelmingly in the Empire's favor, because its preservation was, in their opinion, the best bulwark against the revolution. Before the Empire had disappeared, therefore, concern about the red specter had pushed social conservatives toward electoral union, and after its fall the desire for peace and order prompted them to form the broad conservative coalition which emerged in the election of February 8, 1871.

Because elections were carried out under the trying circumstances created by war and invasion, historians have stressed their abnormality when explaining the monarchists' victory—to the point sometimes of making the circumstances, not the monarchists, completely responsible for the outcome. This attitude, in the case of the legitimists, derives, in part at least, from the assumption about the nature of the legitimist's relationship with his society mentioned in the "Introduction." Legitimists were alienated from nineteenth-

---

[14] Quoted in Pierre de La Gorce, *Histoire de la Seconde République française* (Paris, 1887), p. 134. The manifesto was issued by the Committee of the Rue de Poitier which was composed of Orleanists, legitimists, and Bonapartists.

[15] Louis Girard, ed., *Les élections de 1869*, p. xv.

century France, but observers have often concluded that this alienation meant that they were totally out of contact with political
events. Therefore, the victorious legitimist candidate of 1871, according to this logic, seemed to find himself, as if by a miracle,
suddenly thrust into an office that he neither coveted nor actively
planned to obtain.[16] The relationship between the legitimists and
their society will arise repeatedly in this study, but it is necessary,
considering that it lies at the heart of their success at the polls, to
consider it now strictly with regard to the electoral process.

One reason legitimist political activities in 1871 have been ignored is that the electoral period was very short, too short, it is
believed, for any real preparation to have occurred. As Gouault
pointed out in his study of the elections, "there was scarcely any
electoral campaign. More often than not the decree of January 29
convoking the electors was not known by people until January 31
or February 1. Certain prefects, like the one in the Bouches-du-
Rhône, who opposed elections, put off publishing it until February
3 or 4. And balloting took place on the eighth."[17] It is true that
the elections were carried out at short notice and that many of the
candidates knew nothing about elections until after they happened
because they were away fighting in the war. Among the legitimists,
for example, Cazenove de Pradine, who had been gravely wounded
when the Papal Zouaves charged the Prussian gunners at Patay,
learned about his election in the hospital; and Costa de Beauregard
received news of both his nomination and election by the same
post in an internment camp in Switzerland. Still if the bizarre
aspects of the election should not be overlooked, neither should
they be allowed to mislead. The number of legitimists who fought
in the war never exceeded 5 percent of the total number of candidates elected in 1871, for most of them were too old for military
service. Throughout the war most resided in the departments from
which they were elected, and those who did not had friends and
relatives who did the work on their behalf. Although the electoral
period was officially short, nothing stopped the legitimists from

---

[16] Jacques Gouault, for example, who has written the most thorough
account of the elections clearly supports this idea. See *Comment la France
est devenue républicaine*, p. 72.

[17] *Ibid.*, p. 59. Gouault devotes one page to electoral preparations, primarily to show that they were nonexistent. Others echo his opinion. Jacques
Chastenet wrote, for example, in *Enfance de la Troisième, 1870–1879*
(Paris, 1942), p. 51: "It was only in Paris, as also in Lyons and Marseilles
that the electoral committees showed any signs of electoral activity."

thinking about elections before the decree was issued. Conservatives of all political persuasions had been particularly preoccupied with the necessity to restore order after September 4, and the election of a National Assembly seemed the most appropriate method, under the circumstances, to accomplish their aims. More significantly, the possibility of elections was not a subject of idle speculation. The Government of National Defense first announced the election of a National Constituent Assembly on September 8, 1870. For nearly a month thereafter—despite a number of decrees that first advanced elections to October 2, then postponed them *sine die*, then reestablished them for October 16, and finally postponed them again *sine die* on October 9—Frenchmen believed elections would be held in October 1870.[18] After the postponement of October 9 they had no reason to think that elections would not be held in the immediate future. Elections were only delayed, and whenever there was speculation about an armistice, as in late October, November, and mid-January, the electoral issue arose again. The question, then, never was whether elections would be held but when, and there was no reason why conservatives should have awaited the official opening of the campaign before preparing for them.

Yet this only admits the possibility of electoral preparations. It does not prove they actually took place, for proof of electoral activity is not as easy to find for this election as for others in recent French history. The invasion caused a breakdown in the normal flow of information. Cut off from the rest of France, Paris, the customary center of national electoral activity, did not receive news of events in the provinces to any appreciable extent, although the provinces did receive news from Paris by balloon.[19] During the crisis Frenchmen fell back on local resources. Some information of events in other parts of the nation was reported, but it was incomplete, unverified, and often little more than rumor. Political life, therefore, was restricted to a far greater extent than before the Franco-Prussian War to the local level. Scholars who rely on the capital for information with which to reconstruct events in France suffer from the same dearth of information that Parisians experienced during the summer, fall, and winter of 1870–1871.

---

[18] See Gouault, *Comment la France est devenue républicaine*, pp. 29–31.

[19] Over two million letters were carried out of Paris by balloon during the period of siege, September 20, 1870 to January 28, 1871. Balloons, however, could not fly from the provinces into Paris.

The Parisian press, for example, usually the political pulse of the nation, is of little value in studying this election. Moreover, Paris did not receive copies of provincial newspapers that were customarily sent to the capital and deposited in the national library. Consequently, the collection of provincial newspapers now located in the Versailles annex of the Bibliothèque nationale contains few issues for the wartime period. It is possible, but doubtful, that prefectural reports on electoral activities in the departments eventually found their way to Paris, but, if they did, they must have been destroyed for they are not in the Archives nationales. One is forced, therefore, to look in municipal libraries, departmental archives, and above all in private papers for evidence of electoral activities. This is difficult and often fruitless work because they are scattered throughout the country, are not available for consultation (private archives, for example), and frequently contain few or no documents relating to the wartime period. But if necessarily fragmentary, these provincial sources reveal the active and sustained role legitimists performed in preparing the conservative electoral coalition of 1871.

One such collection of sources is deposited in the archives of the Benoist d'Azy family. Comte Denys Benoist d'Azy, the principal family figure involved in the elections of 1871, had a long and distinguished political and business career. Elected to the Chamber of Deputies from Nièvre in 1841, he left office in 1848 only to reappear in the Legislative Assembly of 1849 as a deputy from the Gard. Although he retired from politics during the Second Empire in order to devote himself to banking, railroads, and metallurgy, he energetically supported opposition candidates in the elections of 1863 and 1869. Benoist d'Azy was a notable of national standing with widespread contacts in Parisian financial and political circles and had immense influence among the notables of Nièvre and Gard. His correspondence, which is probably exceptional because of its volume for the wartime months, offers a sustained, if limited, view into the semipublic conservative electioneering. Correspondence from Paris was sparse, but he did receive a few letters from his daughter, Madame Augustin Cochin, reporting on politics in the capital. Most of his letters came from Marseilles and Gard, where his son Charles was looking after family and business interests. Charles sent lurid accounts of the revolutionary agitation in Marseilles and the Midi. From these Benoist d'Azy, who was in the Nièvre, pieced together an alarming

20

story of impending revolution. Relying on many of the same contacts that he had used in previous elections, he sent numerous letters to notables in the Center and the Midi urging conciliation and union among the various factions of the "party of order."

But he concentrated his greatest efforts in the two departments, Nièvre and Gard, from which he was elected in February. Benoist d'Azy began to consult with notables in Nièvre about organizing a conservative electoral fusion soon after the Revolution of September 4. On September 20, 1870 he wrote his son: "As much as I can judge by opinions expressed in this area, I believe that sensible republicans are afraid of the mob and will be much inclined to make a sort of alliance with reasonable monarchists."[20] His judgment seems to have been accurate, for after participating in a special meeting in late September of all the general and district councillors of Nièvre, he commented: "The conservative list will be formed in such a fashion that honest republicans will be represented."[21] At the same time, he wrote to the legitimists Surville (his son's father-in-law), Larcy, and Hombres (both of whom had been colleagues in the Legislative Assembly of 1849) in Gard urging action and unity. There his principle agent was his son. He instructed him not only "to get to Alais to see Larcy" but also "to see a certain M. Fouges," about whom he remarked, "He is a republican, but he is not a red and he must understand that above all we need men of order."[22] Nor did Benoist d'Azy cease electioneering after the postponement of elections, for, as he warned his son upon hearing of the adjournment of October 9, "it is necessary, nonetheless, to prepare for this election which can spring into being at any moment."[23] It was these preliminary efforts that enabled, as Benoist d'Azy described it, three hundred "of the more respected men in the department [of Nièvre, including] a certain number of moderate republicans" to assemble in Nevers a few days after the last electoral decree and adopt a fusionist list of conservative candidates.[24]

---

[20] Ltr., Denys Benoist d'Azy to Charles Benoist d'Azy, *Benoist d'Azy MSS*. The earliest letters referring to electoral preparations in the *Benoist d'Azy MSS* are dated Sept. 20. The contents of the letters show, however, that preparations had been under way for some days.

[21] *Ibid.*, Sept. 25, 1870.   [22] *Ibid.*, Oct. 25, 1870.

[23] *Ibid.*, Oct. 11, 1870.

[24] *Ibid.*, Feb. 5, 1871. Even Gambetta's prefect, Cyprien Girerd, was included and elected on the republican, Bonapartist, legitimist, and Orleanist fusion.

The personal papers of Baron de Larcy show evidence also of electoral preparation.[25] In 1870 Larcy, a rich landlord in St-Chaptes (Gard), had been active in politics for forty years. He had been a member of the legitimist opposition (from Hérault where he also owned property) during the July Monarchy, a conservative deputy in the Legislative Assembly of 1849, and an unsuccessful opposition candidate in two imperial elections (1863 and 1869). With Benoist d'Azy, Larcy was a sponsor of the electoral fusion in Gard in 1849 (on which both men had been elected), and he corresponded with his former colleague to the same end in 1870–1871, and most certainly (although there is no record of it in Larcy's papers) either spoke personally or corresponded with Charles Benoist d'Azy about the electoral coalition. Larcy's correspondence, moreover, contains letters from other notables (Louis-Numa Baragnon, a Nîmes lawyer; Hombres, a lawyer in Alais; and Ferdinand Boyer, a lawyer in Nîmes) interested in electoral fusion. Both Baragnon and Boyer were elected to the municipal council of Nîmes in September 1870, and they entered into extensive negotiations with conservatives after the first electoral proclamation in September. These men were instrumental in forming an electoral committee in Nîmes in early October 1870 for the purpose of drafting a list of candidates of conservative fusion. This committee, moreover, took advantage of electoral postponements in order to improve its organization. "Yesterday, October 10, 1870" the minutes of the committee record,

> a certain number of delegates from various districts in the Gard came to Nîmes with the idea of drafting a list of candidates for the Constituent Assembly. The postponement of elections depriving this meeting of its immediate purpose, the delegates thought it necessary to profit from the delay in order to organize a more complete departmental representation. They met, therefore, invited M. Larcy to fill the office of president and M. Surville (Charles Benoist d'Azy's father-in-law) that of vice-president. M. Baragon (Louis-Numa) was charged as secretary to draw up a report on the resolutions adopted.[26]

[25] The Larcy papers are part of the private archives of the Lordat family, Château de La Tour, St-Chaptes, Gard. They have been classified. Hereafter cited as *Larcy MSS*.

[26] *Ibid.*, dossier Va, Baron de Larcy, Vie politique (1830–1871), fol. 1871.

One of the resolutions called for the creation of "a committee for each district" and a central committee.[27] "The members separated on promising to make the greatest effort in favor of the above-mentioned organization."[28] When the election came these men had formed a conservative peace list of such appeal that it won every seat in the department's delegation.

The private correspondence of the Marquis de La Guiche contains equally valuable information about the elections.[29] La Guiche, a rich *propriétaire* in Saône-et-Loire and a prominent member of Parisian society, spent a fortune on politics during his lifetime. Elected to the Chamber of Deputies in 1846, he never received enough votes from the anticlerical peasantry in the Charolles (except in 1871) to be elected to a national legislature under the regime of universal suffrage. But he never quit trying. A perennial candidate, he founded a newspaper, *Le Journal de Mâcon*, to support his political ambitions, ambitions which he had seen frustrated most recently in the 1869 elections. Although a captain in the *garde mobile*, La Guiche never left his district during the war; he was in effect engrossed in politics much more than military events. He corresponded with Benoist d'Azy in neighboring Nièvre, with Adolphe Thiers, with his father-in-law, the Duc de Mortemart (who was elected from the Rhône on the conservative list in 1871), about the need for conservative union. But the bulk of the letters in his archives came from various notables or electoral agents in Saône-et-Loire who were busily engaged in reactivating for the coming contest committees that had functioned during the elections of 1869.

As early as September 14 La Guiche began contacting notables in his district. By October 4 a committee for Charolles had selected delegates, who in turn met with delegates from other departmental districts in a central meeting in Mâcon. This central committee adopted a list, alloted by district (La Guiche was chosen for Charolles), of candidates whose political background ran the gamut of conservative politics. As one royalist wrote La Guiche after the Mâcon meeting,

[27] *Ibid.*

[28] Ltr., Louis-Numa Baragnon to Larcy, Oct. 20, 1870, *ibid.*, dossier v, Lettres reçues, A-D.

[29] The archives of the La Guiche family are located in the Château de Chaumont, St-Bonnet-de-Joux, Saône-et-Loire. They have been classified. Hereafter cited as the *La Guiche MSS.*

the results were all the more satisfying because the moderate republican elements were very strongly represented . . . and because our list has the support of this party, which is rather important in Mâcon, Chalon, and Louhan. [Republicans are well represented on the list] but it is better to assure the co-operation of the moderate faction of this party, to give it certain concessions, than to make a purer list based uniquely on a coterie.[30]

Although these elections were abortive, rumors about their possibility continued to spur Conservative preparations in the Saône-et-Loire. In late October *Le Journal de Saône-et-Loire*, when urging conservatives to concentrate on electoral fusion, quoted a news story from *Le Français*: "Most of the former deputies who were assembled in Tours for the purpose of pressing the necessity of elections upon the government (the delegation headed by Gambetta) have left [Tours] in order to promote their candidacy in their respective departments."[31] And a few days later a central committee met again in Mâcon "in order to have a complete plan ready when the moment comes."[32] In fact, in Saône-et-Loire the committee appears to have completed its preparations before the January 29 electoral decree was issued. As a supporter of La Guiche wrote on February 1 after hearing news of elections, "the moment has come for you to be presented and *à propos* of this subject you have already reached agreement with the central committee in Mâcon."[33]

The contents of these three archives are particularly interesting because they show electoral activities of legitimists elected in 1871 during the war on both the departmental and interdepartmental levels. Moreover, these sources are significant because they turned

[30] Ltr., Ganay to La Guiche, n. d. (the letter was probably written on Oct. 9 or 10), *ibid.*, Correspondance, Philibert de La Guiche, dossier 12339, Lettres diverses, Elections A-L.

[31] *Le Journal de Saône-et-Loire*, Oct. 29, 1870. Among those present at Tours were Thiers, Talhouet, Antonin Lefèvre-Pontalis (brother of the legitimist Amédée Lefèvre-Pontalis), Lambrecht, Cochery, Grévy, Barante, and Guyot-Montpayeux. All these men were elected on fusionist lists in February, 1871.

[32] Ltr., Champvans to La Guiche, Oct. 29, 1870, *La Guiche MSS*, dossier 12339, Lettres diverses: *Le Journal de Mâcon*. Champvans was editor of the newspaper.

[33] Ltr., Trouillet to La Guiche, Feb. 1, 1871, *ibid.*, dossier 12335, Lettres diverses, Elections M-Z.

24

up at random in a general search for private archives. The accidental nature of the selection suggests, therefore, that a more plentiful supply of private sources would produce much of the same evidence. In fact, other private and public sources uncovered give occasional glimpses into legitimists' electoral activities before February 1871. When called away to a conservative meeting in Yssingeaux, for example, Florentin Malartre, a silk spinner in Dunières and a member of the department's general council, reported about sincere efforts to form a broad conservative fusion in the department.[34] The agenda of Baron Chaurand contains an entry that lists expenses he incurred in September for a trip to a conservative electoral meeting in a city in the Ardèche.[35] The private papers of Charles Chesnelong include letters from Kolb-Bernard that refer to electoral meetings in Lille. The wartime editions of newspapers, which occasionally turn up in public and private archives and libraries, also comment about electioneering in which legitimists took part. In Basses-Pyrénées a committee in Orthez, headed by Charles Chesnelong, issued an electoral manifesto on September 20 entreating "all good citizens to unite on the terrain of a conservative and liberal Republic," an appeal that obviously reflected conservative opinion in the department, for the central committee in Pau selected a list composed of five monarchists and four republicans.[36] In Eure-et-Loir *Le Journal de Chartres* published a "republican" list that included men of Bonapartist, legitimist (those elected in February), and republican persuasion.[37] After a meeting of the general councillors in Cher, who gathered as an electoral committee for the department, *Le Journal de Sancerre et de son arrondissement* reported that the committee had adopted a list of fusion composed of one legitimist (the Marquis de Vogüé) and four liberal monarchists.[38] And general councillors

---

[34] The Malartre correspondence is in the family home, Les Vignes, Dunières, Haute-Loire. These letters have not been classified. Malartre wrote to his wife constantly while in the National Assembly but there are few letters for the wartime period since he was at home most of the time. Hereafter cited as *Malartre MSS.*

[35] The agenda is kept among the papers of Baron Chaurand, Château de Chanels, Paysac, Ardèche. Not classified. Hereafter cited as *Chaurand MSS.*

[36] The manifesto is in the *Chesnelong MSS.* The conservative list was published in *Le Mémorial des Pyrénées*, Sept. 22, 1870.

[37] *Le Journal de Chartres*, Oct. 6, 1870.

[38] *Le Journal de Sancerre et de son arrondissement*, Sept. 25, 1870.

25

in a similar meeting in Côtes-du-Nord offered the voters a group of candidates—which varied from fervent legitimist to moderate republican in its makeup—"known in the department for their firmness, their moderation, their experience, their fidelity to the great principles of order on which society and public prosperity rest."[39] Like those of Benoist d'Azy these letters and the newspapers show that the radical peril seemed uppermost in men's minds. Louis de Lamberterie's electoral manifesto—"it is necessary to organize a strong and regular government and to reestablish society, so long subverted, on a broad base"—appears to be no more than the public equivalent of the private opinion expressed by Florentin Malartre, who wrote to his wife from the meeting in Yssingeaux, "all of us are directly threatened if the men of disorder win."[40]

Finally, studies of two departments have been done that corroborate the evidence gleaned from primary sources. The first, which is the less important, deals indirectly with elections and is concerned with public opinion in the Sarthe before, during, and following the war. The author notes that the *parti conservateur sarthois*, in which legitimists like La Rochefoucauld-Bisaccia, Juigné, Vétillart, and others elected in 1871 were active, worked diligently to consolidate their electoral position after September 1870.[41] In the second work, which studies elections in Loire, the author writes that beginning in September "the conservatives prepared actively for the campaign; but it seems with moderation, with the sense of action among all factions of the liberal party that was indispensable in the face of the radical peril and foreign danger."[42] Some forty or fifty men of order met in each district of the Loire to select candidates who were incorporated into a departmental fusionist list in early October by a central committee sitting in St-Etienne. As a result of these early efforts "there was

[39] *Le Journal de Lannion et de son arrondissement*, Oct. 13, 1870.

[40] Lamberterie's manifesto is in *Le Courrier du Lot*, Oct. 8, 1870. Malartre's remark is taken from a ltr., Malartre to his wife, Oct. 9, 1870, *Malartre MSS*.

[41] Paul Delaunay, "L'esprit public dans le département de la Sarthe pendant et après la guerre de 1870–1871," *Revue historique et archéologique du Maine*, XXIV-XXV (1944–1945), 13.

[42] Laurent Boyer, "Les élections politiques dans le département de la Loire de 1870 à 1879" (Thèse pour le doctorat en droit, Faculté de Droit, Université de Lyon, 1959), pp. 27–28.

not much to change during the electoral jostling of February 1871; the apparatus was already in place."[43]

Certainly the war reduced the scope and intensity of electoral activity, but these men faced the problem of organizing a coalition of notables in each department, not of wooing the electorate. Since the war was not a total war, the mails continued to function, if irregularly, throughout most of the country, thereby enabling these notables—who were by definition known to each other— to establish the preliminary contacts necessary for electoral meetings. Just how extensive and sustained were their organizational efforts? The answer to this question would be forthcoming only if hundreds of private archives were available with documentation for the wartime period, a probability that makes any detailed reconstruction of events unlikely. But the letters and newspapers cited in this study were located in departments situated in every region of France (except the east, which sent few legitimists to the Assembly), and whenever appropriate documents were found, they invariably led to the reasonable conclusion that electoral activity was widespread. The efforts of legitimists, moreover, are not so surprising because these men were spurred both by the fear of the red specter and the knowledge that they could win. Indeed, just three days after the Revolution of September 4, Jacquier of the newspaper *L'Univers* wrote the legitimist La Guiche that, in the event of elections, the countryside "will be for order."[44] As the war dragged on and as it became more unpopular with the peasantry, the monarchists grew increasingly confident. In Saône-et-Loire, a department where the monarchists were weak, the editor of La Guiche's paper wrote on September 13 that their chances were "good."[45] A few months later (December 6) he wrote enthusiastically: "Evidently, it is our hour which begins to chime."[46] In distant Nord, Kolb-Bernard noted, just a few days before the conclusion of the armistice, that the countryside was antirepublican and anti-Gambetta.[47] Monarchists everywhere seemed to exhibit

[43] *Ibid.*, p. 31.

[44] Ltr., Jacquier to La Guiche, Sept. 7, 1870, *La Guiche MSS*, Correspondance, Philibert de La Guiche, dossier 12339, Lettres diverses, Elections A-L.

[45] Ltr., Champvans to La Guiche, *ibid.*, dossier 12339, Lettres diverses, *Le Journal de Mâcon*.

[46] *Ibid.*

[47] Ltr., Kolb-Bernard to Chesnelong, Jan. 23, 1871, *Chesnelong MSS.*

the kind of confidence that Charles Benoist d'Azy showed on the eve of the election in Gard: "It is," he wrote his father, "the opinion of all that the voting will be good."[48]

Thus, these legitimists promoted the formation of a broad pro-peace conservative union that took advantage of the mood of a war-weary electorate in order to sweep into office.[49] But if the circumstances that surrounded the elections were unique, the behavior of these men was not that exceptional. Many of these same men or their fathers had joined in that conservative coalition (of similar scope for almost identical reasons) that supported Louis Napoleon's presidential ambitions in 1848 and that won a smashing electoral victory in the legislative elections of 1849. During the Empire, moreover, they had always tempered their opposition, no matter how much they disliked the regime, whenever they feared that its collapse would rebound to the benefit of the revolutionaries; and it is one of the ironies of recent history that the progressive weakening of that regime called forth from them increasing support. The legitimists responded after September 4 in the same vein. In the eastern departments where republicans dominated the "party of order," legitimist stalwarts like Lucien-Brun (Ain), Costa de Beauregard (Haute-Savoie) and Quinsonas (Isère) ran on lists that were composed primarily of republicans, and in other departments, such as those in the Center, they readily admitted republicans to the lists. Legitimists were so intent on fusion that they sometimes either publicly declared their allegiance to a republican form of government or consciously allowed their names to be placed on a list that ran under a republican rubric

[48] Ltr., Charles Benoist d'Azy to Denys Benoist d'Azy, Feb. 8, 1871, *Benoist d'Azy MSS.*

[49] It should be noted that the election of February 8, 1871 was conducted under a system called *scrutin de liste* or list-balloting. Each department received its representation in the Assembly according to population and the candidates won a seat in a department's delegation by order of votes acquired from the department's electorate; the first seat going to the candidate who had the most votes, the second to the runner-up, and so forth, until the department's allotted seats were filled. The quota of seats apportioned among the various departments varied from the most populous departments of Seine (43 seats) and Nord (28 seats) to the sparsely inhabited departments of Lozère (3 seats) and Hautes-Alpes (2 seats). In an American context, this system would amount to electing all the members of a state's congressional delegation *at large*, with Democrats and Republicans each presenting a list of candidates for the allotted seats, as opposed to electing each congressman by single member districts.

28

rather than run the risk of splitting conservative forces.[50] In departments where they were strongest, moreover, they cooperated freely with Orleanists and conservative republicans in the electoral meetings. Whenever there were rumblings of partisan legitimist discontent they were quickly squelched, as was the case of some ultras in Maine-et-Loire, who were chastised for being "more preoccupied with their [partisan] interests than with the welfare of France."[51] None of the legitimists elected in 1871 ran on lists that were composed uniquely of legitimists, nor did they mention their dynastic affiliations during the contest. If they had, the coalition which they so ardently desired could never have come into being. Silence on the dynastic issue was the source of their electoral strength. In most departments a single list of conservative fusion won every seat in the department's delegation.[52]

This discussion of legitimist activity in the election and representation in the victorious coalition is based purely on hindsight, for the election in fact does not reveal the dynastic convictions of the candidates on the fusionist lists. From them alone, there is no way, therefore, to identify the legitimist deputies of 1871. Once the peace had been secured, the Commune crushed, and the conservative deputies faced the problem of writing a constitution, the "party of order" came apart; still it did not break along clearly discernible dynastic lines. Political parties with a permanent organizational structure, a publicly announced program, and fixed membership lists, did not exist in France at the time. The deputies took their seats in the Assembly according to the division of the hemicycle (the extreme Right, Right, and Center constituting the monarchist majority), not as Bonapartists, Orleanists, or legitimists. Neither did they, when forming extraparliamentary factions,

[50] Thus Amédée Lefèvre-Pontalis (Eure-et-Loire), Gontaut-Biron and Xavier Dufaur (both of Basses-Pyrénées) publicly adhered to the Republic, and Gaston de Béthune (Ardennes), Adrien Tailhand and Baron Chaurand (both of Ardèche) ran as "republican" candidates. Lefèvre-Pontalis declared for the Republic in *Le Journal de Chartres*, Oct. 6, 1870. Dufaur said, "Today the Republic is the only possible government. It imposes itself on all good citizens." Quoted in Jules Clerc, *Biographie des députés* (Paris, 1875), p. 320. Gontaut-Biron echoed, "The Republic . . . is the form [of government] which divides us the least." *Ibid.*, p. 414.

[51] *Le Journal de Maine-et-Loire*, Feb. 3, 1871.

[52] Most of the lists, along with the political orientation of the candidates, are appended to my dissertation: Robert R. Locke, "The Legitimists: A Study in Social Mentality" (Diss., University of California at Los Angeles, 1965).

give them monarchist names. They referred to a group after the place its members held in the National Assembly (*Réunion Centre-Droite*), after the name of the street (*Réunion des Chevau-légers* and *Réunion Colbert*) or building (*Réunion des Réservoirs*) where they met in Versailles, or after the deputy (*Réunion Changarnier*) who organized the group.

The failure to adopt dynastic labels was perfectly consonant with the political situation. The war had left the Bonapartists confused and discouraged. The Emperor, who lay gravely ill, had used up his capital with the French people, and the Prince Imperial was still a youth. Only the most faithful clung to the Empire in 1871, and many a man who had been an ardent Bonapartist before the war no doubt sought, at least temporarily, new alliances after the Empire's collapse. "The truth is," one deputy wrote, "that the Assembly counted a certain number of former ministers or servitors of the Empire, who, if the occasion arose, would not have refused to recognize [the Empire] again, but who, in February 1871 thought neither of its reestablishment nor of opposing the restoration of another regime.[53] Many whose Bonapartist convictions waned immediately after the election eventually returned to their former allegiances, but this was hardly the case with all of them. For a number of notables Bonapartism had been less a matter of personal faith than intelligent politics. They saw no reason to remain loyal to a dynasty that had fallen in disgrace, and the former Orleanists, who had been in the coalition, faced a somewhat similar situation. They probably would have voted for the restoration of the cadet branch of the Bourbon family had the opportunity arisen, but it never did, for the head of the House of Orleans, the Comte de Paris, refused to be a candidate for the throne. Much has been said about the perfidy of the Orleanists during the campaign to restore the elder branch of the monarchy, and it is certainly true that they refused to bow to Chambord's wishes. Yet if the Comte de Paris offered only qualified support to his cousin, he never tried to be king in his place. In effect, there was only one real candidate for the throne from 1871 to 1875, and the Comte de Paris recognized as much himself by his famous visit of family reconciliation on August 5, 1873. During these years, the deputies had only one choice: either a monarchy under the Comte de Chambord or a republic.

[53] Amédée Lefèvre-Pontalis, *L'Assemblée nationale et M. Thiers. Premiere partie: Les essais de constitution* (Paris, 1879), p. 8.

Therefore the parliamentary groupings into which the members of the "peace" coalition divided did not represent rival claimants for the throne as much as they did different attitudes about the restoration of one claimant, Chambord. For the extreme Right the case was clear—they openly and vociferously supported the exiled monarch. Like Lucien-Brun, Cazenove de Pradine, Gabriel de Belcastel, La Rochette, and Carayon-Latour, many of them had been Chambord's confidants and some had worked actively in his service during the Second Empire. Chambord believed that he was king by divine right. He did not expect Frenchmen to bargain with him for the crown but to submit to their king by welcoming him back, without conditions, to a throne that "ne relevait que de lui, après Dieu."[54] He was not predisposed to compromise his birthright by making any deals for the throne because with such a concession he would, in his opinion, have traded away the substance of hereditary monarchy for an illusion. This does not mean that Chambord would have refused to grant Frenchmen a constitution guaranteeing representative government and civil liberties, but he wanted to bestow them, not have them extorted from him as a precondition for his restoration. For Chambord the principle of legitimacy was inviolable, and to preserve it, he insisted that France accept the white flag that symbolized divine right hereditary monarchy. Most of the extreme Right was upset about Chambord's attitude on the flag issue because they considered it too much a trifle to worry about. Basically, however, they agreed with him about the restoration. Suspecting an Orleanist "plot" to set aside "Henri V" in favor of the Comte de Paris or some sort of Orleanist-dominated republic, they insisted, with the simplicity of faith exhibited by the pretender himself, that the Assembly recognize Chambord without preconditions. Indeed, they denied the Assembly any jurisdiction in the affair.

The former Orleanists, who occupied most of the Left-and Right-Center in the Chamber, rejected the *Chevau-légers'* point of view. They were not divine right monarchists; hence they believed that the Assembly, especially since it was a "constituent" assembly, had complete constitutional jurisdiction. Nevertheless they were divided in their attitude toward the restoration. The Left-Center deputies would not accept Chambord; he smacked too much of the Old Regime. Instead, under Adolphe Thiers'

[54] Quoted in Philippe du Puy de Clinchamps, *Le royalisme* (Paris, 1967), p. 39.

leadership, they rallied to the Republic which after the suppression of the Commune, they were convinced, would offer sufficient guarantees against revolutionary perils. Most of the Orleanists, those who joined the *Réunion Centre-Droite*, did not, however, arbitrarily reject Chambord's restoration. Many of them had been closely associated with the Orleanist family (two Orleanist princes themselves sat in the Assembly), and they wanted to see the Comte de Paris on the throne. Inasmuch as the count was the heir apparent of the childless Chambord, this would be the inevitable result of the restoration of the legitimate monarchy. A certain Vicomte de Bastard perhaps best summarized this point of view when he wrote his father shortly after the Comte de Paris' visit to Chambord in 1873. "One has to admit it, the Orleanist princes act like princes. They strongly affirm that they want to step aside for the Comte de Chambord. Let them always preserve this policy! And you will one day see the Comte de Paris king of France, this time legitimately, because they will not have re-enacted a second 1830."[55] The Right-Center was prepared to cooperate with the Right in order to bring about a restoration. In return for its support, however, it expected Chambord to recognize the tricolor, emblem of national sovereignty. But this was the one concession Chambord could not make since it would permit the Orleanist-dominated Assembly to dictate the form and content of the restored monarchy. He clung, therefore, to the white flag, symbol of legitimacy. Since neither the pretender nor the Right-Center would compromise, an impasse resulted that wrecked the campaign to restore the monarchy.

The remainder of the victorious conservative electoral coalition occupied the benches on the Assembly's moderate Right. About fifty of these Rightists were what one deputy, who obviously considered himself among them, called "monarchists without party attachments."[56] These men, devout Catholics, had been political opportunists, not in the sense that they sought personal advantages, but in that they cooperated with any regime that promised to defend the Church. Most of them had rallied to Louis Napoleon

[55] Ltr., Vicomte de Bastard to his father, Nov. 2, 1872. *Titres et documents pour servir de preuves à l'histoire de la maison de Bastard. XIXe siècle. Branches de Guienne.* Tome XXXII. *Titres et documents concernant Octave Comte de Bastard d'Estang,* 1884. In possession of the Comtesse de Fraguier, Sarthe. Hereafter cited as *Bastard MSS.*

[56] Ltr., Chesnelong to his wife, Jan. 26, 1872. *Chesnelong MSS.*

after the *coup d'état* of December 2, and many had been official candidates for the Legislative Corps during the Empire. Still they had fought bitterly against the Emperor's Italian policy and scarcely regretted the Empire's fall when it came. Some thought of accepting the Republic after the Revolution of September 4, but, quickly convinced that republicanism signified implacable anticlericalism, they rallied to the monarchy.[57] Most of the Rightist deputies, unlike the "monarchists without party attachments," had clear legitimist antecedents. Nonetheless they were not royalists like the extreme Right. They were temperamentally quite different men, *politiques* rather than *doctrinaires*.

The Right's attitude toward the restoration differed from that of its colleagues on the extreme Right and the Right-Center. Whereas the extreme Right adopted the stance of the true believer on the restoration question, the Right approached it pragmatically. As one of the moderate rightists (Comte de Sugny) explained to Chambord himself, the restoration could theoretically come about in three ways: a military *coup d'état*, a favorable plebiscite, or a vote in the National Assembly. Chambord could rely neither on the army, which was primarily Bonapartist and secondarily republican, nor on a ground swell of support among the people in a plebiscite, for the electorate, despite the results of February 8, would be antilegitimist. Success, Sugny concluded, could only be attained by a favorable vote in the National Assembly.[58] Since Chambord needed the votes of the Right-Center and he could acquire these votes only by compromising with the Orleanists, the moderate Right advocated concessions. The extreme Right might clamor for a restoration without conditions, but the Right knew only one answer to the question that one of its number, Arthur de Cumont, asked the editor of the intransigent legitimist newspaper *L'Union*: "By whom will the monarchy be restored without conditions?"[59] That answer was nobody.

[57] Emile Keller, disappointed in 1871 on meeting the Comte de Chambord, decided "to accept openly the constitutional terrain of a conservative Republic." It was the anticlericals' conquest of power which brought him (after the by-elections of July, 1871) into the legitimist camp. See Gustave Gautherot, *Emile Keller, 1828–1909, Un demi-siècle de défense nationale et religieuse* (Paris, 1922), p. vi.

[58] Comte de Sugny, "Voyage à Brengenz, 7 nov. 1872," *Visites au Comte de Chambord, 1872–1883* (typewritten manuscript, personal property of Olivier de Sugny, Paris), p. 5.

[59] Arthur de Cumont, *Les incurables*, 2e ed. (Angers, 1883), p. 30.

The Right, therefore, advocated a policy of fusion; in fact, they organized an extraparliamentary group, the *Réunion Colbert*, precisely for the purpose of promoting a fusion among all monarchists in the Assembly. The rightist deputies became the real driving force at Versailles behind the effort to restore the monarchy. They nagged the Comte de Chambord mercilessly about the necessity to accept the tricolor; and they worked diligently among the deputies trying to build a promonarchist consensus in the Chamber. Many of these fusionists never entirely trusted the good faith of the Orleanists; some were scarcely less skeptical about the Orleanists' accepting Chambord than the extreme Right. Maurice Aubry, for example, deputy from Vosges, said as much in a letter to Charles Chesnelong after hearing of the Comte de Paris' voyage to Frohsdorf in 1873; Martial Delpit, deputy from Dordogne, made the point equally clear when he commented about fusionist activities in his notebook; and Olivier de Sugny pointedly warned the Orleanist Harcourt not to "close the door to the head of the House of France."[60] If they did not trust the Orleanists, they nonetheless had to rely on them completely if they were to have any chance for success. Calculating the strength of the monarchists, the fusionist Larcy cited the forecast of the republican newspaper *La Liberté* on the expected vote for the restoration (fall of 1873) as: 339 deputies *for*, 353 *against*, and 30 *doubtful*. "[B]ut these figures," he continued, "are not exact; and after a rigorous examination they must be rectified as follows: *for* 355, *against* 338, *doubtful* 31. Even with the last hypothesis one sees that we will barely make it. Any mistake will be fatal and we are keeping the greatest vigil."[61]

From Chambord's viewpoint and that of the extreme Right, anyone who advocated concessions to "this ambitious and intriguing heap" (an extreme rightist's epithet for the Orleanists) was something less than a loyal supporter of the king, if not an outright traitor to his cause.[62] In effect, the fusionist Right carried on a

---

[60] Ltrs., Maurice Aubry to Chesnelong, Aug. 21, 1871 and Olivier de Sugny to Chesnelong, Nov. 18, 1874, *Chesnelong MSS*. P. B. des Valades, ed., *Martial Delpit, député à l'Assemblée nationale, journal et correspondance* (Paris, 1898), pp. 190–194.

[61] Ltr., Larcy to his daughter (Mme. Roux-Larcy), Oct. 25, 1873, *Larcy MSS*, dossier: Lettres envoyées aux membres de sa famille par le Baron Roger de Larcy.

[62] The quote is from a ltr., Pierre Soury-Lavergne to his wife, May 15, 1871, *Soury-Lavergne MSS*.

34

veritable dialogue of the deaf with the extreme Right over restoration. "France is going to perish," the fusionist Falloux wrote.

Between a social Caesar and a war of savages in the street there is only one way to salvation—the royalty. It is necessary, then, at all costs and by all the strength at our command to reestablish the monarchy. The flag, a national prejudice, is too rooted in the people's soul to be uprooted; it is necessary to take it as it is. Bend every effort to convince M. le Comte de Chambord that he must accept the arbitration of the Assembly. If we want to save the country this is the inevitable dénouement.

To this plea Falloux's correspondent, the extreme rightist Gabriel de Belcastel replied:

Yes . . . the monarchy will be the salvation of the fatherland, if it is faithful to itself and to its mission; if it acts like an inviolable principle against which neither the intrigues, nor the riots, nor the majorities of the day can prevail; if it no longer fears to uphold the social notion of good and evil, leaving the good its natural right of liberty and suppressing evil which has no rights; if before claiming what is due to Caesar, it gives to God what is his due; if it is, in a word, a Christian royalty, if it is not the revolution crowned.[63]

Many extreme rightists grew to hate the fusionist Right even more perhaps than they did the Right-Center for they felt them to be playing the Orleanist game. The fusionist Right, on the other hand, complained just as bitterly about the ultralegitimists' inability to recognize the realities of parliamentary life. "He thinks," the exasperated Charles Chesnelong said of Chambord's personal secretary, Dreux-Brézé, "that the Assembly must limit itself purely and simply to proclaiming [Chambord] the king. When one speaks to him of finding a majority, he comprehends nothing."[64]

These, then, were the parliamentary groups that emerged when

[63] Both quotations are given in Gabriel de Belcastel, *A mes électeurs, Cinq ans de vie politique, votes principaux, propositions, lettres, et discours* (Toulouse, 1876), p. 39. Falloux was not a deputy in the National Assembly but he was one of the leaders of the moderate Right. For this reason he is included among the legitimists.

[64] C. de Kirwan, *Charles Chesnelong. Son rôle sous le Second Empire et les régimes qui ont suivi.* Extrait de *la Revue des Sciences Ecclésiastiques et la Science Catholique*, Année 1909 (Paris, 1901), p. 19.

the peace coalition of 1871 disintegrated. The Orleanists held out for a tricolor monarchy; the extreme Right demanded unequivocal submission to the pretender; and the Right did its best to reconcile what was perhaps the irreconcilable. None of these groups was fixed, homogeneous, or mutually exclusive in its composition. Membership lists of various *réunions* changed constantly as deputies' political opinions evolved. Membership in one group, moreover, did not prevent a man from belonging to others. Twenty percent of the deputies enrolled in the *Réunion Centre-Droite* and over 10 percent of the members of the *Réunion des Chevau-légers* also belonged to the *Réunion Colbert*. This interpenetration of groups prompted one deputy to remark that he did not know where the Right ended and the Right-Center began; and the same could be said about the juncture between the Left and Right-Center, and the Right and extreme Right.[65] The Right was not composed of distinct blocs, but of groups that gradually merged, the one into the other. As a result there were nuances of opinion in each of the groups described above. Some extreme rightists were less intransigent than others, some Orleanists less liberal than others; some rightists leaned toward the Right-Center and some toward the extreme Right. Even though a group's attitude toward the restoration can be described in polarized terms, the subtleties of human psychology and the absence of complete documentation make it impossible for the historian to decide into which group every deputy should be placed. Perhaps at times a deputy himself did not know exactly where he stood.

Not surprisingly, therefore, estimates of the size of various monarchist groups have varied significantly. In 1872 Charles Chesnelong calculated the Right's numerical strength as follows: extreme Right 50, Right 100, Right-Center 200.[66] A few weeks later *Le Figaro* divided the Right into extreme Right 52, Right 124, Right-Center 174.[67] Etienne Lamy, in *Témoins des jours passés*, quoted Rightist strength as extreme Right 100, Right 120, and Right-Center 150.[68] References to legitimists, moreover, vary even

[65] Charles de Lacombe, *Journal politique de Charles de Lacombe, député à l'Assemblée nationale* (Paris, 1907), vol. I, p. 202.

[66] Ltr., Chesnelong to his wife, Jan. 26, 1872, *Chesnelong MSS.*

[67] *Le Figaro*, March 26, 1872.

[68] Extract, Etienne Lamy, *Témoins des jours passés*, printed in Charles de Lacombe, *Journal politique*, vol. I, Appendix A.

more. To cite the widest divergence, the republican Jules Simon counted 80 legitimists in the Chamber, whereas the royalist Amédée Lefèvre-Pontalis calculated: "Of the 420 deputies who were neither republicans nor Bonapartists, one can count between 200 and 220 who adhered, either of old or by reason of recent conversion, to legitimist opinions."[69] Accounts given by historians only add to the confusion. To mention but two examples, Halévy states that the Chamber contained "more than 100 Legitimists," while Gouault fixed their number at the exact figure of 182.[70] Thus comments by contemporaries and historians do not clarify the numerical strength of the legitimist deputies much more than the elections themselves.

Apparently conflicting estimates about the strength of the groups designated as extreme, moderate, and center Right are a result of subtle subjective evaluations of deputies who are borderline cases. Some observers (Lamy for instance) obviously identified the extreme Right with the hundred deputies or so (membership fluctuated) who joined the *Réunion des Chevau-légers*. But the *Chevau-légers* did not always exhibit the same intransigence vis-à-vis the Orleanist Right-Center. This can best be illustrated by a rather well known incident. In May 1873 the Right joined together to overthrow Adolphe Thiers and elect Marshal MacMahon president of the Republic. The Duc de Broglie formed a cabinet composed of deputies drawn from the Right and Right-Center to replace Thiers' Left-Center oriented government. After the failure of the restoration campaign in October 1873, the Broglie government decided to give priority in the Assembly to drafting constitutional laws. The *Chevau-légers* objected to this procedure because the Assembly presumed to make a constitution before the restoration, something they believed not only violated the theory of legitimate monarchy (because the monarch needed to participate in constitutional decisions) but also practically eliminated the possibility of ever restoring Chambord (who would never agree to this Assembly-made constitution). But opposition to the Broglie government's move posed serious difficulties. If the members of the *Chevau-légers* voted against the government, it would fall.

[69] Both figures are given in Amédée Lefèvre-Pontalis, *L'Assemblée nationale*, p. 9.

[70] Daniel Halévy, *La fin des notables* (Paris, 1930), p. 12. Gouault, *Comment la France est devenue républicaine*, p. 74.

Many argued that the republicans would be the real winners when the rightist coalition collapsed and that, in the long run, their victory would be more disadvantageous to the royalists because the republican triumph would make even more remote the possibility of ever restoring the legitimate monarchy. Overcome by the desire to punish Broglie for his treachery fifty-two *Chevau-légers* joined with the republican Left (and Bonapartists) to bring down the government, thereby contributing to the confusion on the Right that, as predicted, led to the passage of the republican constitutional laws a few months later. However, over forty of the *Chevau-légers* voted in favor of the Broglie government because they feared the consequences of playing the *politique du pire*. Therefore, even though the *Chevau-légers* were legitimists par excellence some observers placed only part of them in the extreme Right, while others applied the label to the entire group. The same sort of subtle distinctions, moreover, were used in estimating the strength of the moderate and Right-Center, for some (Lamy and *Le Figaro*, for example) included men in the moderate Right whom others (Chesnelong, for example) put in the Right-Center.

The different estimates contemporaries made about the numerical strength of the rightist groups resulted from divergent but unexplained estimates of the attitudes of deputies living in a fluid political situation. For this reason it is impossible to determine not only which figure is more correct but also the basis for the differences among them. Faced with this situation, Gouault tried to establish a number of objective criteria that would more clearly delineate rightist groups. He selected various roll call votes in the National Assembly that he considered major determinants in a deputy's attitude toward the restoration. He picked the vote of confidence on the Broglie government, discussed above as the key issue that differentiated the extreme from the moderate Right, and the vote on the constitutional laws in February 1875 to separate the moderate from the Right-Center.[71] He chose the latter issue because he felt that the refusal to accept even the most conservative form of republican government, which these laws established, indicated that a deputy was a staunch royalist (or Bonapartist). Gouault's selections are in themselves somewhat arbitrary. Although fifty-two deputies voted against the Broglie government, this does not mean that they were equally intransigent in their

[71] Gouault, *Comment la France est devenue républicaine*, Annexe i.

outlook. Had Gouault chosen other issues on which to determine this strength he would have had very different results. The election of lifetime senators in December 1875, in accordance with the new constitutional law, offers a good example.

In order to ensure the conservative character of the Senate, the Center, Right-Center, and Right approved of a provision in the constitutional law that made seventy-five of its three hundred senators members for life. They were to be elected first by the National Assembly and then, as vacancies occurred in their ranks, by the Senate itself. A group of rightists drew up a list of candidates for the lifetime Senate that included Bonapartists, liberal monarchists, and legitimists. This fusionist list would have passed if it had received the support of the conservatives in the Chamber. But the Right-Center refused to accept Bonapartists on the list. The Bonapartists, therefore, made a deal with the republicans according to which they would support a republican list that included the names of some Bonapartists. A number of *Chevau-légers*, who were determined to chastise certain Right-Center deputies for having voted for the republican constitution, joined with the republicans and Bonapartists and voted for the leftist list on which some of the ultralegitimists were also carried. Although they defeated the "traitors" in the Right-Center, they also succeeded in giving the republicans an unhoped-for victory in the election, for fifty-seven republicans were elected to the new Senate for life.

The episode is very similar in character to the move against the Broglie government in 1874, for in both cases the extreme Right's attack on the hated Orleanists helped the republicans. But in the case of the Senate elections only eleven members of the extreme Right participated in the coalition. Had Gouault used these elections instead of the vote of nonconfidence against the Broglie government as the gauge for measuring the numerical strength of the extreme Right in the Assembly he would have arrived at the figure of eleven instead of fifty-two. The explanation for the difference seems to be one of expected consequence. The fall of the Broglie government did not change the composition of the National Assembly; it remained a monarchist-dominated body. The senatorial elections, however, eliminated from the Senate royalists who were assured, precisely because they were a majority in the National Assembly, of winning the seats. Members of the extreme Right who were willing to overthrow Broglie's government refused, in the Senate election, to join in a coalition that would

39

have such drastic consequences. Indeed, the *Chevau-légers*, so incensed by the action of the eleven, formally expelled them from their *réunion*.[72]

These examples illustrate the relativity of such a concept as "intransigence." It is difficult to find a more intransigent legitimist than Rodez-Benavent. He resigned a seat in the General Council of Hérault during the Second Empire rather than swear an oath of allegiance to Napoleon III. This act is especially significant because many legitimists who refused to sit in the Legislative Corps out of loyalty to Chambord accepted the positions in general councils on the ground that they were not political bodies. But when it came to electoral contests between Bonapartists and republicans, Rodez-Benavent, who received the praise of the prefect for his efforts, actively supported the Bonapartist candidates in his canton of Grange.[73] Other cases can be cited where the intransigent legitimists openly supported Bonapartists against radicals. One of Chambord's most fervent disciples, Cornulier-Lucinière, who sat on the municipal council of Nantes during the Empire, forgot his anti-Bonapartist sentiments when it came to fighting the radical elements in the port city. All the *Chevau-légers*, moreover, sacrificed their principles by forming the electoral league in 1871. When fear of the red specter became great enough all the extreme Right made common cause with Orleanists in defense of the social order. Some of the most determined Orleanist haters ran in 1871 on the same lists with Adolphe Thiers. This was true even of Ernest de La Rochette, leader of the rebels in the affair of the senatorial elections. Whenever radicalism had threatened, La Rochette had been an energetic champion of conservative fusion (in 1849 and in 1871 for example). Every rightist member of the National Assembly was willing at some point to cooperate with men he disliked from a dynastic viewpoint in the interest of conservative solidarity, but that point differed considerably according to the temperament and judgment of the deputy. Thus, it is somewhat arbitrary to

[72] See the *Procès-verbaux de la réunion des Chevau-légers, en date du 15 décembre 1875*. A copy of these minutes was sent to the author by a descendant of Lucien-Brun.

[73] The prefect praised him for his "aid in various elections carried out in the Canton of Grange, 1862–1863," and the government supported his candidacy, a candidacy violently attacked by the "parti protestant et avancé," once he overcame his royalist scruples and again ran for the general council in 1864. A. D. (Hérault), 2 M⁸25, *Elections, Conseil général, renouvellement partiel du 19 juin 1864*, p. 4.

select one or two votes, as Gouault has done, as a basis for differentiating the various rightist groups. One can never be sure what a vote on a specific issue actually meant. The vote on the constitutional laws, for example, did not necessarily signify that those who favored the laws were Orleanists and that those who opposed their enactment were legitimists. Consider the cases of Arthur de Cumont and Louis Viennet. The former was a legitimist who in family tradition vigorously supported Chambord's restoration through a fusion of all monarchists in the Assembly, and the latter was an Orleanist who also favored a policy of fusion. Yet Cumont eventually voted in favor of the republican constitutional laws, while Viennet voted against them. Cumont's vote appeared to have been the culmination of a long feud he had with the ultras, for as a fusionist he was annoyed with Chambord because of his intransigence and at odds with the ultras in his department (Maine-et-Loire) who censured him for advocating a policy of reconciliation with the Orleanists. He voted for the Republic partly out of a sense of resignation to the inevitable and partly out of a desire to punish the ultralegitimists for having blocked the restoration because of their inflexibility. Viennet, on the other hand, after much hesitation, voted against the constitutional laws because he did not want a Republic. But he did not like Chambord and was suspicious of the legitimists. Moreover, he did not censure those monarchists who approved of the republican constitution. In fact, he praised them for having the courage to accept the laws.[74] If one uses the vote as the test for dividing Orleanists from legitimists, Cumont would be considered more of an Orleanist, and Viennet more of a legitimist which was most certainly not the case.

Still the historian need not despair of the problem that this situation presents for group identification. If every deputy cannot be classified in the extreme, moderate, or center Right according to some completely objective system, most of them can be grouped on grounds that are perfectly reasonable. A good case can be made for Gouault's classification because the criteria he chose offer a really significant basis for dividing the rightists. Contemporary evidence, moreover, supports his conclusions since the men he selected by roll-call vote analysis coincide in number and name

[74] See ltr., Louis Viennet to his wife, Feb. 25, 1875, private archives of Guy Viennet, Bézier (Hérault). Not classified. The Viennet papers include letters written by the deputy to members of his family, 1871–1876. Hereafter cited as *Viennet MSS.*

41

with those mentioned in documents of the time. Gouault put the strength of the extreme Right at fifty-two, a figure with which Chesnelong and *Le Figaro* obviously agreed, and the membership lists of the *Réunion Colbert* and the *Chevau-légers* have the names of most of the deputies whom he places in the moderate and extreme Right. If legitimism can be identified with these two groups of deputies, the problem of selecting the legitimist deputies of 1871 can be solved. While most include the extreme Right in the legitimist camp, opinion splits over where to place the moderate Right. This dispute, which has been perpetuated by historians, began with the deputies themselves. Jules Simon, for example, used the term legitimist when speaking of the *Chevau-légers*, a distinction with which his enemies the *Chevau-légers* would have fully agreed. Intransigent legitimists like Vinols de Montfleury or Félix du Temple never considered moderates like Ernoul, Chesnelong, Sugny, or Benoist d'Azy "true" legitimists. Amédée Lefèvre-Pontalis, on the other hand, plainly included the moderate Right in the legitimist camp, and he counted deputies who had not been legitimists before 1871 but who, in his opinion, had sincerely rallied to Chambord in legitimists' ranks. This is not some picayune debate, for any analysis of the legitimists of 1871 and of legitimism itself would differ significantly according to whether the group included or excluded the moderate Right.

One of the charges leveled against the moderate Right can be dispensed with rather quickly. The *Chevau-légers*, whose accusations have been echoed in the works of Emmanuel Beau de Lomenie, believed that the moderate Right, although ostensibly supporting Chambord, actually worked to block his restoration.[75] No moderate rightist, of course, would have openly admitted that he was "plotting" to set aside the Comte for an Orleanist. And since most records are meant for public consumption the fusionists would not have mentioned a "plot" even had there been one. Therefore, it is difficult to disprove a plot, especially to men who want to believe it existed. Yet these men never present any real evidence (nor does Beau de Lomenie) to prove the faithlessness of the fusionists vis-à-vis the absent monarch. And although the sources that reveal men's most intimate thoughts (letters, diaries, etc.) are rare and inaccessible, those available do not indicate that these fusionists wavered in their support of Chambord's restoration. On

[75] This is the major point of his book, *La restauration manquée. L'Affaire du drapeau blanc.* (Paris, 1932).

the contrary, they indicate that they did everything possible to achieve that end. If the desire to restore Chambord suffices to make a person a legitimist, then, the moderate Right clearly deserves the appellation. But it is most certainly not quite that simple. The Comte de Chambord always said that his person was nothing, his principle everything. It was the principle, not the man, that constituted the specificity of legitimism during the nineteenth century. Then, the question is whether the moderate Right in asking for the man sacrificed the principle. And the answer to the question must be sought within the framework of the ideological conflicts that raged in France during the last century.

Nineteenth-century Frenchmen not only lived in the shadow of their great Revolution but also repeatedly experienced insurrections and revolutionary events. Many men were so dissatisfied with the state of affairs in France, Europe, and the world that they approved of all revolutions, both successful and abortive. Marx and his followers, for instance, saw each revolution as a step along the way toward the eventual liberation of all mankind from the intellectual, moral, and physical bondage that had constituted its lot since the beginning of history. It is important, however, when considering France's revolutionary past, to distinguish between revolution in itself and specific revolutions, for, although some men approved of revolution, others only approved of some revolutions. The men who carried through the Revolution of 1830 obviously fall into this category, but so do the republicans because, if they felt the revolution had stopped short in 1830, they concluded that it had gone too far in June 1848. These revolutionaries, then, were also counterrevolutionaries, depending on the circumstances, but all these men, at some point, had condoned the revolutionary act. In this sense, they were completely different (even though at times they worked with them in the interests of maintaining order) from those counterrevolutionaries who opposed revolution in any form.

In the essay *The Rebel*, Albert Camus pointed out a basic difference between all modern revolutionaries and their opponents. Modern rebellion was born when man killed God and enthroned himself in His place. Even the mildest nineteenth-century rebels, the liberals, operated according to this presumption. In scholarship and science, they made human reason the measure of truth; in poetry and literature, they added sentiment to reason but nevertheless made man alone the arbiter of beauty and good taste. Socially, the

43

liberal presumed that intelligence and talent were the proper gauge of personal worth. In education he championed secular enlightenment, the great hope for the progressive liberation of the human spirit from the dogmas of received truth and monkish superstition. Politically, he held that governments were instituted by men for men and that they were ultimately responsible to the body politic. In short, the liberal presumption permeated every aspect of existence because it constituted an attitude toward life. According to Croce, it signified that "the aim of life is in life itself, and duty lies in the increase and elevation of this life, and the method in free initiative and individual inventiveness. . . ."[76] This liberal mystique admits, of course, a variety of interpretations. The Orleanist oligarchs tried to apply it uniquely to themselves because, they maintained, they had earned the right to dominate society through their achievements. Democrats saw through the smug claims of these men of property and accused them of exploiting the nation for their own sordid material interests. But democrats were themselves attacked for subjecting the individual and his property to the caprice of ambitious demagogues who sought to manipulate the ignorant and voracious masses to their own ends. Yet in stating their principles or in attacking those of others, Orleanist oligarchs and democratic republicans operated on the same assumption, i.e., that man had on his own authority the right to promote mankind's happiness, enlightenment, and freedom in this world. It was this presumption, which for want of a better term has been called the liberal presumption, with which the counterrevolution took issue. Counterrevolutionaries did not just deny the need for change, which is what the Orleanists or democrats themselves did once they got what they wanted. They refused to accept the basic assumption that it was within man's province to arrange the world. On the contrary, they believed that it was precisely the desire to do so that constituted the principal source of evil in modern times.

In effect, the counterrevolutionary opposed the liberal with a Catholic interpretation of man and his environment. The Church, of course, was not a monolith. A great many prorevolutionary or at least proliberal elements had been trying to bring the Church into line with liberalism since the eighteenth century. In its oligarchic form liberalism sought to accommodate Catholicism to an

---

[76] Benedetto Croce, *History of Europe in the Nineteenth Century* (New York, 1963), pp. 20–21.

optimistic belief in the moral and material progress of man, one that would permit him to rid the Church of the baggage of inherited superstitions that ran counter to the dictates of reason in politics, economics, philosophy, science, in theology itself. Liberalism, in its democratic form, endeavored to reawaken Catholicism to the egalitarian humanism with which the life and suffering of Jesus had so long been identified in the popular mind. But the counterrevolutionary Catholics were bitterly opposed to these efforts. "To the liberal conception that the aim of life is in life itself and duty lies in the increase and elevation of this life and the method in free initiative and individual inventiveness," they replied, "on the contrary, the aim lies in a life beyond this world, for which the life of this world is simply a preparation, which must be made with heed to what a God who is in the heavens, by means of his vicar on earth and of his Church, bids us believe and do."[77] They were convinced that the liberal Catholics, in their desire to be children of their times, had let the Church's theology be determined willy-nilly by the latest currents in philosophic and scientific thought and that the "truths" which man presumed to establish by reason were not only errors (to the extent that they were in conflict with received dogma) but posed a direct threat to the faith. Liberal Catholics had, in their opinion, committed the blunder of letting human reason loose in the field of theology where under its pitiless scrutiny theology had been forced to defend itself against the intolerable contradictions that reason exposed. "But what sort of theology is possible," they asked, "that stands in such a forced and precarious relation to reason, constantly threatened with destruction by the very compromises it is forced, in reason's name, to make?" From the conservative Catholic viewpoint liberals had only succeeded in watering down religion to a bland idea of ethical progress, forgetting that the aesthetic and paradoxical elements so essential to religious faith in man could not be satisfied with the merely ethical. The religious position of the liberal Catholics was weak because their moralism and humanism lacked insight into the demonic character of human existence. The counterrevolutionaries believed that man was naturally covetous, capable of the meanest deeds and foulest crimes unless held in check by the strictest authority. Liberalism failed, therefore, to have a true understanding of human nature and the

[77] *Ibid.*

tragedy of life, for man in his vanity would not stop at committing the greatest crime of all, i.e., killing God and putting himself in his place. Indeed, this was exactly what he had done when he gave birth to liberalism. Liberal Catholicism was a contradiction in terms. Not only was liberalism at odds with Catholicism, it was its deadly enemy. Either liberalism had to be stamped out or it would lead, with all its terrible consequences, to the destruction of the Church and with it the faith that was the sole hope of mankind.

This fundamental incompatibility with liberalism marked the counterrevolutionary's approach to the problem of political and social change, disorder and insurrection in his time. These men and women believed that there was a moral order to which men, regardless of their desires, should conform. The following story, related by the Marquis de Belleval, illustrates this conception of moral order. Once while taking a stroll in the countryside at Frohsdorf, Belleval came upon some unknown peasant who, instead of tipping his hat, came to the Marquis and kissed his hand as was the local custom. This act, Belleval testifies, was not done in any sense of self-conscious or belittling servility, for both, at least on the Marquis' word, found the action quite natural, the one to the other.[78] Because of the Marquis' rank he was an authority in the community and the ceremony that accompanied his brief encounter with the peasant simply registered this social fact. The unquestioning acceptance of the situation constituted what the counterrevolutionaries called the essence of moral order. It was predicated on an elitist assumption that societies were composed of a hierarchy of social groups, each of which stood in an intimate but natural association with the other. A belief in a hierarchical organization of society does not in itself make a person a counterrevolutionary. Orleanists and Bonapartists, for example, had strong elitist sentiments. But the counterrevolutionary differed from other elitists in his attitude toward the manner in which the hierarchy came into being. Many modern elitists based their elitism on the enlightenment idea of talent. The best came to the top, the mediocre, by definition the majority, remained at the bottom of the social scale. Men like Pareto, Mosca, and Weber have recognized the importance of inheritance in perpetuating an elite, but they maintained that an elite based on heredity loses its vitality and declines because it is inevitably challenged by capable, ambitious men from

---

[78] Marquis de Belleval, *Souvenirs de ma jeunesse* (Paris, 1895), p. 139.

the lower social levels. This idea is a rough approximation perhaps to what actually happens in history, but the counterrevolutionary would never have accepted it as a valid process since it was based on the idea that the individual advanced as far as his talents or guile could take him. The counterrevolutionary operated on the opposite assumption. He not only realized the importance of environment in determining the fate of the individual but also rejected the idea that man should have any fate other than that proper to the group into which he was born. A peasant was destined *qua* peasant to follow in the family tradition, just as a landlord or artisan was destined to do the same. But why should he deny to man the benefits of talent? The answer is the same that he gave to liberal Catholics. A society could not exist on liberal principles any more than a religion because man needed the check of tradition and religion to control his carnal appetites. The counterrevolutionary claimed that the attitude of respect for traditional ecclesiastical and lay authorities was divinely ordained truth upon which the very existence of society depended. It was this conception of moral order that separated the counterrevolutionary from all his contemporaries. When the counterrevolutionary gave the social order a divine sanction he automatically excluded the possibility of any fundamental change leading to anything good. "What is true . . . ," Lucien-Brun proclaimed, "is that every living society needs authority, that this authority if it is legitimate comes from God, and that all other authority is only an accident of violence and a usurpation. . . . There is no society without hierarchy."[79]

The counterrevolutionary had developed an almost pathological aversion to change, but he was not prepared to admit that there was anything unsound about his interpretation of recent history. If there was anything sick about the world it was, in his opinion, modern man. The counterrevolutionary concluded that society faced a "moral crisis" because men, in their monstrous egoism, had turned their backs on traditional beliefs. Sons fought against father, employees against employers, subjects against rulers, mortals against God. He advanced a monocausal explanation for the most violent revolution and the most peaceful social change. In fact, he hardly distinguished between the two. The peasant lad who longed to obtain the education of a lawyer's son, the farm boy who abandoned his lands to seek his fortune in the city, the

[79] Lucien-Brun, *Introduction à l'étude du droit*, 2e ed. (Paris, 1887), p. 268.

innkeeper who had ambitions to become mayor in the commune, the artisan's son who wanted to become the local school teacher—all perpetrated almost as great a violence against society as did armed mobs in the street. Indeed, the counterrevolutionary saw a direct connection between the two. Once peasant or worker overstepped the natural bonds of his social condition, renounced the traditions of family and class, he became a misfit (*déclassé*), rootless, lonely and profoundly unhappy, subject to revolutionary utopian propaganda, and a potential agent for armed rebellion.

This discussion of the counterrevolutionary mentality bears directly on the problem of identifying legitimists in 1871. Obviously a divine right hereditary monarchy appealed to men who were emotionally attached to traditional forms of authority. But the single most important factor in their struggle to retain moral order was the Church not the monarchy. Opinion among counterrevolutionaries divided. On the one hand, there were the political intransigents who maintained that the restoration of the legitimate monarchy was the *sine qua non* for defending the Church and with it moral order in France. "How do you hope to restore order in the family," one of these intransigent royalists asked the conservative sociologist Frédéric Le Play,

> as long as order does not reign at the summit of the state? Tomorrow is not even assured and you dream of undertaking the long work of social restoration! Tomorrow perhaps the government of the country will be in the hands of the enemies of all order, of every honest custom, of every rule. . . . The political question takes precedence over all others; it dominates everything; resolve it first, the rest will come in turn.[80]

The second attitude could be called opportunistic. For many counterrevolutionaries the practical realities of French politics during most of the nineteenth century made the intransigent royalist position untenable, because there was no chance to restore the monarchy. They preferred to concentrate their efforts on a defense of the papacy and, as the pope himself frequently did, decided to cooperate with and even accept any regime that would protect the faith. This was true, for example, of that implacable opponent of liberal Catholicism, Louis Veuillot, editor of the ultramontane Catholic newspaper *L'Univers*, who rallied to the Second Empire.

[80] Lucien-Brun, *L'union de la paix sociale*, no. 2, Lettre à M. F. Le Play (Tours, 1872), pp. 6–7.

But this does not mean that they were indifferent to the question of regime. Most of them came from legitimist families and would have been happy to restore the monarchy. And those who had no legitimist antecedents were certainly predisposed psychologically and ideologically towards legitimism.

These two counterrevolutionary attitudes were reflected in the extreme and moderate Right approach to the restoration. The extreme Right did not think that the restoration of the monarchy could depend on the vote of the National Assembly. It was an integral part of the divinely ordained social hierarchy; its presence was essential to the preservation of the moral order. The Right-Center's claim, therefore, that the Assembly had the right to decide the issue was itself an act of rebellion, a symptom of that demon in modern man that drove him to question all time-honored values and legitimate authority. A monarchy restored by one assembly could just as easily be destroyed by another assembly; it would have no validity, no durability. Even though Chambord would have been on the throne he would not, if dependent on the Assembly, be a legitimate king. He would be an Orleanist, and this is exactly what Chambord himself feared.

The moderate Right confronted the problem with a radically different temper. They were practical men. As practical men, they had supported the Second Empire, which to them constituted the only effective force at hand with which to defend the Church and the moral order; they cooperated with the Orleanists in the National Assembly; they voted in favor of the *Septennat* after the restoration campaign failed even at the cost of vexing the Comte de Chambord and the extreme Right; they defended the Broglie government from the attacks of the pretender and the extreme Right, even when it proceeded to draft constitutional laws. But they did so not because they approved of the Empire or of the Orleanist Right-Center but because the alternative seemed potentially much more disastrous. Moreover, they were ready to make a deal with the Orleanists in order to restore Chambord. It was this restoration by a "sordid" deal that so distressed the extreme Right because it seemingly violated the very essence of hereditary monarchy. But the moderate Right unlike the extreme Right and the Orleanist Right-Center did not view the intervention of the National Assembly in terms of principle. It was simply an expedient, a means to an end. That end was the restoration of the Comte de Chambord. For the first time since 1830, moreover, this restora-

49

tion seemed possible. Considering this and the unacceptable alternative, the moderate Right believed the restoration essential for the preservation of the Church and moral order in France. Thus, they urged Chambord to accept a compromise and they were bitterly disappointed when he refused. "He did not think," Martial Delpit wrote in his diary shortly after Chambord's last white flag manifesto, "that he compromised all the honest people in the country, that there is no longer a basis for the conservative party in France. The wrath here (Versailles) is great against the Comte de Chambord."[81]

There is no way, of course, to resolve the conflict between the moderate and extreme Right. Whether one agrees with the intransigents' argument that a deal with the Orleanists would violate the moral order or with the moderates' contention that it was the best way to assure its preservation depends perhaps on the personal temperament of the observer. Curiously enough, however, both these groups shared the same concern with the "moral crisis." The moderate Right was not liberal in any sense of the word. Like the extreme Right, it had the same deep antipathy for the liberal presumption, the same concept of the moral order, and the same concern for its preservation. Indeed it was the idea of moral order that separated both the moderate and the extreme Right from other conservative groups in the Assembly. Although fear of the barricades drove them to make common cause with all conservatives during revolutionary crises, the men in the chamber's Center little understood or sympathized with the counterrevolutionary idea of a moral order. This failure, for example, emerges quite clearly in the character of their leader, Adolphe Thiers. Notwithstanding a hate of Jacobinism or a dislike of Bonapartism, the president of the Republic admired the Revolution, especially as embodied in the centralized state. It was, he once observed, the most effective instrument ever devised for retaining order, and hence the envy of Europe.[82] The remarks reveals a person completely at odds with the idea of "moral order"; for Thiers order meant obedience externally imposed, not respect self-imposed. Despite his approval of the spirit of resignation that religion instilled in the lower classes, he did not really appreciate the counterrevolu-

[81] Valades, *Martial Delpit*, p. 54.

[82] France, Archives nationales, C 2866, Assemblée nationale, 1871, *Commission de décentralisation*, Séance du 23 juin 1871. Hereafter *Archives nationales* will be cited as A. N.

tionary's point that an insurrection in the street was only a particular manifestation of a moral crisis in society. He relied on the bayonet to keep the public peace, a remedy which for the counterrevolutionary was no remedy at all. "Son of Voltaire," one of the rightist deputies summed him up, "doubt and skepticism have led him astray."[83] The Right-Center was more socially conservative than the Center because it preferred an oligarchy to the middle-class democracy that Thiers and his friends were fashioning. Moreover, it was wedded to a certain conception of the moral order, for these deputies were convinced that a lack of respect for authority was a significant cause of popular ferment and undesirable social change. Still they were prepared to disregard traditional authority when it suited their purpose. Nothing illustrates this better than the Right-Center's insistence that Chambord accept the tricolor. Its insistence was not a tactic, as with the moderate Right, but the symbolic denial of divine right hereditary monarchy in favor of the liberal monarchy of 1830.

Thus the counterrevolutionary conception of the moral crisis helps explain the very different attitudes that the various groups in the Assembly adopted toward Chambord's restoration. Since the moral crisis meant nothing to Thiers and his followers, the legitimate monarchy had no special significance. They willingly rallied to a republican form of government once assured that it could crush the "mobs" in the street. Because it equated a Republic with democracy and anticlericalism the Right-Center, which was primarily liberal Catholic, preferred a liberal monarchy to a Republic; but it preferred a Republic, especially a patrician Republic, to the monarchy of the Comte de Chambord. Monarchy to them was only a convenience, the instrument through which they proposed to realize their claim to rule France. When Chambord asked them to renounce this "pretention" the Right-Center discarded the monarchy for a conservative Republic. They were neither filled with reverence for legitimism nor convinced that Chambord's restoration was essential to the preservation of the Church and the moral order. Although sharing a common concern for the preservation of moral order, the moderate and extreme Right differed from the Orleanist Right-Center specifically on the latter point. This was true of deputies who had no royalist past or personal affection for Chambord. Charles Chesnelong, for example, who had rallied to the Second Empire was so convinced of

[83] P. B. des Valades, ed., *Martial Delpit*, p. 266.

51

the necessity to restore the legitimate monarchy that he said, for his part, he would gladly have accepted the white flag.[84] "Here is the reality behind these intrigues," he wrote. "The Orleanists prefer the monarchy of the Comte de Paris to a Republic. They prefer a Republic to the monarchy of the Comte de Chambord. . . . France can only be saved by the monarchy; the monarchy is only possible through a union of monarchical forces. This union is compromised. We are impotent."[85] Benoist d'Azy, to cite but one more example from moderate rightist opinion, viewed the restoration in the same light. "Perhaps we have not shown all the political skill needed," he wrote his son sadly after the adoption of the republican constitution, "but at least we have never voted against that which represents the principle of order (the Monarchy)."[86] The vital role that the hereditary monarchy played in their plans to restore order, moral order, in France, makes these moderate rightists legitimists.

In his study of the elections of 1871, Gouault contends that the men on the conservative peace lists ". . . were all equally and firmly conservatives but this does not distinguish them from most of the republican committee's candidates; for the one as for the other there was no social question then. It was only after the Commune that the conservatives were to place themselves on the terrain of social defense and make republicans the equivalent of revolutionaries in their propaganda."[87] Gouault considers the election within the narrow limits of the short electoral period and uniquely in terms of the peace issue. He ignores the long suite of events before and during the war that forms the real cadre of the election. Republicans who formed electoral committees were social conservatives (in the sense that most opposed social revolution), but they were not as alarmed as other conservatives about the prospects of an immediate insurrection, not to the point at least of subordinating their republican convictions, as did the monarchists and conservative republicans on the conservative lists, to the interests of "peace and order." If the republicans did not give priority to the social question (meaning fear of an immediate insurrection), their conservative opponents did, and from this

[84] Ltr., Chesnelong to Olivier de Sugny, Nov. 12, 1874, *Chesnelong MSS.*
[85] Ltr., Chesnelong to his wife, Feb. 26, 1872, *ibid.*
[86] Ltr., Denys Benoist d'Azy to Charles Benoist d'Azy, March 4, 1875, *Benoist d'Azy MSS.*
[87] Gouault, *Comment la France est devenue républicaine*, p. 61 n.

standpoint the social question was very much an issue in the 1871 election. Still Gouault is partially correct when he states that the conservatives, when placing themselves on the "terrain of social defense" made "republicans the equivalent of revolutionaries in their propaganda" (although this occurred long before the Commune). For all conservatives, whatever their political convictions, the prospect of a revolution was a frightful thing. But social defense did not mean the same thing to all these men. When the deputies on the moderate and extreme Right "place[d] themselves on the terrain of social defense," it was against the liberal presumption (in whatever form—popular sovereignty, oligarchic sovereignty, popular insurrection, dictatorship, atheism, agnosticism, scienticism, materialism, etc.) that they took their stand. In 1870–1871 France experienced a humiliating military defeat and a tragic civil war. Both, these deputies believed, were symptomatic of a deep moral crisis within the nation. To them the restoration of the legitimate monarchy was a necessary step toward France's moral regeneration. Therefore, despite their differences in temperament, despite even the hatred that existed among them, the deputies on the extreme and moderate Right shall be considered legitimists in this study.[88] Many of them had no personal affection for the pretender, many were late comers to the legitimist fold, but all actively and ardently sought a restoration. The monarchy was only a step in the right direction. Indeed, it is not the restoration per se but the legitimists themselves and their overall program, the principal concerns of this book, that give the restoration any meaning in French history.

[88] The names of these deputies are given in Appendix.

Chapter Two

THE LEGITIMISTS:
SOCIAL BACKGROUND

A basic assumption often used in social history is that an ideology appeals to particular social groups more than to others and that it is possible to show how ideological outlooks themselves reflect deeper antagonisms that separate various groups within a body politic. Marx made one of the first attempts to establish such an interrelationship when he claimed that the Revolution had brought the political conquest of the state by a class that had been created by the industrial "mode of production" (the bourgeoisie) and consequently the defeat of an older class whose power had been based on the ownership of land (the aristocracy). His analysis, moreover, referred specifically to nineteenth-century legitimists. He hitched legitimism to the buggy of the aristocracy and the aristocracy to a preindustrial system of economic exploitation. On the other hand, he associated Orleanism with the bourgeoisie, creator of a modern capitalist economy. He clearly stated the thesis in the *Eighteenth Brumaire of Louis Bonaparte* by tying Orleanism to "high finance, large-scale industry, wholesale trade, that is *capital*," and legitimism to the aristocracy, that is "large landed property."[1] He gave the ideological conflict between legitimists and liberal monarchists, then, a socioeconomic base: the legitimists' conception of a society of rank held together by a belief in a moral order served the interest of a class of hereditary landlords; the Orleanist conception of a society of merit held together by a belief in individualism served the interests of a rising class of merchants, bankers, and manufacturers.

Marx developed an especially fruitful analysis that not only offered insight into the socioeconomic base of French politics but also established the framework within which most of the subsequent work on the subject has taken place. Nevertheless the Marxist hypothesis has been directly challenged by a number of his-

[1] See *The Eighteenth Brumaire of Louis Bonaparte* (Moscow, 1934), pp. 39–41.

torians who have been engaged in the arduous process of measuring it against historical facts. Studies of the victims of the terror, for example, suggest that the counterrevolution by no means can be identified with the aristocracy. More importantly, work that shows the revolutionary bourgeoisie's conservative occupational situation (e.g., a predominance of lawyers and landlords in their ranks) and conservative economic attitude (a predilection to persist in outmoded business methods and economic routine) have undermined confidence in the idea that it represented a class of dynamic entrepreneurs. Moreover, even the contention that liberalism was the natural philosophy of the new industrial groups has been opened to question by those who insist that modern industry, with a need to rationalize its production, was institutionally more suited to a neofeudalistic policy of industrial management than the operational principles of *laissez faire*. The argument is that liberalism, which appealed to the independent small businessman, professional person, and artisan of the preindustrial urban society, was an anachronistic conception in the modern industrial urban society.

Still all the recent literature on the socioeconomic background of nineteenth-century French politics does not tend to revise Marx. Scholars continue to treat the clash between the aristocracy and the *grande bourgeoisie* in traditional Marxist terms.[2] Moreover, on the basis of present knowledge, it is impossible to decide how much revision of Marx, when dealing with the legitimists, is valid because studies are, with the possible exception of Tudesq's work on the French notables from 1840 to 1849, not based on a systematic and detailed analysis of their economic and social origins.[3] Such a gap is perfectly understandable since it would be an enormous undertaking for the entire nation. But even the works that touch on the more modest subject of legitimist parliamentary political groups suffer from the same lack of research.[4] Hence,

[2] Jean Lhomme, *La grande bourgeoisie au pouvoir (1830–1880): Essai sur l'histoire sociale de la France* (Paris, 1960). Also consult the older work by Emmanuel Beau de Loménie, *Les résponsabilités des dynasties bourgeoises*, Tome I: *De Bonaparte à Mac-Mahon* (Paris, 1943).

[3] André-Jean Tudesq, *Les grands notables en France (1840–1849)*, 2 vols. (Paris, 1964).

[4] In *Comment la France est devenue républicaine*, Jacques Gouault does not seriously discuss the subject of the deputies social origins. Herbert F. Brabant, *The Beginning of the Third Republic. A History of the National*

it is necessary to ask once again: What did the legitimist deputies of 1871, who were so much at odds with their contemporaries, represent in French society? What were their social antecedents? How did they fit into the socioeconomic world in which they lived? Answers to these questions are essential to an understanding of the legitimist deputies, and they can help clarify the greater problem of the meaning of legitimism within the nineteenth-century French political context.

Still it would be presumptuous to brush aside all previous studies as if they were of little consequence. If they have provided few or confused answers to the specific problems tackled here, they have set the guidelines along which the research and analysis have been conducted and they have provided most of the generalizations which will be accepted, modified, or rejected in this and the next chapter. The problem is essentially the one with which Marx was preoccupied more than a hundred years ago and which has been debated ever since, the complex interrelationship between politics, ideology, and social groups in a community experiencing accelerated socioeconomic change. There are many ways the subject could be presented. Here, the legitimist deputies will be discussed as a nineteenth-century extension of the social categories of the Old Regime, and then their relationship to the process of large-scale industrialization, which occurred for the most part after the overthrow of the old Bourbon monarchy, will be analyzed. Moreover, inasmuch as the identification of people is aided through comparisons, the legitimists will be measured against some of their political opponents, especially their colleagues in the Assembly's Right-Center, whenever feasible.

Fifty-five percent of the legitimist deputies descended from families that had belonged to the aristocracy in 1789.[5] Some came from noble houses whose particular history was intimately associated with that of the French royalty itself. The Vicomte Gontaut-Biron, *propriétaire* of the lovely Château de Navailles and deputy from Basses-Pyrénées, claimed among his ancestors four marshals of France, one of whom had fought beside Henri IV in

---

Assembly (February–September 1871) (New York, 1940) and Daniel Halévy, *La fin des notables* (Paris, 1930) are political histories.

[5] Rather than cite the source of each item of biographical information I have limited the citations to what appears to be the more important references. The bibliography lists all relevant biographical sources.

the wars of religion and all of whom look down imperiously at passersby from portraits hung in the ancestral home. La Rochefoucauld-Bisaccia and Emmanuel Crussol d'Uzès, deputies respectively from Sarthe and Gard, were scions of two rich and powerful ducal houses, which for centuries had ranked among the first families of France. In a Europe still largely monarchical and aristocratic in character, the prestige of these names was so great that Adolphe Thiers immediately put the deputies to work for the Republic. On the conclusion of the Treaty of Frankfurt he sent Gontaut-Biron to Berlin and La Rochefoucauld-Bisaccia to the court of Saint James to represent the provisional republican government. These three men were the most prominent aristocrats in legitimist parliamentary circles, but others could also boast a proud past. There was the Marquis de Vogüé, deputy from Cher, whose family had been *seigneurs* in Vivarais during the Middle Ages; and Comte Diesbach de Belleroche, from Pas-de-Calais, whose family had provided the monarchy with Swiss guards for generations, one unit of which had the doubtful distinction of being slaughtered by the Parisian "mobs" in 1792. And many deputies from the western and southwestern departments—Louis de Lorgeril, Henri de Tréveneuc, Félix du Marhallach, Emile de Kermenguy, Gabriel de Belcastel, Amédée de Lur-Saluces, Cazenove de Pradine, Abbadie de Barrau—could trace their ancestry to the medieval feudatories of Brittany and Acquitaine.

The deputy, however, who could date his nobility from the high or late Middle Ages was certainly an exception. Most could trace their ancestry to families who appear to have established themselves in the Second Estate sometime during the sixteenth or seventeenth century. This was certainly true of Roger de Larcy, deputy from Gard, whose grandfather had been a *conseiller* at the *Cour des aides* in Montpellier; Louis de Ventavon, deputy from Hautes-Alpes, whose family sat in the *Parlement* in Grenoble; Rességuier, deputy from Gers, who came from prominent *parlementaires* in Toulouse; La Borderie and Gouvello, deputies from Ille-et-Vilaine, who descended from respected *parlementaires* families in Rennes, and a number of others whose ancestors had belonged to the much more recent *noblesse de robe*. Then, there were a few legitimists whose titles of nobility were of even more recent and perhaps dubious origins. The families of Denys Benoist d'Azy, whose grandfather Pierre Benoist had been mayor of Angers (1751–1755), a charge which conferred titles of nobility on its holder, and Joseph de La Bouillerie, whose grandfather had purchased the lands of La Bouillerie in 1713 (whence the family took its name), for example, had scarcely managed to acquire a footing in the Second Estate before the Revolution eliminated all these juridic distinctions.[6] An exact reckoning of the social status of the deputies' families before 1789 is not easy to make, but the following chart gives as precise a representation of their noble lineage as sources permit.

TABLE 1

Titles of Nobility of 106 Deputies
in the National Assembly, 1871

Date	No. of Deputies
Pre-1600	44
Post-1600	29
Post-1700	13
Unknown	20

Thus the family histories of these legitimist deputies mirror five hundred years of the social evolution of the French nobility. Some had claims to the oldest titles, while others came from families that had acquired noble status as the French aristocracy recruited members from the Third Estate. It was the sudden appearance of these quaint and often colorful noblemen in the National Assembly that made such an impression on the Frenchmen of 1871. At the moment of crisis, Frenchmen seemed to have used the power of modern democracy to resurrect the Middle Ages in their anachronistic form. Their presence in the ranks of the legitimists has so impressed historians that they have sometimes in rhetorical flights, identified the legitimist deputies with ". . . these old distinguished *gentil-hommes*, vestiges of the past, the Larcys, Cazenove de Pradines, Carayon-Latours, all perfectly honest men, mystically attached to God and to their prince growing old in exile, believ[ing] that

[6] The biographical information on the La Bouillerie family was given to me during a personal interview with the deputy's descendant. For Benoist d'Azy, see Paul, Jean, et Henri Drouillet, *Histoire de Saint-Benin-d'Azy* (Paris, 1937), p. 486.

58

the hour of the Comte de Chambord had come and unceasingly thank[ing] Providence for it."[7]

Forty-five percent of the legitimists, however, had no claim to membership in the nobility.[8] A few had titles conferred by a Restoration monarch or a pope during the nineteenth century. Florentin Malartre, for example, had been made a Comte and Chaurand a Baron of Saint-Empire by a grateful Pius IX for services rendered the papacy, and Dahirel and Guiraud had inherited titles that their fathers had received from Charles X. None, however, had imperial titles. But, if the Revolution is considered the watershed in the history of the French aristocracy, all these men unmistakably had bourgeois backgrounds. Some of their families had been engaged in commerce and manufacturing before 1789. Florentin Malartre's grandfather, for example, operated a small silk mill in the mountain commune of Dunières (Haute-Loire) in the eighteenth century; the grandfathers of both Courbet-Poulard and Léonce de Guiraud manufactured textiles, the former in Abbéville (Somme), the other in Limoux (Aude). The Monjaret de Kerjégu brothers, Louis and François, were grandsons of a cloth merchant of St-Brieuc (Finistère), and Jean Journu inherited a prosperous wine business in Bordeaux that had been in the family for generations. Most, however, had belonged to the professional bourgeoisie. Of these, a few had served the nobility. Baron Chaurand's grandfather had been *bailli* for the Seigneur de Chambonas, a wealthy noble in Vivarais, and Adolphe Laurenceau's grandfather had been a feudist for the Poitevin nobility. The majority, however, had served the monarchy in one capacity or another. Kolb-Bernard's grandfather had been a sergeant major in a Swiss regiment; Théophile Bidard's grandfather was *inspecteur de l'enregistrement* for the king's domain in Rennes; and Ferdinand Boyer's grandfather was a syndic to the *procureur municipal* of Nîmes. Still others had been lawyers. Emile Carron's grandfather practiced law in Rennes as did François Dahirel's in Ploërmel and Felix Monteil's in Ber-

---

[7] Gouault, *Comment la France est devenue républicaine*, p. 74.

[8] Nonnobles were more numerous in the moderate Right than the extreme Right. Still a fourth (12 out of 52) of the extreme rightists who voted to bring down the Broglie government in 1874 belonged to this category. They were Lucien-Brun, Combier, Chaurand, Amédée Lefèvre-Pontalis, Ferdinand Boyer, J-B Dumon, Pajot, Théry, Paulin Gillon, Dahirel, Martin d'Auray, and Charles du Bodan.

gerac. Soury-Lavergne's grandfather had been a notary in Rochechouart (Haute-Vienne), and some came from both professional
and business family backgrounds; Raudot and Chesnelong, for example, were descendants of a long line of merchants and lawyers.

How do the prerevolutionary origins of the legitimist deputies'
families aid in understanding their position in nineteenth-century
France? First, their aristocratic antecedents are of particular importance. For the families of many of these noblemen, the Revolution had been a bitter, unforgettable experience. Indeed, the present
generation still recounts the suffering of their ancestors during those
troubled times. The Marquis de La Guiche, for example, when
showing a rococo portrait in his château of a pretty young boy,
pointedly remarks that this innocent youth had been guillotined
during the Terror as an enemy of the Republic. The Vicomte
Benoist d'Azy narrates how his great-great-great grandfather, Vincent Benoist, who, implicated in a plot to save Marie Antoinette,
fled to England on the very day the police came to his house to
place him under arrest.[9] The Comte Pierre Cornulier-Lucinière
notes with regret how the family's properties had been sold as a
bien national during the Revolution. These and numerous tales of
the same genre no doubt often give a false impression, particularly
regarding the loss of property. Although Vincent Benoist lived in
penury for a while in England, he managed, on his return to France;
not only to keep but also to expand his territorial fortune in subsequent years. Although an *émigré*, Diesbach de Belleroche's lands
remained immune from confiscations on a technicality—he was a
Swiss citizen. Other *émigrés*, who did not enjoy such immunity,
often reacquired their lands, which had been bought by a friend or
an agent, after the Restoration or purchased new lands, while those
who remained quietly in France through the radical phases of the
Revolution never lost their property. "The great crisis which
opened in 1789," Bloch wrote, "did not destroy large property. . . .
The survival of noble fortunes in certain regions of France—notably in the West—is one of the least studied but most incontestable
facts of our recent social history."[10] The family history of most of

---

[9] While in England Benoist had to live off his wits. He wrote some racy
novels under a pseudonym but he also has the distinction of translating
Arthur Young's studies of French agriculture into French.

[10] Marc Bloch, *Les caractères originaux de l'histoire rurale française*,
2e ed., Tome I (Paris, 1960), pp. 246–247.

these deputies certainly supports such a conclusion. Despite their ability to survive the revolutionary epoch without irreparable property losses, the horror of watching old friends disappear in the revolutionary whirlwind, the experience of exile and emigration, and the constant if largely successful fight to keep the family's properties intact produced intense anxieties in that uprooted generation. It was these anxieties that the stories of the present-day descendants reflect, if in an attenuated manner, and that were felt by the postrevolutionary generation, to which the deputies of 1871 belonged, in an even more aggravated form.

These bitter family memories might have been forgotten had not the deputies grown up in an environment that constantly kept them alive. Many had been educated at home by private tutors chosen for their "correct" political and religious opinions, and those sent away to boarding schools invariably attended schools (often, like the Collège of Fribourg in Switzerland where five of these noblemen had been classmates, in a foreign country) that exuded an ultramontane Catholic-royalist atmosphere.[11] The values learned at home and at school, moreover, undoubtedly discouraged these young aristocrats from engaging in state service. A few had joined the diplomatic corps or some other state administration during the Restoration. Benoist d'Azy, for example, who was blessed by his father's patronage and with a great deal of talent besides, became the youngest *directeur de la dette inscrite* in French administrative history, a feat which is still a topic of conversation among French civil servants.[12] An even larger percentage had become army or naval officers under Louis XVIII or Charles X. But after the Revolution of 1830 few continued to serve. Of those who did most followed army careers. General Aurelle de Paladines, who commanded the Army of the Loire during the Franco-German War, had an illustrious career, although Lt. Col. Rocquemaurel, who retired in 1870 after thirty-six years of service, had a long if undistinguished record. Two nobles were naval officers. Dompierre

[11] Quinsonas, Diesbach de Belleroche, Saint-Victor, Abbadie de Barrau, and Cintré, deputies respectively from Isère, Pas-de-Calais, Rhône, Gers, and Ille-et-Vilaine. Hence they came from various regions of France. See Henri Beaune, *Lucien-Brun: Notice biographique* (Paris, 1901), p. 45.

[12] Guy Thuillier who is known for his works on banking and business history and is a magistrate in the Ministry of Finance provided this information.

d'Hornoy concluded a brilliant career as an admiral and navy minister in one of Thiers' cabinets; Félix du Temple rose to the rank of frigate captain before he interrupted his service to enter the National Assembly. In all, ten nobles served more than fifteen years on active duty. This is a small proportion of a group from families traditionally associated with the military. Furthermore, it was the only state function with which they identified. Except for one deputy, Bois-Boissel, who held a minor post in his native department of Côtes-du-Nord, all the descendants of the old robe families abandoned the magistracy; none could be found in the various branches of the civil service.

This does not mean that they refrained from politics. Of the nobles, 65 percent sat on a general council and 29 percent in a national legislature (other than the National Assembly) after 1830. But their participation was usually limited to short terms. Most had served in the Legislative Assembly of 1849 (only 7 percent had been in the Legislative Corps), and thus in 1871 their legislative experience lay some eighteen years behind them. Furthermore, although some had distinguished legislative records, none ever held a ministerial portfolio before 1871. Even their legislative activities, therefore, confirm that they had cut themselves off from the governmental and administrative life of the nation. But how else could it have been, considering that they were legitimists?

These noblemen tended, therefore, to withdraw into a private world. A minority, perhaps no more than 10 percent, although it is hard to calculate the number precisely, circulated in the *société* of Faubourg St-Germain, an exclusive, clerical-legitimist aristocratic milieu located in an elegant quarter of Paris on the left bank of the Seine, where the richer and often more illustrious families, like the Costa de Beauregards, La Guiches, Gontaut-Birons, and Benoist d'Azys, kept an apartment or *hôtel particulier*. Even though they sometimes participated in Parisian *société*, most of the aristocrats maintained their apartments or *hôtels* in Nantes, Rennes, Angers, Lille, Abbéville, Nancy, Montpellier, Nîmes, Lyons, Toulouse, Bordeaux, or some other provincial city. In short they belonged to a set provincial aristocratic *société*. If Comte de Diesbach de Belleroche was any judge "the old and aristocratic society" of provincial France was very active during the first half of the nineteenth century. It was only after the building of the railroads that, as he wrote in his memoirs (the memoirs of a veritable fox-hunting man), "the beautiful *hôtels* [were] sold and Lille, like so many other provincial cities [saw] itself deserted to the profit of Paris."[13]

The distinction between Parisian and provincial has become somewhat legendary. The witty and urbane Parisians usually considered the provincials country bumpkins. The Marquis de Belleval, for example, expressed a typical Parisian outlook when he described the *société* in Abbeville that he knew so well in his youth. *Société*, he wrote,

> was the reunion of all the nobility in the city, the *faubourg, banlieue*, and district. It was the sum of the titled and nontitled families, who displayed their coats of arms on the doors of their more or less antedeluvian carriages and on the buttons of the copiously embroidered baroque liveries of their servants, families for whom the *nec plus ultra* of elegance and good taste consisted in vegetating during the summer in their *gentilhommières* and in peopling during the winter the houses that they had conserved in their little cities which they decorated with the name of "hotel."[14]

Most provincials, on the other hand, considered Parisian *société* artificial and insincere, although many secretly yearned to escape the boredom of the provinces, particularly in their youth. Still, despite the intellectual and artistic superiority of Parisian *société* and its fashionable elegance, the Parisian life style was remarkably similar to that of the provinces. The seasonal shift from city to countryside was followed by members of both milieux, although the pattern was interrupted more frequently by Parisians with visits to some winter resort (like Nice) or watering place (like Bex in Switzerland), and the break in the routine became increasingly popular as the century wore on. Usually, however, all the aristocrats spent at least part of their summers on their lands engaging in fox hunts and other social customs followed by the rural gentry. And in winter they participated in the balls, receptions, and intimate *soirées* characteristic of the urban social season. Whether Parisian or provincial all were locked into a social ritual that kept them isolated in their own peculiar aristocratic group.

Time, however, was not spent uniquely or even principally in

[13] Eugène de Diesbach de Belleroche, *Souvenirs et mémoires de 1817 à 1905* (Namur, 1911), p. 229. Edition reserved exclusively for the Diesbach de Belleroche family. The copy consulted is in the possession of Ghislain de Diesbach de Belleroche of Paris.

[14] *Souvenirs de ma jeunesse*, p. 42.

entertainment, for these men were far from frivolous people. Some devoted themselves to historical study and *belles lettres*. The Comte de La Monneraye, deputy from Morbihan, wrote a book on the religious architecture of eleventh and twelfth century Brittany; Marc de Lassus, deputy from Haute-Garonne, published brochures on the archaeology and history of his *pays*, St-Gaudens; Eugène de Montlaur and Audren de Kerdrel acquired a certain if limited renown for works on travel and poetry; and Costa de Beauregard eventually earned the laurels of the French Academy for histories about his native Savoy. Another, Félix du Temple has gained fame for studies that looked to the future rather than the past. In 1857 he patented a design for a powered airplane that was the most advanced for his time. Its wings were set in a shallow "V" to keep it from tipping sideways, and it had a propeller set at the front of the fuselage to pull it through the air. Temple tested a scale model that rose into the air under its own power, the first fixed-wing machine ever to do so. He experimented with a full sized machine for several years but no one is quite sure whether he managed to fly it under its own power. Actually, considering that it was powered by a hot air engine, it is unlikely that it ever left the ground because the successful flight of heavier than air machines depended on the invention of the internal combustion engine. Nonetheless, Temple's experiments counted among the more important in the history of flight.

All nobles devoted at least some effort to defending Pius IX, especially when he seemed menaced by the Italian patriots in the 1860s. In France they wrote pro-Vatican articles and books, attended gatherings that protested the government's Italian policy, and either ran themselves or campaigned for clerical candidates in the legislative elections of 1863 and 1869. Some of them, in fact, directly aided the papal military cause. Charette de La Gontrie was commander of the Papal Zouaves; Henri de Saintenac, after resigning a commission in the French army, became one of its lieutenants, and the sons and nephews of other nobles who were themselves too old to fight, joined the papal armed forces.[15] This support did not stop short of illegality. The La Guiche family archives contain correspondence between La Guiche and Benoist d'Azy which indicates that they and a number of others were

---

[15] La Guiche's brother, Benoist d'Azy's grandson, Chaurand's two sons, and Dampierre's son were officers in the Papal Zouaves.

clandestinely engaged in purchasing and running guns and ammunition to the papal forces in Rome.[16]

Devout Catholics, these nobles also took their Christian obligations as members of the "directing classes" very seriously. Diesbach de Belleroche published a "greeting" that he received from the villagers on the occasion of his arrival at Gouy after his marriage. The document illustrates his conception of his family's relationship with the population in the village where his lands were located. The delegate of the villagers, Delattre, received Diesbach and his bride on August 28, 1844 as follows:

Monsieur le Comte et Madame la Comtesse:

The inhabitants of the Commune of Gouy (Pas-de-Calais) wish to express to you today on the occasion of your first arrival in this commune as our lord (Diesbach's father had just died) . . . their joy, affection, and hopes. . . . For everyone, today is a holiday; you see the cultivator, the artisan, all the conditions coming in order to acknowledge their lord and the lady whom they are avid to know, to see, and to greet. As in the old days when your glorious ancestors, returning from a military expedition, saw themselves surrounded by their vassals and soldiers, today the same haste, same affection, same confidence; for, if it is no more the brave soldier who wants to beg that his services be continued, it is the cultivator, the father of a family, who wants you to bless his position which he hopes to maintain in the same condition as in the past, considering that we are exposed without respite to all the troublesome vagaries of the seasons; it is the groups of poor who, drunk with joy, loudly proclaim their hopes and say that they are going to see the good days once more and find again a mother in Madame la Comtesse.

It is only your return, your arrival as lord among us that can heal the wounds that the loss of your amiable father has made in our hearts. . . . The rich will never forget his affability, his tenants, his kindnesses; and the poor his gifts, his liberality. We shall find in you our benefactor, for virtues are hereditary in your family.

. . . [G]ouy, of which the great part is the property of your ancestors is not an unfamiliar place to you; everyone here is

[16] See the correspondence in *La Guiche MSS*, I[e] dossier 12291: Prélats et Ecclésiastiques.

conscious of the name of your beloved father; at Gouy everyone has grown up obligated to your amiable family; and among the obligations that we must acknowledge are those we owe to you. Moreover, we hope that our holy religion will find once again in its protector and particularly in Madame la Comtesse, your wife, a sincere friend, a wife who recognizes the needs for the decoration of the house of God. . . .

Finally, homage, respect, and obedience to the Diesbach family that we have always cherished; this has always been the motto of the inhabitants and this it will always be. . . .[17]

This is a curious document because of its very subservience. Perhaps Delattre was an obedient servant, but one suspects that he was a sly but hardly humble fox who was trying to obtain the most from the richest man in the commune. In order to do so, he had to cast his speech in the form that would make the greatest impression on his "lord," and he apparently succeeded since Diesbach was so proud of the speech that he published it *in extenso* in his memoirs. In short, the speech reveals the sense of obligation that Diesbach was expected to have and did have toward the village, and it was this sense of obligation that the deputies from the aristocracy shared. "He has a noble fortune, of which he makes a noble usage," one prefect wrote of the Baron de La Grange during the Second Empire.[18] References of this sort praising the nobles' largesse vis-à-vis their peasantry are legion. It was the Vicomtesse Gontaut-Biron who cared for the poor in Navailles (Basses-Pyrénées), the Comtesse Benoist d'Azy who dispensed food and clothing to the indigent in St-Benin d'Azy (Nièvre), the Marquise de La Guiche who occupied herself with the poor in the commune of St-Bonnet-de-Joux (Saône-et-Loire), and the Comtesse de Durfort de Civrac who looked after the poor in Beaupreau (Maine-et-Loire). In sum, it was the ladies, who practiced charities during the summer months. But their husbands, especially when greater expenses like the building of a village church or a parochial school were entailed, were active as well.

During the nobles' winter *sejours* in the cities, moreover, the clergy enlisted their support on behalf of the urban poor. Wives and the future deputies often devoted time and contributed money to

---

[17] Eugène de Diesbach de Belleroche, *Souvenirs et mémoires*, Appendix.
[18] Ltr., Subprefect of Hazebrouck to Prefect of Nord, Feb. 4, 1852, A. D. (Nord) M 30/6, *Elections*. The baron in question was the deputy's father.

the parish or helped the St-Vincent-de-Paul societies that were being formed in Paris and provincial cities for the specific purpose of alleviating poverty. Charity, however, was not their only concern. The members of Parisian *société* in particular were familiar with the latest and boldest Catholic thinking about the "social question" which tended to conclude that the war between the haves and have-nots could not be stopped by individual and institutional charities. One, Benoist d'Azy, who was *directeur-gérant* of the *Cie. des Forges et Fonderies d'Alais* for almost forty years, tried to deal with the specific problem of working-class distress in large-scale industry through a policy of company paternalism. He spent hours reviewing plans for buildings—houses, churches, and parochial schools—that the company constructed at Alais, for he had to convince the board of directors of the financial as well as the social soundness of every construction before it could be made. He also sponsored a mutual aid society that paid sickness, accident, and death benefits to his workers and their families, and the highlight of his industrial career occurred when, against the opposition of many board members, he put through an old age retirement scheme at Alais. "Everyone," he noted, "who spends his life laboring is entitled to financial security in his old age. It is the least we can do,"[19] and he intended that pensions be just. "Tell me," he asked his son Charles, "what is a good pension, one that will really take care of the needs of the workers and their families."[20]

Benoist d'Azy and nine other legitimist deputies of aristocratic origins, moreover, became deeply involved in the work of organizations that were concerned with finding solutions to social problems. Of these, four belonged to Armand de Melun's *Société d'économie charitable*, perhaps the best known social Catholic group in France before 1870; the others and some of Melun's group too were members of Frédéric Le Play's *Société d'économie sociale*.[21] In fact, Benoist d'Azy, Anatole de Melun (Armand's twin brother),

[19] Ltr., Denys Benoist d'Azy to Charles Benoist d'Azy, Apr. 25, 1873, *Benoist d'Azy MSS.*

[20] *Ibid.* For information about this paternalism at Fourchambault in which the Benoist d'Azys were also involved see Guy Thuillier, "Les problêmes sociaux à Fourchambault de 1840 à 1870," *Actes du quatre-vingt-unième congrès national des sociétés savantes*, Section d'histoire moderne et contemporaine (Rouen-Caen, 1956), 47.

[21] The Melun group's activities are discussed in J-B. Duroselle, *Les débuts du catholicisme sociale en France (1822–1870)* (Paris, 1951), pp. 198–235 and pp. 434–474.

and Louis de Kergorlay were vice presidents of Le Play's association.[22] Whereas the members of Melun's group were preoccupied with workers' unions during the 1860s, those in Le Play's addressed themselves to a broad range of social issues. Le Play himself excelled in the method of analysis now called *sociographie microscopique.* He spent a great part of his life observing the social behavior of many agricultural and manufacturing communities (he visited Benoist d'Azy's factory in Alais in 1843) throughout Europe in order to discover the causes of social discord and harmony. Le Play's "empirical" investigation simply verified his organic conception of society in which the family was the basic unit in a hierarchical social structure.[23] These nobles, therefore, were impressed by Le Play's conclusions, as was the Comte de Chambord himself.[24] They participated regularly in the society's meetings that were devoted to discussions of the investigations of social problems undertaken by members of the group and the formulation of specific proposals for *la réforme sociale.*

The nobles' public and private activities affected their identity as a social group. Obviously, the rhythm of life that existed in *société* tended to isolate them from the rest of the French community and to reinforce their aristocratic exclusivity. The less serious activities (fox hunting, receptions, and balls) were often the most important social determinants because they involved the entire family. Indeed, the winter social season was an earnest affair, for it provided a means by which families concluded matrimonial alliances. The results of such arrangements are shown by the family connections that existed among the deputies of 1871. The Duc de Mortemart, for example, was La Guiche's father-in-law, Costa de Beauregard was Quinsonas' son-in-law, Rességuier's daughter married Benoist d'Azy's son, and Vogüé's granddaughter married Benoist d'Azy's grandson. Some marriages were contracted with families who were not members of *société.* Crussol d'Uzès's marriage with an heiress whose fortune had been made in the

---

[22] There were twelve vice presidents. Four other legitimist deputies—Humbert Grange, Kolb-Bernard, Maurice Aubry, and Saint-Victor—were members. For lists of members consult the *Société internationale des études pratiques d'économie sociale, Bulletin,* Session de 1869 (Paris, 1872), and *ibid.,* Session de 1872–1873 (Paris, 1873).

[23] A clear presentation of Le Play's ideas can be found in Frédéric Le Play, *La réforme sociale en France,* 6e édition, 4 vols. (Tours, 1878).

[24] For Chambord's appreciation of Le Play, see Marvin L. Brown, Jr., *The Comte de Chambord* (Chapel Hill, N.C.), p. 15 and p. 164.

sardine industry is perhaps the best known example of such a *mesalliance* but there were others. Roger de Larcy married a contractor's daughter; Diesbach de Belleroche wed the daughter of a rich bourgeois landlord; and Eugène des Rotour's mother, born Plichon, came from a wealthy but very bourgeois family in Nord.[25] These marriages were usually contracted for calculated financial reasons, in order, as the aristocrats so quaintly phrased it, to re-gild the family crest. *Société* rarely accepted the spouse's family into its midst. In fact, a spouse's acceptance by *société* depended on his (or usually her) disassociation from his (or her) previous social antecedents. Such marriages, therefore, hardly signified a precipitous change in the predominantly aristocratic character of the families in question. Since the newcomers adopted attitudes of *société* instead of the reverse, their inclusion in the routine of *société* did not undermine its tendency to remain socially apart.

It is true that their more serious activities often brought these aristocrats into contact with other elements in French society. The Jesuit *collèges*, where many studied, enrolled middle class students. The St-Vincent-de-Paul societies were composed of middle-class as well as aristocratic patrons. Neither Melun's nor Le Play's group was composed solely of aristocrats or for that matter of legitimists. Still all these groups attacked the rhetoric and the reality of the liberal conception of society that had been introduced into France by the Enlightenment and the Revolution. Contact with the middle classes could only have significantly affected noblemen if it had brought them under the influence of the ethics of individualism. Therefore, participation in these groups resulted in strengthening the counterrevolutionary attitude of these aristocrats who had been attracted to them because of their ideological outlook in the first place. These activities contributed to those conditioning factors which, along with their abstention from public life, their relatively closed social existence, and their family memories and traditions, kept the nobles in the counterrevolutionary camp.

[25] The Right-Center deputy Plichon was Rotour's close relative. Plichon informed an agent of the Prefect before the elections of 1869 in which Rotours was a candidate against Thiers: "My political opinions are no doubt closer to those of Monsieur Thiers than those of M. des Rotours, but in the final analysis the difference is not too great; besides my family ties with Monsieur des Rotours prevent me from supporting Monsieur Thiers against him." A. D. (Nord), M 30/27, *Elections de 1869.*

The correlation—ideological outlook and social background—exhibited between these nobles and legitimism is noteworthy when the aristocratic composition of the National Assembly is considered. In 1872 *Le Figaro* published a breakdown of membership as shown in Table 2.[26]

TABLE 2

Ideology and Aristocratic Composition
of the National Assembly, 1872

Ideological Outlook	No. of Deputies	Titled	With Particule
Extreme Right	52	28	11
Right	124	39	28
Right-Center	174	31	25
Bonapartists	13	3	2
Left-Center	99	4	11
Left	160	1	9
Extreme Left	67	0	0

These figures show that twice as many legitimists (extreme Right and Right combined) as Orleanists (Right-Center), and four times as many legitimists as conservative republicans (Left-Center) were nobles, but do not present an exact tally of the number of aristocrats in the Assembly. Some of the deputies had Bonapartist titles and many, despite the *particule*, are bourgeois (among the extreme Right legitimists, for example, Bodan and Martin d'Auray). But these correctives do not weaken the conclusion that the great majority of the aristocrats in the Chamber were legitimists since the titled Bonapartists and most bourgeois with a *particule* in their name did not sit among the legitimists.

This correlation between the legitimist and the aristocrat is one example of the deeper social tensions that lay behind the ideological conflicts in nineteenth-century France. The aristocrats came from a social group stripped of the last vestiges of its privileges by the Revolution. It was naturally predisposed to reject any ideology that it blamed for destroying the legal and institutional framework in which it had held an honored place. To be sure, there

[26] *Le Figaro*, March 26, 1872.

were members of the old aristocracy who not only accepted the Revolution in one form or another but who had actually contributed to its success. They had not allowed social origins to dictate their ideological outlook but, to some extent at least, had permitted an ideological viewpoint to determine their place and their attitude toward postrevolutionary society. For example, Henri de Saint-Simon advocated the principle of merit as opposed to rank based on either birth or wealth and became the prophet of industrialism; Alexis de Tocqueville, who certainly regretted the passing of aristocratic values, nevertheless frankly confronted the democratic age despite a fear of the tyranny of the masses. However, most were content to find a place in the liberal oligarchy that ruled France under the censitarian monarchies. They mingled freely with the bourgeois notables. They accepted cabinet, prefectural, and other posts in government and administration. These aristocrats—the Harcourts, Broglies, Audiffret-Pasquiers, and the Orleanist princes themselves—were represented in the National Assembly on the Right and Left-Center. But they were always a minority of the old aristocracy just as they were a minority among the nobles in the chamber itself.

If legitimism and the legitimist nobles in the Assembly represented and were representative of dispossessed, estranged, self-contained nineteenth-century groups of aristocrats, what can be said of their bourgeois colleagues? One possible social explanation for their ideological position is that they had been assimilated into aristocratic society or had become its lackeys. "There is," Bodley noted,

> many a weather beaten château, wherein the combination of rustic discomfort and faded good breeding gives the impression that the masters are relics of an ancient caste, fallen into decay in a democratic age. Yet on inquiry, it will be found, sometimes even in regions of aristocratic tradition, that these mouldering guardians of the prejudices of the Old Regime are of Revolutionary origins. They are descendants perhaps of a regicide of the Convention, or perhaps of an obscure provincial Jacobin, who got his share of confiscated lands for the aid he gave to Carrier in drowning the royalists yonder at Nantes, or for his services on the infernal column of Westermann, which scoured the loyal Vendée with rapine.[27]

[27] J.E.C. Bodley, *France* (London, 1899), p. 558.

71

The above quotation illustrates a process of assimilation that occurred in many regions of France, but particularly in the West, for a century. As one scholar, who studied the sale of national lands in Côtes-du-Nord concluded: Once the bourgeoisie had acquired land in the department, it "was no longer at the head of reform movements. . . . [It] became resolutely conservative and [was] only interested in fusing itself with the old nobility which it had politically supplanted but whose names and memories it envied."[28] The phenomenon, moreover, was hardly limited to France. Rosenberg points out that the bourgeois acquired a considerable amount of property in East Prussia during the eighteenth and nineteenth centuries but that the influx of these newcomers did not change the character of the landlord class since they simply assumed the attitudes and social habits of the old Junker group.[29] It was not an easy matter to enter into aristocratic company in Prussia or France, but some bourgeois often did. Their legitimism could either have been assumed in order to smooth the way into or have resulted from their acceptance by aristocratic *société*, but in either case it could be considered as a characteristic acquired from another social group. Despite their background, therefore, these men would really have become socially as well as politically indistinguishable from the old aristocracy.

Undoubtedly the legitimist deputies of *roturier* origins had more contact with the aristocracy than did nonlegitimist bourgeois because of their common political interest. They formed electoral committees, organized campaigns, and met to map out political strategy when elected. Furthermore, the bourgeois had associated with the aristocracy in a number of Church-related activities, often beginning at school. The *Collège* of Fribourg sent five bourgeois classmates (three of whom joined the legitimist Right), five aristocrats mentioned before to the National Assembly, and both aristocrats and bourgeois were proud that they had attended the same school.[30] The bourgeois, moreover, had worked closely with nobles in the defense of the papacy during the 1860s. Kolb-Bernard, Baron Chaurand, Paulin Gillon, Charles Combier,

---

[28] Léon Dubreuil, *La vente des biens nationaux dans le département des Côtes-du-Nord (1790–1830)* (Paris, 1912), p. 650.

[29] Hans Rosenberg, "Die Pseudodemokratisierung der Rittergutsbesitzerklasse," in Hans-Ulrich Wehler, ed., *Moderne deutsche Sozialgeschichte* (Cologne, 1968), 287–309.

[30] Combier, Grange, Lucien-Brun, Laprade, and Lefébure.

Charles Chesnelong, Emile Keller, and Florentin Malartre distinguished themselves as zealous advocates of the papal cause. These men and others participated in associations that were preoccupied with the social question that brought them together with their colleagues from the nobility. Baron Chaurand, who worked with Ozanam in Paris, was cofounder of the first St-Vincent-de-Paul society in Lyons, Kolb-Bernard was vice president of the St-Vincent-de-Paul society in Lille over which Armand de Melun presided. Jules Maurice, Paulin Gillon, and Emile Dépasse while mayors respectively of Douai, Bar-le-duc, and Lannion, enlisted the support of the nobility for the promotion of mutual aid societies, hospital care for the poor, and town orphanages.

These relations do not prove that the bourgeois legitimists had become sufficiently involved in the dynamics of aristocratic society to have been assimilated. Examples of this sort of metamorphosis exist. Two deputies of the extreme Right, Charles du Bodan and Martin d'Auray, men who were received in the most exclusive salons of Western aristocratic *société*, almost fit the stereotype described by Bodley, for they probably were not only *hobereaux* of *roturier* origins but also descendants of bourgeois radicals who had acquired confiscated lands during the Revolution and who had even favored the death penalty for Louis XVI.[31] Moreover, the wine grower Mayaud, *propriétaire* of the Château de La Tremblay in Maine-et-Loire, and Laurenceau, owner of the Manoir de Joffre in Vienne and of a "sumptuous" residence in the aristocratic quarter of St-Hilaire in Poitier, although they had a less disreputable inheritance from a legitimist viewpoint, fall into this classification because they had adopted the life style and mannerisms of the aristocracy.[32] But besides them and a few others, the rest of the bourgeois did not.

Social historians frequently measure the distinction between aristocrat and bourgeois in occupational functions or some other quantifiable form, and such criteria can also be applied to the legitimist deputies. Whereas only 24 percent of the nobles were engaged in a profession or a business, 81 percent of the bourgeois were. These statistics alone show that the bourgeois were essentially

[31] Edouard Drumont, who is hardly an unimpeachable source, claimed as much. See his *La fin d'un monde: Etude psychologique et sociale* (Paris, 1889), p. 13.

[32] On Laurenceau see Etienne Salliard, *Les Laurenceau Vouillé au siècle dernier* (Poitier, 1950).

urbanites since their professional and business activities were a vital part of city life. The nobles, on the other hand, despite their periodic stay in the cities, served no real function in the city's commercial or professional environment. Most did not enter the lawyer guilds, merchant associations, or municipal governmental councils on which the bourgeois oligarchs sat. They were an alien colony in the city's midst. Other figures reveal the lack of social fusion between the two groups. Although examples of bourgeois and aristocratic intermarriage are fairly common among the nobles, the bourgeois deputies rarely intermarried with the aristocracy (less than 2 percent). This indicates that they were not sufficiently rich or influential to be accepted into an aristocratic family, a privilege that was primarily extended to members of the *haute-bourgeoisie*. The bourgeois legitimists were middle-class. They belonged to what Kolb-Bernard called the *vieille et bonne bourgeoisie* of provincial France that formed a social milieu quite distinct from the old aristocracy and the Parisian *haute-bourgeoisie*.[33]

If such quantifiable information is indispensable for describing the external attributes of the bourgeoisie and aristocracy, the gulf that separated each group cannot be fully appreciated unless qualitative characteristics are taken into account. The words bourgeois and middle class have always been highly connotative. The bourgeois honored thrift and hard work. They tended to lack taste, to be impressed by wealth, no matter how vulgarly displayed. These qualities are real enough, but they are not easy to measure. Nevertheless evidence occasionally appears in a deputy's correspondence or some other document that gives some insight into the mind of the bourgeois. One of the more illuminating sources of this kind is a notebook belonging to the silk spinner Malartre.[34] Malartre, a man of modest means, kept a detailed record of all his expenditures in the book during his stay in Versailles, painstakingly noting every last penny spent for taxis, food, and lodging, and the receipts he carefully collected for these expenses are still located in the attic of the family home in Dunières. He was a model of bourgeois thrift, parsimony, and sometimes avarice. After voting for a state loan, he wrote to his wife. "If I only had the money what good business the loan could be. It is an affair to earn back a third of the capital in three years, plus the interest at six percent!!! There

[33] Ltr., Kolb-Bernard to Chesnelong, June 13, 1876, *Chesnelong MSS.*
[34] Located among the *Malartre MSS.*

will be enough for everyone."[35] The long newsy letters that Malartre sent to his wife (whom he had left at home primarily because he could not afford to maintain a family in Paris or Versailles) reveal his character. The vividness of detail that he uses to recount the receptions and balls, which he attended in his capacity as a deputy, makes these letters a rich source for the social life of the time. But Malartre wrote with the enthusiasm of the indiscriminate awe-struck child who was impressed by almost everything he saw, from the decor of the rooms to the gowns and coiffures of the ladies in attendance. In these letters, there was never a word about the lack of taste in the immediate aftermath of the gaudy Second Empire. Benoist d'Azy's son Charles remarked of Maurice Aubry shortly after meeting him for the first time that he was a good and generous man but a bit common in his actions and tastes.[36] The aristocrat could forgive anything but vulgarity, and this is what he found in the middle classes. They confused ostentation with style. They were impressed by money: nobility was not. They did not know when to be quiet or when and how to speak. In short, they lacked sophistication. One constant complaint bourgeois deputies leveled at Chambord's representatives in France was that they never treated them socially with the informality that sincere and loyal legitimists deserved. One suspects that the reason for this coldness was that these men, whom Chambord chose primarily from the aristocracy, were not accustomed to receiving just anybody into their company. The terms bourgeois and aristocrat, therefore, really apply to these legitimist deputies. They not only differed in their origins and their occupations but also lived in groups whose conception of style and taste were quite distinct.

The legitimist opinion of the bourgeois deputies, then, cannot be attributed to their adoption of aristocratic ways. On the contrary, it must be explained in terms of the experiences and attitudes peculiar to this group of bourgeois. One attitude that the bourgeois held in common was their religious faith. All were fervent Catholics. In most cases, their Catholicism was a strongly rooted family tradition. Although Bodan and Martin d'Auray might have descended from Jacobins, the families of others had become conscious counterrevolutionaries when events had led to a conflict between the Church and the Revolution. Indeed, some of them had paid heavily

[35] Ltr., Malartre to his wife, June 25, 1871, *ibid.*

[36] Ltr., Charles Benoist d'Azy to Denys Benoist d'Azy, July 27, 1870, *Benoist d'Azy MSS.*

for their convictions. Ferdinand Boyer's grandfather was guillotined in Nîmes, Jean Journu's guillotined in Bordeaux, and Emile Carron's, who narrowly escaped a similar fate, languished in a Rennes prison for over a year while the radicals were in power. But religious faith is not properly speaking a social phenomenon. It can and did exist more among some social groups than others, but this fact, which cannot be attributed to religion itself, must be explained either socially or by individual psychology. While faith might help explain why the bourgeois deputies or their families joined the counterrevolution, it does not show any purely social reasons for their ideological opposition.

When the immediate social effects of the Revolution are considered, it is difficult to see how they could have been socially antagonistic to the families of the bourgeois. There are instances where the bourgeois might have held the Revolution responsible for material as well as personal losses. The Chesnelong family's fortune, for example, disappeared when the slaves revolted in Saint-Dominique, and the Malartres' silk mills were confiscated because of the aid they had given to refractory priests. But most families survived the Revolution with little, if any, property loss and some undoubtedly experienced a net gain. Since the bourgeois appear on the whole more prosperous after the Revolution than before, they could not have detested the Revolution for having consummated their material ruin. Whereas the nobles could resent their loss of privilege, the bourgeois could make no such complaint. Of the bourgeois legitimist deputies, 20 percent had pursued careers from which their families by tradition had been socially barred. Of these, 14 percent were judges on appellate courts or *procureurs généraux* in the magistracy and the remaining 6 percent became military men. General Ducrot had performed well in his profession. He caught the eye of the entire nation for a brief moment after he was appointed MacMahon's second in command just before Sedan, but his moment of greatness eluded him when he became involved in the tragic-comic command muddle that preceded the army's defeat and surrender.[37] Still, there were no great captains in Du-

[37] Convinced that the army's march to relieve Marshal Bazaine at Metz was a fatal mistake, Ducrot counseled a rapid retreat on Paris in order to escape encirclement. If Ducrot had been permitted to carry out his retreat, he might have saved MacMahon's army, and he almost got his chance, for after MacMahon was wounded, Ducrot assumed command and ordered a general retreat. Before the retreat began, he was himself removed from

crot's generation. He, Admiral François Monjaret de Kerjégu, the descendant of the cloth merchant, the younger military men like Colonels Jean Brunet and Emile Carron, the judges, and public prosecutors could look back on their careers with a sense of achievement that would not have been possible had the Revolution not opened up new careers to members of their families. The bourgeois deputies' ideological opposition to the Revolution, therefore, could not have stemmed from the harmful effect that the specific social and economic reforms adopted during the Revolution had on their actual position in French society.

Nevertheless the social impact of the Revolution cannot be restricted to its immediate consequences. For the bourgeois deputies the Revolution was never specifically aimed at a social group or institutions. If it had been, it would have come to an end. It was revolution against any social order that tried to maintain itself by the weight of traditions and religious orthodoxy that the legitimist had in mind when he condemned revolution. The bourgeois may have gained from the reforms of 1789, but they believed in a society of permanency. This belief, which they sought to defend with the ideology of legitimism, really did effectively mirror a social conflict that had arisen between the class to which they belonged and the rest of French society. It is particularly noteworthy that the bourgeois deputies, with few exceptions, were elected from departments where their families had long been established members of the Third Estate. This does not mean that the deputies necessarily resided in the departments themselves on a permanent basis. Many of them had, in fact, gone elsewhere in order to practice a profession, but they became candidates in their native departments. This applies to the Parisian banker Maurice Aubry, who ran in Vosges where his family owned a lace business in Mirecourt; the railroad engineer Charles Combier, who, although chief engineer for the *Chemin de Fer des Ardennes*, became a candidate in Ardèche where his family's silk mills had long been located; the lawyer Lucien-Brun who, despite his prominence in the *lyonnais* bar, was a candidate in Ain where the family had been important notaries in the town of Gex; Baron Chaurand, who, if a member of the *lyonnais haute-bourgeoisie*, ran for the Assembly in Ardèche

---

command by a general Wimpfen who arrived on the battlefield from Paris with orders that the army join with Bazaine. See General Ducrot, *La journée de Sedan* (Paris, 1871).

where the family had been involved in the legal profession for generations and had lived in the same home, as one of his descendants proudly observed, before Columbus discovered America; Adrien Tailhand, a judge in the appellate court at Nîmes, who was a candidate and a member of the general council in Ardèche, where his family owned property. Their professions may have taken them away from home, but the claim to candidacy that resulted from their family's traditional importance in a department's oligarchy far outweighed any claim they could make, or even sought to make, on the basis of individual talent.

Deputies who were newcomers to the department they represented, moreover, did not break this pattern of oligarchic supremacy. Several examples could be chosen to prove this contention but that of Charles Kolb-Bernard will be given because his family had not been associated for long with any community. Kolb was the son of a sergeant major in a Swiss regiment that served the monarchy. He began his career as a minor official in the *Régie de Tabac*, holding posts in several provincial cities. He was what the legitimists called *déraciné*. But Kolb quit government service during the Restoration in order to take a position with the Lille sugar refinery, *Bernard Frères*. Although Kolb had no personal fortune, his talents were such that he caught the eye not only of his boss but also of his boss' daughter. Kolb married Mlle. Bernard with full parental blessing and eventually succeeded his father-in-law as company director and inherited the Bernard fortune besides. Kolb, who added Bernard to his family name, was completely accepted by his adopted family and through them became assimilated into the bourgeois society of Lille. He responded by fully identifying himself with his new family and their social milieu.[38] The legitimist deputy Vinols de Montfleury when commenting on the elections of 1871 noted that, in contrast to the republicans "who owed their seats to their knowledge or talents, to their audacity, to their ardor, to their ambition . . . , most of the deputies on the Right had been elected because of their social position, of their fortune, of their honorableness."[39] Kolb-Bernard may have been a self-made man, but he owed his success to the ease with which he transformed himself from a Kolb into a Ber-

[38] See Mgr. Baunard, "Kolb-Bernard," *Reliques d'histoire: notices et portraits* (Paris, 1899).

[39] Baron de Vinols de Montfleury, *Mémoires politiques d'un membre de l'Assemblée nationale constituante de 1871* (Le Puy, 1882), p. 199.

nard. In the final analysis, therefore, his candidacy was no less a result of his family's social position, fortune, and honorableness than it had been for the other men.

The bourgeois legitimists' conception of ethics was group based. They believed that "honorableness" and "honesty" were family traits, and they taught their children, as Chesnelong wrote to his son Pierre, to love God, work hard, and honor the family because the family's social standing and good name were sacred.[40] They believed that the old Catholic town oligarchy, their oligarchy, was characterized, to use Kolb-Bernard's words, by "religious fidelity, habits of work, probity, holiness, thrift, and, when needed, saintly prodigality in doing good works."[41] When the bourgeois legitimists insisted that family count more than individual talent in selection of a candidate, they were asserting the supremacy of the traditional town oligarchy in local affairs. It was the same sort of claim to social preeminence made by the aristocracy—indeed, the kind of pretension against which the old Catholic bourgeoisie had historically chaffed in its encounter with the nobility. But the Revolution removed the basic cause of friction between the two when it abolished aristocratic .privilege. Now the old Catholic bourgeoisie saw its political and social standing challenged by the dogma of individualism. The bourgeois legitimist deputies' ideological struggle with the Revolution, therefore, reflected the social antagonism that existed between the old Catholic oligarchy and the newer middle class, which challenged the position of the former as the ruling elite in the towns of provincial France.

Still, if legitimism seems a reasonable ideological outlook for members of the old Catholic bourgeoisie, the correlation between the two is less valid than that between legitimism and the aristocracy. This is apparent from the diversity of political opinion within the families of the legitimist deputies themselves. A few of the aristocrats had relatives who professed nonlegitimist opinions. The Orleanist minister Vicomte d'Argout, *gouverneur* of the *Banque de France*, was Belcastel's uncle; the Orleanist industrialist Delahante, the *Chevau-léger* La Bouillerie's father-in-law; and the republican Lur-Saluces, cousin of his legitimist namesake in the National Assembly. But these men were not members of the immediate family of the legitimist deputies and were quite rare cases

[40] Ltr., Charles Chesnelong to Pierre Chesnelong, date not legible, *Chesnelong MSS.*

[41] Ltr., Kolb-Bernard to Charles Chesnelong, June 13, 1876, *ibid.*

even among members of their extended families. With the bourgeois deputies, however, the incidence of nonlegitimists in the
family is greater and extends into the immediate family circle.
Armand Fresneau's father had been an Orleanist prefect and his
uncle was a Bonapartist senator; Amédée Lefèvre-Pontalis' brother
was a Thierist republican; and Charles du Bodan's father served
the July Monarchy, Second Republic, and Second Empire with
equal loyalty. On occasion, the fervent legitimism of a deputy
appears rather the exception than the family rule. This was probably the case with Paulin Gillon's family that seemed devoted first
to the liberal Orleanist Monarchy (his brother was a faithful Orleanist deputy during the July Monarchy) and later to a conservative Republic (his nephew was the future president of the Republic, Raymond Poincaré).[42]

The evidence shows the limitations of trying to find a purely
cause-effect relationship between social background and ideological convictions. Some men are temperamentally predisposed to
adopt ideological positions; others are not, and those that are
need not adopt the same ideology. The subjective factor of individual psychology can never be eliminated without falsifying social history. Although most legitimists followed family political
traditions, some members of legitimist families did not, and some
members of nonlegitimist families became legitimists. The psychological condition of the individual need not have remained constant. Paulin Gillon, for example, appears to have adopted an intransigent legitimist attitude rather late in life when he became
convinced that a return to traditional beliefs was the only alternative to social upheaval. At times the ideological differentiation
among members of a single family could have embarrassing, if not
outright painful, results. Armand Fresneau's uncompromising legitimism while a deputy to the Legislative Assembly of 1849 hurt
his father's career because it prompted Louis Bonaparte to dis-
miss the elder Fresneau from a prefectural post.[43]

[42] For Paulin Gillon's family, see Charles A. Salmon, *Paulin Gillon,
1796–1878* (Bar-le-duc, 1881), pp. 4–6. For Bodan's father's career, see
M. du Bodan, *Discours prononcés de 1838 à 1858, précédés d'une lettre à
ses fils* (Corbeil, 1868).

[43] After serving in various subprefectures Fresneau's father was named
prefect of Corsica on May 16, 1845. On January 11, 1849 he was made
prefect of the Pas-de-Calais and then, as a result of his son's opinions, he
was dismissed from his post in March 1851. There is a letter, March 10,
1851, from Jean Fresneau to the minister of the interior protesting that

Since these examples are restricted to the individual deputies and their families, they do not indicate whether limits to social determinism spring from anything other than psychological factors. They do not, for example, prevent the conclusion that the Catholic oligarchy of provincial France, with exceptions resulting from the idiosyncrasies of individual character, inevitably became legitimist. On the other hand, evidence based solely on the legitimist deputies and their families certainly cannot be used to prove the contrary since, without a general knowledge of the political behavior of the Catholic bourgeois oligarchy in France, it is impossible to know whether the specific comportment of the bourgeois legitimist deputies is typical or atypical, and without this information it is not possible even to make a qualified statement about social determinism.

No detailed studies of the political and religious behavior of the notables on the local level have been done for every region of France. But Tudesq, who spent years working in national and local archives, produced a study of the notables in France during the 1840s.[44] Tudesq also faced the difficult problem of deciding who was a notable, but, because he was working on the subject during the July Monarchy, he found an easy and satisfactory answer. He simply identified the notables with the body of men (about 180,000) who were the electors of France. This permitted him to measure the strength of the legitimist notables by noting the percentage of votes cast for legitimist candidates in the municipal elections of 1837. The results, which are given in Map 1 were not perfect, for many legitimist notables did not vote. But they do provide a reasonably good picture of legitimist representation among the notables in the various regions of France.

The map shows that there were pockets of legitimist strength (areas I, II, and III) in the Northeast, the East, and the Center. Legitimists constituted a strong minority group in Belfort (1), Haute-Saône (2), Haut-Rhin (3), and Jura (7); a weaker but

---

his career should not be broken because of his son's actions. These documents were deposited in the private papers of the Fresneau family, which are located in the family home, Bourg-des-comtes, Ille-et-Vilaine. Hereafter cited as *Fresneau MSS.*

[44] A-J Tudesq, *Les grands notables en France*, 2 vols. (Paris, 1964). This analysis of the geographical distribution of Legitimist strength leans heavily on Tudesq's study. See in particular, Tome premier, livre premier, *La puissance régionale des notables*, Chapters II ("La France légitimiste. Répartition géographique") and III ("Le légitimisme; comportement et idéologie").

81

MAP 1. Percentage of the Legitimist Vote in the
Municipal Election of 1837

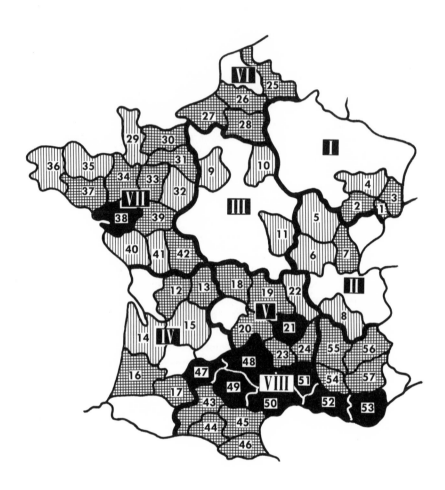

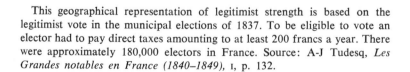

5 TO 9%   10 TO 19%   20% OR MORE

This geographical representation of legitimist strength is based on the legitimist vote in the municipal elections of 1837. To be eligible to vote an elector had to pay direct taxes amounting to at least 200 francs a year. There were approximately 180,000 electors in France. Source: A-J Tudesq, *Les Grandes notables en France (1840–1849)*, i, p. 132.

still measurable group in Vosges (4), Côte d'Or (5), Saône-et-Loire (6), Isère (8), Eure-et-Loir (9), where they were concentrated in the district of Châteaudun, Seine-et-Marne (10), and Nièvre (11), where they were especially numerous in the district of Château-Chinon (Benoist d'Azy was elected to the Chamber of Deputies from this district in 1841). But the map really reveals the relative absence of legitimist notables in these three regions of France. The legitimist vote was very weak in seven of the departments located in the Southwest, the Central Massif, and the North (areas IV, V, and VI), but in three departments, Gironde (14), Dordogne (15), and Loire (22) between 5 and 9 percent, in thirteen departments, Charente (12), Haute-Vienne (13), Landes (16), Gers (17), Creuse (18), Puy de Dôme (19), Cantal (20), Lozère (23), Ardèche (24), Nord (25), Somme (26), Seine-Inférieure (27), and Oise (28), between 10 and 19 percent, and in one department, Haute-Loire (21) over 20 percent of the electors cast a ballot for legitimist candidates. Legitimist notables, therefore, were much more numerous in these areas than in the Center, the East, and the Northeast. But the areas of greatest legitimist influence were undoubtedly the West and the South (areas VII and VIII). In the West between 5 and 9 percent of the electors in six departments, Manche (29), Sarthe (32), Côtes-du-Nord (35), Finistère (36), Vendée (40), and Deux-Sèvres (41), 10 and 19 percent in seven departments, Calvados (30), Orne (31), Mayenne (33), Ille-et-Vilaine (34), Morbihan (37), Maine-et-Loire (39), and Vienne (42), and over 20 percent in one department, Loire-Inférieure (38), voted legitimist. Still the results are deceptive because legitimist abstentions were particularly pronounced in these departments. The legitimist notables, therefore, were even more numerous in the West than the balloting suggests. In fact, the West was "le foyer de l'intrigue légitimiste par excellence."[45] But if this is true, the South was not far behind. In seven of the fifteen departments, Tarn-et-Garonne (47), Aveyron (48), Tarn (49), Herault (50), Gard (51), Bouches-du-Rhône (52), and Var (53), over 20 percent of the notables voted legitimist, and in the other eight, Haute-Garonne (43), Ariège (44), Aude (45), Pyrénées-Orientales (46), Vaucluse (54), Drôme (55), Haute-Alpes (56), and Basses-Alpes (57), their vote amounted to between 10 and 19 percent of the ballots cast.

Thus Tudesq's study shows some regions where legitimists were

[45] *Ibid.*, p. 133.

an isolated and insignificant minority; others where they may have been an important group in a canton or a district but counted for very little in a department; and still others where they formed a solid political group among the notables within one or more departments. These results are significant when compared to those indicating areas of legitimist strength in the elections of 1871. In 1871 elections were conducted by *scrutin de liste*. This electoral method permitted the conservatives to form one broad fusionist list behind which their constituency could unite. However, when drafting the lists the conservatives did not allot places to legitimists, Orleanists, or conservative republicans according to a uniform formula. The political opinions of the notable varied regionally, and because this was an effective fusion the political composition of the electoral lists reflected this variation. Theoretically, then, a map which gives the political composition of the "peace" lists should reveal the strength and weakness of the legitimist notables within a department's conservative community. However, two practical difficulties limit the possibility of constructing such a map. In the first place, the conservatives did not produce a single list in many departments. Where several lists of peace candidates of differing political nuances appear, it is impossible to know on the basis of the lists themselves which list, if any, best mirrors conservative opinion. In the second place, the lists are not easy to find because of the paucity of source material resulting, as previously mentioned, from the effects of war and invasion. This is particularly the case in departments where conservatives lost, for the newspapers followed the disturbing practice of printing the names of the victorious lists while ignoring the losing conservative fusion. Even when the defeated conservative lists appear in print, they are often useless because no information about the candidates' political persuasion was published, and since they were not elected, little information about them could be found. Still these obstacles to the construction of a map are not insurmountable. Although conservatives cannot be easily identified politically in departments where republicans won, republicans lost in most departments. When several conservative lists appear in a department, moreover, usually one of them won. This indicates that the victorious list was the principal list of fusion and that the others represented ineffectual splinter groups.[46] Even more important, in

[46] When more than one conservative list appeared in a department, moreover, the division among conservatives was often more apparent than

most departments only one conservative fusionist list existed. Accordingly, a map that indicates only the departments where a single conservative list won should offer an approximate representation of the varying strength of monarchist groups in the French conservative community.

Map 2 gives legitimist representation on the victorious "peace" lists. In the Northeast, the East, and the Center (areas I, II, and III), the Gambetta republicans won in Moselle, Meurthe-et-Moselle, Bas-Rhin, Haut-Rhin, Côte d'Or, and Yonne. Hence these departments are excluded from consideration in this discussion. The legitimist part in Seine-et-Oise, Seine-et-Marne, Meuse, and Haute-Savoie, moreover, cannot be measured by the schema presented here since there was a multiplicity of lists in each department, none of which won most of the seats in the elections. Elsewhere, however, a propeace conservative list triumphed. In these twenty-three departments, the legitimists numbered more than 50 percent of the candidates; in only two, Belfort (1) and Nièvre (four of seven) (18); between 25 and 50 percent in three, Eure-et-Loir (13), Haute-Marne (4), and Allier (19); less than 25 percent in fourteen, Haute-Saône (2), Vosges (3), Ardennes (5), Doubs (6), Jura (7), Saône-et-Loire (8), Rhône (9), Ain (10), Isère (11), Savoie (12), Loiret (14), Loir-et-Cher (15), Indre-et-Loir (16), and Cher (17); and were not represented in four. On the average they held 12 percent of the positions on the winning lists in these departments.

The legitimists' minor role in the coalition, therefore, discloses the same lack of influence among the notables in these areas as shown in the municipal elections over thirty years before. To be sure, legitimist representation on the lists in Haute-Marne, Rhône, and Allier seems to exaggerate their numbers measured in the municipal elections. In fact, legitimists generally received a larger

---

real. There were four lists in Gard, for example, but of the nine candidates on the victorious list two ran on all four lists, three on three lists, three on two lists, and only one on one list. In Loire, the two conservative lists were identical, except for one man; in Lot, there were two conservative lists, but four of the six candidates on the list that won appeared on the other list. In the Deux-Sèvres there were five lists, but four of the seven candidates on the list that won ran on four lists, one on three lists, and two on two lists. In Vendée, one of three conservative lists won all the seats, but of the candidates elected two were on all three lists, four on two lists, and two on a single list.

MAP 2. Percentage of Legitimist Representation on the Peace Lists, February 8, 1871

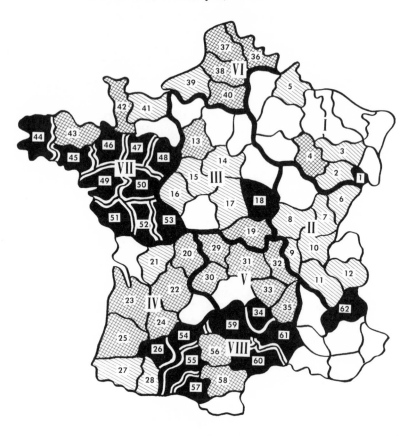

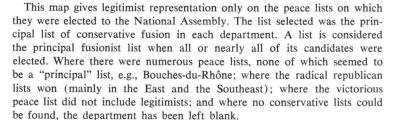

LESS THAN 25%   25 TO 50%   50% OR MORE

This map gives legitimist representation only on the peace lists on which they were elected to the National Assembly. The list selected was the principal list of conservative fusion in each department. A list is considered the principal fusionist list when all or nearly all of its candidates were elected. Where there were numerous peace lists, none of which seemed to be a "principal" list, e.g., Bouches-du-Rhône; where the radical republican lists won (mainly in the East and the Southeast); where the victorious peace list did not include legitimists; and where no conservative lists could be found, the department has been left blank.

When comparing this map with Map 1, it should be remembered that it does not give the lists in departments where legitimists may have figured prominently on peace lists that lost, i.e., the Southeast (Drôme, Vaucluse, Basses-Alpes, and Var).

share on the lists than the municipal elections show they warranted. But usually they were given only token representation. In Ardennes, Haute-Saône, Vosges, Doubs, Jura, Ain, Isère, Savoie, Loir-et-Cher, Loiret, Indre-et-Loir, and Cher only one legitimist appears on the fusionist list. But the weakness of their party is revealed by the conditions of their candidacy as well as the smallness of their number. Often the legitimists seemed to be selected because they were war heroes. This was the case with Costa de Beauregard (Savoie), Ducrot (Nièvre), Aurelle de Paladines (Allier), Vaulchier (Doubs), and Keller (Belfort). The conservative notables appeared, therefore, to have chosen them despite rather than because of their political opinions. Moreover, they sometimes ran as republicans. Costa de Beauregard appeared on a republican list on which he was the only nonrepublican among the candidates (but not designated as such); Lucien-Brun in Ain and Béthune in Ardennes ran similarly. The legitimists could not have counted for much in these departments if they had to accept fusion under republican auspices.

In the Southwest, the Central Massif, and the North (areas IV, V, and VI), the departments of Lot and Charente-Inférieure are excluded from consideration because no single list of conservative fusion won. In all the others, however, conservatives backed one victorious "peace" list. In two of these departments, Gers (26) and Lozère (34), the legitimists composed 50 percent or more of the coalition; in fifteen, Haute-Vienne (20), Dordogne (22), Gironde (23), Lot-et-Garonne (24), Landes (25), Creuse (29), Corrèze (30), Nord (36), Pas-de-Calais (37), Somme (38), and Oise (40), they amounted to between 25 and 49 percent; in four, Charente (21), Basses-Pyrénées (27), Hautes-Pyrénées (28), and Seine-Inférieure (39), less than 25 percent; and in one they were not represented. On the average, legitimists constituted 32 percent of the candidates on the principal lists of conservative fusion. They were much more important in these three regions than in the East, the Northeast, and the Center. Undoubtedly, in some departments their strength is exaggerated. Their presence on the coalition in Hautes-Pyrénées, Basses-Pyrénées, Lot-et-Garonne, Corrèze, and Pas-de-Calais cannot be justified in terms of the municipal elections of 1837. Moreover, this evidence is corroborated by information about their candidacy in 1871. In Basses-Pyrénées, for example, their lack of influence was apparent despite their candidacy, for the legitimists ran as republicans on a list dominated by republicans. It was only because the republicans accepted them in the interest of conservative unity not because the legitimists carried much weight in conservative councils that they were selected. In Lot-et-Garonne, the legitimists' sudden prominence in 1871 can be explained by the momentary eclipse of the Bonapartist notables who were the real magnates in the department. Indeed, since Bonapartists were predominant throughout the Southwest, the slump in their prestige gave the legitimist and Orleanist notables a disproportionate influence in conservative electoral meetings everywhere in this region. But generally the correlation between legitimist numerical strength among the departments' notables and their representation in the coalition holds.

This conclusion is reinforced by the municipal elections of 1837, and is also supported by the greater prominence of the legitimist candidates here than in the East, Northeast, and Center before their election. Whereas candidates in the latter areas were rarely office holders during the Second Empire, those in the North and the Central Massif usually and those in the Southwest occasionally held local offices.[47] Some had been so well entrenched in their electoral district that they successfully braved the hostility of the imperial bureaucracy in order to gain their seat. Partz de Pressy, for example, won a general councillor's seat in the canton of St-Pol (Pas-de-Calais) despite governmental efforts to defeat him. Kolb-Bernard was so influential in his district that the minister of interior, "regretting that it was not possible to choose a candidate whose antecedents offered more guarantees," instructed the prefect of Nord to support his candidacy for the legislature rather than try to find a more suitable candidate whose inevitable defeat by Kolb-Bernard's would embarrass the government.[48] Most of the legitimists, however, could never have won a seat even in a general

[47] In Nord, Pajot and Théry were municipal councillors (Lille); Leurent both a municipal councillor (Tourcoing) and a general councillor; Maurice, mayor of Douai; La Grange, a general councillor; Kolb-Bernard and Rotours general councillors and deputies to the Legislative Corps. In Pas-de-Calais Partz de Pressy was a general councillor. In Somme Blin de Bourdon was a general councillor and Courbet-Poulard municipal councillor (Abbéville). In Oise, Kergorlay was a general councillor and Labitte a municipal councillor (Beauville). In Seine-Inférieure Bagneux was a general councillor. In Central Massif most of the legitimist candidates were general councillors.

[48] Ltr., minister of interior to prefect of Nord, July 16, 1859, A. D. (Nord), M 30/9, *Elections.*

council much less the legislature against imperial opposition. In fact, most had received the support of the government in their electoral district. But the government approved of them because they were important men in the community who agreed to back a regime, of which they fundamentally disapproved, in the interests of order. If they had not been powerful notables, the regime could have easily brushed them aside for more enthusiastic supporters. It chose not to, precisely because it preferred their cooperation to their opposition. And governments habitually fear only the opposition of the powerful.

Of the twenty-two departments in which the conservative fusionist list won (areas VII and VIII), legitimists constituted 50 percent or more of the coalition in seventeen departments, Finistère (44), Morbihan (45), Ille-et-Vilaine (46), Mayenne (47), Sarthe (48), Loire-Inférieure (49), Maine-et-Loire (50), Vendée (51), Deux-Sèvres (52), Vienne (53), Tarn-et-Garonne (54), Haute-Garonne (55), Ariège (57), Aveyron (59), Hérault (60), Gard (61), and Hautes-Alpes (62); between 25 and 49 percent in four, Manche (42), Côtes-du-Nord (43), Tarn (56), and Aude (58); and less than 25 percent in one, Calvados (41). On an average legitimists made up 53 percent of the candidates in the thirteen western departments and 51 percent of those in the nine southern departments covered on the map. Since the republicans won in the southeastern departments and in Pyrénées-Orientales, legitimist representation in the conservative coalition there is not noted, but, if the municipal elections are any basis for assessing their strength among the conservative notables of this region in 1871, it was certainly as great where they lost as where they won. On the other hand, the comparison between 1837 and 1871 is deceptive for the western departments because legitimist electoral abstentions in 1837 do not reflect the strength of legitimists as well as their participation in the coalition of 1871. The composition of the conservative electoral lists in both areas, therefore, reveals the presence of a large and influential group of legitimist notables within the conservative community.

As in the North and the Central Massif, moreover, the legitimist candidates were themselves *primi inter pares* in the legitimist group. Again their general preeminence on the local level is shown by the fact that many were mayors or members of municipal or general councils when the Empire collapsed. In the West this was especially so. Here most of the officeholders had not acquired their positions as implacable foes of the Empire; they had struck the same uneasy compromise with the regime that legitimists had elsewhere. But the acceptance of the government had not been a confession of impotence. If they cooperated with the Empire to maintain order, they cooperated from a position of relative independence. Indeed, some of them enjoyed almost impregnable electoral positions on the cantonal level. The prefect of the Maine-et-Loire, for example, complained about his helplessness in Durfort de Civrac's canton. ". . . [T]he influence of this Civrac family is indeed extraordinary in this little hamlet (*petit pays*) where they possess 120,000 *livres de rente* in the environs of Beaupreau and in the city, to the point that we pay them rent on the tribunal and the jail which are their property."[49] When they wanted to exert their independence, they often did so successfully. Prefectural hostility failed to dislodge Civrac from a seat in the general council; in fact, the prefect was forced to appoint him mayor of Beaupreau because he could find no one in the commune who dared risk the enmity of the Civrac family by accepting the office.[50] Durfort's decision to become an official candidate in the election to the Legislative Corps extricated the prefect from a difficult situation. Similarly, La Rochejacquelain in Deux-Sèvres and Champagny in Côtes-du-Nord, with the support of the local notables, overcame the powerful patronage machinery of the imperial bureaucracy that tried to block their elections to the general councils. But again occupation of a local office is not a completely reliable gauge of the legitimists' influence just before their selection as candidates in 1871, for many of them had remained aloof from politics during the Empire. Had they entered local electoral contests, the number of offices in their possession would have been even greater.

In the South legitimist candidates had also been local office-holders. Ferdinand Boyer and Louis-Numa Baragnon were members of the municipal council of Nîmes; Bonald was a general councillor in the Aveyron; Grasset was a general councillor in the Hérault, and a number of others also held offices. But if this confirms their significance in departmental affairs, it does not show it to the fullest extent. The reason, however, is very different from that given for the West. In the South the notable could not rely

[49] Ltr., prefect of the Maine-et-Loire to the minister of the interior, July 18, 1852, A. N., F[ic] III, Maine-et-Loire.

[50] In 1852 the government's candidate for the general council lost to Durfort de Civrac, 1,119 to 486.

on the support of the electorate to the same degree that he could in the West. That he did not win local elections, therefore, was not a sign of his lack of influence among the notables as of the notables' inability to get the local population to support them against the government. The prefect could choose his candidates with more freedom here. But the subject of the electoral behavior of the population in the South will be taken up in Chapter Six. The point at issue now is the political attitude of the notable. There can be no doubt that the legitimist candidate was a prominent notable in 1871, the best proof of which is not that he held local office before the election, which he often did, but that he was placed on the ballot by the leaders of the legitimist faction of the fusionist camp. In the South legitimist candidates were, like those in the West, both the leaders and representatives of a large and influential legitimist society. This society was much more important than those existing in the North and the Central Massif because of its number and density. Indeed, half (102 deputies) of the legitimists in the National Assembly came from these two regions (73 from the West and 29 from the South) which graphically indicates their strength there.

Thus, a comparison of the elections of 1837 and 1871 helps identify legitimism within a larger social context than is provided by the deputies themselves. Moreover, the elections provide data that, with the aid of information coming from other sources, assist in coming to grips with the question of social determinism. Tudesq devotes considerable space in his study to the social composition of the legitimist faction in areas of its concentration. Unfortunately, he does not produce statistical data to support his generalizations, but they are based on a thorough knowledge of the notables in each area. His analysis supports the conclusions that can be drawn from the legitimist deputies themselves. The legitimist notables were both members of the old aristocracy and the old Catholic bourgeois oligarchy of provincial France. Tudesq does not merely offer a conclusion that applies vaguely to every area of legitimist strength. He refers specifically to legitimists in a city, a canton, a district, a department, or a region, showing how the actual social mixture differed from place to place. In particular, he notes that legitimist society in its two principal regions of strength was, despite the fact that it contained aristocratic and bourgeois notables in each area, a study in contrasts. In the West the landholding aristocracy dominated. They were rich and numerous among the

91

rural notables and with the aid of the clergy controlled much of the countryside. This contention is not surprising since it confirms the conclusions made by electoral sociologists for over sixty years. Moreover, it is verified by the social background of the legitimist candidates of 1871 because 65 percent of them were aristocrats and many of the others were bourgeois landlords who lived in the style of the rural gentry. The center of legitimist *société* in the West was clearly in the countryside.

In the South, on the other hand, Tudesq describes legitimism as primarily an urban phenomenon. In this region, the nobility was not unimportant among the legitimist notables, but the nobles were more fully integrated into town life than their Western counterparts. Tudesq also points out that a large segment of the town oligarchy embraced legitimist opinions. For example, in Toulouse at least one-third of the magistrates were legitimists as were many of the university professors; in Nîmes and Montpellier members of the professional bourgeoisie were frequently legitimists and in Marseilles notables from the liberal professions, businessmen, and merchants (*négociants*) were often royalists. In some Southern cities the middle and even the working classes supported the clerical-royalist cause. In no other area of France did the legitimist play such a vital role in town life. The legitimist representation from the South seems to corroborate Tudesq's findings because 45 percent of the candidates in 1871 were not only bourgeois but also bourgeois who participated in the professional and business activities of the towns.

Since all members of the old Catholic town oligarchy and the aristocracy were not legitimists in these areas an absolute cause-effect relationship between social background and ideological outlook cannot be asserted. But the high incidence of legitimism among the Catholic oligarchy and the aristocracy suggests that an approximate correlation might exist. This would be true, however, only if areas of legitimist strength coincided everywhere in the nation with areas in which the aristocracy and the old Catholic bourgeoisie were prominent notables. As far as the aristocracy is concerned, this is certainly the case. There were some nonlegitimist areas of aristocratic concentration as noted, but, generally speaking, regions in which the aristocracy was numerous were legitimist, and regions where it was not were not. With the Catholic bourgeoisie, however, the hypothesis is much less tenable. Before this point can be established, however, it is necessary to identify the areas where the old Catholic oligarchy predominated.

There is no study that clearly delineates on a national scale between the staunch Catholic bourgeois oligarchy and liberal, Voltairian, or Protestant bourgeois groups. But the religious outlook of the bourgeois can be surmised from the religious attitudes that existed in an area. One of the characteristics of nineteenth-century Catholicism is that it integrated diverse social elements into a community in which the institutions of the Church formed a focal point. When the Catholic community was strong in a region, it encompassed broad segments of the upper, middle, and lower classes. The religious vitality of any one group in the area seemed to be nourished from the whole. A small body of militant Catholics could flourish in an area of anticlericalism or religious indifference. But the old Catholic oligarchy's religious life and its influence among the notables were especially intense wherever the Church had a large following. Thus, one way of noting the old Catholic bourgeois oligarchy's strength is to find the areas where a Catholic culture was firmly rooted among the people.

It is not easy to determine whether a population was ardently Catholic because questions of faith are deeply personal, qualitative, and hence hard to measure. Religious sociologists, however, have tried to overcome the problem of quantification with a reasonable assumption: People who attend mass on Easter are considered devout, whereas those who stayed away are anticlerical or religiously indifferent. Bishop Dupanloup, who was a deputy in the National Assembly, sponsored a study based on this hypothesis at the beginning of the Third Republic, and he found less than 5 percent of the men in most of the cantons of his diocese attended Easter mass.[51] Neither the legitimist vote in the municipal elections of 1837 nor their participation on the conservative electoral list of 1871, it might be added, was significant in Dupanloup's diocese. With the exception of Dupanloup's survey, the religious practices of Frenchmen at the beginning of the Third Republic have not been analyzed on a territorial basis. Studies of other periods, however, provide information that can be usefully projected into the Third Republic. In 1947 Canon Boulard prepared a map of Catholic areas and areas of religious indifference in rural France

[51] Gabriel Le Bras, *Etudes de sociologie religieuse*, Tome I, *Sociologie de la pratique religieuse dans les campagnes françaises* (Paris, 1955), pp. 69–71.

according to the criteria employed in Orleans by Bishop Dupanloup.[52] Because religious practice in rural France had changed
since 1870, the map could not be accepted as completely valid for
the earlier period. But the changes have generally been detrimental
to the Church, that is, change has meant de-Christianization. The
assumption, therefore, that the areas which were staunchly Catholic
in 1947 were at least as Catholic three-quarters of a century earlier seems valid.

Canon Boulard's findings unfortunately do not completely identify the Catholic bourgeois notables because they pertain uniquely
to the countryside, and rural and urban religious practices sometimes differed radically. There were cities, like Avignon, where
the Catholics were numerous but where the Church's influence
was negligible in the surrounding countryside. Boulard's map,
therefore, fails to show Catholic presence in such cases. But what
about the reverse? Did the city constitute an anticlerical speck
in a Catholic ocean and if so does this mean that the old Catholic
oligarchy would be unimportant in the area? Studies of the religious sociology of urban France are very rare, and thus it is
impossible to formulate any precise answer to the question. Most
authorities claim, however, that as a general rule cities are more
antireligious than the countryside. If this is true, does it follow
that a strong Catholic oligarchy did not exist in the towns? Exact
answers must await studies based on statistics, but the available
evidence suggests that even when strongly anticlerical lower and
middle classes were present in the city, the clerical party was
especially strong among the town oligarchy when the surrounding
rural area was Catholic. The bourgeois, in fact, could rely on the
countryside to buttress its position since with peasant votes its
members could be elected to the department's general councils,
the national legislature, and, with gerrymandering, which put extra-
mural peasant communities within the municipality, to a town
council. Furthermore, a Protestant or anticlerical "menace" within
the city's walls prompted the Catholic notables to exploit every
opportunity to assure their ascendancy in local affairs. If de-
Christianization in the countryside did not always drastically reduce the influence of Catholic notables in adjacent cities, the
presence of a devout peasantry did signify that a strong group of
Catholic notables existed in neighboring towns. Since bourgeois
notables lived in rural as well as urban areas, the departments and

[52] *Ibid.*, p. 325.

regions Boulard designated as Catholic offer a good guide to the relative geographical strength of the clerical party among the bourgeois notables.

When Boulard's Catholic areas are compared with the legitimist strongholds outlined on Tudesq's map the coincidence is striking. There were many rural regions in the South where the legitimist notables were numerous, but the countryside was indifferent to Catholic tradition, such as in Bouches-du-Rhône, Var, and in most places in Vaucluse, Basses-Alpes, Hérault, the Ariège. In these departments the Catholic oligarchy was strong in the towns. In the rest of the South, the Central Massif, the North, and the West, the legitimist and the Catholic areas are nearly congruous. However, Catholic areas appear where the legitimist notables were sparse. This occurred in Basses-Pyrénées, Hautes-Pyrénées, Doubs, Meurthe-et-Moselle, Meuse, Moselle, Haute-Marne, and Pas-de-Calais. In these departments (and in Haute-Savoie and Savoie that cannot be compared because they were not part of France in 1837), the Catholic oligarchy was very strong. It fought just as strenuously throughout the early years of the Third Republic to protect the Church and the social order from the radicals as Catholic notables did in legitimist areas.

Legitimist deputies Paulin Gillon, Xavier Dufaur, Charles Chesnelong, and Paul Besson came from these departments, and there is no reason to suppose that they were more certain that family ranked above individual talent as the measure of a man, more interested in maintaining their position in society, or less disturbed by the revolutionary threat to the Church and the oligarchy's social position than other members of their group. But unlike these deputies, the Catholic oligarchic group to which they belonged believed with few exceptions that these aims could be accomplished within the framework of a liberal monarchy or conservative republic. Since legitimist opinion did not exist to any appreciable extent in these areas, it cannot be concluded that the old Catholic oligarchy was attracted by legitimism; and unless this sort of attraction occurred in each place where this oligarchy was strong, it is impossible to say that a sizable portion of the group, even if it was a minority, adopted a legitimist viewpoint because it was the ideological expression proper to an oligarchy threatened by a social revolution. In short, the fact that a man might be a member of a socioreligious category called *Catholic notables of old bourgeois extraction* is not in itself even an approximate cause for his being a legitimist.

Thus the social background of the legitimist deputies rather confounds a purely sociological interpretation of legitimist ideology. To be sure, the aristocracy fits well into a sociological view of the French Revolution, but what is to be made of the presence of so many bourgeois on legitimist benches in the National Assembly? They were not unusual members of French society, but neither were they representatives of any clearly distinguishable social or socioreligious group which, because of a common social experience, adopted a common ideological outlook. If social logic breaks down, then, what can take its place? Perhaps nothing, except description, since the manifold accidents of historical experience touched the individual, the family, and the specific social group in ways that are not subject to social categorization. Historical experience did indeed affect the old Catholic oligarchy differently. The devout Catholics in the Savoy, to take an obvious example, had no French royalist tradition. The Savoy had not even belonged to France until the Second Empire. Although there were compelling reasons for the Catholics in Savoy to have organized a defense of their class and religion historically, there were none that coupled this defense with French royalism. In the legitimist areas, on the other hand, the royalist tradition was strongly rooted. It could be argued that this happened because of social factors. The nobility was legitimist and was strong in the legitimist areas, but weak in Catholic areas that were not legitimist. Hence, wherever the nobility was strong, the Catholic bourgeoisie tended to be influenced by its royalist opinions. This obviously occurred in the West. But the nature of legitimism varied so much even in these legitimist regions that its character cannot be attributed solely to the presence of the nobility. The aristocracy and the Catholic bourgeoisie in the North were never the ardent sort of legitimists that they were in the rural West or urban South. They put conservative solidarity ahead of dynastic convictions more than their counterparts in the other regions. And the strident legitimism that appears among the bourgeois notables in the South was never matched by the bourgeois in the West. The peculiar unrepeatable blend of regional history led to the creation of attitudes that caused the reaction to the Revolution to be translated into a legitimist culture that was never exactly paralleled from area to area.

Still, if the unique historical experience is indispensable to a description of the regional basis of legitimism, social factors are important. The French Revolution, which propounded the principle of equal citizenship, undermined the rigid orders of traditional dependence in France, and constituted a threat to the social authority of the aristocracy and the Catholic bourgeois oligarchy, both of which based their claim to leadership on the inequality of family and class relationships. Legitimism was not the only possible response to this revolutionary threat, but it was the answer that the legitimist deputies of both aristocratic and bourgeois antecedents gave, and comparative sociological data support the conclusion that their opinions reflected that of most of the descendants of the aristocracy and a significant part of the old Catholic oligarchy in France.

Chapter Three

THE LEGITIMISTS:
ECONOMIC BACKGROUND

Usually the legitimists' economic background, which is the subject of this chapter, and their social antecedents, which was the subject of the last, are discussed together. Here, however, they have been separated because, if interrelated, they are nonetheless different topics. Legitimists have been considered an economically antiquated group within nineteenth-century society, a group whose political and social outlook corresponded to the backwardness of their economic function. The subject of backwardness is somewhat involved because of the very different meaning it entails for a preindustrial and an industrial economy. In the preindustrial French economy of the late eighteenth and early nineteenth centuries, commerce, manufacturing, and banking existed, but these activities were quite distinct in terms of productive techniques and business organization from those of the large-scale industrial market economy that subsequently appeared. On the other hand, when the banking, commerce, and manufacturing of preindustrial France are compared with the predominantly premarket agricultural activities of the previous centuries, they obviously represent new economic forms. The question of backwardness, then, is one of time. The business organization or productive techniques which were progressive in 1800 would have become retrogressive if practiced in the mid-nineteenth century. This distinction bears on the problem of the relative economic backwardness of social groups. Legitimists have been traced socially to two groups, the old aristocracy and the old Catholic town oligarchy of provincial France. The former might be considered economically retrograde and the latter economically progressive in the context of a preindustrial economy, but the judgment could easily change when the descendants of these social groups are evaluated according to the degree of adaptability to conditions of modern industrialization. Moreover, although the legitimist deputies descended from prominent social groups in a preindustrial economy, it seems only logical, that their relative economic backwardness and that of their contemporaries be considered in relation to the Industrial Revolution since they themselves lived during this era of accelerated change.

The legitimist deputies' economic position can be measured first of all in terms of property holdings. Ownership of property is in itself an economically passive state since property is something that somebody has, not something that he does. But property forms are an important indicator of a man's place in the economic process. Wills and other financial documents of the nineteenth century usually distinguished between real and liquid forms of property. Real property existed as land or buildings or fixed equipment, but in an economic sense it is best perhaps to consider it in terms of agricultural properties and business properties (factories, mines, commercial houses). Liquid property was generally held in the form of industrial stocks and bonds or state rents. State rents are liquid securities that did not bear directly on economic development, and the tendency to invest heavily in them certainly did divert funds from more productive enterprises.[1] It is, then, the ownership of industrial stocks and bonds that offers the surest guide for judging the deputies' contribution to large-scale corporate industrialization.

Most of the aristocrats' families survived the Revolution with

[1] Of the 20 to 22 billion francs of liquid securities invested in concerns quoted on the Paris stock exchange in 1863, 9 billion was in municipal or state bonds. Another 6½ billion was invested in railroad stock. Since the railroads were created and supported by the state, which guaranteed interest payments to their stockholders, the income earned from only 5½ billion of these stock exchange values was not supported by the public treasury. Of this 5½ billion 2½ was invested in foreign companies. This left 3 billion for French companies, half of which was in credit institutions. Another 550 million was invested in public service companies (transport, gas lights, and building societies). Of the 20 to 22 billion, therefore, only 1 billion was invested in joint-stock corporations engaged in productive enterprises (mines, factories, textile mills, machine workshops, etc.). The 20 to 22 billion francs invested produced an annual revenue of about 1 billion 50 million francs. Of this amount 450 million was paid on state and municipal bonds. Another 325 million went to railroad bondholders. Credit societies took 75 million; the corporations engaged in public services 25 million, and the foreign companies 125 million. Thus the profit from French joint-stock industrial firms only amounted to 50 million francs. This evidence shows the relative capital starvation of French industry. See Auguste Vitu, *Guide financier, répertoire général des valeurs financières et industrielles* (Paris, 1864), pp. 14–16.

agricultural properties. After the Restoration, moreover, their fathers and the future deputies themselves did their best to reconstruct or expand their holdings. For many aristocrats, who associated it with the family's most vital interests, the acquisition of land became a lifelong passion which they pursed as relentlessly as any of Zola's tight-fisted, land-hungry peasants. Sometimes they simply purchased farms. But skillfully exploited matrimonial arrangements brought quicker and more fruitful results. The possession of an "old and respected" name could be advantageous because rich bourgeois were willing to pay handsome dowries in order to acquire one. The fathers of Roger de Larcy, Crussol d'Uzès, and Eugène des Rotours counted among those nobles whose land holdings were considerably augmented from such practical compacts. But an improved fortune did not necessarily turn on a *mesalliance*. Benoist d'Azy's marriage with Mlle. Brière d'Azy, which eventually brought him over 2,000 hectares in the Nièvre, and Vogüé's marriage with the daughter of one of Louis XVIII's finance ministers, which helped to reconstruct a territorial fortune lost during the Revolution, were hardly disadvantageous socially. Deputies of bourgeois extraction had also come into the possession of agricultural properties through direct inheritance, purchase, or marriage. Baron Chaurand and Lucien-Brun, who married daughters of rich *lyonnais* merchants, and Ernoul, whose marriage with an heiress in Haute-Vienne, made their fortunes, particularly benefited, for example, from the last of the three methods of acquiring lands.

An absence of documentation makes it impossible to furnish precise data on the deputies' land holdings.[2] But the numerous if fragmentary sources available—biographical aids, prefectural reports, wills and testaments—prove that the legitimists were important landlords. Some of the nobles were among the richest *propriétaires* in France. Carayon-Latour, whose father had been *receveur général* in the Gironde during the Restoration, reputedly earned 400,000 *livres de rente*, an immense sum considering that Henri de Saintenac, the richest landlord in Ariège, and Eugène des Rotours, one of the richest in Nord, were considered extremely

---

[2] In 1872 the minister of the interior ordered the prefects to forward information about the deputies' income to his office. Copies of the reports have turned up in a few departmental archives but the reports the minister received, if he in fact got them all, could not be found in the Archives nationales. If these reports could be found, they could provide information for a statistical breakdown of all the deputies' income.

wealthy with an income of 150,000 *livres de rente*.[3] These aristocrats, plus the Comte de Bouillé, deputy from Nièvre, the Marquis de Vogüé, deputy from Cher, Crussol d'Uzès, deputy from Gard, and the Marquis de Rességuier, deputy from Landes, were certainly not only the most important landlords in their native departments but also among the richest in France. But even the poorest aristocrats appear to have received incomes that rarely fell below the comfortable figure of 15,000 *livres de rente* and more frequently amounted to 30,000 or 40,000.[4] The bourgeois, on the other hand, were not such wealthy landlords. A few (Baucarne-Leroux from Nord, for instance) may have ranked with the wealthiest nobles in their landed fortunes (150,000 *livres de rente*) but the majority probably earned between 10,000 and 20,000, a substantial sum but one considerably less than the average earned from their agricultural properties by the nobles.

If the bourgeois' landholdings were smaller than the nobles', their ownership of other kinds of real property was greater. A few nobles owned small manufactories—mostly forges or iron foundries—which were located on their agricultural properties, but they were not important sources of revenue. The Marquis de Vogüé's iron works near Bourges was, for example, simply a luxury supported from his other revenues since it usually operated at a loss. Eighteen percent of the bourgeois, however, possessed commercial or industrial properties that were their family's major source of revenue. A man like Jules Leurent must have earned a great deal from his textile mills in the Nord and his linen mills in the Midi because he was reputedly a wealthy man, although contemporary

[3] Income from land was quoted in *livres de rente* in nineteenth century France and not in francs. There was, of course, no *livre* currency. The value of the livre was the same as the franc. The figure on Carayon-Latour is given in *Le Figaro*, supplement entitled *Tribune électorale*, Feb. 11, 1876; that on Saintenac in A. D. (Ariège) 2 M 41[1], Prefect report to minister of interior on deputies' incomes. Rotours married a Van der Kerke, one of the prominent families in Nord. For information about the lands, which he received through his marriage and his income, see A. D. (Nord) M 6/9 *Police générale*, dossier on Rotours.

[4] See, for example, the prefect's report for Ille-et-Vilaine in which the nobles' income ranged between 25 and 30 thousand *livres de rente* and for Hérault where they ranged between 15 and 40 thousand. A. D. (Ille-et-Vilaine), 3 Me 18, *Elections législatives-1871*, and A. D. (Hérault), 2 M[s] 25, *Conseil général, Renouvellement partiel du 19 juin 1864*, p. 3 and p. 17. The conclusion in the text is based on frequent references to deputies' incomes from sources too numerous to cite.

references to a man's wealth cannot be taken at their face value. Florentin Malartre who had to live very modestly from the limited sums he received from his rented factory during his tenure in the National Assembly, was very amused when a contemporary referred to him as a "grand industriel."[5] Charles Chesnelong's business properties, on the other hand, were obviously more valuable than Malartre's but of less value than Leurent's. In fact, Chesnelong left a will that gives a detailed account of his properties. In 1844, when he married Ernestine Lacoste, he only had, with his wife's dowry, 93,000 francs. Twenty years later his fortune had increased to 483,000 francs. Of this amount 110,000 francs had come from his parents after their death, and the rest of the increase (280,000 francs) he had earned from his merchant house in Orthez. By 1883 he was worth 775,000 francs, the major part of which (about 500,000 francs) represented the value of his business.[6] But it is impossible, because of the lack of sources, to present a statistical representation of the value of the bourgeois deputies' business properties. Probably Chesnelong's holdings are more representative of the group than Leurent's or Malartre's. Moreover, since 17 percent of the legitimists were lawyers or notaries many must have owned offices or buildings wherein they practiced their professions. No doubt to some extent the value of these properties depended on the lawyer's or notary's professional reputation as much as on the physical conditions of the property itself. And in any event it is not known what the value of these properties was nor how many deputies might have rented an office space or building instead of owning it outright.

Information about property in the form of liquid securities is even more difficult to obtain than that on real estate. Reports on a deputy's wealth that appear in prefectural records refer almost exclusively to real estate, the value of which could be calculated from the tax rolls. The sort of prefectural reports that reveal the value of the deputies' agricultural properties, therefore, are useless when it comes to stocks and bonds. In fact, an official could not even make an educated guess about a man's holdings in liquid securities because, unlike land and buildings that were open to public view, they could be hidden in a desk drawer or wall safe. The only good sources that give detailed information about a

[5] Ltr., Malartre to his wife, June 26, 1873, *Malartre MSS.*

[6] Chesnelong's will is in the hands of his descendant, Monsieur Jean d'Iribarne of St-Jean-Le-Vieux (Basses-Pyrénées).

deputy's holdings in stocks and bonds are family financial records; but since the deputies (and their descendants, too, it might be added) released these documents reluctantly, private references are difficult to obtain. Only three families produced documents (last wills and testaments in each case) that list (among his other possessions) a deputy's worth in liquid securities. One, Denys Benoist d'Azy, left his heirs 2 million francs in industrial stocks and bonds and 1 million in *rentes d'état*; another, Philibert de La Guiche, left 24 million of which 4 million was in industrial securities; and a third, Charles Chesnelong, had 52,832 francs in liquid securities when he died, 24,699 francs of which was in railroad stocks and the remainder in state bonds.[7] Obviously no valid generalizations can be made about 200 legitimist deputies from these documents. But information drawn from other sources indicates, if without precise figures, that fifteen deputies had important holdings in industrial stocks and bonds. These were the legitimists who sat on the boards of direction of financial and industrial corporations. Since ownership of considerable stock in a company was a statutory requirement for membership on its board, these fifteen men had to be major stockholders, at least in these companies. No doubt others, who did not sit on boards of direction, also owned stocks in industry, and in some cases (like La Guiche) substantial sums were invested. "Everybody nowadays," Benoist d'Azy observed during the Second Empire "arranges his affairs so that a part of his fortune is held in liquid securities."[8] A deputy did this not only because he expected a greater return but also because liquid securities could be exchanged more easily than land (for the purpose of paying a dowry, for example) without suffering the higher fees and undergoing the involved and expensive legal formalities that were associated with real estate transactions.

Still their investments in industrial stocks and bonds should not be exaggerated. Probably no more than 10 percent of the deputies owned significant amounts of industrial securities, and when they bought liquid securities, they usually purchased *rentes d'état* that

[7] Partage des successions confondues de Monsieur le Marquis et Madame la Marquise de La Guiche, *La Guiche MSS.*

[8] Ministère de l'agriculture, du commerce et des travaux publics. *Enquête sur l'agriculture, 1866–1870,* 38 vols. The reference is from the *Enquête agricole,* 2e série, 9e circonscription (Paris, 1867), p. 377. See the bibliography for a discussion of how the inquiry's work was published. Hereafter referred to as the *Enquête agricole.*

were considered, with some justification, a much safer investment than industrial stocks and bonds.[9] When compared with their holdings in buildings and lands, especially agricultural lands, the stock portfolios of most deputies were most certainly modest affairs. Even a capitalist-industrialist of Benoist d'Azy's stature left most of his fortune in real estate.[10] The bulk of their property undoubtedly was in agricultural holdings.

To some extent the preponderance of real estate among legitimists' property holdings could be considered natural since the greater part of their fortunes had been acquired before liquid securities, especially industrial stocks and bonds, had begun to attract investors on a large scale from the French public. Deputies of modest income never had sufficient capital available to permit them to invest heavily enough in stocks and bonds to shift the base of their holdings into this newer property form. Malartre's complaint about his inability to take advantage of the opportunity to buy state rents after the Franco-German war because of a lack of ready cash illustrates this.[11] But it can also be explained by a certain reluctance on their part to invest money in liquid securities, a reluctance induced by both social and individual considerations. These deputies believed that the ownership of liquid securities had a morally harmful effect on people. The land, Gavardie stated, "can only be acquired by great efforts and extended formalities: the value of liquid securities changes according to the desires of men."[12] Even men who sat on corporation boards echoed this sentiment. Benoist d'Azy, for example, disapproved of liquid securities because they were "so easy to hold, to exchange, to hide, lend themselves to speculation and favor the gaming spirit which seduces everybody."[13] Moreover, legitimists felt deeply that the accumulation of a personal fortune should have economically productive and socially useful results, and they distinguished, therefore, between profits gained through speculation on the stockmarket and

[9] Even an entrepreneur of Emile Martin's stature (he was a republican) invested heavily in land in order to "détacher sa fortune des chances industrielles." Guy Thuillier, *Georges Dufaud et les débuts du grand capitalisme dans la métallurgie en Nivernais au XIXe siècle* (Paris, 1959), p. 90.

[10] Benoist d'Azy's will is in the *Benoist d'Azy MSS.*

[11] Ltr., Malartre to his wife, June 25, 1871, *Malartre MSS.* He did manage to scrape up 800 francs which he invested in the new bonds.

[12] E. de Gavardie, *Etudes sur les vraies doctrines sociales et politiques* (Pau, 1862), p. 182.

[13] *Enquête agricole*, 2e série, 9e circonscription (Paris, 1867), p. 376.

those made in industry and agriculture, for the former occurred on paper alone while the latter, they reasoned, required the creation of jobs and the production of goods. Their individual objections stemmed from a long-standing distrust of liquid securities as a reliable form of investment. Convinced that the value of paper securities could disappear almost overnight, they were not prepared to risk the loss of the family's fortune by investing the bulk of it in stocks and bonds. This prejudice applied particularly to investments in industrial securities but state rents were also considered less trustworthy than the land because the fortunes of state treasuries were subject to catastrophies while the land endured.

Yet disapproval of liquid securities was not the same thing as dislike of commerce and industry. All the deputies thought highly of agricultural property in terms of its economic soundness and social desirability. But the small businessmen or manufacturers among them would never have conceded that they were engaged in economically and socially unproductive activities. Moreover, the corporate industrialists considered their industrial stocks to be more than purely paper values. Benoist d'Azy, for example, always felt that his stocks in railroads and metallurgical firms were "liquid securities in form . . . which had a solid land base."[14] Legitimists regretted the machinations of the stock speculator, but, like the family merchant and manufacturer, they found their industrial securities represented far from sterile forms of property. Perhaps statements like Benoist d'Azy's were only rationalizations. Legitimists were, after all, not adverse to making money. In any event, if most of their fortunes remained in agricultural lands out of preference, their property base as a group shifted, as the century wore on, from agriculture to commerce and industry. The growth of the joint-stock company, as opposed to the family-owned industrial firm, facilitated this shift.

Although property holdings are important, they are only one of the factors that helps explain the legitimists' relation to the economy. Their active economic role, about which greater information is available, reveals more. People with money and talent had many economically creative possibilities before them in the mid-nineteenth century. They could, of course, engage in a profession or run a family-owned business. But it was the classic age of the capitalist entrepreneur and the greater the entrepreneur, the less he was occupied or preoccupied with any specific profession or

[14] *Ibid.*

business. His hallmark was the very ubiquitousness of his economic interests. Rather than discuss the entrepreneur as an abstraction, it is best to describe the manifold interests and activities of the legitimists themselves. The most important capitalist-entrepreneur among them will be discussed first and then be used as a yardstick against which the other deputies' contributions to the industrialization of France can be measured.

The man in question, Comte Denys Benoist d'Azy, was not a self-made man.[15] He came from a rich bourgeois family of Angers that, as noted, had been ennobled in the eighteenth century, and he received at birth, therefore, the advantages of money and a respected name. His father, Vincent Benoist, moreover, because of his loyalty to the Bourbons, had emerged from the Revolution and the Empire not only a wealthy but also a man of influence in the Restoration government and administration. Deputy from Maine-et-Loire, *Directeur général des contributions indirectes* in the Finance Ministry, a member of Charles X's Privy Council, the elder Benoist cut an attractive figure in the political, financial, and social circles of the capital, and the younger Benoist, who was handsome, intelligent, and hard-working in his own right, benefited from his father's position. Other associations were equally important. As a young man Benoist became a close friend of Henri de Kersaint, descendant of an old noble family, and through this friendship gained entry into the fashionable salon of Kersaint's sister, the Duchesse de Duras (who was one of Chateaubriand's literary friends and herself a writer of ability) where he also made the acquaintance of the Duchess' future son-in-law, destined to inherit the title of Duc de Rauzan.[16] In this social milieu Benoist mingled with a segment of the old aristocracy that was involved in banking and corporate finance. Kersaint and Rauzan were, for example,

---

[15] For information on Benoist d'Azy's early industrial career see Robert R. Locke, "Drouillard, Benoist, et Cie.," *Revue d'histoire de le sidérurgie*, VII: 4 (1967), 277–299.

[16] According to the literary critic Sainte-Beuve young Denys Benoist fell in love with the Duchess' daughter but lost out, because of his lesser birth, to the Duc de Rauzan's eldest son. Sainte-Beuve claims that Denys' suffering from this disappointment inadvertently gave birth to a literary masterpiece because the Duchesse de Duras wrote a novel, *Edouard*, which was based on her observations of the unhappy Denys and that Stendhal got the idea for his character Julien Sorel from reading *Edouard*. See C-A Sainte-Beuve, "Mme. de Duras," *Portraits des femmes* (Paris, 1870).

both members of the board of direction of St-Gobain in which Benoist himself held stock, and Kersaint, who introduced Benoist to one of the family in 1836, was apparently on familiar terms with the Rothschilds.

Another group with which Benoist established contact was also of paramount importance for his subsequent industrial career. In 1822 he married the daughter of Brière d'Azy, the richest landlord in Nièvre and one of the department's leading iron manufacturers. Nièvre was, after the Napoleonic wars, a region in which the metallurgical industry underwent rapid development. The first English type rolling mill built by a Frenchman was installed at Fourchambault for the Boigues by Georges Dufaud, and it operated in conjunction with one of the first sophisticated machine workshops built by a Frenchman, the remarkably skilled engineer Emile Martin, Georges Dufaud's son-in-law.[17] Brière d'Azy was well acquainted with the men who had brought about these technological developments in his own backyard. He was also a friend of Aaron Manby and his son Charles, two of the more imaginative English engineers of the nineteenth century. The Manbys, who constructed the first steamboat to sail on the Seine, installed the first gas lights in Paris, and ran a famous machine workshop at Charenton, had acquired in partnership with the Frenchman Wilson the coke-burning blast furnaces in Le Creusot where they installed an English type rolling mill and foundry. When Benoist married, he moved to Nièvre where he became Brière d'Azy's companion as well as his son-in-law. Because of this he acquired an intimate knowledge of both the men and the technology responsible for the breakthrough that led to mass production in French metallurgy.

These family and social connections would probably have brought Benoist into industrial affairs as a matter of course, but they did not automatically turn him into the industrialist that he later became. In fact, during the 1820s he devoted his efforts primarily to government service. He began in the diplomatic corps but soon shifted into fiscal administration where he had the short but brilliant career previously mentioned. In 1830 he left government service out of loyalty to the old monarchy. Legitimist resignations from government and administrative posts—the so-called *émigration à l'intérieure*—have usually been cited as sympto-

[17] See Guy Thuillier, *Georges Dufaud et les débuts.* Also see André Thuillier, *Emile Martin* (Nevers, 1968).

matic of the legitimists' general withdrawal from the economic and social life of the nation, but there is no reason why this should have automatically been true. Since government or administration was time-consuming, it actually interfered with the pursuit of private economic interests, and once they had quit politics and administration legitimists had far more time, if they chose, to devote to economic matters. This was the case with Benoist, for he was too curious, too vital a man to remain idle for very long.

In 1835 a cousin of Brière d'Azy, Hyppolyte Drouillard of the financial house *Blacques, Certain, et Drouillard*, became interested in the *Cie. des Forges et Fonderies d'Alais*. Organized in 1829 in order to build a mass production English style ironworks, the company had exhausted its capital before having even completed the construction of the factory. Drouillard wanted to lease the factory from the nearly bankrupt company for twenty years but he needed financial and technical assistance in order to accomplish his project. Benoist, who decided to join Drouillard, brought both to the new farm company *Drouillard, Benoist, et Cie.* He used his Parisian contacts (in a tight money market) to raise sorely needed capital for the projected firm, for Kersaint, Rauzan, and their friends responded to Benoist's call by investing in the company. Its capital came primarily from Benoist and his aristocratic friends. To assure success, Benoist moved to Alais with his wife and children to direct the factory operations. The task Benoist assumed was much greater than either he or his associates had at first imagined. They had taken over an enterprise in which men with greater financial resources had failed, when the difficulties of mounting a large metallurgical plant were not only great but also to some extent unknown, and at a time when new but better established firms like Le Creusot and Decazeville were also in serious financial straits. But Benoist, who had an enormous capacity for work, met each difficulty with skill and determination. He traveled extensively in France, Belgium, and Britain, taking notes on equipment design and production procedures for future reference. He enlisted the technical aid of Charles Manby and Emile Martin; recruited skilled workers in Britain, Belgium, and France; supervised personally the construction of new blast furnaces, a foundry, and a forge; and worked ceaselessly once they came into production to cut costs and control quality. Moreover, realizing the importance of the rail market to the forge at Alais, he helped negotiate a rail purchase agreement with the Grand'Combe-Beaucaire railroad, used his business contacts in Marseilles (when he realized its failure would endanger the contract) to raise private capital for this financially crippled railroad, and after private efforts failed to secure enough capital for it, brought pressure to bear on his friends inside and outside the Chamber of Deputies and the Chamber of Peers to secure the government guarantee of interest for the Grand'Combe-Beaucaire line that assured its and with it Alais' success. In short it was primarily through Benoist's efforts that the company succeeded in the early 1840s, after months of frustration that seemed to indicate it might suffer the fate of its predecessor, in building a thriving iron factory in the Midi which became one of the biggest producers in France.[18]

Between 1836 and 1840 Benoist devoted his time almost exclusively to Alais, but after the farm company prospered, he left the routine technical and business operations to others in order to exploit new business opportunities. Because of his interest and experience, it was natural that these efforts occurred in metallurgy. During the 1840s, in association with Kersaint and a group of *nivernais* ironmongers and *lyonnais* capitalists, he built a number of coke-burning blast furnaces in Montluçon which became one of the principal units (along with the coal mines of Commentry and the forges and foundries of Fourchambault) in an interdependent complex of factories located in Nièvre and Allier; and in partnership with Drouillard, he helped construct the foundries and forges of Bouquiès and Fumel, near Decazeville. At the same time he was a zealous and indefatigable railroad man who participated directly in the organization and development of the *Chemin de Fer du Gard, Avignon-Marseilles, Lyon-Avignon, Paris-Orléans, Centre et Ouest*, and, after his election to the Chamber of Deputies in 1841, took a direct part in the crucial legislative struggles on whose outcome the future of the railroads depended. By 1848, therefore, Benoist (who added the "d'Azy" to his name by Royal ordinance in 1846) not only found himself one of the nation's leading iron manufacturers but also entrenched on the boards of directors of many of the more important railroad companies.

From this vantage point he made a major contribution to the extraordinary industrial expansion of France during the Second Empire. At its beginning he helped organize two of the largest railroad networks in Europe (Paris-Orléans and Paris-Lyon-à-la-

[18] In 1847 Alais produced 21,264 tons of pig iron, ranking among the top five producers in France. It was the largest producer of iron rails.

Méditerranée), participated in the creation of new credit institutions, and played an important role in the negotiations that led to the amalgamations of several metallurgical firms into new, more powerful, corporations—while simultaneously, as *directeur-gérant*, keeping a close watch on the forges and foundry in Alais. By 1870 Benoist d'Azy had long been one of the leading financier-industrialists of France. He held the following positions: head of the *Cie. des Fonderies et Forges d'Alais*; president of the board of directions of the *Cie. des Mines de Houille de Commentry et des Forges et Fonderies de Fourchambault, Montluçon, et Imphy*; vice-president of the boards of direction of both *Paris-Orléans* and *P. L. M.*; a board member of both the *Cie. des Mines de Villefort, Vialas, Comberdonde et Auzonet* and the *Cie. des Mines de La Grand'Combe*. Through his influence his eldest son Paul had become a member of the following boards of directors: the *Cie. Française de Réassurance contre l'Incendie*; the *Cie. des Mines de Houille de Commentry et des Forges et Fonderies de Fourchambault, Montluçon et Imphy*; the *Société générale des Chemins de Fer Romains*; and the *Chemins de Fer de l'Ouest*. His son-in-law, Augustin Cochin, sat on the boards of several corporations, including the Paris-Orléans railroad. Benoist d'Azy had family and personal relations that extended into almost every branch (excluding textiles) of French corporate industry.[19]

Still this catalogue of achievements does not tell the whole story. Once when traveling in northern England on a tour of British metallurgical factories, he noticed the now famous Durham bulls and decided to import some for his farm. This was not an idle gesture because Benoist d'Azy was keenly interested in agriculture. "A great part of my life has been occupied with agriculture," he told members of an agricultural committee in 1866,

> my father-in-law, then myself, we counted among the *propriétaires* who were the most concerned on a rather large scale with agriculture. Today, between my sons and myself, we cultivate directly almost 2,000 hectares, that is personally, and with the aid of an overseer, field hands or sharecroppers. . . . If I have not held the plow in my own hands I have at least followed it many a time. . . .[20]

[19] See Auguste Vitu, *Guide financier.*
[20] *Enquête agricole*, 3e série, p. 506.

Agriculture, which underwent almost as drastic a transformation as manufacturing during the nineteenth century, was itself subject to capitalist marketing practices. The agriculturist who specialized in market gardening or the sheep and cattle man who bred superior beasts in order to furnish meat to the rapidly growing urban market was just as creative a capitalist-entrepreneur as the manufacturer who mass produced shoes for their tired feet. In fact, agriculture became in many instances (tanning, sugar beets, sericulture, for example) inseparable from the manufacturing process. Benoist d'Azy's interest in stockbreeding as well as in the other agricultural improvements (reforestation and irrigation, for example) he successfully carried through on his own farms expressed this faith in the economic possibilities open to the imaginative agriculturist. Moreover, realizing that French agriculture suffered from a lack of capital be helped organize the *Crédit Foncier de France* and the *Crédit Agricole*, expressly for the purpose of providing cheap loans to enterprising farmers. These institutions never lived up to his expectations but not through his fault because they subsequently fell under the control of men whose loan policies betrayed the founder's original intention.

Benoist d'Azy was not the most important capitalist-entrepreneur in nineteenth-century France, but he was in the front rank. Civil servant, financier, head of a large corporation, member of the boards of direction of many of the major financial and industrial firms of the nation, agriculturist, legislator—any one of these jobs would have been sufficient to fill the lifetime of most men. But Benoist d'Azy was not an ordinary man. He thrilled at the speed (30 miles an hour) of the train that took him from London to Newcastle. He marveled at the immense size of the machine tools at Fawcett and Preston. "This district of Dudley," he wrote in his notebook while touring British factories,

> is a black city. Smoke, rain—the fires which make it seem like day through the thick atmosphere, each blends with the other, then the pretty well-kept houses . . . , a beautiful greenery. The miners with their long flannel shirts, the forge workers, . . . the boats on the canal, the wagons on the roads, omnibuses everywhere. Here is the laboratory where the products of the entire world are being prepared![21]

[21] "Notebook," *Benoist d'Azy MSS.*

The range and scope of his activities were never dictated purely by pecuniary gain. He was simply amazed by the creative results that intelligent and hard-working men could achieve in their environment and drew great satisfaction from his participation in this collective enterprise.

Probably, as entrepreneurs, none of the deputies in the National Assembly equaled Benoist d'Azy; certainly none of the legitimists did. Yet a deputy need not have been involved as intensively or extensively in economic affairs to have made a substantial contribution to the nation's development. The matter is clearly relative; some made great, others modest, and others negligible, if not negative, contributions. Fourteen of the legitimists, like Benoist d'Azy, were preoccupied with corporate business. This does not mean that they did not engage in other activities. Amédée Lefèvre-Pontalis, for example, member of the boards of direction of the *Messageries Maritimes*, the *Cie. des Mines de La Loire*, and the *Crédit Industriel et Commercial*, was a lawyer, and most of the others were agriculturists. Indeed, the Marquis de Vogüé undoubtedly made much more money from agriculture than industry, and his industrial interests were considerable. Still the fourteen can be distinguished from the other legitimists precisely because they played a role in corporate industry.

Ten of the fourteen were uniquely concerned with corporate affairs *autour du tapis vert*, and of these ten eight were members of the nobility. The nobility, of course, had a long standing prejudice against engaging in "trade," but there was a radical difference between corporate industry and the traditional family-owned business. The board members of corporations or financial institutions were the *grands seigneurs*, the captains of industry, of the nineteenth century, who differed as much from the preindustrial family businessmen as the rich landlords did from the middle class farmers. Although prejudiced against actually running a small business remained firm, these nobles accepted positions in large corporations not only because they were lucrative but also because they were seats of power, prestige, and privilege in modern society.

Of these nobles two, the *Chevau-léger* Comte de Béthune and the moderate rightist Comte de Melun, were not involved in manufacture or commerce. Both were members of the boards of directors of insurance companies (Béthune of *La Providence*, Melun of *Le Nord*), nothing exceptional in itself because the nobility

112

seemed to be particularly attracted to the insurance industry. Others were involved in businesses that seemed a natural extension of their activities in agriculture. This was certainly true of the *Chevau-léger* Comte de Bouillé who was a member of the board of direction of the *Crédit Foncier Colonial*, but it also applied to men engaged in industry. Studies of corporations have shown that certain industries, mining and metallurgy especially, had a high proportion of nobles sitting on the boards of direction.[22] Before the age of coal in metallurgy iron foundries were usually located in forested areas because they depended heavily on charcoal fuel. It was normal, therefore, since they owned forests, for the nobility to own forges and foundries. As a result of this experience, they were naturally drawn to these industries when the technological transformation occurred. Moreover, often the coal mine or the iron ores essential to the operation of the large-scale metallurgical firm were located on nobles' lands, and they were given stock in the newly organized company in payment for the rights to use the ores or mine the coal. Both the *Chevau-léger* Lagrange and the moderate rightist Vogüé appear to have entered corporate industry in this manner. Lagrange, who was a rich landlord in the Nord, was one of the five *régisseurs* of the mines of Anzin, and Vogüé was active in metallurgy. Through his ownership of the foundry near Bourges, he developed extensive relations with the ironmongers of Cher. (One of these ironmongers, Comte Jaubert, who was also an important stockholder in the forges and foundries of Fourchambault in neighboring Nièvre, was a Right-Center deputy in 1871.) Vogüé's interest in metallurgy, like Benoist d'Azy's, also led him to railroading. He sat on the board of directors of the *Cie. Paris-Orléans* on which Benoist d'Azy and Comte Jaubert sat. These business acquaintances developed into family relationships, for Benoist d'Azy's grandson's marriage with Vogüé's granddaughter and his (Benoist d'Azy's) son Paul's marriage with the daughter of Comte Jaubert happened after these three men joined the railroad company.

The other three nobles, on the other hand, did not enter industry initially through developing minerals on their lands. Neither the moderate rightist Pontoi-Pontcarré, member of the board of direction of the *Cie. Universelle du Canal Maritime de Suez*, nor his colleague the Comte de Vaulchier, member of the board of

---

[22] See Jacques Boudet, *Le monde des affaires en France de 1830 à nos jours* (Paris, 1952).

113

the *Sous-Comptoir des Chemins de Fer*, was involved in metallurgy. The other noble, the *Chevau-léger* Joseph de La Bouillerie did have metallurgical and mining as well as banking interests. He was not, however, a rich landlord and unlike Vogüé, Lagrange, and Benoist d'Azy, did not come to metallurgy through agriculture but primarily through his marriage with the daughter of an even greater financier-capitalist than Benoist d'Azy, Gustave Delahante. (La Bouillerie's brother, moreover, married another Delahante daughter, thus further cementing the family alliance.) Inasmuch as the La Bouilleries were fervent legitimists they disapproved of the political attitudes of their father-in-law, who had been an Orleanist, but these political differences did not prevent them from working closely with Delahante in finance and industry. Joseph de La Bouillerie's manifold industrial activities brought him to the boards of directors of the *Société Anonyme des Mines de La Loire*, the *Société Générale du Crédit Industriel et Commercial*, the *Sous-Comptoir du Commerce et de l'Industrie*, and the *Société du Dépôt et des Comptes Courants* during the mid-1860s.

The remaining six deputies were from the bourgeoisie. One, the lawyer-financier Amédée Lefèvre-Pontalis, was a member of the Parisian *haute-bourgeoisie*. Two others, Baron Chaurand, who was a member of the board of directors of the forges and foundries of Bessèges and C. Princeteau, a board member of the *Société pour l'Éclairage au Gaz de la Ville de Libourne*, were important in the bourgeois *société* respectively of Lyons and Bordeaux. The fourth, the financier Maurice Aubry, began his business career in the provinces. During the Restoration Aubry's father had started a lace business in Mirecourt which his son eventually inherited. But it was not a "modern" textile operation since it was based on the putting-out instead of the factory system. The Aubrys were simply the middlemen who provided the raw material and collected the finished products from the peasants who manufactured the lace in their cottages during the slow agricultural seasons. Had Aubry limited himself to the lace business, he could hardly be classified among the capitalists. But Aubry shifted his interests to finance capitalism. At first he became director of the *Comptoir d'Escompte d'Epinal*; then, without relinquishing his provincial ties, he moved to Paris where he helped organize the important financial house, *Donon, Aubry, Gautier, et Cie*. Thereupon he became a motive force in the financial revolution that was France's greatest single contribution to the process of rapid industrial change—the industrial development bank. Specifically he helped found the *Crédit Industriel et Commercial*. His brother became a member of the *Crédit Industriel et Commercial*'s board of direction on which La Bouillerie and Amédée Lefèvre-Pontalis sat.

The last two legitimist corporate industrialists, Montgolfier and Jullien, unlike the others, were engaged in the daily operation of a specific industry. Montgolfier, directed the *Cie. des Aciers de La Marine*, and Jullien headed the forges and foundries of Terrenoire. Of the two Jullien's work is noteworthy. He took over at Terrenoire when the company faced the enormously expensive and technically complicated process of converting from iron to steel production. Jullien installed and successfully operated some of the first Bessemer converters and Siemens-Martin open-hearth furnaces in France. Moreover, convinced that ultimately success would depend on a larger industrial base than Terrenoire offered, he set about gathering a number of firms into one large metallurgical complex. After considerable negotiations, La Voulte and Bessèges were amalgamated with Terrenoire. Jullien wanted to finish the complex by acquiring Alais, but this company refused to join the consortium. Nonetheless Jullien brought the forges and foundries of Alais into the combination, for he managed, in contract negotiations concluded between him and Benoist d'Azy during the National Assembly, to lease the forges and foundries of the Alais company (but not the mines). Finally, Jullien had a hand in creating the capital source on which the expansion of his company depended, for he was a charter member of the board of direction of the bank that lent most of the capital needed, the *Crédit Lyonnais*. Jullien was a bold entrepreneur. Unfortunately his plans ended rather badly, for Terrenoire failed in the 1880s. But the failure could really not have been foreseen. He was deeply committed to his venture when the business depression of 1873 destroyed his markets and what depression started scientific invention completed. In 1877 Thomas and Gilchrist discovered the process which removed phosphorus from iron ores, thereby making the Lorraine ores commercially exploitable. Once this occurred there was little future for the steel industry (because of the high costs of raw materials) outside the northeastern corner of France. Terrenoire succumbed with many factories located in the Central Massif and its littoral, but during the Second Empire and the first few years of the Third Republic, under Jullien's leadership, it was one of the most technologically advanced and economically dynamic metallurgical firms in France.

It was stated above that Benoist d'Azy was the greatest financier-industrialist among the legitimists. He belonged to the first generation of industrialists who faced the task of introducing English methods into France while most of the others belonged to the next generation that built on the foundations Benoist d'Azy and his contemporaries laid. Moreover, whereas Benoist d'Azy felt equally at home in the boardroom or the plant, most of his colleagues spent the bulk of their time in one or the other. Indeed a man like the Marquis de Vogüé, a *grand seigneur* in habit as well as name, did not have the technical knowledge or capacity for sustained work and rigorous attention to detail without which no director of a large corporation could hope to succeed.[23] But this hardly means that their economic contributions were insignificant. The second generation company director like Jullien or Montgolfier may have built on past efforts but he did not just repeat earlier techniques. Jullien was in fact much more adventurous than the older Benoist d'Azy during the 1860s. While Jullien experimented, Benoist d'Azy watched the installation of the Bessemer converters and Siemens-Martin furnaces, which had been developed by Emile Martin and his son, in Terrenoire and elsewhere with growing apprehension, for he fully realized that unless Alais adopted the production methods of its competitors, it would be forced out of the iron business. On the other hand, Benoist d'Azy feared the heavy investments and risks involved in making the changes. As it turned out he was right, for Alais, a very successful iron factory, could no more survive in the age of steel than Terrenoire. One reason, in fact, Benoist d'Azy was willing to lease Alais to Terrenoire is that Jullien planned to install open-hearth furnaces in Alais at no expense to the parent company. He promised, that is, to make the capital investments that the Alais company had refused to make because of anxieties over costs. Still, if Benoist d'Azy's caution seems justified with hindsight, Jullien and not he carried through the technical innovations, and this is the significant fact.

Neither do the deputies from the generation of financiers who grew to maturity during the Second Empire suffer too much by

---

[23] Still, because of Vogüé's social rank and grace he was a valuable man in the kind of high-level financial negotiations that required impressive entertainment.

116

comparison. Two scholars have written of the men responsible for the founding of the *Crédit Industriel et Commercial* that all

> were pioneers of a new economy; that of the industrial era. All were open to modern ideas and only saw in the success of one venture the way to create others: railroads, steamship companies, coal mines, docks, and warehouses. All were equally interested in the invention of a method of credit which the expansion of their business affairs necessitated. . . .[24]

Since Aubry, Lefèvre-Pontalis, and La Bouillerie belonged to this group, this description applies directly to them. Benoist d'Azy may have helped organize some of the first metallurgical firms and railroad companies, but the second generation continued this work on a scale that dwarfed the accomplishments of the July Monarchy. Benoist d'Azy shared in the later developments too, but he did not dominate the younger men.

A second group of legitimists, some sixteen deputies in all, also engaged in commerce and industry, but they were family not corporate businessmen. None of them came from the old aristocracy. A few nobles owned a forge, foundry, or blast furnace, but they did not personally supervise the operation of the establishment, preferring instead to farm them out to *régisseurs*. By no stretch of the imagination, then, could these nobles be called small businessmen. But this is exactly what the sixteen bourgeois were since each actively conducted the family's business. All these men were involved of course in a traditional business in the sense that the family-owned enterprise was typical of the pre-mass production industrial economy. Often the deputy inherited a business that had been in the family for several generations. Moreover, most of their businesses were traditional because they were not based on any products or production techniques of recent innovation. This was obviously true of merchants—half of the sixteen were merchants—like Journu, who ran a wine business in Bordeaux, Monjaret-de-Kerjégu, who had a cloth store in St-Brieuc, and Chesnelong, who operated a general merchandising wholesale house in Orthez. But it applied too to manufacturers like Malartre, the silk spinner, or Vétillart, the canvas manufacturer, whose businesses fell into a familiar pattern of industry. Still there were businesses based on new technology. Kolb-Bernard's sugar refinery depended on the

[24] Guy Beaujouan and Edmond Lebée, "La fondation du Crédit Industriel et Commercial," *Histoire des entreprises*, no. 6 (Nov., 1960), 24.

117

recent development of a commercially profitable process for extracting sugar from sugar beets, and Leurent's textile mill in Tourcoing was a modern factory which employed steam powered machinery in the mass production of cotton cloth.

The specific entrepreneurial ability of the deputies, however, was not dictated by whether they were involved in an old or new business. Any small businessman has to work hard for his firm to prosper, and there are numerous examples among the deputies of such dedicated hard work. This applies most obviously to men like Leurent and Vétillart who started a business but also to men like Malartre and Chesnelong who followed their fathers' practices. Although the Malartre family had been in the silk textile business in the Dunières valley for centuries, its business had been ruined once during the wars of religion and again during the Revolution.[25] The factory which the deputy inherited had been rebuilt by his father and uncles after years of sacrifice and frugality in postrevolutionary France. So, as a youth, the future deputy not only shared in these privations but also, while serving long years under his father's tutelage, made his own contribution to the business' initial success. When he became head of the firm in his own right, Malartre continued to devote the same energy to the family concern. He repeatedly installed new equipment in order to keep pace with the technological developments in the silk industry. Indeed, he introduced a new industry at Dunières, "le tissage des larges étoffes de soie."[26] Keenly aware of the railroad's importance to the market, Malartre incessantly and successfully intrigued for the construction of the line from Firminy to Annonay which, passing through Dunières, offered an outlet for his silk textiles. Because of his industrial achievements he exercised "une sorte de magistrature suprême dans le pays."[27] Chesnelong's business career followed a similar pattern.[28] His family came from the West where they had been *négociants* during the Old Regime. After the deputy's grandfather had lost his fortune when the slaves revolted in Saint Dominique, his father, Jean Chesnelong, settled in Orthez, without money but

[25] For the Malartre family's association with the textile industry in the Haute-Loire, see A. Boudon-Lashermes, *Les origines de l'industrie de la dentelle et de la soie en Vélay et en Forez* (Le Puy-en-Vélay, 1930).

[26] *Ibid.*, p. 53.   [27] *Ibid.*

[28] For Chesnelong's background see Chapter I of the three-volume biography, M. de Marcey, *Charles Chesnelong, son histoire et celle de son temps* (Paris, 1908).

118

with a great deal of ambition. As with Malartre, it was Chesne-long's father who began the business, but, as with Malartre too, the son worked diligently beside the father to make it a success and then expanded the business considerably when it became his sole responsibility. Chesnelong was exceedingly proud of the fact that he left his sons a merchant house that was more flourishing than the one he had acquired and he admonished them to trade skillfully but honestly, in order to do the same for their sons. In fact, Chesne-long's letters express what Max Weber called the Protestant ethic, which, apparently, was not a Protestant trait but one equally opera-tive in the Catholic middle classes. At any event it appeared fre-quently in the letters and public pronouncements of these legitimist deputies. They were frugal, hard-working, God-fearing men, whose sensibility to new business and technical developments and attention to detail in execution accounted for the prosperous state of their various enterprises during their lifetimes.

Nonetheless they should be classified quite differently from the corporation financiers and industrialists. Some of them had con-nections in the corporate-industrial world. Malartre's daughter, for example, married Montgolfier's son, and Chesnelong was not only a stockholder of an industrial corporation but also a director. Un-like other men, who began as family businessmen (for example, their colleague Maurice Aubry), these men did not become cor-porate businessmen. They remained, despite an occasional con-nection with corporate affairs, essentially family businessmen who contributed therefore little to the financial, technical, or business innovations associated with large-scale corporate enterprise. To the extent that modern industry can be identified with corporate financiers and industrialists, these men were not at the vanguard of economic change.

These two groups of legitimist deputies (the fifteen corporation board members and the sixteen family businessmen) were prin-cipally preoccupied with commerce, banking, and industry. Yet the contribution made to economic change can also be measured in terms of professional activities. Thirty-eight percent of the deputies were regularly employed in a profession, but their pro-fessional interests were quite varied and of unequal importance from the point of view of the dynamics of economic development. Although nearly 10 percent of the deputies followed military careers (thirteen noblemen and six bourgeois), their accomplishments here cannot be used as a yardstick for measuring an impact on economic change. To be sure, they may have stimulated industrial development by advocating the adoption of new ordnance, but we are too prone perhaps to see things in terms of a military-industrial complex. In the nineteenth century the military was more strictly speaking a noneconomic activity than today, and both the professional thinking and service of these men should be considered as noneconomic in orientation. The same generalization applies to the two clergymen who sat in the legitimist group. On the other hand the professions practiced by the two *Chevau-légers* Charles Combier and Adolphe Boisse clearly indicate an economic function.[29] Combier, a graduate of the *Ecole Polytechnique*, was chief engineer for the *Chemin de Fer des Ardennes*, and Boisse was the engineer in charge of the mines and railroad of Carmaux (Tarn). Since neither was a financier nor an industrial promoter, they cannot be classed with a Benoist d'Azy, an Aubry, or a Vogüé. They were professional engineers who were concerned uniquely with the construction and technical operation of an industrial establishment, but their profession, which was the creation of and the creator of big business, automatically involved them in the process of industrialization.

However, the other professional groups into which most legitimists can be placed do not clearly indicate an economic or a noneconomic function. Fifteen percent of the deputies were lawyers, 7 percent magistrates, slightly more than 2 percent journalists or scholars, and 2 percent civil servants. Most of the lawyers practiced in some provincial towns, often where their fathers had been lawyers before them. For example, Ferdinand Boyer, although a bit deaf, felt compelled to take his father's place at the bar in Nîmes, and Félix Monteil followed the paternal profession in Bergerac. There were no Berryers among them, no men with a national reputation, but several had talents that were recognized in the provinces from which they came. Talent sometimes explains their preeminence in the bar. Lucien-Brun, for example, one of the leading legitimist spokesmen in the National Assembly, acquired a first-rate reputation in Lyons. Author of several articles and a book on jurisprudence, repeatedly elected *bâtonnier* of his order, professor of law at the Catholic faculty of Lyons, he is a splendid but by no means unique example of a self-made man. Lucien-Brun, Ernoul (another able lawyer from Poitier), Dahirel from Brittany, and a

[29] Robert *et al., Dictionnaire des parlementaires français.* . . . erroneously places the *Chevau-léger* Adolphe Boisse in the Right-Center.

few others spoke frequently in the Assembly. They were not the best orators at Versailles but they were good and on occasion represented the royalist cause with distinction. The magistrates were what magistrates usually are, solid, respectable, serious citizens who sat on courts of first instance or courts of appeal and dispensed justice. As for the scholars and journalists, one, Martial Delpit, who studied under Augustin Thierry at the *Ecole des Chartes*, was a historian who is remembered not for his histories but for a diary kept at Versailles, which offers excellent commentary on parliamentary life at the beginning of the Third Republic; another, Joseph de La Borderie, a historian who wrote extensively about Brittany, was one of the most distinguished regional historians in France; two others, Pierre Callet, who wrote for the *Gazette de France*, and Octave Depeyre, editor of the *Gazette de Languedoc*, were newspapermen; and another, Douhet, was a scientist of merit. The civil servants were either, like Bodan, *procureur généraux* or subprefects.

The professional activities of these lawyers, magistrates, scholars, journalists, and civil servants had led neither to great fame nor to anonymity. But the question of professional achievement is somewhat different from that of a professional contribution to economic change. The lawyer could be responsible for developing new forms of corporate law, or he could be concerned with traditional affairs. The scholar could, especially if an economist or journalist, advocate industrialization or oppose it. The imaginative civil servant could promote the industrial development of the region under his jurisdiction or leave it to languish. Fame could come from a progressive economic attitude, but it could also come from great skill exercised within the traditional framework of economic life. And a man, of course, could be much less famous than another during his lifetime while being more economically innovative than his more illustrious colleague. Legitimist professional activities, therefore, must be viewed in this manner.

No precise evaluation of their specific contribution to economic change can be made without details of their professional life, something which is unavailable for most of these men. However, it can be said that none of them acquired a professional reputation primarily because of work done on behalf of industrialization. The scholars and the journalists wrote on political, social, and religious subjects when they discussed the contemporary scene or on events far removed from economic or financial questions when they dealt

121

with history. Moreover, the lawyers and magistrates, aside from Amédée Lefèvre-Pontalis, largely ignored corporate legal affairs. On a practical level, they dealt with older property forms covered in the *Code civil*. Even in the late 1860s, the corporation was not common outside Paris. On a theoretical level they certainly did not consciously advocate the extension of the limited liability joint-stock corporation. They really produced few works on jurisprudence, and when they did, as in the case of Lucien-Brun, they touched on social, religious, and political subjects rather than purely economic topics. It was on social rather than economic grounds that they voiced complaints against the joint-stock company. Therefore, the actual contributions these lawyers, magistrates, journalists, or scholars made to the transformation of the nation was much like that of the family businessmen—negligible.

Still the active economic life of the deputies was not confined to business or the professions. Forty-five percent of these men (76 percent of the noblemen and 18 percent of the bourgeois) had little to do with the traditional family type of commerce, industry, or profession, much less with high finance or corporate industry. They belonged to the very large socioeconomic category that is usually designated in biographical dictionaries as *propriétaires*. The business and professional people were also *propriétaires*, and when combined with these 45 percent, the term *propriétaire* became a sort of common denominator for all the legitimist deputies. None of them, of course, tilled their lands with their own hands, but they had the options of thinking and acting—to use an ugly twentieth-century term—as agribusinessmen or simply living as *rentiers*. Benoist d'Azy had adopted the same vigorous entrepreneurial attitude toward his agricultural properties that he exhibited in industry. To what extent did his fellow *propriétaires*, who played almost no role in commerce and industry, follow suit when it came to the exploitation of their land? This is a very important question considering the number of legitimists to which it applies.

Evidence suggests that many of the legitimist *propriétaires* continued to think about agriculture in premarket economic terms. Some, testifying before the agricultural investigating committees of the 1860s, insisted on the need for agricultural protection, while others belittled the importance of machinery for agriculture, argued that machines took work from able farm hands, and complained incidentally about the difficulty of finding laborers during harvest time.[30] Others, moreover, claimed that each locale grew grain in order to insure self-sufficiency, thereby obviously failing to comprehend that a market economy required specialization in crops particularly suited to an area's soil and that this was possible because the railroads had ended the threat of local famine and the need, therefore, to grow grains on lands little suited to their cultivation.[31] The late Michel Augé-Laribé, one of the leading French agricultural historians, maintained that these protectionists sought to survive through the tariff rather than through an improvement of their farming techniques. It might be said in their defense that even with huge capital investments in farm equipment the French farmer could never have been able to compete with the grain-growing and wool-producing farmers of the New World, Australia, and Russia. British farmers made large investments between 1850 and 1870, and lost heavily once improved transportation permitted the products from the non-European agricultural regions of the world to enter their unprotected home market.[32] Survival in free trade came from specialization in crops that were not subject to such competition, but this meant that a nation would have to rely on foreign producers for basic staples and most continental nations refused to take this course. Still the argument that protection was a way out for the legitimist landlords who clung to economic routine cannot be overlooked.

Even so, the incidence of retarded thinking among the legitimist deputies concerning agricultural improvements is fairly rare. Most were very much aware of the advantages that the nineteenth-century urban market offered to an enterprising agriculturalist. There is a brochure in the Bibliothèque nationale, written by the *Chevau-léger* Armand Fresneau, which is an entrepreneurial model in this respect.[33] Fresneau was convinced that the railroads and steamships could permit the Breton farmer, specializing in market gar-

[30] See, for example, Questionnaire répondu par M. le Mis. de Franclieu, *Enquête agricole*, 2e série, 17e circonscription (Paris, 1868), p. 353.

[31] See, for example, the Extrait d'une brochure adressée par M. Edouard de La Bassétière à M. Le Président de la Commission, "Les souffrances agricoles dans l'arrondissement des Sables-d'Olonne," *Enquête agricole*, 2e série, 7e circonscription (Paris, 1869), p. 157.

[32] For a discussion of this problem see J. D. Chambers and G. E. Mingay, *The Agricultural Revolution, 1750–1880* (London, 1966), Chapter VII.

[33] Armand Fresneau, *Rapport adressé à M. Le Cte. de Ségur, le 6 septembre 1868* . . . (Versailles, 1868).

123

dening, to take advantage of the seemingly unlimited market which the population centers of London and Paris offered. He understood, however, that this opportunity would be missed if the farmers did not prepare, and to this end he invested large amounts of capital in his own farms. In the brochure Fresneau not only urged the landlords to follow his example by specializing in market gardening but also, based on the improvements he had made on his lands, outlined the technical steps and capital needed to modernize a farm. Moreover, realizing that such an enterprise depended on regional cooperation, he urged the Breton landlords to form a producers' cooperative that could negotiate with the railroads and steamship lines for cheap rates and rationalize the marketing process on a regional basis. Although Fresneau's account is especially noteworthy because of its details, the kind of mentality he exhibited was by no means exceptional. The great expansion of the railroads during the Second Empire had made these men extremely sensitive to the national if not the international market. Sometimes their entrepreneurial schemes were contradictory. Louis de Kergorlay, for example, had visions of making France into a great flour-producing country that would service markets in Britain and the continent. To accomplish this he wanted to import cheap Russian wheat through Marseilles for transshipment to French mills, a project which shocked other landlords who were themselves wheat producers.[34] On the other hand, the Marquis de Vogüé favored a protective tariff on grains precisely because he realized that the communications revolution made Kergorlay's scheme a practical possibility.[35] But if Vogüé's ideas seem regressive on this point, they were certainly advanced on others. He was, for instance, a convinced advocate of stockbreeding because of the urban meat market that the railroads opened to stockmen.

During the 1850s and the 1860s, these legitimists urged the agricultural community to modernize. They were, with rare exceptions, members of or presided over local or regional agricultural associations, and the more prominent among them (Bouillé, Dampierre,

[34] If we do this, he noted, "France will become the largest and most important center for the milling of flours at the same time that England will provision itself more from French flours than from those made directly from imported foreign wheats." *Enquête agricole*, 3e série, p. 117.

[35] He observed, "Speed of transportation has placed the [French farmers'] struggle with the consumer under new conditions. I do not complain of progress, . . . but, after all, the telegraph [and] the railroads [easily put foreign grains on French markets]." *Ibid.*, p. 365.

Aboville, and Saint-Victor) helped organize the Agricultural Society of France. Indeed, it was because of their standing among agriculturalists on a regional as well as a national level that many of them were called to testify before the imperial agricultural investigating committees. They not only advised their fellow landlords to make capital improvements and conduct experiments vital to agricultural progress but also cursed the state for having neglected the farmer's plight either through its indifference to or outright abuse of agricultural interests. In particular, they singled out the heavy tax burden on the land, the failure to provide agricultural education, and the lack of any support for a banking program that would provide money, at reasonable interest rates, to capital-starved landlords and peasants. And these legitimist landlords, after their election to the Assembly, installed themselves as a significant if not dominant group in the *Réunion des Agriculteurs des Députés de l'Assemblée nationale* that sponsored legislative programs designed to correct these abuses.

But the claim that the legitimist landlords were progressive agriculturists rests as much on their accomplishments as farmers as on the interest they took in promoting agriculture in general. Many experimented with stockbreeding, crop specialization, and viticulture, and began irrigation projects on their lands, and some were involved in a combination of these activities in order to increase the commercial value of their properties. The products marketed by these men, moreover, reveal the broad scope of their agribusiness methods. Baucarne-Leroux, who kept a model farm at La Croix, and Rotours were sugar beet growers in the Nord; Grasset was in sericulture in Gard; Belcastel in Garonne and Delavau in Anjou were winegrowers; and Vogüé in Cher, Dampierre in Landes, Bouillé in Nièvre, and Béthune in Ardennes were big livestock producers. The efforts which these agriculturists put into their lands did not always bear fruit. Fresneau lost heavily in his market gardening venture in Brittany. He was just too far ahead of his time. Grasset, Belcastel, and Delavau suffered with other legitimists when disease destroyed sericulture and the dreaded phylloxera almost wiped out the vineyards of France. But adversity also brought out ingenuity. Nothing could be done to preserve sericulture, but the winegrowers avoided extinction by introducing disease-resistant grafts from California vines into their fields. Belcastel, for example, was particularly noted for his efforts to save his vineyards. Those, moreover, who had been lucky and intelligent enough to have specialized in sugar beets or livestock succeeded brilliantly. Indeed, Rotours, Vogüé, Bouillé, and Dampierre made fortunes marketing these products.

Thus many legitimist landlords rivaled or even surpassed Benoist d'Azy as agribusinessmen. It is probably safe to say that among French *propriétaires* the legitimists were a very progressive element. Yet even the most advanced agronomists among them were not receptive to some innovations. Few, if any, favored corporate farming—they wanted the land to be owned by an individual or a family. This attitude reflected their general distaste for corporate as opposed to family ownership of any economic enterprise. Unlike Benoist d'Azy, most of the legitimist landlords restricted their economic activities to agriculture and disapproved of mining and manufacturing. Often their remarks show they fully understood that agriculture's progress depended on the growth of an urban population but, as enthusiastic agrarians, they rather incongruously favored agriculture in order to offset industrial growth. Since these landlords made up such an important part of the legitimist group, this fact alone would prevent them from being characterized as builders of commerce and industry. Furthermore, although several legitimists were important figures in the big business community, most of the deputies engaged in commerce and manufacturing were not. Considering that the legitimists' professional efforts, with the exception of those of the two engineers Boisse and Combier, had nothing to do with trade and commerce, the legitimists counted even less as a group in the economic process that was bringing about large-scale mining and manufacturing.

If this indicates that the legitimist deputies could not be considered economic progressives, it does not necessarily prove anything about the correlation between dynastic allegiances and economic functions and attitudes in the National Assembly of 1871. Judgments of this kind can only be made if the economic positions of the nonlegitimists are known. In this regard, it is instructive to compare the legitimist deputies with the group immediately to its left, the so-called Orleanist Right-Center, because the Orleanists have been identified with big business. Table 3 gives the occupations of the deputies in the Right-Center and the Right.[36] The com-

[36] The deputies were placed in the classification that best reveals their relationship to the economy. Thus anybody who sat on the board of direction of a financial or industrial corporation has been put in this category, even though he may have been a *propriétaire*. The logic here is that as-

TABLE 3

The Professional and Business Background of the Orleanist
Right-Center and Legitimist Right

Occupation	Right-Center (180 Deputies)		Right (200 Deputies)	
	No. of Deputies	% of Group	No. of Deputies	% of Group
Professions	77	42.8	79	40.5
Lawyers	27	15.	30	15.
Notaries	4	2.2	3	1.5
Magistrates	12	6.7	14	7
Journalists	2	1.1	2	2.0
Scholars	7	3.9	4	2.0
Bureaucrats	7	3.9	4	2.0
Clergymen	1	.6	2	1.0
Military men	17	9.4	19	9.5
Other	0	0	1	.5
Businessmen	46	25.4	31	15.5
Family-owned	29	16	16	8
Manufacturers	19	10.5	8	4
Merchants	6	3.3	3	1.5
Other	4	2.2	5	2.5
Corporate (Banks, Mining, Railroads, Textiles, etc.)	17	9.4	15	7.5
Industrial Technicians	3	1.7	2	1.5
Landlords	40	22.2	77	42
Unable to Classify	14	7.9	1	.5

sociation with big business is more significant than another occupation.
Anybody who was a professional man is classified under this heading, even
though he may have been a rich landlord, but not, of course, if he were
in corporate business. Landlords, therefore, are those deputies who had
no significant business or professional connections. The group "Unable
to Classify" is of interest because of the relatively high number in the
Right-Center. These were rather obscure men about whom little or no
biographical information could be found. Because of their obscurity it is
doubtful whether they could have been important financiers or industrialists. My guess is that most of them were *propriétaires*, although many
may have been professional people or family businessmen.

parison shows that the professions claimed about as many deputies in both groups. There were some variations among the professional groups. A slightly higher percentage of Orleanists, for example, were scholars; more eminent scholars no doubt, than the legitimists since all seven were university professors. But the most significant difference in occupations occurred in the categories of businessmen and *propriétaires*. Almost twice as many Orleanists as legitimists (men like the Duc de Decaze, of the forges and foundries of Decazeville; Deseilligny, director first of the forges and foundries of Le Creusot and then of those of Decazeville, Talhouet, *régisseur* of the mines of Anzin; Cornélis de Witte, member of the boards of direction of the Grand'Combe and the Lombard railroad) belonged to the big business community, and twice as many Orleanists as legitimists operated family-owned businesses. These men were no more important as financiers, industrialists, or small businessmen than their legitimist colleagues, but they were certainly more numerous. On the other hand, whereas most of the Orleanists were, like the legitimists, *propriétaires*, only half as many were exclusively *propriétaires*. Many of them were as rich and as influential landlords as the legitimists, but they were not as numerous as the rightists.

Obviously, because there were more of them, the financier-industrialists in the Right-Center contributed more to the creation of the corporate industrial economic structure than the legitimists. But did they as a group, in contrast to the legitimists, promote the industrialization of France? The answer is no. The Orleanist lawyers, like the legitimists, practiced in some provincial city. They were not corporate lawyers, and they did not aid, especially in fact or theory, the development of the corporation. The scholars were not economists but, for the most part, professors of literature, and the military men, like their legitimist colleagues, were preoccupied with tasks that were only tangentially connected with economic development. The testimony of the Orleanist *propriétaires* before the agricultural investigating committees demonstrates that they were frequently enlightened agriculturists but no more so than the legitimists. It is true that the Orleanists were greater figures in French society. Whereas no legitimist had ever held a cabinet office before 1871, Jaubert and Talhouet had been ministers of public works; Batbie, minister of public instruction; Buffet, minister of finance; and Daru, minister of foreign affairs. This political preeminence extended into literary and journalistic fields. The Or-

128

leanists often wrote for the more respected periodicals in France. Cornélis de Witte, Chasseloup-Laubat, Passy, and Vitet, for example, contributed articles to the *Revue des Deux Mondes,* and others wrote scholarly books or literary works that earned them a reputation far exceeding that enjoyed by the legitimists. There were occasions when the Orleanists used their political positions to back industrial development. During the July Monarchy, for example, Comte Jaubert, while minister of public works, had strongly supported government subsidies for the railroads. Still the number of Orleanist deputies who sponsored large-scale industrialization or were directly engaged in big business was, if larger than the number of legitimists, quite limited.

This conclusion, moreover, is buttressed by an analysis of the financial guide compiled by Auguste Vitu during the Second Empire. Vitu named the members of the boards of direction of most of the 1,000 companies listed on the various stock exchanges of France. His study is not complete since some companies did not provide him with the names of their board members. Usually, this happened with very obscure provincial companies, but board members are not listed for a few large concerns (for example, the mines of Anzin, the five *régisseurs* of which sat in the National Assembly). Since members of the boards of direction of these companies are listed for a single year, the guide obviously overlooks men who had sat on a company board before and after this time. Nonetheless the study is quite comprehensive, despite the occasional omissions and time limitation, because it names the great majority (over two thousand) of the men who directed the corporate banking, financial, commercial, industrial, and public service businesses of France. It also offers a useful base for analyzing the corporate background of the deputies of 1871. Deputies who were board members of corporations at some point during their life other than the year (1863) considered or on companies which did not give names to Vitu are not on the lists. This was true for the legitimists Lagrange, Vogüé, Chaurand, Lefèvre-Pontalis, and Montgolfier, and for a number of Center deputies, including Witte, Deseilligny, Thiers, and Audiffret-Pasquier. But the guide's scope suggests that most of the deputies who were prominent board members of French industry during the last decade of the Second Empire were included in the presentation.

Thirty-five of the deputies elected to the National Assembly sat on the boards of directors of at least one of the corporations listed *de Paris*, sat on the Assembly's extreme Left and four others (Du-by Vitu. One of them, Edmond Adam, of the *Comptoir d'Escompte* coux of the *Cie. Impériale des Voitures de Paris*; Ducuing of the *Banque d'Emission et de Placement* and the insurance company *Le Sémaphore*; Mangini of the *Crédit Lyonnais*; and Flotard, of the *Société Anonyme des Houillères de Montrambert et de la Béraudière*) sat among the Left-Republicans.

Nine deputies were members of the Left-Center and closely affiliated with Adolphe Thiers: Germain (*Crédit Lyonnais, Société des Forges de Châtillon et Commentry, Société Anonyme des Houillères de Montrambert et de la Béraudière, Société d'Eclairage au Gaz et des Hauts-Fourneaux et Fonderies de Marseille et des Mines de Portes et Sénéchas, Cie. Française d'Assurances Maritime*); Target (*Cie. Française de Réassurance contre l'Incendie*); Pallotte (*Société des Houillères d'Ahun, Cie. Anonyme des Houillères du Chemin de Fer de Saint-Eloi*); Gouin (*Sous-Comptoir des Chemins de Fer*); Say (*Nord* [railroad], *Cie. Française de Réassurance contre l'Incendie*); Ancel (*La Préséverante* [insurance]); Pourtalès (*Cie. Générale des Eaux, Cie. Nouvelles d'Assurances Maritimes du Havre*); Teisserenc de Bort (*P.L.M.* [railroad], *Société des Polders de l'Ouest*); Rivet (*P.L.M., Lyon à Genève* [railroad], *Cie. Française de Réassurance contre l'Incendie*).

Eleven deputies were members of the Right-Center: Ternaux (*La France* [insurance], *Société Civile des Mines de Houille de Dourges*); Rainneville (*Orléans* [railroad], *Dauphiné* [railroad], *Crédit Foncier de France, Crédit Agricole, La Réassurance*); Peulve (*Cie. d'Armaments Maritimes*); Talhouet (*Cie. de Béthune* [coal mine], *L'Impériale* [insurance]); Barante (*Société des Mines de Plomb Argentifère et de la Fonderie de Pontgibaud*); Lacombe (*Société Anonyme de Houillères de Rive-de-Gier*); Plichon (*L'Indemnité* [insurance]); Paultre (*Bessèges à Alais* [railroad], *Société d'Eclairage au Gaz et des Hauts-Fourneaux et Fonderies de Marseille et des Mines de Portes et Sénéchas*); Duc de Decaze (*Cie. des Houillères et Fonderies de l'Aveyron*); N. Johnston (*Cie. du Midi et du Canal Latéral à la Garonne, Société des Mines de Plomb Argentifère et de la Fonderie de Pontgibaud*); Jaubert (*Cie. des Mines de Houille de Commentry et des Forges et Fonderies de Fourchambault, Montluçon et Imphy*).

Ten deputies were members of the legitimist Right. They were Béthune, Vaulchier, Pontoi-Pontcarré, Princeteau, Jullien, La

Bouillerie, Benoist d'Azy, Bouillé, Melun, and Aubry. One deputy, Martenot of the *Société des Forges de Châtillon et Commentry* and the *Caisse Générale des Assurances Commerciales contre les Risques Maritimes* was a Bonapartist. Although six years before their election to the National Assembly twice as many of the Left- and Right-Center deputies had been members of boards of directors as legitimists, the Orleanist Center could hardly be described as dominated by corporate business. There were 727 deputies in the National Assembly of whom only 35 were listed as board members by Vitu. If the comparison made here indicates anything, it is that members of boards of direction did not dominate French political life at the beginning of the Third Republic.

Other studies seem to corroborate this evidence. Sherman Kent, for example, has shown that the Orleanist notables who were members of the *pays légal* during the July Monarchy were not captains of industry but landlords and, as such, scarcely different from the legitimists.[37] He offers convincing evidence that the Revolution of 1830 did not bring the triumph of high finance, wholesale trade, and large-scale manufacture over a landlord class since the occupational background of the deputies in the Chamber of Deputies hardly varied from one regime to the other. The analysis of the relationship between occupational function and political comportment moreover has been extended back into the Old Regime and the Revolution. A good case has been made for the contention that the rise of the bourgeoisie resulted primarily from the growth of the royal and Church bureaucratic institutions which it manned and that a principal source of revolutionary agitation was the desire of the middle classes to gain access to top positions in the army, the magistracy, the Church hierarchy, and the government ministries from which they were barred. The conflict, then, was not economic in the sense that the bourgeois liberals represented a new mode of production. The reformers of 1789 were interested in economic and fiscal issues. They wanted, for example, to eliminate the last vestiges of manorialism. But this was a step against privilege which was not directly prompted by any desire to introduce changes in economic production in the country. Even the clash over property (i.e., the sale of national lands) was not concerned with different property forms but with who should own land. Indeed the late Alfred Cobban has gone to considerable lengths to show that

[37] Sherman Kent, *Electoral Procedure Under Louis Philippe* (New Haven, 1937).

the revolutionary bourgeoisie was a class of economically conservative landlords.[38]

It is, of course, somewhat illogical to argue about the political attitudes of financiers or industrialists with examples taken from a society that did not undergo much large-scale industrialization until the Second Empire. In a preindustrial society the economic power of the notables, whether Orleanists or legitimists, of necessity had to be rooted in the ownership of land. But evidence collected in societies in which great wealth had been accumulated in manufacturing and industry indicates that the presence of a Benoist d'Azy, a Maurice Aubry, or a La Bouillerie among the legitimists is not some abberation in the "normal" political and ideological attitudes that the big financier or industrialist would assume. A scrutiny of the membership lists of Frédéric Le Play's *Société d'économie sociale*, for example, shows that at least half of its members were manufacturers or engineers—Le Play himself was a renowned metallurgical engineer who was familiar with the great metallurgical factories of France.[39] And Le Play's group rejected the laissez-faire individualistic philosophies of liberalism in favor of corporate social theories. Le Play tried to remain neutral in political questions and many of the members of the *Société* followed his example. But there is no doubt that legitimists felt at home with the social philosophy espoused in the Le Play group. Since many of its members were legitimists and the Comte de Chambord let it be known that he greatly admired and agreed with Le Play's social philosophy, it is not unreasonable to believe that the industrialists in Le Play's group, who were politically neutral, would have accepted the legitimist monarchy had it been restored because they shared the legitimist conception of social organization.

However, the best examples of industrialists adopting political and social attitudes similar to those of the French legitimists occurred on the other side of the Rhine. Antiliberalism seemed to grow among big businessmen in Germany with the increased tempo of industrialization. The Germans were notorious for their feudal mentality, and, although the industrialists destroyed the old

[38] Alfred Cobban, *The Social Interpretation of the French Revolution* (Cambridge, 1964). See Chapter VIII.

[39] For lists of members consult "Liste générale des membres de la société d'économie sociale au 1e déc. 1869," *Bulletin, Société internationale des études practiques d'économie sociale*, III (1872), 228–240; and "Liste générale des membres de la société d'economie sociale," *ibid.*, IV (1875), 883–894.

handicraft system of production, they incorporated many of its features (regulation of production and consumption, the prerequisite of a thorough professional and occupational training) into the new industrial order. They quickly abandoned any earlier flirtation with political liberalism for the neofeudalism of the Bismarckian state. The conservative alliance between East Elbian landlord and industrialist that emerged in Imperial Germany proves the extent to which the political and social mentality of the old landlord class and the new captains of industry could coincide.

Apparently, then, nothing inherent in the process of industrialization prevented the financier or manufacturer from adopting antiliberal social conceptions. To be sure the nineteenth-century industrialist objected to those aspects of preindustrial society that hampered the recruitment of labor, production, and the marketing of his products. He was happy, therefore, to see the workers' guilds and other economically restrictive characteristics of the Old Regime swept away, but he did not want to see them replaced by anarchy. The penchant of iron manufacturers and railroad builders to ask for state aid is well known but less known perhaps was their effort—particularly in technologically advanced industries —to tie their labor force to the factory just as the feudal lords had tried to stabilize their labor force through serfdom. French iron manufacturers, for example, agreed on several occasions in the 1840s not to raid each other's establishments for skilled workers, although they repeatedly violated these agreements because of the scarcity of qualified men.[40] Moreover, if they did not rely on the sort of legal measures used in serfdom, large companies often adopted policies that bound their working population to their factory since a constant turnover in labor seriously impaired efficiency. Companies built schools and housing, founded mutual aid societies, and even implemented pension schemes in order to bring their workers into a community. Workers, especially those who had been employed for a long time, were reluctant to leave since they often had to forfeit any money that they had paid into a mutual aid or pension fund when quitting the company. Also the industrialist sought not only to build a community but also to develop in his workers a corporate spirit. In the social context of the modern factory, neofeudalism was just as pertinent eco-

[40] For a discussion of business combination in the earlier period, see Bertrand Gille, *Recherches sur la formation de la grande entreprise capitaliste (1815–1848)* (Paris, 1959), Chapters II & V.

133

nomically as laissez-faire ideas about a free and uninhibited labor supply.

In fact it has been argued that the philosophy of individualism was not particularly suited to an industrial community. Individualism was born and flourished in a preindustrial society. It appealed mostly to the middle classes, the independent small businessman, and the professional person who were uneasy with, if not hostile, toward big banks and big industry. The political and economic attitudes usually associated with liberalism have survived within this middle class group into the twentieth century. However, Jürgen Habermas has pointed out that the decline in liberalism which occurred during the third quarter of the last century resulted inevitably from the change in the economic and social structure introduced into Europe by the process of large-scale industrialization.[41] The most obvious example of how this transformation affected attitudes is the change which occurred among the German National Liberals when, after the industrialists supplanted the merchants in the party, it adjusted its economic program and its politics to the needs of the new men. But there are other examples. Proudhon's anarchistic individualism that appealed to the artisans employed in the small workshops gave way under the impact of industrialization to the highly structured, centralized, bureaucratic corporate existence of the industrial union and Marxist party that were rooted in the new proletariat.

The point, however, is not so much that industrialization produced socioeconomic groups which adopted specific political and social attitudes peculiar to themselves but that it produced groups which could accommodate a number of preexistent political and social systems to their situation. "Citizens of a country which has not passed through a feudal age," Val R. Lorwin has written, "cannot easily imagine how long its heritage conditions social attitudes."[42] The rapid and massive industrialization of a Germany so little removed from "feudalism" certainly appears to underscore the truth of such a statement. As early as 1916, Thorstein Veblen analyzed the feudalistic character of German industrialization. Similar comments, moreover, have been made about Japan. In

[41] Jürgen Habermas, "Strukturwandel der Oeffentlichkeit," in Hans-Ulrich Wehler, *Moderne deutsche Sozialgeschichte* (Cologne, 1968), pp. 197–221.

[42] Val R. Lorwin, *The French Labor Movement* (Cambridge, Mass., 1954), p. 37.

the course of modernization Japan imported many Western cultural elements but the importation of Western culture did not drastically affect the basic cultural structure of the country. This cultural structure contained interpersonal attitudes that could be called "feudalistic," the emotional commitment of the junior to the senior and vice-versa, the pattern of loyalty on the one side and responsible loving care on the other. The relationship, which existed in the family and in the bureaucratic world of preindustrial Japan, was transferred to business. The Japanese worker developed a remarkable emotional attachment to the business organization and the company responded in kind with a paternal solicitude for his welfare.[43]

If the citizen of a country which has not passed through a feudal age cannot imagine the effect this heritage has on industrialization, by the same token, it can be said that citizens of a country which has not passed through a liberal-democratic revolution cannot imagine how its heritage conditions social relations in the developing industrial state. For Veblen, Schumpeter, and many others who were familiar with the British experience, the feudal hangover in Germany was some sort of aberration in the normal evolution·of an industrial society. It was an atavism, something to be cursed for the distortions it caused in the country's history. But there was nothing inherent in the process of industrialization that made people more liberal. France had undergone a liberal-democratic revolution before large-scale industrialization began; Germany had not, and the social political attitudes of industrialists varied accordingly. The legitimist might have been an anachronism in France because he lived in a society in which the majority of his compatriots rejected his ideas, but the reason for their rejection cannot be determined on the basis of their relationship to the process of industrialization. Legitimists were industrialists. Moreover, the form of their political and social ideas was not necessarily incompatible with the social and economic requirements of an industrial society. Most French industrialists were probably Orleanists or liberals of some sort but this occurred because most Frenchmen were liberals before industrialization began. That French, British, or American businessmen clung to certain liberal principles in economics as well as politics long after (the prejudice against trusts is a good example of the difference between these men and the Germans) they could be justified on rational economic grounds

[43] See Chie Nakane, *Japanese Society* (London, 1971).

135

is sufficient testimony to the strength of this heritage from pre-industrial times.

These general considerations bear directly on the complex subject, to which we have and shall repeatedly refer, of the correlation between the legitimists' socioeconomic background and their ideological outlook. Since the appearance of legitimist and Orleanist political groupings preceded industrialization; since the majority of the deputies in both groups in the National Assembly were not professionally or occupationally involved in the corporate large-scale industrial transformation of France; since industrialists themselves could and did adopt various and conflicting sociopolitical attitudes; and since these attitudes were, to a large extent, a heritage from the preindustrial period of a nation's history, it appears that neither the legitimists nor their Orleanist opponents can be identified on the basis of their relationship to the process of industrialization per se. This does not mean that industrialization did not damage the vested economic interests of many of these men and, as a result, arouse their animosity. But the economic harm (or benefit) it caused affected men of quite different ideological beliefs. The family businessman, whether a republican, an Orleanist, or a legitimist, a clerical or an anticlerical, was equally menaced by the rise of corporate industry and frequently reacted in the same hostile way. There are numerous examples of the expression of this hostility among small businessmen of various parties in the Assembly. Indeed, the inability of the merchants and manufacturers to adjust to the institutional and psychological demands of modern business practices is well known. The landlord, whether a bourgeois liberal or an aristocratic legitimist, moreover, was equally distressed by the rural exodus which accompanied urbanization and responded with similar economic complaints, both inside and outside the Assembly. Instances of this sort of common economic grievance can easily be multiplied. These people did not band together politically because they were often at each other's throats over ideological issues that had a greater hold over their imaginations than purely economic ones. In other words, the political and social cleavages existing in France during industrialization did not correlate with the problems induced by industrialization.

Neither does it appear that the legitimists can be separated from other Frenchmen on the grounds of differing economic functions in a preindustrial society. Although traditional merchants and manufacturers often behaved like Luddites when faced with large-scale industrialization, they did represent a different form of wealth from that of the landlord. To the extent, therefore, that the legitimists could be related to the land and their opponents to this "new mode of production" (manufacture and commerce), their conflicts might be considered economic in origin. If the legitimists had been aristocrats, this contention might have great validity. The old aristocracy did not participate appreciably in the trade and manufacture of the preindustrial economy. But half of the deputies were from the bourgeoisie, and among them were many merchants and manufacturers. The merchants and manufacturers of preindustrial France, in fact, cannot be grouped neatly among the revolutionaries. More significantly, the liberal bourgeoisie is not identifiable with merchants and manufacturers. The fact that liberal bourgeois were important landlords and that many had acquired the money to purchase land not through trade and commerce but through capturing lucrative positions in the royal bureaucracy is especially significant in this regard.

Thus the economic background of the deputies indicates that the conflict between legitimists and Orleanists was not the political and ideological manifestation of a social struggle that resulted from the replacement of an old economic elite, based on land ownership, by a new economic elite, based on modern industry. Could, then, the basis of the struggle be social instead of economic? Legitimists came from the old aristocracy and the old Catholic oligarchy. It would be convenient if these two social groups could be identified with legitimists since it would mean that their ideology reflected the opinion of fairly clearly definable social groups that were at odds with new "social elites" forming in France. But, as Chapter Two indicated, too many of the descendants of the old aristocracy and the old Catholic oligarchy were not legitimists for this to have been true. Still this does not deny the social roots of legitimism. Stendahl, writing specifically about the legitimists of Nancy, remarked that the great evil which afflicted the nineteenth century was "la colère du rang contre le mérite."[44] None of these men accepted the idea of individual merit as an operative principle for society. Family and class counted for much more than talent as criteria for political and social leadership. Since such ideas could only lead to the perpetuation of the power of the traditional social elite from which the legitimists came, they must be seen as an

[44] Stendhal, *Lucien Leuwen* (Monaco, 1947), Tome I, p. 158.

137

extension of the struggle of that elite to survive in a rapidly changing society.

Nor does it deny that this social struggle was essentially noneconomic. Many legitimists disapproved of industrialization. They
resented the political and social ambitions of the *nouveau riche*,
particularly when based on a philosophy of individual merit and
a lack of respect for traditional social authorities, and they really
objected to the social not the economic effects of industrialization.[45]
This might sound nonsensical to people who think that these social
consequences were the inevitable result of economic change, but
this is not necessarily what occurs. There are several instances in
history where an old social elite performed a dynamic role in the
economy. In the sixteenth and seventeenth centuries, the Prussian
Junkers developed into a group of rather hard-nosed capitalistic
landlords; in the late eighteenth and early nineteenth centuries
British peers invested heavily in new industries. In France aristocratic landlords provided much of the capital needed for the
new mining and iron industries. The part that the legitimist aristocrats Kersaint and Rauzan played in financing Benoist d'Azy's
metallurgical establishment at Alais is a case in point. In each instance the staying power of the old elite was strengthened by its
progressive economic function. Moreover, the social groups that
had challenged and were continuing to challenge the authority of
the older elites were not always the specific creations or creators
of economic change. Bourgeois revolutionaries of 1789 who acquired fortunes from government service instead of trade and
manufacture fall into this category as do the Orleanist landlords
and middle-class lawyers who attacked the pretensions of the old
aristocracy and the Catholic oligarchy in 1830 while ensconced in
conservative economic functions.

In a society undergoing rapid industrialization, there are two
variables: the economic process of transformation and the preindustrial socioeconomic and political world in which the industrialization takes place. The process of industrialization greatly

[45] For an example of how a legitimist considered industrialization primarily from a social instead of an economic standpoint see, D. K. Cohen,
"The Vicomte de Bonald's Critique of Industrialism," *The Journal of
Modern History*, 41:4 (Dec., 1969), 475–484. Bonald would have considered the social results of industrialization as inevitable. The point here
is that they were only inevitable because of the preexistent social context
in which the industrialization took place.

modifies the preindustrial relationships in order for it to occur (i.e., abolishes those forces that resist industrialization), but at the same time the preexistent political, economic, and social norms incorporate the industrialization process into their own environmental patterns insofar as these patterns do not hinder industrialization itself. Germany and Japan were more "feudal" societies when massive industrialization came; France had experienced the French Revolution. In Germany and Japan, where the traditional authorities and their social ethic were deeply rooted, economic transformation did not destroy their influences but adapted them to the new conditions. In France, where society had undergone a fundamental sociopsychological revolution before industrialization on a large scale, industrialization only hastened the spread of social-ideological outlooks already developed in the preindustrial era.

As a method for understanding the legitimists, therefore, economic and social factors should be separated in the sense that the socioethical norms adapted to industrialization were those hammered out in the social conflicts of preindustrial France. Legitimists, of course, criticized the social results of industrialization. It was not, however, industrialization itself but industrialization considered within the framework of a society wherein the moral order had been undermined through political, social, and ethical developments not specifically attributable to technological change that alarmed them. Their criticism of industrialization, therefore, was inseparable from their general criticism of all those factors in French society which they blamed for undermining the moral order. To their analysis of these factors—which sheds light on where the legitimists stood in the preindustrial but postrevolutionary society—we now turn.

Chapter Four

THE SOCIOLOGY OF MORAL ORDER

George Orwell, in an excellent essay on Charles Dickens, touches on one of the problems that most perplexes modern man—the origins of evil and injustice in society. Orwell points out that two completely opposite views prevail on the subject. On the one hand, some maintain that evil and injustice are a product of society. The most sophisticated presentation of this environmentalist position was propounded perhaps by Marx. Marx believed that men's ideals and values were class-based and therefore held that the behavior of men differed in a class-ridden society. In particular, he argued that greed, selfishness, callousness, and inhumanity were characteristic of the modern bourgeoisie. But the subtlety of Marx's argument is that he did not think these evils were an intrinsic part of human nature. Man in a bourgeois world had been alienated from his humaneness by a private-property system. Abolish the system and human beings will be able to find the spiritual enrichment and genuine ethical existence that was being denied them. A similar view had been expressed by many important Enlightenment thinkers. Rousseau, for example, claimed that man was born free but everywhere in chains because his essential goodness was corrupted by the artificiality of civilization. Voltaire, although more pessimistic about man's basic nature, was convinced that much injustice could be corrected through educational and institutional reforms. The opposite viewpoint is much older and simpler to state. It is that evil exists in the world because it is part of man's nature. Since evil is irremediable, it will exist in all societies regardless of socioeconomic relations. The view is usually associated with Christians, but it does not have to be. Many agnostics and atheists have come to the same conclusions simply from observing their fellow man. This pessimism has been reinforced in our own century by the actions of the Marxists. Much of Orwell's own work deals specifically with the soulless inhumanity of the Communist world which seems to have arisen

140

from the inability of man, even Communist man, to overcome the human weakness of using power to exploit others.

The debate over the source of evil is of interest in this study because it helps clarify the legitimists' approach to the problem. When they looked for the cause of immorality among men, they inevitably fell back on the Christian doctrine of original sin. People were evil not because they were alienated from themselves but because they were alienated from God. Albert Camus who makes a great deal of the revolt against God in *The Rebel* asserts that in order to be free man killed God—an act accomplished philosophically by Enlightenment philosophers like Helvétius and actually when the Convention ended divine right monarchy by beheading Louis XVI. But Camus relates the sad tale of cruelty and murder that has transpired since men made themselves the measure and judge of all things. Systematically slugged, beaten, and killed in concentration camps by democrats, communists, and fascists alike, men have been exterminated, in the name of humanity, on a vast scale with a ruthlessness that inspires awe because of its incredible efficiency. Camus was not asking for a return to God. He was a humanist pleading for a moderation that would spare people such fates, but he offers no convincing reason why his pleas should not be uttered in vain since there is little evidence in the chronicle of the recent past to substantiate such a faith in moderation. The legitimists lived before Camus, but they would have quickly pointed out that his mistake like that of all humanists before him was to base the salvation of man on man himself. Man fell when he revolted against God, and since Camus approved of this revolution, the legitimists would have accused him, despite his moderation, of committing crimes against his fellows.

The legitimists considered evil inherent in man, and this accounts for their unabiding pessimism. The worker's strike against his employer, the employer's neglect of his workers, the husband's infidelity toward his wife, the son's disrespect for the father—theft, war, and revolution, all were but particular manifestations of the greed, lust, and unbridled ambitions that had dwelt in the hearts of corrupt human beings since the Fall. They believed the high-minded ideals expressed in socialist, red republican, and liberal propaganda to be but a front for the baser motives of ambitious men or proof of the foolish misunderstanding of human nature by those of purer inspiration. Nothing good had come from man

141

without God in the past, and only worse could be expected in the future. Still, if the cause of misfortune could be easily identified, it was apparent to the legitimists that its actual presence in society could not be explained simply in Christian terms. Some people respected the social hierarchy; others rebelled. Some were good Christians, others were atheists or anticlericals. All men might be morally tainted, but some were less tainted than others. Moreover, the incidence of "good" and "bad" men was not distributed accidentally throughout society; it varied according to social situations. The legitimists, therefore, had more in common with Voltaireans or Marxists than one might think, for like them they were disgruntled environmentalists. They did not approach the subject in a systematic manner, but their criticism of society indicates that they felt a person's mental outlook was conditioned by the totality of complex social-psychological experiences which he encountered in the community. They did not believe that a change in environment would make men "good," but they did think it would lessen the influence of "evil."

In order to understand the deputies' social critique, it is necessary to review their conception of legitimate authority. The idea of legitimacy is open to various interpretations. Republicans too could be considered legitimists inasmuch as they held that all legitimate authority in the nation came from the people. The legitimists, of course, rejected such a contention. Deeply religious, these deputies believed that man was lost without the guidance of his Creator. This was true not only in a personal sense (without God man forfeited the possibility of eternal salvation) but also in a civic sense (God provided the ethical foundation for all social life). The deputies shared the firm conviction that any society which had to be maintained by force was no society at all because social groups were more than a collection of individuals related in some physical way; they were moral entities or they were nothing. It was religion that breathed life into these collectivities, and its absence that caused them to disintegrate into anarchy. "Do you believe," Louis-Numa Baragnon asked a Catholic audience in the late 1870s, "that the principal guardian of order in society is the *gendarme*? Ah! If we only had him we would be in bad straits. The real guardian of society is religious belief."[1]

[1] M. Baragnon, *Les écoles populaires et le droit des pères de famille, discours prononcé à la salle Rivoli le premier juillet 1879* (Paris, 1879), p. 11.

Very few people of religious conviction would have argued with this. What distinguished the legitimists is that they let traditional religious authority and not individual religious conscience decide the questions of whom and what the Christian must believe. Thus the specific historical content of their credo was quite clear. They fervently supported the Roman pontiff and were the arch enemies of Protestantism. "I do not see anywhere in Protestantism," Kolb-Bernard remarked "that which is the life of humanity. I mean authority."[2] Kolb-Bernard's remark distorts history since Protestanism obviously had its authoritarian character. The teachings of the Lutheran Church in Prussia are sufficient testimony to this fact. But the essential point for legitimists is that Protestantism was born out of revolt against the vicar of Christ, and any set of beliefs, whether religious or secular, which denied the supremacy of the Holy Father could not be forgiven. The legitimists, of course, extended this respect for traditional authority to the monarchy. They would in fact have agreed with Camus that the death of Louis XVI reflected the pervasive desire of modern man to kill God and deny the divine authority personified in this man.

The alliance between throne and altar was the pillar of the Old Regime, and for the legitimists, the assault on the two divinely instituted authorities that began at the end of the eighteenth century was the great crime of the Revolution. If, however, they wanted to restore the Church and the monarchy to the place that they had held in national life prior to 1789, they did not seek specifically to reestablish the Old Regime. This assertion is self-evident perhaps if its economic aspects, like the incredibly inefficient system of weights and measures or the complex internal tariffs that existed in the country, are remembered. No doubt some staunch reactionaries in 1789 would have opposed their abolition, but one searches in vain for any evidence that nineteenth-century legitimists sought their return. Indeed the ideas would have been idiotic, if for no other reason than personal economic interests. Many of the legitimist deputies, especially the winegrowers, were fervent free traders in the mid-nineteenth century, but even those who were protectionists were not interested in erecting any internal impediments to trade since they sold their own agricultural and manufactured products within a regional and sometimes national market.

[2] Mgr. Baunard, "Kolb-Bernard," *Reliques d'histoire, notices et portraits* (Paris, 1899), p. 246.

More importantly, legitimists professed no desire to restore the social structure of the Old Regime. Many aristocrats might have regretted the lost privileges of their ancestors, but they realized that they were gone forever. As the Marquis de Franclieu, one of the most reactionary legitimists in the Assembly, noted in 1874, "It is undoubtedly impossible to restore the Estates general as it once existed. Two of the elements of which it was composed, the nobility and the clergy, have been irrevocably assimilated into the Third."[3] If this was true of the nobles, it was doubly so of the bourgeois. They would have gained no advantage from such a turn of events; it would have reduced them to second-class citizens. Nor do these men ever suggest that serfdom or any legally defined form of servitude reappear. They accepted the equality before the law which had come out of the Revolution. No antiquarians with an overriding interest in the past, these men were passionately interested in preserving what was "best" or eliminating what was "worst" in the society in which they lived, a society that had been profoundly affected by the Revolution. The monarchy and the Church were important to them because of their relevance to the immediate social situation.

Legitimists, therefore, were reduced to defining this "best" and "worst" against the shadowy figures of nineteenth-century French society, and not surprisingly they found it difficult to establish precise social categories. About the only social group for which they had uniform praise was the family. In contradistinction to philosophical radicals they considered the family and not the individual to be the basic component of society. For them the individual's existence was not just lonely and unbearable unless he was well integrated into a developed family life but meaningless because the essence of a person's life came from membership in this blood-related group. By family, moreover, they meant what sociologists now call the hierarchically organized extended family—the nuclear family was, in their opinion, the first step on the road to the anarchy of individualism—in which each person's roll and function were sharply defined by sex and age.[4] This reverence for the family resulted no doubt from the experiences of a lifetime of informal and

[3] Marquis de Franclieu, *Rapport au roi sur le vote universel honnête-ment pratiqué* (Tarbes, 1874), p. 12.

[4] Contemporaries called the extended family *la famille souche*. The term and concept was made popular by Le Play in his studies.

144

formal conditioning acquired in families that were inordinately proud of their own achievements. The deputies went to great lengths to protect their family name. It was said of one, for example, that he paid the large debts of a relative who was threatened with financial collapse uniquely because the shame of a bankruptcy would besmirch the family honor.[5] Respect for God and family was the guiding principle that they taught their own children, for they took their responsibilities as family head seriously. They infused these deeply felt sentiments, moreover, into their general conception of society because they thought them valid for all men whatever their family's place in society.

When legitimists dealt with social groups larger than the family, their analysis became blurred. Members of the aristocracy valued the *société* in which they lived, but *société* was not everywhere the same. In the provinces it tended to be rather exclusively aristocratic and efforts to introduce men of *roturier* origins into its midst encountered resistance. This is what happened, for example, when the Marquise de Rességuier tried to bring a bourgeois friend into the aristocratic salons of Toulouse. She was snubbed and never returned.[6] But in Paris, where the old aristocracy and the *haute bourgeoisie* mixed freely, the praise of *société* did not have such a purely aristocratic ring. Parisian aristocrats, moreover, were socially quite distinct from the provincials because of their greater contact with the literary, business, and governmental elite of the nation. This accounts for that disdain, mentioned earlier, often expressed by aristocrats in the provinces toward the "artificiality" of the life led by aristocrats in the capital and the Parisians' contempt for the stultifying witless boredom of provincial *société*. Legitimists of middle-class origins also did not feel subservient to the descendants of the old aristocracy. Emile Keller, for example, considered them a singularly inept social group.[7] But if they disliked or were indifferent to the old aristocracy, they did not reject the idea of an aristocracy. Lucien-Brun for one considered the presence of an aristocracy essential for the preservation of a social

[5] Pontoi-Poincarré, deputy from Eure-et-Loir.

[6] "Rapport sur la situation des partis—1866," presented by the sub-prefect of Muret to the prefect of Haute-Garonne, A. D. (Haute-Garonne) 4 M 86 *Police générale*, p. 15.

[7] G. Gautherot, *Emile Keller (1828–1909). Un demi-siècle de défense nationale et religieuse* (Paris, 1922), p. 254.

145

order.[8] His aristocracy, however, could not be identified with the old aristocracy or in fact with any social group then existing in France because it was a new elite. He would not have objected to remnants of the old aristocracy finding their place in this new elite, but it would also have included the bourgeois. A certain tension existed between legitimists of bourgeois and aristocratic origins, but neither could have condemned the other without dividing the group badly. The deputies' origins and the great changes in the relationship between the old aristocracy and the bourgeoisie ushered into France since the Revolution precluded the possibility of defining an aristocratic elite in terms of the prerevolutionary social categories, and few of them ever really tried. This was true of aristocrats as well as bourgeois. Although the aristocrats lived in their *société*, nowhere in their writings do they suggest that the old nobility's privileges should be reinstated or that it should be granted new ones. It was much easier to imagine an hereditary aristocracy as something that did not actually exist but that would exist in the future.

A similar lack of consistency appeared in the legitimists' evaluation of the economic and professional basis of the elite. All the deputies recognized that a landlord class possessed virtues which made it especially gifted for leadership. Although he was not talking of the aristocracy but of any group of landlords, whether composed of bourgeois or aristocrats, General Ducrot felt that they made the best soldiers, and Lucien-Brun conceived of his new aristocracy as primarily a landlord class.[9] On the other hand, legitimists like the small businessmen Chesnelong, Kolb-Bernard, Malartre, and Journu, or the big industrialists like Benoist d'Azy, La Bouillerie, or Aubry, while not disparaging the landlords, would not have conceded that they or the groups to which they belonged were less responsible or less capable of holding positions of civic and political trust, nor would they have thought their activities less economically productive or socially useful. In short, they would not have demoted the merchant or industrialist to some inferior status vis-à-vis the landlord among the nation's elite. Of the professions, legitimists generally approved of the military and the magistracy. But they often complained about lawyers. "These miser-

---

[8] Lucien-Brun, *Introduction à l'étude du droit* (Paris, 1887), p. 117.

[9] A. N., C 2809, *I^e Sous-commission, réorganisation de l'armée* [*Recrutement*], Procès-verbaux, séance du 9 juin 1871.

able lawyers," Florentin Malartre wrote about the republicans in the National Assembly,

> are unable to say anything in the language of a common mortal and, *a propos* of everything or nothing, there they are, their mouths often empty and more or less sonorous, believing themselves obligated to hold up the solution of an article for three hours. . . . Instead of telling themselves that they are [in the Assembly] to conduct the nation's business naturally, simply, and honestly, they tell themselves that they are here above all to shine, to show off their wit, and to conquer a more or less sham notoriety and a popularity on the outside [of the Chamber] while burying the heart of the question in a flux of words.[10]

These were not the strictures of an aristocrat against the middle classes but of a pure bourgeois, and they were frequently echoed by bourgeois and aristocrat alike. Other legitimists would not have assailed the lawyers because of the attitude of some republicans. Indeed, the numerous legitimists who were themselves lawyers were hardly ashamed of a profession with which their families had often been associated for generations.

The disagreements that appear among legitimists when commenting about the social elite also emerge in their judgments about groups further down the social scale. Usually, they eulogized the peasantry. "It is in the fields," the historian Martial Delpit wrote, "it is among the agricultural population that the power of our country resides. There our impoverished blood enriches itself, there our solid armies are formed."[11] On the other hand, there were frequent complaints about artisans and industrial workers. Yet if these were customary attitudes, quite different ones can be found. Often legitimists were annoyed with the peasantry. For instance, in a statement about agricultural workers, Vogüé noted, "Relations with workers often become difficult. There is a certain spirit of adventure, and I would not say of independence—his attitude is good everywhere for everyone—but of resistance in the workers which gives birth to a state of things that is not hostile

[10] Ltr., Malartre to his wife, July 19, 1871, *Malartre MSS.*

[11] "Procès-verbaux des séances de la réunion libre des agriculteurs de l'Assemblée nationale," séance du 13 février, *Journal de l'agriculture*, II: 263 (Apr. 25, 1874), p. 150.

but more tense than before. . . ."[12] Le Lasseux, who was much less diplomatic, stated the complaint quite bluntly: The agricultural workers have "pretensions which border on insubordination."[13] Opinions about artisans and workers, moreover, were far from uniform. Benoist d'Azy and Vétillart, for example, never considered their factory workers basically bad. In fact, when Benoist d'Azy heard that his iron workers at Alais had voted against their foremen in a local election, he was shocked. Roger de Larcy "spoke to me yesterday of the votes of our workers," he wrote to his son in 1874, "who have not even voted for their foremen. . . . I avow that I will be very upset if this is true. . . . In the end it is nothing more than another example of the great sickness that is consuming France."[14]

Although dissension among legitimists about the basis of the social elite often reveals a resentment between aristocrats and bourgeois, and landlords and industrialists that existed in nineteenth-century French society, it would be wrong to make too much of these conflicts. When referring to the social elite, the deputies employed the term *notable* much more frequently than any other, and they did so with reason. Legitimists really did not think of society in terms of collectivities. To them a notable was a person who belonged to a family that was respected because of the position its members held in a community, and this position resulted from the direct personal paternalistic relations the family members had within the community. The notable, for example, was not a capitalist who had relations with labor—an impossible abstraction—but a particular factory owner who gave employment and occupied himself with the welfare of his workers. Traditionally the old nobility had performed this function in the village. Like any group in such a position they had resented attacks on their "legitimate" authority and the friction between aristocrats and bourgeois within the legitimist ranks proper was the residue of this resentment. But by the mid-nineteenth century the old battles had been fought. The aristocrats had lost their privileges. Many remained notables because of the wealth and prestige of their

[12] *Enquête agricole*, 3ᵉ série, p. 379.

[13] Ernest Le Lasseux, *Enquête parlementaire-questionnaire agriculture*, Comices agricoles du canton du Grez-en-Bouère (Château-Gontier, n. d.), p. 4.

[14] Ltr., Benoist d'Azy to his son Charles, Dec. 2, 1874, *Benoist d'Azy MSS.*

families but they had been joined by bourgeois who now counted themselves and their families among the notables of France. If the legitimist aristocrats, bourgeois, landlords, or manufacturers had accentuated their economic and social differences, they could not have been in the same political camp, but they did not do this. What they had come to recognize when they used the word *notable* was that the social grounds of the hereditary elite, which united them more as notables than divided them in another capacity, had really changed. What the legitimist landlord (whether of bourgeois or aristocratic extraction), industrialist, merchant, and professional wanted to preserve or even restore was the community in which the position of his family, and the *société* to which it belonged, was respectfully acknowledged.

Comments about social groups other than the notables were prompted by this quest for community. La Bassétière, in written testimony before the agricultural investigating committee, outlined the moral order that reigned among the peasantry in Vendée.

Enter our religious and moral countryside, visit some honest laborer, sit down before his hearth where, under the venerated authority of the family head there still reigns that union which God blesses, and those modest desires which He loves to satisfy; where a share made for everyone, a share set aside for the future, there still remains a share for the poor who never knock in vain at this hospitable door. Here is one of the mildest, most enviable, in a word, the happiest existences that one could ever find.[15]

When the legitimists praised the peasantry it was because they possessed, as Ventavon phrased it, "love for family and all conservative instincts."[16] Indeed, these men developed a veritable "myth of the garden" according to which the soil and air of the countryside had a moralizing effect on those who came into contact with them. On the other hand, they condemned other social groups because they lacked these qualities. The agricultural day laborers

[15] *Enquête agricole*, 2e série, 7e circonscription, Dépositions orales reçues par la commission supérieure (Paris, 1869), p. 153.

[16] M. de Ventavon, *Rapport sommaire fait au nom de la 7e commission d'initiative sur la proposition de MM. Paul Morin, le Comte Abbadie de Barrau et plusieurs de leurs collègues, pour étendre les associations syndicales et autoriser les départements à garantir ces associations en vue des besoins de l'agriculture*, Annexe aux Procès-verbaux de l'Assemblée nationale, Session—1871, No. 659.

whom they despised belonged to the most depressed segment of the rural population. Shifting about the countryside in search of a livelihood, these laborers at least had the independence of their poverty and they displayed it in that instinctive distrust of authority that is common among the most degraded members of a society. The lawyer, of course, could not be compared socially with the agricultural day laborer, but he was not appreciated by legitimists because he was the most vocal, politically capable, and effective propagandist of the middle-class democrats who were challenging the supremacy of the notables. "To an outstanding degree politics today," Max Weber noted, "is conducted in public by means of the spoken word. To weigh the effects of the word properly falls within the range of the lawyer's task."[17] This was true only where public opinion was the stepping stone to prominence, that is, in a democracy; in the legitimists' conception of society a man's prominence depended on tradition. They both feared and detested the lawyer when he catered to the populace because this violated their conception of the social hierarchy. As for the industrial workers about whom they complained, they too lacked the respect for the notables—specifically in this case their employers—which the legitimists automatically expected of them. All three groups, therefore, had this much in common: they did not fit into the legitimists' idea of a society in which everyone kept his place.

Still the conflicting opinions which legitimists uttered indicate that the mentality of peasants, industrial workers, lawyers, and members of other groups as well was hardly uniform. Legitimists, in fact, when praising or condemning a group, usually described characteristics in connection with it that were not its essential attributes. Compared to the Vendéen peasant, La Bassétière observed,

the industrial worker, the city worker, ordinarily earns a higher salary; if you see him during a holiday he will appear better dressed, perhaps more fortunate. But do not believe any of this. Visit the garret which serves him for lodgings, where light and air, which the country worker enjoys at his pleasure, have been sparingly parceled out; see how he is isolated, lost in the middle of this immense multitude, how he does not know to whom to

[17] H. H. Gerth and C. Wright Mills, eds., *From Max Weber* (New York, 1958), p. 95.

150

turn if in need of advice. . . . You will understand that frequently poverty, wretchedness, and always a painful inability to count on tomorrow are hidden beneath these brilliant appearances.[18]

It was the family housed in urban tenements that lost its cohesiveness, the isolated individual, uprooted from his place in society, and as a result, ridden with anxiety and feelings of insecurity who listened to the siren of revolution. It was not the industrial workers per se but the industrial worker in the city, in fact the city environment proper they hated. The city was characterized by flux and change, by great wealth ostentatiously displayed by the *nouveau riche*, and by great poverty that was all the more conspicuous because of its concentration in densely populated squalid quarters. These deputies denounced all classes of urbanites. They disliked their materialism, their promiscuity, their waste of material resources, and their callous disregard for the suffering of others. Above all, they detested, as the Lille manufacturer Kolb-Bernard wrote, "the furor for pleasures, for luxury, and for business that reigned in Paris."[19] Paris possessed all the attributes of the city writ large and in proportion as it towered over other cities in France it received the greater censure. Even Baron Haussmann's renovations aroused their disgust, a disgust centered particularly on the new Opera, "monument to decadence," Gabriel de Belcastel exclaimed, "of which the frontispiece was only a short time ago an outrage to public decency."[20] No human trust, they alleged, could be developed in such unstable and depersonalized surroundings, only soulless isolation and loneliness could exist. When in the city they felt themselves "lost in the immense multitude," and they realized that the kind of social relations they desired could not exist in such a place.

After praising his peasants for being "very respectful and very susceptible to authority, regardless of its origins," the Vicomte de Falloux immediately outlined the environment in which this mentality of submission took place. In Anjou, he stated, "each exploitation encloses a dwelling place and everything necessary for a family. The tenant remains on the same land . . . and everything takes place there between the family head and his children

[18] *Enquête agricole*, 2e série, 7e circonscription, p. 151.

[19] Ltr., Kolb-Bernard to Chesnelong, Oct. 23, 1871, *Chesnelong MSS.*

[20] Gabriel de Belcastel, *A mes électeurs. Cinq ans de vie politiques, votes principaux propositions, lettres et discours* (Toulouse, 1876), p. 111.

[and] landlord and tenant live from one generation to the next in close association with each other (*en face les uns des autres*).[21] Although they believed in a general way that agriculture had a moralizing effect on the peasantry—"this immense mass for whom order is a prime necessity," as Eugène de Montlaur put it—they actually recognized that this peasant mentality depended on a social situation.[22] This social situation, first of all, had a property base. Property, the Comte de Melun pointed out,

> stops the nomadic life which renders men heedless of the future, forgetful of the traditions of their home town, disrespectful of the opinions of those who have always known them. . . . Property makes he who possesses it more tidy, more industrious; it removes him from fatal distractions, keeps him near his hearth, in the bosom of his family, and usefully occupies his leisure time; it augments the authority of the parents who have the right to pride themselves on the results they have obtained and thus to set the example for those who profit from their spirit of order and economy.[23]

Legitimists believed most certainly that the peasant *propriétaire* offered, in Meaux's words, "a guarantee of stability, for all society,"[24] but they were not advocates of a general distribution of property in equal shares among all French rural families. "I prefer," the Marquis de Vogüé once explained in a typical view, "the property arrangement that makes of an [agricultural day] worker a sharecropper, later on a tenant farmer, and perhaps one day a *propriétaire*."[25] Since the social hierarchy required a class of large landlords with properties needing to be farmed, this progression of dependent peasant family farms seemed the natural complement of the social order because it permitted the peasant family to work the land as a unit while at the same time remaining economically dependent on the landlord. The results from the legitimists' perspective were highly satisfactory. "My relations with the rural populations," Vogüé remarked, "are among the more gratifying

---

[21] *Enquête agricole*, 3e série, pp. 532–533.

[22] Eugène de Montlaur, *L'ordre social* (Moulins, 1849), p. 73.

[23] Comte de Melun, *Rapport fait au nom de la commission chargée d'étudier la situation des classes ouvrières en France, situation matérielle et économique des ouvriers* (Paris, 1875), pp. 9–10.

[24] Vicomte de Meaux, *Les conclusions de l'Enquête agricole* (Paris, 1869), p. 9.

[25] *Enquête agricole*, 3e série, p. 373.

aspects of my agricultural life. I have personally only to congratulate myself because of their excellence and if I speak only of my experience I would say that they get better everyday. . . . I find, as far as I am concerned, that these relations, above all in the rapport I develop with my sharecroppers, are excellent."[26] Second, the social situation of which Falloux spoke had a religious character. Falloux realized that the peasant's respect for the landlord in Anjou depended on religious belief, but this belief in its social manifestation stemmed from the manner in which religious practice hinged on property relations. Legitimist landlords conscientiously filled their charitable responsibilities toward their sharecroppers and tenant farmers because they believed that the "law of a Christian social order was charity at work in a respected hierarchy."[27] When the legitimist landlord married or had children, he encouraged his peasants to participate in a *fête* in honor of the event; or when there was a baptism, a confirmation, or a marriage in the families of his peasants, he recognized these events with favors or gifts; and the priest who was always present on such occasions sanctified the social relation upon giving his blessing. Legitimists were generally conscious of religion's social role. They welcomed, for example, the village festivals that blended religious practice with the major economic events of the agricultural season (i.e., the harvest) and often participated in them because they sensed their importance in preserving respect for the traditional social order. It was because he saw how religion had been incorporated into the life of the village that Gavardie could claim, "It is the rural commune traced upon the parish and acting with it like the union of body and soul that formed and still forms today all political order in France."[28] Religion supported the village social order but was itself strengthened by that order.

Thus the legitimists interpreted the mentality of the social group in respect to the environment in which it was enmeshed, and this helps explain how their comments about workers or peasants could vary so much. Benoist d'Azy built company housing, a church, and a parochial school for his workers at Alais. He helped select the parish priest and approved of the member of the *Frères des écoles chrétiennes* who taught in the company school. The

[26] *Ibid.*, p. 379.

[27] Lucien-Brun, *Introduction à l'étude du droit*, p. 292.

[28] E. Gavardie, *Etude sur les vraies doctrines sociales et politiques* (Pau, 1862), p. 349.

company management—frequently Benoist d'Azy himself or his son—the priests, and the factory population joined in local holidays as, for example, in the annual *fête* celebrated in honor of the local workers' patron saint. When the legitimists praised the worker, they saw him incorporated into this kind of socioeconomic structure, and it was precisely this workers' community that they found wanting in the city. With the city worker living in rented quarters, often no larger than a hotel room, and dispersed among the population, with the extended family giving way to the nuclear family or no family at all, with the clergy unable to know even the physical whereabouts of his flock, the interaction between family, religion, and property that the legitimists saw buttress the social hierarchy in the industrial as well as the agricultural village could not take place. The same criteria, moreover, apply to their criticism of the peasantry. The groups they singled out were those that had escaped environmental influences which Falloux described. This was true of the agricultural day workers and the peasant *propriétaires* who were not only economically independent of the large landlords but also, when plentiful enough, supplanted them entirely.

The core of the legitimist social criticism was not specifically the occupational or economic function of particular groups but their relation to the community. In this community men lived in time-honored associations in which separate institutions existed for each function in life. There was nothing wrong with the industrial worker, the peasant, the artisan, or the lawyer, only something wrong with workers, peasants, artisans, and lawyers who were not integrated into a family that belonged to a corporation proper to their function in life, which formed part of a larger community. And this latter point is of supreme importance, for it was not just the uprooted individual with whom the legitimists were at odds but any association of men that did not form part of a community in which the local "social authorities" (the large landlord in the village, the industrialist in the factory, the oligarch in the municipality), joined by bishops and the local clergy, oversaw the great events of personal life, sponsored the social activity, and formulated the public conscience in the interests of a social harmony that to legitimists was the essence of community itself. Clearly their insistence on social harmony reflected their own class consciousness, for in denying the possibility of class consciousness to others they refused to admit that groups could have legitimate interests that were fundamentally opposed to each other and to their own. The desire for this community was the legitimists' chief concern, and concomitantly the dynamics of its subversion was their principal preoccupation.

From what has been said so far obviously both the physical growth of the city and the penetration of city influences into the countryside disturbed legitimists. In fact, they saw these two as part of a whole. One reason frequently cited for the rural exodus was the discrepancy between the economic prosperity of city and countryside. "Faced with a remuneration more than double than that which they have formerly been able to obtain," the Marquis de Franclieu stated, "and enticed by still greater promises, all those who are able have hurried to profit from these circumstances in order to leave a hard and ungrateful metier, in which he who possesses only his hands is assured of never being able to improve his position, [to flee to the city]."[29] Statements like this show the legitimists' concern for poverty and the urgent social reasons for which they felt it must be alleviated, but they never would have considered material want a sufficient cause for the depopulation of the countryside. In their eyes, the modesty of one's material desire distinguished the "moral" from the "immoral" man. "It was," as La Bassétière put it, "the exaggerated desire for well-being that is felt in the most remote regions of the countryside . . . that prompts the population to abandon agriculture."[30] The rural exodus was only symptomatic of the breakdown of the community in the countryside itself. The legitimists' fixation on the dynamics of subversion, therefore, forced them to examine the process by which the socioeconomic and religious foundation of community was being undermined. This meant that they were interested in the causes of economic backwardness in the countryside and the alteration in proper property relations, in the people and institutions which, either directly or indirectly, challenged the position of the "social authorities," in the methods they used to seduce the public, and in the reasons why the public was susceptible to this seduction.

Certainly the oldest major menace to the social order, and the

[29] *Enquête agricole*, 2e série, 17e circonscription, p. 352.

[30] *Ibid.*, 7e circonscription, p. 151. For a good example of their concern with rural poverty see R. de La Pervanchère, *L'agriculture en Bretagne* (Nantes, 1867).

subject of constant complaint on their part, was the modern bureaucratic state.[31] Legitimists numbered in a long line of antistatists,
stretching from the old feudal nobility through the *frondeur* of the
seventeenth century to the notables of 1787 and beyond. They
were the spiritual descendants of Montesquieu and the admirers of
Tocqueville, for even though royalists, they did not hesitate to
criticize the absolutist kings, the great state builders, of the Old
Regime. Louis XIV was not their favorite monarch. The state acquired power by force, but statists developed a theory of sovereignty legally and morally to justify this use of force. Briefly, the
statists claim that the collective needs of a community require the
erection of a single authority to which the entire country, in the
interest of the general welfare and the continuity of the community
itself, owe allegiance. The chief executive, the supreme administrative and police power, delegates his sovereignty to a host of subordinates who are his instruments. They are appointed and dismissed
at his pleasure and exercise whatever powers he chooses to delegate. Neither individual nor group rights take precedence over that
of the state; in fact, if the state decided that the existence of an individual or group was not in the general interest, they could be
suppressed. It is easy to see why the legitimists opposed such a
theory. The state's claim to a life of its own violated their conception of a society in which the father held his position in the family,
the priest's in the parish, and the notable's in the community by
prescriptive right. For legitimists it was an important part of their
function as social authorities to head councils and dispense justice;
in fact it was essential to the preservation of social order. When
the state placed agents into the community, it dissolved the social
hierarchy because the people transferred their allegiance from the
notable to the state official. Even if the state appointed the richest
notables from the most important families as prefects, mayors, or
judges, legitimists objected, since their tenure in office depended
on the good will of some bureaucrat sitting in Paris rather than on
the social position of the appointee per se. The state could not guarantee social harmony since it was itself a disruptive force in society.

---

[31] Legitimists' attacks against the state appear repeatedly in their
speeches and writings. See the bibliography for works specifically on the
subject, and in particular the minutes of the parliamentary committee on
decentralization in whose deliberations legitimists played a great part. A. N.,
Assemblée nationale—1871, C 2866, *Procès-verbaux de la commission de
décentralisation, 1871–74.*

Still if the legitimists found the state obnoxious in principle, they did not necessarily oppose it in fact. When in power neither the Restoration monarchs nor their supporters seemed in any hurry to dismantle the formidable bureaucratic instrument fashioned by Napoleon. Louis XVIII and Charles X had not hesitated to use the prefects for partisan political purposes, to pack the judiciary with their men, and to put clerical royalists into positions of authority in state institutions.[32] Their actions had been dictated less by hypocrisy than by a realistic effort to seek a modus vivendi with the state, according to which it supported the position of the notables in the community in return for their support of the state. This is what the Junkers worked out in Prussia with their king, and it explains their remarkable longevity as leaders in the local community as well as in the state itself. Except for the Restoration period, no such "holy alliance" had, in legitimist opinion, existed in France, not only because the legitimists had lost the state through the action of a usurper but also because constitutionally the notables did not control the state on any level. The Napoleonic state controlled them.

Obviously this applied to the prefect and his council. Prefects were government officials appointed by the minister of interior who were transferred frequently from department to department precisely because the government wanted them to retain their independence from the local notables. Prefects usually did everything possible to win the support of the notables, but it was winning the notables over to the regime, not supporting the local hierarchy, that was the operative principle, and since legitimists found every regime after 1830 distasteful, if not detestable, the prefects were their natural enemies. Moreover, there was no way the notables could effectively oppose the prefect's will had they so chosen. Although the government in Paris selected mayors and their adjuncts in the larger communes, the prefect appointed them elsewhere. He also selected the communal school teacher; appointed the *commissaires de police*; the *gardes champêtres* (rural police); commanded the cantonal *commissaires de police*; selected (on the minister of

[32] In respect to one such state institution, for example, Bertier de Sauvigny points out that during the Restoration when "the clergy found itself able to infiltrate and dominate the institution of the *Université*, one ceased to ask for its suppression and henceforth thought only of comfortably installing oneself in the conquered fortress." *La restauration* (Paris, 1955), p. 431.

interior's approval) the *officiers*, who presided over the municipal and general councils, which were intended to represent local notables but were completely at the prefect's mercy since he chose their officers, prepared the departmental budget, kept the tax rolls, issued public works contracts, "tutored" municipal government (he had veto power over decisions taken in the municipality), administered state forests and lands, and, through the surveillance of the press and public assembly, mastered local politics.[33]

To these political, police, and administrative powers can be added the broad judicial functions exercised by the prefects' councils. Throughout its long history, the state had developed a system of "preventative" justice that, distinct from the "repressive" justice dispensed by the regular courts, governed the relations between the administrative authority and the citizenry.[34] The state theorists justified the administrative law on the grounds that private citizens could not be allowed to bring suit against administrative officials in the regular courts without undermining the legitimate authority of the state. Since the notables who felt aggrieved by the state's action only had recourse to the administrative courts and the state expanded its jurisdiction continually, increasingly more of them had to deal with administrative courts. The court of first instance was the prefect's council that, presided over by the prefect, rendered judgments on all complaints arising from tax assessments, tax payments, the condemnation of unsanitary or unsafe private property, the confiscation (with compensation set by the state official) of private property by right of eminent domain, and a host of other economic or fiscal complaints raised by notables against the state. In addition, the prefectural councils could protect the police from any suits arising from charges of police malpractice simply by refusing to let the case be tried before the regular courts. The plaintiff could appeal the prefectural council's decision to the Council of State, the supreme administrative court sitting in Paris, but the Council of State was itself appointed by the executive. Thus the state's administrative courts judged cases in which the state was an interested party.

The notables' inability to control the selection or action of the prefect and his council was typical of each branch of state adminis-

[33] For a good discussion of the prefect's power see Brian Chapman, *L'administration locale en France* (Paris, 1962).

[34] See Howard C. Payne, *The Police State of Louis Napoléon Bonaparte, 1851–1860* (Seattle, 1966), pp. 3–34 and passim.

tration. The regular judiciary, where the offices had been hereditary and the *parlements* had offered sustained opposition to the encroachment of the state into local affairs, had been, if not a perfect system to legitimists, at least one in which the notables possessed their offices by right instead of by government fiat. But the notables lost the hereditary right to these offices after 1789. Indeed, in the reform of 1810, which remained in vigor after Napoleon's fall, the emperor gave the executive the power to appoint and promote magistrates. Even the educational requirement for entry into the magistracy was insufficient to place much of a check on the emperor's choices, for, if the candidate had the *licence en droit*, a diploma that was relatively easy to acquire, he qualified for appointment. Once on the bench, moreover, the only guideline the government had to follow in making promotions was age, and again, this was not much of a hindrance inasmuch as a *substitut* could be advanced to *juge* at age twenty-five, to *président* or *conseillier* at twenty-seven, and to *président* of a court at age thirty.[35] But the point for legitimists was not so much the actual qualifications that the state set up for appointment and promotion as the fact that the state assumed this jurisdiction, for it thereby deprived the notable of his "natural" right to these offices. Legitimists felt most keenly about the justice of the peace (whom they viewed as a sort of father figure in the community), whose office should automatically go to a member of the most prominent family rather than be tossed around by the state like a political football.

The same logic applied to their evaluation of the state system of education. Before the Revolution education had fallen primarily under the jurisdiction of the Church, but after 1789 the Church's monopoly had been destroyed and under Napoleon a centralized state system, the *Université*, was created.[36] The *Université* was a hierarchically organized public corporation that directed every aspect (teacher recruitment and training, pedagogic methods, curricula, examinations, granting of diplomas [*collation des grades*], finance, and administration) of primary, secondary, and higher education. The chief of state appointed the head of the *Université*, the *Grand Maître*, who in turn, filled the various administrative and pedagogic positions in this vast organization. Of course, there were

[35] For a discussion of the Napoleonic reform see relevant sections of Jacques Godechot, *Les institutions de la France sous la Révolution et l'Empire* (Paris, 1951).

[36] *Ibid.*

requirements that a candidate had to fulfill in order to qualify for appointment, but these were set by the *Université* itself, i.e., the candidate had to have the diploma or degree from the appropriate faculty or normal school in order to be eligible. The institution Napoleon created, therefore, was self-perpetuating, with immense influence because its diplomas and degrees were required by law for almost any professional or administrative career. Whoever controlled the state system, moreover, had a powerful instrument in his hands with which to shape public opinion. In neighboring Prussia there was also a state educational system but one that legitimists, from a social, if not religious, point of view, admired, especially in the countryside, because the landlords chose the pastors and the two together selected and supervised the school teachers. The Napoleonic system prevented the local notables and the clergy from exercising either prerogative.

Another state institution about which legitimists complained was the army. They were not antimilitarists. On the contrary, they considered military discipline beneficial for the people since it instilled in them the idea of obedience to authority, but they felt that the military system extant in France throughout most of the nineteenth century escaped the notables' control. Again it is instructive to compare briefly the Prussian system, which so many of the legitimist deputies eulogized, to the French system, which so many disliked. In Prussia the army was divided into an active and a reserve force. The reserve trained annually with the active force in the regions where the reserve soldiers and officers lived and, when war broke out, could be rapidly incorporated into the regular army units with which they had served. The regular army officers were drawn from the aristocracy and the "feudalized" bourgeois who had accepted the social and political values and traditions of the nobility. Since the regular officers elected their units' reserve officers, the reserve officers were also drawn from the same group of notables from whom the regulars came; since these reserve officers were also the community's "social authorities" in civilian life, this meant that the recruitment and training of the civilian population was under the command of the community's notables. The French army was also divided into an active army and a reserve, but they did not train together. The active French army was a professional service that took its recruits from the community to a military post usually near some provincial city where they underwent training and subsequent service. The army officers were either promoted from the ranks or taken from the military schools (*St-Cyr, Ecole Polytechnique*) where success was attained through competitive examinations. Soldiers and officers, therefore, were strangers to the areas in which they were stationed, and this alienation from the local population was reinforced by the practice of shifting the regiments of the French army periodically from one post to another. Training in the French reserve was never very seriously pursued because the regulars took little interest in a reserve that was considered militarily valueless. The legitimists considered the French army organization reprehensible in that it institutionally divorced military service from the community and weakened the position of the notables.

Thus the legitimists found the state bureaucracy in its various institutional manifestations to be an alien force in the social order. It produced a loss of social purpose among the notables and many, frustrated by the absence of a meaningful function in the locality, emigrated to the city where they could occupy themselves more enjoyably. "One reproaches the *propriétaire* for his absenteeism," the Vicomte d'Aboville sadly commented, but this results "above all from the decline in influence that an intelligent man can exert around him (*autour de lui*) [in the village]."[37] However, consequences were much greater to the legitimists than this. The state, legitimists stressed, had a "demoralizing" effect on the entire population which caused it to abandon its traditional beliefs and occupations. This was so first of all because the people transferred their loyalties from the old social authorities to the state officials who had become the real authorities in France. Moreover, by multiplying petty bureaucratic jobs in the village, the state turned the peasants into an ambitious group of office seekers. Peasants, tired of manual labor and enamored with the prestige and authority of officialdom, readily left the fields to become postmen, *gardes champêtres*, or, if they were literate, minor clerks in the administration, and some even left the village to find similar employment in the cities. Legitimists contended that the Napoleonic state, by its size and voraciousness, was an urban institution. It was the city that housed most of the state's army of civil servants in huge buildings erected at immense public expense, and that built the greatest and most expensive monuments to the state's glory. Because of this people left the countryside to serve their new masters in the chief adminis-

---

[37] *Enquête agricole*, 3e série, p. 245.

trative centers of the nation. Legitimists did not see the damage coming uniquely from the movement to the city. It was the reciprocal movement between city and countryside that caused so much harm. In this respect, they singled out two institutions, the army and the *Université*, for special criticism.

The sociologist Daniel Faucher has noted the traumatic psychological effect that exposure to the outside world had on peasants drafted into the French army. "Events like [World War I]," he explained,

> have been factors of unheard of transformation [in peasant mentality]; peasants in the *Midi* believed, for example, that all the houses of France were the same as those they lived in; when they discovered the houses of the Paris basin, of the Somme, of the East of France, they were astonished in the strongest sense of the word and even upset by this astonishment; their deepest mentality, their intellectual dispositions completely changed.[38]

Legitimists were not sufficiently knowledgeable, living in a pre-Freudian world, to engage in an analysis of the traumatic psychological effects of such a phenomenon, but they had observed that the peasant taken to the city was lost to them forever. "After seven years (the length of military service before 1872) spent in the city," Monjaret de Kerjégu concluded, "in the center of pleasures of every sort [the recruit] refuses to come back to the countryside or comes back reluctantly."[39] If he returned he refused to work in the fields. ". . . [B]arracks' life," Le Lasseux observed, "sickens one of rural life."[40] Most legitimists also extended this complaint to reserve army training. "The reserve," the Marquis de Meaux wrote, "weighs on agriculture. It takes the cultivator from the fields a certain length of time, makes him lose his taste for [work], increases habits of instability, and prevents marriages."[41] These men, then, were saying that the barracks-billeted army (*armée de caserne*) encouraged the rural exodus. And this result had serious implications for the future of the army itself as well as the social order, for an army was only as good as the raw materials of which it was composed. As General Ducrot stated, "the urban worker" is "an

---

[38] Georges Friedmann, ed., *Villes-et-campagnes*, p. 393.

[39] *Enquête agricole*, 2e série, 3e circonscription, p. 357.

[40] Ernest Le Lasseux, *Enquête parlementaire*, p. 4.

[41] *Enquête agricole*, 2e série, 27e circonscription, p. 397.

element of indiscipline and disorder in the army."[42] Since army training accelerated the urbanizing process, it quickened the "demoralization" of the army, for once the city worker predominated in the service, both it and the nation itself would be lost to the urban revolutionaries.

Legitimists believed that the *lycées, collèges,* university faculties, and *grandes écoles,* since they were located in the cities, produced the same effect on the middle class and upper class, but the effect that the state normal school had on the peasantry upset them even more. "For the most part," Martial Delpit observed,

> the people who come to these establishments belong to peasant families whose resources are mediocre. They spend three years [in school] and receive a much broader instruction than they will have the mission to teach . . . and after this preparation they go back and establish themselves in a village where they have every chance of finding themselves misplaced (*déclassés*) and unhappy. They fulfill, against their will, their ten-year engagement contracted with the state and then leave their position in order to augment the number of misplaced, dissatisfied, and ambitious people.[43]

Thus the *Université* uprooted the teacher recruit from the peasantry, brought him to a normal school where he learned to scorn the ignorant population from whence he came, and then sent him back to the village where he infected the youth with his own disgust for agricultural life, the Church, and the traditional social order. Is it any wonder, the Vicomte d'Aboville remarked, that peasants "coming from primary schools," sought to leave the fields and emigrate to the cities?[44]

Since institutions are not only made but also staffed by men and men adopt policies, the legitimists also criticized the social consequences of the policies assumed by the leaders and implemented by their bureaucratic minions. This distinction between institutions and men, moreover, is not a fiction. During the July Monarchy, the French magistracy was subject to the same in-

[42] A. N., C 2809, Assemblée nationale—1871, *Réorganisation de l'armée,* Procès-verbaux, 1e Sous-commission, séance du 29 juin 1871, p. 18.

[43] A. N., C 3129, *Instruction publique,* Procès-verbaux de la commission de l'instruction primaire, séance du 21 fév. 1872.

[44] *Enquête agricole,* 3e série, p. 247.

stitutional dominance that it had been under every post-Napoleonic regime, but it gained a reputation for probity that stood in marked contrast to that of the magistracy under the Empire and the Restoration.[45] This could have occurred only because the executive chose to respect the independence of the magistracy, for it could have exerted great political pressure on judges. During the Second Empire, on the other hand, legitimists had been annoyed precisely by the government's practice of appointing and promoting magistrates friendly to the regime and of using them, especially the justices of the peace, in clearly partisan political activity. Indeed, the regime's obsessive preoccupation with the manipulation of the electorate irritated the notables because all too frequently, from their standpoint, the prefects, subprefects, and mayors consciously promoted the influence of the more "unsavory" elements in the community in order to manage local and national elections. Specifically, legitimists accused the administration of working with cabaret owners in elections, thereby enhancing their position. "A person cannot doubt the cabaret owner's influence," the Vicomte de Falloux protested before an agricultural investigating committee,

> when he lives in the countryside and when he sees that the cabaret owners are treated as sort of authority in the area. People come to their place, certain newspapers are read, certain influences are exercised, certain umbrages upheld. Does a person have such and such a grudge, or such and such an administrative personality to serve? It is in the cabaret that this action begins to take effect, that it is nurtured and that it develops in relation to the electoral crisis which is renewed every six years.[46]

Falloux thought that the state used its power to help cabaret owners replace the notables as fonts of authority. Even though he saw this happening during the Empire, legitimists perceived the same combination of middle-class elements in the village working through the bureaucracy to undermine the notables under the Republic. "These rascals," Charles de Lacombe wrote of the middle-class republicans who were active in his department (Puy-de-Dôme) "by virtue of the fact that they proclaim themselves Republicans and we are in a Republic believe that they are officialdom (*le*

[45] See Marcel Rousselet, *La magistrature sous la Monarchie de Juillet* (Paris, 1937).

[46] *Enquête agricole*, 3e série, p. 539.

164

monde officiel)! Not only do they believe it but they are known as such. . . ."[47]

But the range of the state's interference cannot be limited to the political manipulation of men and groups. In fact, most of the legitimist criticism about policies concerned the ill effects of particular programs. They asserted, for instance, that successive regimes, whether autocratic or ostensibly democratic, had consistently followed fiscal and financial policies that had exploited the countryside in favor of the city. The state taxed the land oppressively, while leaving liquid securities almost tax free; it exacted heavy fees from landlords for registering property titles while letting owners of stocks and bonds escape similar impositions.[48] These complaints were voiced by legitimists who were themselves owners of liquid securities not in the interest of raising more money through taxes on liquid securities (although, if necessary, they were willing to pay taxes on liquid securities providing land taxes were cut) but to reduce taxes on real estate, especially since so much of the money went to what legitimists considered "sterile" expenditures on the bureaucracy. Protests about expenditures were in fact usually coupled with those about taxes, for legitimists believed that the state compounded its injustice by spending the revenues taken from the countryside on urban public works and charities. Again the imperial regime was the greatest offender in their eyes. Legitimists bitterly resented the huge public works programs carried out during the Second Empire and were among the more caustic critics of the *comptes fantastiques* of Baron Haussmann. The legitimists maintained that fiscal policy contributed to the impoverishment of the countryside and to that rural exodus which was fraught with such evil promise.

Indirectly, legitimists blamed these tax and fiscal policies for abetting the investment in liquid securities which drained capital needed for agricultural and industrial development from rural areas, while concurrently destroying the material foundation of the moral

[47] Charles de Lacombe, *Journal politique*, p. 69.

[48] For comments about the tax inequity see the testimony of Benoist d'Azy (*Enquête agricole*, 3e série, p. 512) and Comte de Gouvello (*Enquête agricole*, 2e série, 8e circonscription, p. 301) before the agricultural committees: Ltr., Malartre to his wife, June 30, 1872, *Malartre MSS*; and the "Procès-verbaux des séances de la Réunion libre des agriculteurs de l'Assemblée nationale," especially for the year 1871–1872 which were published in the *Journal de l'agriculture*.

165

order. In Chapter Three, the legitimist tendency to oppose liquid securities was explained as an example of a backward economic attitude. But their repugnance toward liquid securities stemmed from social rather than economic considerations. Even if financially advantageous, legitimists generally considered liquid securities to be socially harmful. Most of these men identified the family with property. For aristocrats like Crussol d'Uzès, the family name itself had come from a medieval manor, but even when this was not the case, their families had a deep emotional attachment to a particular property that symbolized in their minds family continuity. It applied to men like Chesnelong, Malartre, and Kolb-Bernard whose factories or businesses were treasured as both a source of income and a patrimony to be guarded in the interests of the preservation of the family itself.[49] Legitimists argued quite simply that liquid securities could never evoke the memories of childhood, provide the place for family reunions, show the material results of generations of collective family effort, or even, because of their risk, guarantee the long-range financial security that was imperative for a family's survival. Legitimists thought, moreover, that liquid securities depersonalized social as well as family relations. *Rentes d'état* only brought the holder into contact with an abstraction, the state. Industrial stocks or bonds usually did not allow their owners to participate in the operation of factories or mines, and many never saw the enterprise in which they owned stock. Consequently, legitimists felt that the stockholder neither acquired the sense of paternal responsibility toward the workers nor the workers the respect for the social authorities which was possible in a family-owned and operated firm or farm. Some legitimists thought a company's directors could develop this paternalism, but most really considered the joint-stock corporation and particularly the *société anonyme* to be a threat to the social order. Oddly enough, few deputies commented about the law of 1867 that liberalized the rules governing the foundation of limited liability joint-stock corporations. But it is difficult to imagine their general approbation of the measure. In any case, they did complain and frequently about the fiscal and tax policies that, in their view, encouraged investment in liquid securities.

[49] This attitude is rather typical of French Catholic bourgeois family mentality. See Charles P. Kindleberger, "The Post War Resurgence of the French Economy," and Jesse R. Pitts "Continuity and Change in Bourgeois France," in Stanley Hoffmann et al., *In Search of France* (New York, 1965), pp. 118–158, 235–304.

An even older and perhaps more common complaint, however, was about the situation produced by the inheritance law passed on March 7, 1793, and subsequently incorporated into the *Code civil*. This law, which was supposed to break up large property by requiring every offspring to receive an equal share of an inheritance, the legitimists agreed, had succeeded only too well. Again, they were concerned with the economic results of this change because, convinced that the large landlord provided the capital and know-how for agricultural improvement and the funds for charity, they believed that the law had caused the disappearance of the large landlord through dividing inheritances into smaller and smaller plots, and had contributed to economic distress in rural areas and to the depopulation of the countryside. "[I]n three-quarters of France," Comte Raudot claimed, "agriculture, delivered up to ignorance, to routine, to want, even to misery, practiced laboriously on small difficult-to-work plots, moves at a snail's pace and the masses suffer."[50] Even more shattering, legitimists felt, was the law's social results. By depriving the family head of the right to dispose of the patrimony, it weakened his authority in the home, fostered a spirit of disrespect in his children, and destroyed the property base on which the survival of the extended family depended. Since it was axiomatic among legitimists that no society could exist in the countryside without the presence of a class of large landlords to whom the peasantry were tied in an economic as well as a moral and social sense the inheritance law eliminated the basis of the rural social order.

Finally, the legitimists' criticism of the content of state education should be mentioned. In an address to a group of landlords in 1867, Baron Chaurand recalled:

> One must not forget that the principal end of primary education is first to form the heart and mind of those for whom it is destined. Our devotion to agriculture should not make us lose sight of this essential point. It is incumbent upon us to watch over the tendency of our character to exaggerate everything. In order to repair the grievous neglect from which agriculture suffers, we must not want to make farmers before we make men and Christians. Religious and moral instruction must always provide the principal and most numerous subjects for dictation and reading in primary education.[51]

[50] M. Raudot, *De l'agriculture en France* (Paris, 1857), Part II, p. 11.
[51] Baron Chaurand, *De l'enseignement de l'agriculture* (Paris, 1867), p. 6.

Because legitimists thought that a social ethic could not be founded uniquely on civicism but had to be based on the teachings and sanction of the Church, it was imperative that education give proper moral instruction, and in their opinion the men who had run the *Université* and the state since 1830 had nothing but disdain for the Church. Their greatest allegation against state education was that it ignored God.

Still legitimists condemned state education for reasons quite apart from religious instruction. They held Napoleon III primarily responsible for the fact that France, a predominantly agricultural country, was almost bereft of any worthwhile system of agricultural education. During the Second Republic, the government and legislature had made a belated step in the right direction. A farm-school program was started that provided on-the-job training for peasant youth. The *propriétaire* who set up a *ferme-école* promised to teach agricultural day laborers practical farming techniques in return for a state subsidy and the right to sell the crops produced to his profit. Although there were complaints that *propriétaires* were more interested in exploiting a cheap labor supply than in instructing the peasants, most legitimists supported the *fermes-écoles*. At the same time, regional agricultural schools, which were intended to give instruction to the sons of peasant *propriétaires*, and a national institute for advanced agricultural study, which was designed to teach agronomy to the sons of larger landlords, had been created. Since Louis Napoleon had abolished the national institute for reasons of economy, and reduced the number of *fermes-écoles* and regional schools, the program had been short lived and almost ineffectual. These were but further examples of how state policy led to rural backwardness. However, legitimists were just as unhappy with the subjects taught in the regular schools. In the *lycée* or the *collège*, they pointed out, the landlord's son studied classics and mathematics; in the university faculties, liberal arts and the professions; in the *grandes écoles*, engineering and administration. In their opinion, these subjects taught a nation of landlords to despise agriculture, to leave the countryside in order to practice a profession in the city, or, worse still, simply to indulge in its sterile distractions as *rentiers* instead of remaining in the countryside as farmers.

The absence of proper instruction in the state primary schools had the same results. "To read, write, and do arithmetic well," Vicomte Gontaut-Biron stated, "to know his religion thoroughly will suffice for a man destined to live in the countryside and ask the land for subsistence."[52] Gontaut-Biron's criteria were too restrictive for most legitimist landlords who wanted the peasantry to acquire some knowledge about agriculture by the time they left school. Nothing in the primary school curricula, they asserted, pertained to agriculture; nothing fostered a generous love for the soil in the peasantry. On the contrary, and this was Gontaut-Biron's concern, the peasant received a smattering of knowledge about history and geography that, legitimists claimed, was not only useless but also aroused a distaste in him for his calling. "The most important thing," Vogüé urged, "is to persuade [the peasant] that he is not being instructed at school to acquire the means to leave the fields," and this depended, legitimists thought, as much on what he was not taught as on what he was.[53] This preoccupation with uprooting people from their place in society is characteristic of all legitimist thinking about state education. They disapproved of the Duruy law of 1867 that organized primary education for girls because they thought young girls, who were destined for the home and motherhood, should not be taught intellectual subjects that would encourage them to forsake their God-given role in society. They also generally opposed the idea of using education to promote social advancement. During a committee hearing on the advisability of creating state scholarships for the poor, the legitimist Arthur de Cumont observed "that the application of such a proposal would conjure up a real social peril. It would create an army of ten thousand misfits for whom it would be necessary under threat of real danger, to furnish positions commensurate with their knowledge."[54] Education was important to legitimists, but they wanted it to equip a person psychologically and technically for the function corresponding to his place in the social hierarchy. This,

[52] *Enquête agricole*, 2e série, 17e circonscription, p. 478.

[53] *Ibid.*, 3e série, p. 381.

[54] A. N., Assemblée nationale—1871, C 3129, *Instruction publique*, Procès-verbaux de la commission, séance du 5 fev. 1872. Vogüé criticized the peasant for saying: "'. . . [W]e learn in order to become something other than what we are. . . .' I consider this an evil; when the new outlets which are opening are saturated with competitors what will become of these misfits (*gens déclassés*)? They will return to agriculture with pain and sorrow; they will no longer know how to apply their knowledge to the land, and they will augment the number of discontented. For a long time there has been danger, then, in the direction which this very excellent thing called primary instruction has taken." *Enquête agricole*, 3e série, p. 381.

169

in their opinion, state education failed to do, for, while it did not train people to perform essential economic tasks, neither did it teach them to respect the social order.

Even though the state ranked high on the legitimist list of culprits, neither its institutions nor the policies followed by those in power account for the sum total of their critique of the dynamics of subversion. Legitimists were terrified by the spread of "socialist" sentiments among rural industrial workers and artisans to which they attributed the rash of strikes and disorders that occurred in France at the end of the Second Empire and the beginning of the Third Republic. Moreover, although they did not really distinguish clearly between "socialists" and "radicals," legitimists were equally alarmed about the spread of egalitarian ideas among the peasantry. Typically, they saw urban socialists and radicals contaminating the rural population, but they also saw them working in league with certain elements in the countryside, like the socially ambitious petty bourgeois in the village, to overthrow the social order. It was the process of radicalization, as well as the revolutionaries, upon which legitimists focused.

They accused journalists, writers, and publicists of producing socialist and egalitarian tracts that corrupted the people, of writing trashy novels and serial stories that destroyed the basic beliefs in conjugal fidelity, family solidarity, honor, duty, obedience to authority, and religion, all of which made the people susceptible to revolutionary propaganda. Moreover, they blamed publishers for sins of omission as well as commission. "I do not ask for books that would be completely scientific or moral," Benoist d'Azy noted in a criticism of this lacuna in reading material, "but for books which can hold the interests of the rural population: tales of travel, for example, agricultural works which will develop in them a love of the land."[55] They were disturbed too with the licensed colporteurs who distributed the products of the mass press in the countryside. These men, they claimed, were tinged with the ideas of the products they sold and were as a result doubly dangerous because their personal influence on the people was as subversive as the books, novels, pamphlets, brochures, and newspapers they peddled. Indeed, legitimists thought agents of "secret societies" roamed the

[55] *Enquête agricole*, 3e série, p. 554. For other remarks on the bad influence of the press, see Ltr., Malartre to his wife, March 4, 1872, *Malartre MSS* and Ltr., Kolb-Bernard to Chesnelong, Oct. 29, 1872, *Chesnelong MSS.*

countryside fomenting trouble. "These voracious interlopers," as Florentin Malartre described them, "scum of every place, who without possessing a penny, with neither hearth nor home, without any interest under the sun, come from time to time to dictate the law to the peaceful inhabitants of an area (*pays*)."[56] It was they who organized *La Marianne*, Ducrot claimed, that waged a relentless campaign among the industrial workers of Cher and Nièvre during the Revolution of 1848; they who founded the International that, legitimists believed, stirred up industrial and agricultural workers during the Commune.[57] The agricultural day laborers had been so manipulated by the agents of "secret societies" in his area (Ariège), Franclieu avowed, that, despite their basic honesty "tomorrow all will act in a manner contrary to the influence that I might want to exercise."[58]

When the legitimists sought the center in which and from which all the revolutionary influences were unleashed, their eyes fell invariably upon the cabaret. Like many Frenchmen they blamed the cabaret for causing the physical brutalization of the people that resulted from the excessive consumption of alcohol, for keeping the father from the home, and for taking money needed for food, clothing, and shelter from the family. Although they never set foot in the people's cabarets themselves, they were also sure that within their walls the peasants and workers heard the egalitarian propaganda of the agents of "secret societies," read the literature carried in by colporteurs and itinerant workers, plotted strikes, electoral agitations, and even revolutions. The legitimists' tendency to make the cabaret the clearing house for public disorder helps to explain the intensity with which they assailed drunkenness, for booze and rebellion were intimately associated with each other in their minds. General Ducrot related how he could not understand why industrial workers in the Cher, far removed from city influences, had gone on strike until, while taking a stroll in a wooded

[56] Ltr., Malartre to his wife, Sept. 6, 1875, *Malartre MSS.*

[57] A. N., Assemblée nationale—1871, C 2806, *Commission relative au recrutement et à l'organisation des armées de terre et de mer*, 2e registre des procès-verbaux, séance du 11 juillet 1872.

[58] *Enquête agricole*, 2e série, 17e circonscription, p. 353. For the International's supposed activities in the countryside see Olivier de Sugny, *Rapport fait au nom de la commission d'enquête sur les actes du gouvernement de la défense nationale* (Sous-commission du Sud-Est), 13 nov. 1872, p. 7. Annexe aux procès-verbaux de l'Assemblée nationale, Année 1872, No. 1416 K.

area, he came upon a *café-chantant* filled with drunken workers.[59] If, for legitimists, the Church sheltered the social order, the cabaret housed the forces of disorder. This explains the underlying despair that accompanied observations such as that made by the Vicomte d'Aboville. "Formerly," he lamented, "each religious holiday was a holiday for the people. Today things have changed. In an ever-expanding zone around the capital the men go to the cabaret and there are no more holidays, distractions, or pleasures in the life of the countryside."[60]

Thus the growth of the centralized state and the activities of revolutionary social groups combined to form the complex mutually reinforcing factors that the legitimist deputies saw undermining the moral order. Still if they thought of human experience as a dense net of interrelationships that had a massive psychological effect on people, they did not evaluate all the phenomena in the same way. Since they feared a social revolution most, they applauded the state's use of force to ferret out revolutionaries, break strikes, and suppress radical literature, and they frequently worked openly with state officials to these ends. But, in the final analysis, legitimists could not rely on the state to prevent social revolution. After all, in their scheme of things, the state itself created social groups (i.e., the lay school teachers, the army veterans) who were just as subversive as the free masons, Jacobin clubs, or the International. It weakened the authority of the Church and the lay notables and made the lower classes responsive to "revolutionary propaganda." The state, through its fiscal policies, inheritance laws, and economic policies, contributed to the rural exodus that promised to urbanize and hence radicalize the nation. In the long run, the state would itself fall victim to the democratic revolution, and when this happened, the destruction of the social order would be consummated. For legitimists, therefore, the threat that the state

[59] A. N., C 2809, *I^e sous-commission, réorganisation de l'armée*, Procès-verbaux, séance du 9 juin 1871, pp. 86–87. For other remarks on the cabaret, see the *Enquête agricole*, passim, specifically Falloux (3e série, pp. 538–540), Bidard (2e série, 17e circonscription, p. 650), and Franclieu (2e série, 17e circonscription, p. 353); and see Sugny (Rapport No. 1416 K, Annexe aux procès-verbaux, p. 3), Le Lasseux (*Enquête-parlementaire*, p. 5), La Rochette (*Espérance du peuple*, Jan. 6, 1876), and Gavardie (*Etude sur les vraies*, p. 255).

[60] *Enquête agricole*, 3e série, p. 247. Aboville came from Dupanloup's diocese of Orléans where the *déchristianization* of the population was especially marked.

and the social revolutionaries presented to the social order was really one and the same.

This, then, was the legitimists' sociology of moral order. Two questions come to mind when evaluating it: how did their analysis differ from that of their opponents and how valid was their perception of this changing society? In seeking an answer to the first question, the legitimists' conception of the notable is particularly significant. They believed that social rank not individual talent was the chief determinant of a man's function and position in society, and although they did not attempt to define the notable in terms of the old nobility, they generally limited them to the descendants of the nobility and the town oligarchy. The radical republicans in the Assembly who represented what Gambetta called the *nouvelles couches* of society obviously opposed such a view. Moreover, moderate republicans and former Orleanists like Adolphe Thiers, who frequently came from the *haute-bourgeoisie*, were willing to share political power with the rising middle classes. There were, however, deputies on the Right who supported the political and social ascendancy of the notables just as the legitimists did. Some of them sat among the Bonapartists, but the great majority, followers of the Duc de Broglie and Marshal MacMahon, sat in the Orleanist Right-Center. The question is how did their view of the notable differ from the legitimists'?

Even though bitterly divided, the nature of the antagonism among the rightist deputies cannot be defined on the basis of differing views about the socioeconomic constitution of the notables. The Right-Center and the Bonapartists certainly denied any special privileges to descendants of the old aristocracy, but since the legitimists made no special claims for the nobility as distinct from the bourgeoisie, this former conflict no longer serves to set the Bonapartists and Orleanists off from the legitimists. Nor can differing conceptions about the economic function of the notable be utilized to show this distinction. More Orleanists and Bonapartists respected financier-industrialists than legitimists but neither, on the other hand, would have considered the rich landlord to be inferior to the manufacturer or merchant. Indeed, often Orleanist and Bonapartist notables were agrarians like their legitimist colleagues. But if conceptions of the social composition of the notables' class were similar, those dealing with the origins of the notables' authority differed. Napoléon III's Minister of the Interior, Persigny, wrote in 1852: "We have given the legislature to the upper classes.

173

We have openly supported and chosen our candidates but from the highest ranks of society, from the great landowners, wealthy mayors, and so on."[61] Persigny failed to realize perhaps that the Bonapartists presumed to "give" the notable what the legitimist considered to be his by birthright, and that constituted the offense. Bonapartists in fact based their propaganda on an *appel au peuple*, which ostensibly rooted power in the masses. This hardly amounted to a democratic impulse since they were more interested in manipulating public opinion for the benefit of the notable than following it, but it does indicate that the Bonapartists did not think of the notable's position as part of any natural order of things. As for the members of the Right-Center, although they would not have subscribed in theory to the legitimists' conception of the notable's prescriptive rights, they did share their concern with the moral order in so far as they expected members of the middle and lower classes to accept, unquestioningly, the political and social as well as the economic dominance of the notable, and they were duly alarmed when they did not.

This difference in opinion about the source of the notable's power explains the attitude the Bonapartists and Center-Rightists assumed towards the sociology of moral order. Bonapartists could not have differed more from the legitimists in their appreciation of the state. They relied on its intervention in the economic and educational life because for them the state provided the motive force behind the nation. They plunged into the rough and tumble of politics, using the methods of mass propaganda at the state's disposal in order to capture a following among the masses that the notable needed to perpetuate his power, because they did not believe in some moral order in which the masses would respect the positions of the notable. The Right-Center, on the other hand, was just as repelled by Bonapartist techniques as the legitimists. Indeed, what is striking about these men is that their critique of society is so often indistinguishable from the legitimists'. Liberal landlords professed the same moral repugnance for the big city. Louis Viennet, for example, the Orleanist deputy from Hérault, characterized the Parisians as "this horrible population which seeks pleasures and distractions of every sort, as if the Commune and its destructions had never laid the country to waste."[62] Other liberal landlords

[61] Theodore Zelden, *The Political System of Napoleon III* (London, 1958), p. 11.

[62] Ltr., Louis Viennet to his wife, Jan. 1, 1872, *Viennet MSS.*

voiced the same alarm about the rural exodus and the state's economic role in promoting such an unwanted event. It is necessary, the Marquis de Lafayette noted, to "redirect capital and labor towards the fields, to stop the disastrous current, which for too long has been favored by the state, that has led to the desertion of the countryside and caused dangerous urban accumulations."[63] Members of the Right-Center showed the same concern as the legitimists for the need to protect family, property, and religion. They were upset with the omnipresence of the state, objected to the powers of the prefects, and denounced the dependence of the judiciary. They complained about stocks and bonds and the multiplication of small property, and attacked the army veteran, the lay school teacher, the colporteur, the itinerant workers, the agents of "secret societies," and the cabarets as socially subversive. They were disturbed by the lack of religion in the state educational system and the harmful effect of the subject matter taught. It is impossible to say whether the pattern of social criticism within the Right-Center was consistent for the group or identical with that of the legitimists. Only a detailed study of the Orleanist deputies could lead to definite conclusions. But it can be said that it was impossible to ascertain solely on the basis of comments deputies made before agricultural investigating committees, legislative commissions, or private Catholic associations whether the speaker was an ultra-legitimist, a moderate-legitimist, or a member of the Orleanist Right-Center. Although the Right-Center did not view the restoration of the monarchy in the same way as the legitimists, their social critique was remarkably similar, and this is important because it made members of both groups close allies in the struggle for the restoration of moral order.

When answering the second question (How valid was the legitimists' perception of their changing society?) the theme introduced at the beginning of this chapter, the legitimists' conception of evil, is very important. The problem is not so much to determine whether human beings are inherently evil (a question that is probably impossible to answer) but to define in what this evil, even if basic to human nature, consists. Because legitimists believed that every man had a place in society, they could not understand that rage which exists in the heart of a man when he confronts his social

---

[63] "Procès-verbaux des séances de la réunion libre des agriculteurs de l'Assemblée nationale," séance du 13 mai 1871, *Journal de l'agriculture*, II: 117 (1871), 66.

"betters." Perhaps this is what the republican deputy Jules Simon meant when he described his legitimist colleagues as men "no longer in touch with anything."[64] Legitimists were, in effect, psychologically and intellectually alienated from most of their contemporaries. They did not understand the customs or the aspirations of people who lived in the cities, and, more significantly, they had, despite their agrarianism, lost contact with people living in the countryside. This is all the more interesting because of the legitimists' insistence on personal contact as the cement of the social order. Legitimists did have contact with their peasants, but they did not necessarily know them. They did not drink with them in the cabaret or rub shoulders with them in the village square, and it would never have occurred to them to establish such intimate personal relationships. Peasants were meant to till the soil, to respect God and the social order. Many of them did just that, but they became fewer and fewer as the century progressed. The legitimists were simply unable to comprehend that some men no longer wished others to look after and to determine their interests and that affirmation of the self gave life meaning. They considered such sentiments unnatural, the very essence of immorality itself.

This inability to accept egoism or egalitarianism as perfectly natural aspects of human nature obviously impinged on the legitimists' idea of "reality." Because they believed that no sane peasant would be irreligious, want to have more material comforts than his ancestors ever did, or prefer not to live in a society in which the guiding principle was a stern paternalism, legitimists interpreted discontent in rural society in purely pathological terms (i.e., as a highly contagious disease spread by those already tainted to those who on their own would never have developed such symptoms). Their pathological approach to society in fact colored their agrarianism. Nothing suggests that the peasant acquires respect for authority and a love of Spartan-like austerity through some magical contact with the soil. Various kinds of social ethics exist in peasant communities as the cult of agrarianism itself attests. American agrarians, in contrast to the legitimists, for example, usually laud rural life for fostering the democratic egalitarian spirit in the freeholding, freedom-loving yeomanry.[65] Contact with the soil does

---

[64] Cited in Amédée Lefèvre-Pontalis, *L'Assemblée nationale et M. Thiers, Première Partie, Les essais de constitutions* (Paris, 1879), p. 9.

[65] See Henry Nash Smith, *Virgin Land, The American West as Symbol and Myth* (Cambridge, Mass., 1950).

not infuse any specific social ethic in people. Unable (or unwilling) to admit this fact, the legitimists were forced to find the sources of "demoralization" in the countryside to a large extent in the corrupt influences that contriving outsiders exercised on the villagers' susceptible but normally pure hearts. This led the legitimists to attribute too much to bogeymen. Every strike was hardly the result of a plot. The International, a weak and disorganized association in 1871, exercised little influence in rural industrial areas, and all disgruntled peasants were not manipulated by agents from "secret societies."

The distortions induced by ideology, however, did not mean blindness to what was going on around them. Legitimist vocabulary was studded with verbs used in approval (*fixer* or *limiter*) or in opprobrium (*déraciner* or *déclasser*)—words that reveal minds longing for security. Perhaps the very anxiety they felt permitted them to sense the alienation and loneliness, to which they so frequently referred, that has assailed the individual in the modern industrial-urbanized society. At least it appears that the men out to build the brave new world of the Third Republic less understood the negative aspects of freedom than these pessimistic legitimists. Moreover, there is a great deal in what the legitimists said about society that has a familiar ring to students of nineteenth-century France. In his famous study *Tableau politique de la France de l'Ouest*, André Siegfried tried to explain the electoral behavior in that section of the country where the legitimists enjoyed the greatest respect from the peasantry.[66] When, he noted, the land in an area was owned by large landlords and farmed by tenant or sharecropping families, when the peasant families lived on isolated farm units instead of in villages, when they were devout Catholics and not anticlericals, and when landords were not guilty of absenteeism, the peasantry tended to submit to the authority of the notable. Although the legitimist deputies did not think of the geological-geographical factors cited by Siegfried in determining a *pays de soumission*, they often saw the same correlation between property, religious practice, and habitat, corresponding to the mentality of the peasantry. This hardly means that the legitimists had discovered the sociological key to explaining political comportment in the West because they had partially anticipated Siegfried. Siegfried's work has itself been criticized, especially for its geological

[66] André Siegfried, *Tableau politique de la France de l'ouest sous la Troisième République* (Paris, 1913).

determinism.[67] But it was so impressive that it served as a model for an entire school of electoral sociologists who have thrived since World War II, and the specific book in question is still one of the best explanations for the political comportment of the Western peasantry during the first forty years of the Third Republic.[68] The fact that so much of what Siegfried said appears, if in a nonscholarly and nonsystematic manner, in legitimist writings and speeches shows that they were rather astute observers.

Furthermore, much of what the legitimists said about the dynamics of subversion seems perceptive enough. Two decades ago a group of experts—historians, economists, geographers, sociologists, political scientists—met in Strasbourg to discuss the relationship between city and countryside in recent French history. Their comments offered a brief résumé of some of the most advanced thinking at the time on the process of social change and it is striking how often the experts discussed subjects which had been very much on the minds of the legitimists eighty years before.[69] Georges Duveau, for example, pointed out the disturbing impact, which legitimists had noted, that the itinerant industrial workers had on a community. Assi came to town, he remarked of one worker in Le Creusot during the great strike of 1870, with a copy of Quinet's *Les révolutions d'Italie* in his knapsack.

> He was a kind of metal worker who roamed from factory to factory and never settled down, and who, by his gift of gab, by his frame of mind was yeast to the popular dough. After he had spent a few weeks at Le Creusot, Father Schneider no longer had the same men shaped by the *Frères des écoles chrétiennes*, as supple, as tranquil, as serene: the visit of Assi had left its mark.[70]

Daniel Faucher, to cite another example, when commenting on the unique catalytic role the peasant colporteur played in the transformation of the village, remarked about his "completely different

[67] Siegfried developed a theory of geological determinism according to which the composition of the soils produced a physical habitat (the *bocage*) in which the property and social relations characteristic of the *pays de soumission* flourished.

[68] For a discussion of Siegfried's method, its validity, and the school of electoral sociologists who have continued his work, see A. Brimo, *Méthode de la géo-sociologie électorale* (Toulouse, 1968).

[69] Friedmann, *Villes-et-campagnes*.

[70] *Ibid.*, p. 166.

notion of space" from that of members of the colporteur's family which came from his travels and permitted him to assimilate new ideas readily and transmit them to the villagers.[71] Others drew attention to the special part the mass press, military service, primary schools, and above all the cabaret performed in the "education" of the village. In recent years, moreover, a number of studies have appeared on similar themes. Gabriel Le Bras, in his work on religious sociology, has commented about the degree to which religious practice depended on social circumstances. "Of a hundred peasants who move [from Brittany] about ninety cease to practice their religion on leaving Gare Montparnasse."[72] Others have written about the migrant farm workers as elements of discontent in the countryside.[73] In short, if the subjects of scholarly inquiry are any indication, the legitimist deputies were able social critics.

Nonetheless one must be careful not to exaggerate the social analytical skill of the legitimists. Aside from overemphasizing the influence of subversive groups, they clearly possessed neither the intellectual tools nor the motivation of the social psychologists. Therefore, they did not delve into the psychological attitudes or experiences of a group that drew their attention. They did not know, for instance, that a peasant's exposure to totally different styles of architecture from those in his village had such an unsettling effect on his psyche, nor did they care. They were not interested in understanding the psychology of any group any more than they were interested in understanding the attitudes of most of their contemporaries. They only knew that there was something very different about some groups of men, that they were not as respectful of the social hierarchy as others, and they condemned them accordingly. Moreover, much of what they said was not particularly

---

[71] *Ibid.*, p. 393.

[72] *Etudes de sociologie religieuse* (Paris, 1956), II, p. 480. As an example of this phenomenon he also cited (p. 481) the results of an interview of twenty-five Breton women who immigrated to Paris. ". . . [O]f the twenty-five, not one failed to go to mass in her village, and we knew who were secretaries of the *Enfants de Marie*; once in Paris none continued to practice (her religion) and one of them is now a dancer in Pigalle."

[73] Examples of the impact of migrant workers on politics are Georges Bourgin, "Les migrants temporaires et la propagation des idées révolutionaires en France au XIXᵉ Siècle," *Revue des révolutions contemporaines*, no. 188 (May, 1941), 6–18; and S. Derruau-Boniol, "Le département de la Creuse, structure sociale et évolution politique," *Revue française de science politique*, VII:1 (jan.–mars 1957), 38–66.

179

original with them. The notion that the centralized state had a debilitating effect on local life was almost as old as the state itself and a commonplace to men of their generation. Ideas about the effect that the proliferation of small property had on the family and the social order were in vogue among conservatives throughout most of the century, especially after they had been so forcefully presented in the works of the popular sociologist Le Play. The newspapers, whenever strikes or public disorder occurred, were filled with fulminations about the sinister influence of the *meneurs* and the "secret societies." The legitimists' concern with the International was shared by most middle-class Frenchmen, a fact which, incidentally, shows that the legitimists were no more influenced by a plot theory of history than other men of property. The middle class's struggle with the notables for dominance in the village and the cabaret's function as the focal point for malcontent in the city and the countryside were such familiar themes to Frenchmen that they were treated in popular literature. Witness the novels of Balzac, Flaubert, and Zola. Most of the ideas the legitimists had were in the air because people in the last century, as in our own, lived during a period of rapid social change and understandably fixed their attention on the social process that they experienced. But, if their comments were frequently too vague for the modern sociologist, sometimes simply erroneous from a modern standpoint, and often not very original, the legitimists were about as observant a group of laymen as existed in France. It was particularly important for these men who believed in a world of immutable values and social forms to try to determine the process by which these values and forms were being undermined. It was quite natural too for them to consider the attack on these values and institutions as a complex series of phenomena, for, having an organic conception of society, they saw a change in one part inevitably affecting the whole. However, legitimists would not have been particularly impressed to know how perceptive they were. The problem for them was not to describe "demoralization" in France. It was to prevent it from taking place.

Chapter Five

AGAINST THE GRAIN

Because few legitimists had held national public offices, they had been forced to criticize society without the power to pass effective reforms. Prior to 1871 legitimists had a voice only in the Legislative Assembly of 1849 in which they supported the successful conservative efforts to establish the *fermes-écoles*, the national institute for agronomy, and the Catholic reform in education that resulted in the Falloux law. The Falloux law, on which some of the deputies of 1871 worked, helped conservative-Catholic education in two ways.[1] First, the law created a Superior Council of Public Instruction and subordinate academic councils located in each department. These councils were composed of educators and representatives from "society" elected by the major corporative interests—authorized religious groups (Catholics, Protestants, Jews), the magistracy, and members of various local and national governmental councils.[2] Legitimists approved of the presence of non-educators on the councils because the corporate bodies which elected them were socially conservative in character. Second, by permitting students in Catholic *collèges* to receive baccalaureates, the Falloux law broke the *Université*'s monopoly in secondary education. Many legitimists were disappointed with the law because it did not allow Catholic *collèges* to confer the baccalaureates outright and left higher education under state control, but the law

[1] M. Hébert and A. Carnec, *La Loi Falloux et la liberté d'enseignement* (La Rochelle, 1953).

[2] The Superior Council of Public Instruction's membership included: the minister of public instruction; four bishops or archbishops elected by their colleagues; a Calvinist pastor elected by the consistory; a Lutheran minister elected by his consistory; a rabbi elected by his peers; three councillors of state elected by their colleagues; three members of the *Cour de cassation* elected by the court; three members of the *Institut* elected by the same; eight educators named by the government from the *Université*; and three members named by the government from private schools. The academic councils were composed of a rector, an academic inspector, the prefect or his delegate, the bishop or his delegate, a Protestant minister, the *procureur général*, a member of the *Cour d'appel*, and four members elected by the general council. The full text of the Falloux law is given in *ibid.*

181

had been a significant breakthrough. Subsequently, however, the legitimists saw many of these gains nullified when Napoleon III closed the national institute for agronomy and curtailed the *fermes-écoles* program. Moreover, a decree of March 1852, which made the Superior Council of Public Instruction appointive instead of elective, modified its composition in favor of the *Université*.[3] A law of June 14, 1854 transferred the right to appoint school teachers (*les instituteurs*) from municipal councils to the prefects and the Duruy law of April 10, 1867, provided in the newly organized girls' primary schools "the same obligatory teaching program as in the boys' schools, including the geography and history of France," and the subjects were taught by public school teachers who were "state officials in the full sense of the word."[4] The educational reforms that legitimists had favored were partially abolished, and education had been the only major area in which they had seen a modicum of success. Practically speaking, therefore, almost all their reforms had yet to be passed in 1871.

On entering the Chamber these deputies neither individually nor collectively produced a legislative blueprint which they tried to enact. The most comprehensive program advanced, embodied in various proposals like Vicomte de Gouvello's *Vues sur la réorganisation de la France*, envisaged administrative decentralization, but this reform ignored the broad socioeconomic problems with which they were concerned.[5] Still the deputies, after years of protest, did not lack legislative ideas. Despite a piecemeal presentation, legislative initiatives on education, decentralization, industrial organization, the magistracy, freedom of association, agriculture, inheritance, the army, and a number of other subjects were put forward and justified by the need to preserve the social order. Designed to provide the necessary framework from which a new moral order could arise, their reform proposals stemmed from the logic of their social analysis.

Profoundly disturbed by the Commune, the legitimists turned their attention initially to the supposed continuing threat of insurrection. One of the first steps they took as deputies, therefore, was to support a bill to outlaw the International, whose activities legitimists alleged had fostered the Commune.[6] Thereupon they spon-

[3] *Ibid.*, p. 214.   [4] *Ibid*, p. 223.

[5] Amédée de Gouvello, *Vues sur la réorganisation de la France* (Vannes, 1871).

[6] Legitimists overwhelmingly supported the law and some thought it

sored a series of measures against social groups which they thought spread revolutionary ideas. To check on labor agitators they insisted that the law requiring industrial workers to carry personal identity cards (the *livret*) be rigorously enforced. The *livret* contained a record of employment that helped employers and police keep tabs on the movement of workers and establish their "reliability." Some legitimists too wanted a new law that would require agricultural day laborers to carry a *livret*, although others thought the requirement might provoke too much discontent among the workers, thereby undoing any advantage. "We must," Cintré had observed about the *livret* for agricultural workers, "require farm help to have personal identity cards. They cannot be kept at work unless constantly given advances and often they leave the sharecropper in difficulties. By noting the day they began work for a cultivator and the length of time they remained with him the personal identity card would be a method of moralization."[7] Moreover, the legitimist wanted to retain article six of the law of March 27, 1849, which specified that "all distributors or colporteurs of books, writings or brochures, gravures or lithographs, must have authorization which would be given by the prefect of police in the department of the Seine and by the prefects in other departments. These authorizations could be withdrawn by the authorities who deliver them."[8] This proviso permitted the government to select reliable colporteurs, to survey closely their activities, and to get rid of the ones who turned out, despite all precautions, to be "dangerous." Legitimists also advocated a reduction in the number of cabarets, regulation of drinking hours in those left open, prohibition of the sale of alcohol to minors or to those who were intoxicated, and the closing of all these establishments on Sundays. In addition, the legitimist deputies generally favored the prohibition of public meetings without police permits.

Even though insisting after 1871 that republicans apply their principles of freedom of the press and speech when dealing with

---

was too soft on the reds. See A. N., Assemblée nationale, C 2841, *Procès-verbaux des séances de la commission nommée pour examiner le projet de loi présenté par M. le Garde des Sceaux contre l'association internationale des travailleurs et contre les séparatistes*, séances du 29 août et 4 sept. 1871, et 8 et 12 jan. 1872.

[7] *Enquête agricole*, 2e série, 3e circonscription, p. 693.

[8] For a discussion of the press see Irene Collins, *The Government and the Newspaper Press in France, 1814–1881* (London, 1959).

royalists, these were not legitimist principles, and they favored a stringent libel law that would prevent newspapers from publishing articles attacking religion, property, family, and the social order, or fostering disrespect for authority. To control the nonperiodic press, the state would have greater power over publishers than had existed under previous governments, including that of the Second Empire. Whereas the imperial authorities prosecuted the offending publisher and author after publication, i.e., after, as far as legitimists were concerned, the damage had been done, they leaned toward a system of censorship that would have, as one royalist newspaper editor wrote, "required the publisher . . . to obtain a special authorization for each work he intended to print under a popular format."[9] Censorship was the most effective method of throttling unwanted publications, but most legitimists hesitated in applying it to the periodicals and newspapers out of fear that it could be used against royalists and Catholics. They fell back on an indirect method that would discourage the proliferation of radical publications: the requirement that "caution money" be deposited by publishers which would be forfeited in case they were convicted under the libel law. "Caution money," a standard technique employed by conservatives against the leftist press during the nineteenth century, hurt radical journalism in two ways. First, because only men of means (who were usually conservatives) could raise the large sums required for deposit, leftists were prevented from even organizing newspapers, and second, if one of their newspapers did come out, it was punished severely financially once it violated the law. To insure that newspaper publishers, editors, and authors indicted under the libel law would not escape conviction, legitimists felt that they should be tried by magistrates instead of juries. Juries, they argued, would too often be composed of radical sympathizers while magistrates—particularly those sitting in any judicial system they would provide—would be social conservatives. However, as restrictive as these measures were, most legitimists thought them too liberal to implement right away. In fact throughout their four-year tenure, they strongly urged that the state of siege proclaimed during the war be maintained.[10] This permitted the generals to

[9] Henri Jouin, *Le livre et l'ouvrier* (Paris, 1873), p. 19. Jouin was a legitimist but not a deputy in the National Assembly. Also see his *L'Assemblée nationale et les ouvriers* (Angers, 1872).

[10] *Annales de l'Assemblée nationale de 1871*, vol. 44, pp. 241–266. Consult the debate over the press law given here and especially the roll call

prohibit public gatherings or censor publications in the districts under their command. Legitimists expected generals to deal harshly with radicals and subversives, and wanted the state of siege perpetuated until they were silenced.

Repressive steps were, of course, only stopgaps that legitimists knew did not confront the basic sources of discontent in modern society. In an effort to formulate proper responses to the underlying causes of "demoralization" legitimists sanctioned the Assembly initiative to establish a legislative committee that would investigate the conditions of the working classes in France. Although all socially conservative deputies backed the investigation, legitimists played an important role in the committee work. The quest began in a certain spirit of magnanimity but with no real zest for inquiry. The legitimist deputies involved felt a responsibility toward the poor and honestly intended to investigate their physical situation—health, sanitation, diet, housing—but they approached the task as members of the "directing classes" and were guided by a long-standing preoccupation with morality. Nothing indicates this ethical focus more than a questionnaire addressed to various individuals and groups in France by the subcommittee examining the workers' intellectual and moral plight. The first question ("What is the moral condition of the workers in your industrial area?") set the tone of interrogation and the questionnaire proceeded to ask if the workers were frugal, if Sunday was observed as a day of rest, if the women did manufacturing in their home rather than in factories, if public drunkenness was prevalent, and what methods were being used "to improve the religious and moral conditions of the working population?"[11] In brief the document is as revealing because of the questions it asked as the answers it tried to evoke. The answers in fact were implicit in the questions, for the legitimists, who were particularly numerous on this subcommittee, and the other conservatives present had already concluded that workers suffered from an insatiable materialism and were profoundly disrespectful toward social authority. This disrespect was itself a disease, not a symptom. Nobody thought of asking the worker's opinion about his "moral" condition for the

---

vote on an amendment to raise the state of siege which the legitimists opposed.

[11] A. N., Assemblée nationale, C 3025, *Enquête sur la situation des classes ouvrières*, dossier de la sous-commission D.

185

questionnaire was addressed to prefects, subprefects, magistrates, priests, employers, and similar notables.[12] As members of the "directing classes" the legitimists could never have understood any worker resentment about not being asked. They had made up their minds about the nature of the moral crisis long in advance and, as a result, thought they knew the remedies.

In the case of the industrial workers, legitimists framed their long-term reform proposals to create an environment, in regard to personnel, location, and social organization, that would inculcate a mentality of respect. Because they believed the peasant's environment superior to that of the urbanite, many extolled the social results of employing the peasantry itself part-time in manufacturing. The merchant and financier Maurice Aubry, for example, emphasized the advantage of this type of production in the lace industry. This industry, he noted, "employs two hundred thousand women and young girls in over sixteen departments"; it coordinates well with household chores and field work "because the women work on the lace only when agriculture does not need them"; and it is particularly suited for the preservation of health and morals "of the country women in the sense that it does not gather the young girls into the sometimes unhealthy large manufacturing centers and that it is undertaken in the domestic foyer."[13] When the workers were engaged exclusively in manufacture, legitimists wanted them to work, if possible, in a rural setting. One of the factory inspectors in the Nord, the Comte de Melun, was very impressed with "putting out" in the textile industries of the Nord and the Rhône. "The weaving is done in the home," he reported,

> where the parents and the children work together on different tasks. This system has great advantages from the moral point of view. It strengthens family ties and preserves the family from the dangers of community life in the workshops. The paternal eye is always more vigilant than the most active surveillance of strangers. From the social point of view it avoids the inconveniences of urban agglomerations which are easily subject to popular emotions. The transformation of the large manufactories which congested the city of Lyons into small workshops

[12] *Ibid.* The answers to the questionnaire given by these authorities are also contained in these dossiers.

[13] Maurice Aubry, *L'Enquête parlementaire sur le régime économique* (Paris, 1870), p. 8.

dispersed throughout the countryside has produced the happiest results.[14]

Such recommendations were not economically feasible in mines and large-scale factories, and legitimists realized this. However, they still urged that these production units would be better socially if located in the countryside. Indeed some thought that this would permit the industrial workers to experience the moralizing influence of agriculture. Alexander Jullien, the director at Terrenoire, believed this a special necessity for miners, and he counseled employers to release their men from the pits periodically so that they could take part in the harvest.[15] Others advised companies to provide each worker with a detached or semidetached dwelling "surrounded by a little garden" which would bring the worker and his family into contact with the "moralizing" influences of the soil while at the same time permitting them to supplement their diets with fresh fruits and vegetables.[16]

Legitimists, however, not only planned to isolate the industrial workers from the city but also sought, in the case of the rural factory community, to mold the population's mentality by bringing it into the institutional structure of the Church which in turn would be incorporated into the everyday life of the industrial village. They favored organizing various social groups religiously—Christian Mothers, Children of Mary—thus making religion an ever present factor in social behavior. Some even wanted to introduce religious services into the factory proper. Kolb-Bernard, for example, recommended that priests lead the workers in prayer at the beginning of the day.[17] Some Catholic reformers advocated the use of religious orders for factory management especially where young girls were concerned, and with this some legitimist deputies might have agreed, although there is no evidence.[18] Whether or not they ap-

[14] Comte de Melun, *Rapport fait au nom de la commission chargée d'étudier la situation des classes ouvrières en France. Situation matérielle et économique des ouvrières* (Paris, 1875), pp. 9–10.

[15] A. N., Assemblée nationale, C 2857, *Commission relative à l'abrogation de la loi sur les coalitions*, séance du 24 jan. 1872.

[16] Comte de Melun, *Rapport fait au nom de la commission chargée d'étudier la situation des classes ouvrières*, p. 7.

[17] Baunard, "Kolb-Bernard," *Reliques d'histoire: Notices et portraits* (Paris, 1899), p. 313.

[18] See the report on Catholic worker groups prepared by the *Direction*

proved of industrial convents, most favored the participation of lay management in workers' socioreligious activities. Maurice Aubry advocated the personal intervention of employers in the lives of their factory population, to honor "the worker's household in the great acts of the Christian family, such as baptism, first communion, marriage."[19] Kolb-Bernard, who counseled similar steps, founded an *Oeuvre de la Sainte-Famille*—an association that brought worker and patron together in common worship in the local church—in Lille in order, as he explained, to strengthen the union of "our brothers and us under the eyes of God."[20] Legitimists wanted to solve the problem of workers' disaffection by creating a series of religious groups to at least one of which every individual in the community would belong and to combine these groups into an overall Christian association patronized by the families of the factory management. The ultimate goal was to establish a series of industrial villages in which the corporate conditions of life would weld each individual into a harmonious hierarchical society that would effectively shield itself from evil urban influences.

The deputies did not produce any legislative plans forcing the socioeconomic reorganization of industry. Such plans would have required state interference to a degree inconceivable in the last century and would have created a state bureaucracy that would have been the negation of everything in which legitimists believed. Rather, they wanted such a reorganization accomplished through private initiative and cooperation between lay and ecclesiastical social authorities. Still this transformation of the industrial community could not be done individually. It required the free development of corporate life. To achieve this, legitimists, among the more vociferous critics of individualism throughout the century, staunchly advocated freedom of association because of the necessity to allow the notables a free hand in the organization of socioreligious corporate bodies. Since associational life had been closely regulated after the Revolution, the deputies generally advocated legislation removing government restrictions. Yet the question of freedom of association raised problems that seriously complicated their legislative intent because its implementation without restrictions would

---

de la sûreté générale for the minister of interior in A. N., F⁷ 12478, *Agissements cléricaux, 1872–1908.*

[19] Maurice Aubry, *Le travail des femmes dans les ateliers, manufactures, et magasins* (Nancy, 1875), p. 23.

[20] Baunard, "Kolb-Bernard," p. 282.

have meant that any group could associate, even the workers, in any way it desired.

This was not something that suddenly occurred to the legitimist deputies in 1871. After the partial removal of antiunion, antistrike restrictions and the rapid growth of trade unions in the late 1860s, Catholic legitimists had engaged in a lively discussion about trade unions, and the legitimist deputies continued the debate inside and outside the National Assembly. The problem arose for the legitimists because of the varying estimates of the character of trade unions. To the extent that they judged them as social revolutionary associations, legitimists universally condemned unions, but to the extent that they viewed them as organizations uniquely preoccupied with the social and economic interests of their membership, they assumed a much more tolerant attitude. Even under the latter assumption, however, legitimists were not necessarily prounion. One reason for this was economic. Although legitimists detested liberalism, many, if not most, believed in an economic law according to which prices and wages were regulated by competition in the market place. "[T]he industrialists do not have the right to organize in order to raise prices," Benoist d'Azy rather speciously maintained (he had tried in the 1840s to organize iron producers in order to keep the prices high).

> If the workers have the right to organize in order to ask for increases in wages, it is an impossible situation. If the workers want to exact an increase in salaries you will have strikes and violence. But, if an intelligent employer has understood that one must do a great deal for the workers; if he occupies himself with housing his (the worker's) wife, children, and family, if he helps him prepare for old age and retirement (for one must not only find satisfaction for present needs but for the needs of old age)—all come from charity, from paternal sentiment but not from the law. The system of unions does not appear to me to be a proper institution for solving the difficulty.[21]

Even if legitimists had been willing to let unions interfere with the market in order to raise wages, many opposed them for compelling social reasons. Unions operated on the premise that workers have legitimate interests that are distinct from and even opposed to those

---

[21] A. N., Assemblée nationale, C 3206, *Commission d'enquête sur les conditions du travail en France,* 1873, 3e vol., p. 63.

of their employers. This assumption really violated the legitimists' conception of society because they condemned the politics of conflicting interests in favor of one of a harmony of interests protected under the watchful eye of social authorities in a community where all "legitimate" interests were represented. ". . . [W]orkers' unions without employers or employers' unions without workers," Armand Fresneau once commented, "are nothing but arms of war in the hands of the ambitious."[22] This was the period when Albert de Mun, a legitimist who himself was elected to a national legislature in 1876, began to organize the *Cercles des ouvriers catholiques* that were composed of workers and *patrons*. Legitimists welcomed these groups since they fit their social conceptions much better than trade unions. Still some legitimists had developed a more sympathetic attitude toward unions. One group, the *Société d'économie charitable*, under the leadership of the legitimist Armand de Melun (twin brother of the deputy in the National Assembly from the Nord and himself a deputy in the Legislative Assembly of 1849) began to move toward open acceptance of trade unions in the late 1860s. In one of the *Société*'s meetings, Melun approvingly remarked, "The worker goes astray and becomes dangerous when he poses as defender of the indefinite and general rights of the working class, but when he comes simply to defend a corporate, a professional interest, he is perfectly reasonable and his actions can inspire no fear."[23] Statements like this have convinced J-B Duroselle, the historian of social-Catholicism before 1870, that Melun's group approved of unions, which is undoubtedly true, but they did so while emasculating them. Melun, for example, opposed national or international organizations and insisted that union membership be limited to those who had lived in a community for at least two years (thus excluding migrant workers) and to those who had no criminal records (thereby excluding men who had been involved in strikes and labor disturbances). Apparently, the Melun group also opposed the right to strike,[24] but their attitude was much more favorable to unions than that of other legitimists.

These misgivings about trade unions shaped the legitimists ap-

[22] Armand Fresneau, "Les syndicats," *Fresneau MSS*. Article kept in the family papers.

[23] "Société d'économie charitable: Enquête sur les associations syndicales, séances des 5, 8, et 29 mars, 1873," *Le Contemporain*, 3e série, 5e vol. (juillet, 1873), p. 689.

[24] *Ibid.*

proach in the National Assembly to freedom of association. After the Commune whatever sympathy trade unions had received seemed to wain, and voices in their favor were drowned by those who, like Benoist d'Azy, observed that unions were the basis of the International, and Martial Delpit, who added that the International is only "a form. Everywhere workers want power, their place in the sun."[25] The deputies were in no mood, therefore, to liberalize laws governing trade unions; indeed some wanted to withdraw the limited rights trade unions had been granted under the Second Empire. Fear of revolutionary clubs and unions led the legitimists in practice to abandon the principle of freedom of association. This does not mean that the deputies relinquished the hope of taking some legislative action to free the "healthy" segments of society from restrictions on association. The problem they faced, as the Vicomte de Meaux noted, was to decide "which are the innocent, the inoffensive, and the useful associations and which are the useless associations, and how one can distinguish between them."[26]

Although seeking above all to find ways to bring the workers into a hierarchicized socioreligious environment, the legitimists did not ignore the workers' material conditions. Concerned with the physical degradation that accompanied work in factories and mines, the deputies directed their attention primarily to drafting an effective child labor law. However, the regulation of child labor was not a simple matter. Left-wing republicans sought a child labor law in order to provide for the education of the youth as well as their physical protection, but the two were not quite the same. Education for the republican idealists had social connotations because it was designed to give the talented and ambitious youth the wherewithal, despite his low social origins, to rise in society. Moreover, an age differential could exist in a child labor law according to whether it was supposed uniquely to protect the child's physical health or promote his education, for in the former case the age limit for work would normally be set higher than for the latter. A child who needed to be kept from work for school could work without its harming his physical well-being.

Opinion among the legitimists varied considerably about child labor restrictions. Deputies, like Vétillart, the cloth manufacturer

[25] Valades, *Martial Delpit, député à l'Assemblée nationale, journal et correspondance* (Paris, 1898), p. 209.

[26] A. N., Assemblée nationale, C 3206, *Commission d'enquête sur les conditions du travail en France*, p. 65.

from Le Mans, wanted to prohibit any child being taken from primary school and employed before age twelve, a liberal attitude at the time.[27] There were, on the other hand, some deputies, like Malartre, who wanted the age limit set at eight, a specification that would have made the child labor law derisory.[28] Unquestionably Malartre and a few others, like the Tourcoing textile manufacturer Jules Leurent, were much more interested in protecting the manufacturer than the child, but they were exceptions. Most adopted a compromise. They could see no reason for keeping children from the work that their station in life destined them to perform, merely to fill their heads with a lot of useless knowledge. As the Comte de Melun observed, child labor might seem hard, but life's duty calls the children of the lower classes to toil in the factory just as it calls the children of the upper classes to toil in the *lycée*.[29] Nevertheless, the deputies did not want the children's health undermined through too early or too excessive labor. There was some debate about the restrictions required to accomplish this. Comte Benoist d'Azy, who remarked that hard work made strong men, seemed to be of the opinion that the earlier a child started work, the sooner he would become a strong man.[30] Most, however, wanted to forbid child labor before age ten and to limit labor to six hours "divided by a rest period" for girls between ten and fourteen with the same stipulation for boys between ten and thirteen.[31] In this way they thought the health of the youth would be protected. Indeed, the six-hour work day appealed to these men from a moral as well as a physical point of view. Since idle boys, as the Comte de Melun cautioned, learned dangerous habits, it was best to have them in the regular discipline of the workshop for six hours a day rather than running about the streets.[32]

[27] *Journal officiel*, vol. 15, p. 413.

[28] A. N., Assemblée nationale, C 2873, *Commission relative au travail des enfants dans les manufactures*, Procès-verbaux, séance du 12 sept. 1871.

[29] *Journal officiel*, vol. 15, p. 280.

[30] *Ibid.*, p. 281. In fairness to Benoist d'Azy it should be noted that in his factory children under twelve were not employed.

[31] *Ibid.*, p. 242. This was the provision for which all legitimists voted.

[32] A. N., Assemblée nationale, C 2873, Commission relative au travail des enfants dans les manufactures, *Rapport de la section du contentieux et de législation sur les modifications à apporter à la loi du 24 mars 1841 concernant le travail des enfants dans les manufactures, extrait du compte-rendu de l'Assemblée générale des comités catholiques des 4, 5, et 6 avril 1872.*

The penchant to draft legislation that would improve the physical condition of the working classes while simultaneously "moralizing" them, was rather typical. Thus legitimists sought to write an article into the child labor bill that would prohibit all night work for young girls and protect them from the promiscuity of the workshop that was thought to be especially prevalent after dark, and they also favored making Sundays a legal day of rest in order to increase Church attendance in manufacturing centers. To these measures can be added others designed to promote material prosperity and to bring about a realignment in social structure. This was the goal of many of the proposed tax and fiscal changes, such as the tax on liquid securities (*rentes d'état* excluded), the elimination of urban public works programs, and the curtailment of state financed social services that had been constantly blamed for contributing to the depopulation of the countryside. Here legitimists were trying to engineer social results by creating economic hardship in selected areas of the country. On the other hand, they also planned to foster economic prosperity in rural areas for the same social reasons. This was the motive behind efforts in the Assembly to create *une école supérieure d'agriculture*, to expand and reform the *fermes-écoles* program, to foster the teaching of agricultural subjects in primary and secondary schools, and to establish a ministry of agriculture that would devote itself full-time to agricultural interests. And it was the motive behind the long-awaited reform which Lucien-Brun now offered in favor of *liberté de tester* in matters of inheritance. This would stop the impoverishment of the countryside which came from the division of the lands into uneconomically small plots and have excellent social consequences as well. "Enact such legislation," Lucien-Brun prophesied, and "despite the immense development of fortunes in the form of liquid securities you will see, after several generations, the political and social constitution profoundly modified by the restoration of a territorial aristocracy."[33]

Still proposals to use economic measures to foster social change often led to disagreement among the legitimist legislators, especially when they affected agriculture. Generally the deputies would have preferred to let private enterprise produce the desired economic improvements. This did not preclude the possibility of helping rural areas through tax relief, education, and other indirect stimuli,

[33] Lucien-Brun, *Introduction à l'étude du droit* (Paris, 1887), p. 197.

but there were strong prejudices against state intervention. "Agricultural improvements must come from local initiative, departmental initiative," one of the leading legitimist agriculturalists remarked. "We do not need government agriculture (*agriculture officielle*)."[34] Nonetheless many felt that the government would have to take a greater hand in rural affairs for real progress to be made. Spurred by the immediate need to recoup agriculture's wartime losses, they supported a bill that authorized the government to lend money to local cooperative societies which in turn would give long term credit to their members for the purpose of purchasing draft animals, agricultural equipment, fertilizer, and seed.[35] Several deputies, moreover, wanted credits to be made available at low interest rates to capital-starved *propriétaires* on a regular basis. Monjaret de Kerjégu, for instance, called for the creation in each department of a bank with 300,000 francs capital which, "on the advice of three previously designated notables of the canton," would make loans to peasants.[36] Similarly, legitimists sponsored legislation favoring the creation of local associations of *propriétaires* (*associations syndicales*) which, collectively, would undertake "works of irrigation, warping, drainage . . . , and other agricultural improvements."[37] Other legitimists concluded that the state needed to provide social services in rural areas if the peasants were to remain on the farm. The Marquis de Gouvello in arguing for these benefits repeated the story of a farm worker in the Midi:

> "If I were to take myself to the nearest city, my children would have, first, a nursery school, then kindergarten, then free schools, the mutual aid societies, the hospital or help in the home. . . . Here they will be lucky if they are able to go to the village school for a few winter months; if they are sick they will have no right to protection, neither during their childhood nor during their adulthood, and their old age will be like mine, a charge to their family. . . ." One cannot repeat too often [he concluded] it is into the countryside that one must transport the sick aided

---

[34] Monjaret de Kerjégu, see "Procès-verbaux des séances de la Réunion libre des agriculteurs de l'Assemblée nationale," séance du 13 mai 1871, *Journal de l'agriculture*, II:117 (1871), 67.

[35] *Journal officiel*, vol. 15, p. 378.

[36] *Enquête agricole*, 2e série, 3e circonscription, p. 357.

[37] A. N., Assemblée nationale, C 2841, *Proposition de loi ayant pour objet de modifier l'art. 9 de la loi de 21 juin 1865 sur les associations syndicales.*

by charity; it is in rural establishments and not in the middle of large population centers that one must raise the orphan, guide and support the aged.[38]

Gouvello certainly thought that it might have been possible for private institutions to pursue these goals, and he personally had done all he could to organize orphanages in the countryside. However, many of the same men who had sought to cut state programs in the cities now thought of beginning them in rural areas and asked for the creation of a special parliamentary committee "charged to study ways to organize public welfare in the countryside." Indeed others, going even further, sponsored a bill that would have given indigent peasants free medical care.[39]

To the extent that this legislation encouraged local initiative, legitimists would not find it objectionable, but some believed it might do more harm than good. Doubts were raised about the advisability of forming cooperative financial societies that would offer cheap credit to *propriétaires*, for it was feared that the small landlords would either go hopelessly into debt or move away, owing large amounts to the credit association, thereby rendering it insolvent. An even more significant point—because it arose entirely from social concerns—was the misgiving about state-run credit institutions that would lend money to sharecroppers and tenant farmers. "The *propriétaire*," Le Lasseux remarked in response to the idea, "must be the banker of his tenant farmers. . . . If you weaken the privilege of the *propriétaire*, you will make him defiant, and he will not continue this toleration toward his tenant when he is behind in his rent."[40] Perhaps Le Lasseux's consideration for the tenant farmer was genuine, but the state's role in lending money to these peasants was certainly alarming since it interfered in the notable's cherished relationship with "his" tenants, and, for this reason, many legitimists were against state-run credit institutions. The chief difficulty with the *associations syndicales* arose from the necessity of forcing uncooperative *propriétaires* to join such an association, provided that a majority of the *proprié-*

[38] Amédée de Gouvello, *La dépopulation des campagnes: Les asiles ruraux et les orphelinats agricoles* (Paris, 1869), p. 24.

[39] A. N., Assemblée nationale, C 2841, Assistance publique, *Proposition presentée par M. de Lestourgie pour une commission chargée d'étudier les moyens d'organiser l'assistance publique dans les campagnes.*

[40] "Procès-verbaux des séances de la réunion," séance du 7 fév. 1873, *Journal de l'agriculture,* III (1873), 266.

195

taires favored its formation. Many legitimists insisted that the co-operative association would not work if left on a purely voluntary basis because a *propriétaire* whose participation was essential to the success of an undertaking could hinder the effort by refusing to join. Unless all interested *propriétaires* enter the association, Ventavon stressed, "the minority can obstruct the work by refusing to aid in the costs even though in most cases they would profit from [a project]."[41] Others, however, opposed this stipulation because forcing a *propriétaire* to pay for improvements he did not want would, as the legitimist lawyer from Lille, Antoine Théry, noted, constitute "an infringement on property rights."[42] Furthermore, proposals to organize state welfare programs in the countryside excited fears of social dislocations. Although some thought that a state program, administered by the notables, was preferable to see-ing peasants migrate to the cities for want of these services, others maintained that the program would be more harmful than benefi-cial. Private charity, Kolb-Bernard pointed out, binds the social classes together while state aid acts as a social dissolvant.[43] These men simply counseled their fellow *propriétaires* to pay greater at-tention to their social obligations rather than run the risk of seeing their authority weakened once more by the state.

Thus legitimist attempts to draft positive economic reforms de-signed to reorganize the social basis of work and "moralize" the working classes ended in considerable frustration. Even though they sought to create an environment that would allow "healthy" groups privately to implement the desired restructuring of society, legislative proposals meant to encourage this development were not easy to formulate. Freedom of association raised the specter of the proliferation of political clubs and revolutionary unions that caused deputies who believed in it in theory to hesitate in practice. State aid which many thought could shore up the social order by increasing agricultural prosperity provoked a countercurrent of op-position within legitimist ranks because some felt it would foster bureaucratic control at the expense of the notable's authority. Fre-quently, therefore, legitimists, hopelessly divided about their de-

[41] A. N., Assemblée nationale, C 2841, *Proposition de loi ayant pour objet de modifier l'art. 9.*

[42] *Ibid., procès-verbaux de la commission chargée d'étudier la proposi-tion de loi.* The Marquis de Vogüé echoed that "he considered the bill as constituting an infringement on property rights." *Ibid.*

[43] Ltr., Kolb-Bernard to Chesnelong, June 2, 1868, *Chesnelong MSS.*

sirability, did not constitute an effective bloc in favor of legislative measures. General agreement, however, did exist about legislative actions in some areas. Most favored a child labor law that would eliminate the physical abuse of children, tax reforms that would shift the burden from the land to stocks and bonds, more money for agricultural education, the creation of a ministry of agriculture that would actively promote agriculture, greater freedom of association, and a reform of inheritance laws in favor of *liberté de tester*. This was a modest program considering the depth of the socioeconomic changes sought, but it was real enough, and the legitimists seized on the opportunity that their election presented to secure its passage in the National Assembly.

Still the legitimists devoted most of their legislative attention to a reform of the noneconomic institutions—army, education, magistracy, administration—on which they had concentrated their criticism before the election. The intent was clear: to recast the institutional framework of the nation in order to eliminate harmful social effects. The chief target was undoubtedly the central state, but the attack on the state was tempered once again by their fear of revolution. Indeed this issue created the broadest range of opinion among the deputies. There were legitimists who were very sensitive to a revolutionary danger and questioned the wisdom of any weakening of state authority. "As far as I am concerned, I have serious doubts," Léonce de Guiraud told the National Assembly during the debate on decentralization, "and these doubts arise primarily from the situation that has been created for us by the insurrection in Paris."[44] Vinols de Montfleury echoed these sentiments in the same debate when he cautioned, "If one wants a strong nation do not weaken the authority of the government."[45] Kolb-Bernard went so far in his counterrevolutionary zeal as to propose a strong dictatorship in order to silence "demagoguery." "The social evil from which we suffer so greatly," he wrote Chesnelong in 1873, "is the weakening of the principle of authority. The immediate remedy is a period of honest dictatorship. It is, if I may say so, a *2 décembre* made not to the profit of one man but to the benefit of society."[46] Some ardent supporters of decentralization, on the other hand, were so convinced of the evil of state power that they persisted in their plans despite the current excitement

[44] *Annales de l'Assemblée nationale, 1871–1875*, vol. 3, p. 363.
[45] *Ibid.*, p. 894.
[46] Ltr., Kolb-Bernard to Chesnelong, Oct. 29, 1873, *Chesnelong MSS.*

over revolution. One of their chief spokesmen, Comte Raudot, for example, advocated the complete dismantlement of the prefectural system and the creation of regional governments welded together on federalist principles.[47] Most legitimists, however, vacillated between these extremes. Although theoretically agreeing with Raudot, they drew back in practice whenever the application of antistatist ideas, in their opinion, might prove socially dangerous. There was, however, much room for disagreement and the legitimist group splintered according to various subjective estimates about the social peril that might be induced by a reform and the specific reform under consideration.

The deputies probably performed the quickest about-face when they approached reform of the army. No real difference of opinion existed about the undesirable social effects of the *armée de caserne*. The conflict arose over whether the population was so "demoralized" that it could not be trusted to defend property and the social order. The subject, moreover, had been complicated, since the legitimists had last thought about it, by the defeat of 1870. Because the victorious Prussians had instituted universal military training, many Frenchmen concluded that the French army had been swamped in 1870 by a nation in arms. France had to follow suit and adopt universal military training if she were to have a force of sufficient size to defend herself in the future. Ancient sailors found rough passage in the straits of Sicily between the rock of Scylla and the whirlpool of Charybdis. Legitimists found themselves in the same boat, trying to avoid the Scylla of German armed might while at the same time keeping the army from being sucked into the revolutionary whirlpool.

About seventy-five legitimists believed a mass army and a socially reliable one could be organized. They supported a regional system of recruitment and training that would supposedly eliminate the defects of the *armée de caserne* without peril. General Trochu outlined the social basis of this system before the army commission.

> I do not believe that barracks and garrison life as understood by the law of 1832 will permit the expansion of military training without danger to the social order. . . . But [by having the soldier trained in his village], you will end the danger of this

[47] A. N., Assemblée nationale, C 2866, *Commission de décentralisation, procès-verbaux 1871–1874*, Iᵉ registre, séance du 1 mai 1871.

barracks-trained army. This will no longer be the barracks soldier, too much of a barracks soldier—this will no longer be the traveling soldier, this will be the soldier operating in a four or five league radius from his birthplace. This soldier, why could he not, under one form or another, spend a certain time (say six or eight months) in basic training and why could he not at various intervals during this training return to the village or farm in order to guide the plow or take part in the harvest.[48]

Local training, the legitimist advocates of this system claimed, would keep the peasants in the villages and not subject them to the urban environment. They would no longer become social misfits during their military service, but according to Audren de Kerdrel, they "will know their officers, which is a great advantage. They will be under the same influences which moulded them in their youth."[49] Conscription of urban youth posed difficulties, but the regionalists felt that the threat of troublesome urban recruits contaminating the peasants could be overcome by either exempting the urbanites from military service or isolating them from the rest of the army in their own units.[50] With the bulk of the officers drawn from the landlord class and the soldiers from the peasantry, the mass conscript army would provide the manpower that would enable France to confront the Germans on an equal footing with little menace to the moral order.

But three-quarters of the legitimists shrank from such an untried system, no matter how splendid the theory. "We need an excellent army," one of their leaders, General Ducrot, explained,

disciplined, well imbued with principles of order, of devotion to duty, an army that would moralize the nation. . . . Today we are

[48] A. N., Assemblée nationale, C 2808, *Réorganisation de l'armée, Sous-commission (Recrutement), procès-verbaux*, séance du 9 juin 1871.

[49] A. N., Assemblée nationale, C 2806, *Commission de l'armée*, 2e registre des procès-verbaux, séance du 16 juillet 1872.

[50] While military *gouverneur* of Paris during the war Trochu had tried to keep the army safe socially by restricting recruitment into the combat army to men between thirty and forty and letting a national guard composed of family heads keep order in the city. But as Ducrot, who was with Trochu in the capital, noted, the revolutionaries armed everybody and "demoralized" the troops. A. N., Assemblée nationale, C 2878, *Enquête sur les causes de l'insurrection du 18 mars 1871, dépositions des témoins—Ducrot.*

in a situation completely different from that under which Prussia achieved her great military reforms. Prussia was a perfectly disciplined and hierarchical nation in which ideas of order and duty predominated. . . . France has become an overly demoralized, a very undisciplined nation. If we wish suddenly to induct every social element into the army we will not end up with anything worthwhile.[51]

Even the prospect of a peasant-conscript army that regionalists thought reliable was viewed with suspicion. "There is a danger which preoccupies me a great deal," the Marquis de Vogüé confessed in the committee hearings. "It is that we would not only have obligatory service for everybody but that we would also arm everybody. . . . I am afraid that in a day of popular agitation we might see the same thing in our countryside that we have just seen in Paris. This possibility of an entirely armed population makes me uneasy."[52] Arguments in favor of a small socially reliable professional army, however, did not resolve the problem of defeating the Germans. In part the opponents of universal military training countered the thesis that victory had gone to the big batallions with that of lions-led-by-asses. They maintained in sum that the French army could have beaten the Germans if its leaders had prepared skillfully and conducted operations with the talent commensurate with their high responsibility. But these professions of faith in the capacity of a smaller professional army to defeat the Germans were not altogether convincing. Probably General Ducrot revealed the opinion of many when he remarked in an army committee meeting that "he did not believe that our generation is destined [to measure swords again with the Germans]. It is uniquely from the point of view of my country, from the point of view of national interest that I speak."[53] In other words, he expected the army to settle accounts with the revolutionaries not the Prussians. Whether or not these men sincerely believed a smaller professional army could suppress the revolution and the Germans too or whether they thought that priority in the reorganization of the army had to be given to the internal over the external threat is not clear, but what is clear is that most legitimists abandoned any idea of basic reform. They preferred, after the Commune, to keep the *armée de caserne*, despite its social dis-

---

[51] A. N., Assemblée nationale, C 2808, *Réorganisation de l'armée, Sous-commission (Recrutement)*, séance du 22 juin 1871.

[52] *Ibid.*, séance du 9 juin 1871.   [53] *Ibid.*, séance du 22 juin 1871.

advantages, rather than run the risk of mass recruitment into the armed forces.

When the deputies took up educational, judicial, and administrative reforms, they faced problems similar to those confronted in military reorganization. Although intent on destroying the "evil" effects of centralization, they did not want to render to the local democrats what they had taken from Caesar. Support for thoroughgoing reform, therefore, hinged on their ability to devise measures that would set aside such dangers of democratization. For the magistracy they sought an acceptable alternate mode of recruitment and advancement of judges to the one established by the law of 1810. Several options were possible: selection and promotion by popular election; selection and promotion by competitive examination; selection and promotion by members of the bar or by the judges themselves; or some combination of these three. Needless to say, to legitimists popular election was anathema, but they also hesitated about the other options. Although many accepted the idea that candidates for the magistracy be examined in order to ascertain their legal knowledge, they did not want to make appointment or advancement contingent on competitive examination. "In a republican mind instruction is the measure of a man's morality," Gavardie complained.[54] But for legitimists social status counted more than knowledge or intelligence. "The competitive examination (*concours*)," Ventavon argued, "only proves one thing—knowledge. But knowledge is not the only condition which the candidate for the magistracy must fill: rectitude, judgment, promptitude, decisiveness, the moral purity of domestic life are also necessary. Moreover, it is not just necessary that the private life of the magistrate be worthy. It is necessary too that his family have a spotless reputation."[55] Opposition to competitive examination was outspoken when it came to the justices of the peace. Legitimists admired the English system of local government where the gentry had historically monopolized the office of justice of the peace and they wanted France to emulate the English example. Since the justice of the peace had to be, in their opinion, a father figure, a paragon of personal and family virtue in the community, the competitive examination would not produce the desired results. How can you expect "influential and respected elderly men who hold a considered position in their locality (*pays*)," Paulin Gillon asked, to undergo a public examination before an audience of "twenty-year-

[54] *Annales de l'Assemblée nationale, 1871–1875*, vol. 7, p. 75.
[55] *Ibid.*

old" baccalaureates?[56] Social position, not technical knowledge, was their chief criterion for a justice of the peace. Indeed the competitive examination would permit men of questionable social background to flood the magistracy.

Similar objections were raised to the bar's having a decisive voice in the selection of magistrates. Unlike America, where the bench is often the conclusion of a professional career at the bar, in France tradition and training have clearly distinguished between bar and bench, each of which constituted in 1871 a separate career and, to a great degree, a different social milieu. The magistracy, despite executive control (or perhaps because the upper classes had dominated the executive throughout most of the century), still remained the stronghold of the gentry, many of whom descended from old robe families. Legitimists feared that, if recruitment and advancement were placed in the hands of the bar, it would mean turning the magistracy over to the revolutionaries, the politically and socially ambitious middle class lawyers.

Because of these misgivings some seventy-five legitimist deputies eventually decided to oppose any reform. As long as the notables controlled the executive, they felt, the retention of the Napoleonic system offered the best guarantee for the social order. Indeed, one legitimist lawyer, Ventavon, even claimed in defense of the anti-reform position that "the evil comes not from the institutions but from the men who have directed them."[57] Ventavon's statement clearly contradicts legitimist testimony in favor of decentralization and is, therefore, scarcely creditable. Apparently Ventavon, who probably did not believe what he said himself, argued speciously against reform. But whether he believed this argument or not, the great majority of the legitimists certainly rejected his idea. They wanted to end executive control. Moreover, if they dreaded popular elections, competitive examinations, or election by the bar, they considered selection and promotion by the magistracy itself without dangers. It offered sufficient insulation against democracy for them to push hard for the elimination of executive interference.

The general and municipal council's role in local affairs presented the chief problem for legitimists, when contemplating governmental decentralization. They were ready to make these councils the core of local government provided that they were not controlled by radicals. Decentralization, therefore, depended on the mode of

[56] Dehesdin, *Etude sur la recrutement et l'avancement des magistrats* (Paris, 1908), p. 82.
[57] *Ibid.*, p. 77.

selection of the councils' members. Traditionally, the upper classes kept control over these councils by imposing property qualifications on candidates and voters alike. Since the Revolution of 1848, however, councils had been elected by universal suffrage. Considerable ambiguity surrounds the legitimists' attitude about both these systems. The historian Beau de Loménie, for example, maintains that the Comte de Chambord favored universal suffrage and was disliked on that account by the Orleanist oligarchy.[58] Yet when Chambord approved of universal suffrage he invariably added the modifier "wisely practiced," which suggests something vastly different from the suffrage advocated by a Léon Gambetta. As the legitimist Gabriel de Belcastel explained, "in the 'king's' manifestoes the words universal suffrage are invested with a sense that sets aside the perils."[59] Perils in legitimist terminology meant voting against the social authorities. On the other hand, legitimists have been admired for their deep hatred of the property qualification, which supposedly expressed vulgar Orleanist materialism. This stereotype too is open to question. One legitimist deputy, Fresneau, for example, bitterly attacked property qualifications in public, but no man worked harder in the Committee on Decentralization to have a property qualification set for the municipal electorate. How can such contradictory behavior be explained? There is little doubt that these deputies, if forced to choose between an electorate limited by property qualifications and one allowing one man one vote, would favor the former. "Property," Amédée Lefèvre-Pontalis admitted, "would be an excellent proof that one has a stake in the [community]."[60] But a rash of legislative initiatives illustrates the legitimists' interest in finding an alternative to the *cens*. Thus Comtes Raudot and Douhet, believing in the conservative instincts of the family man, proposed that the head of the family cast two votes while another legitimist recommended that the head of a household be given a vote for each dependent.[61] Belcastel devised an electoral system in which one man could cast as many as four votes (family head, property owner, university graduate, adult male).[62] Others attacked the problem from the point of view

[58] Emmanuel Beau de Loménie, *La restauration manquée. L'Affaire du drapeau blanc* (Paris, 1932), p. 30.

[59] Gabriel de Belcastel, *A mes electeurs. Cinq ans de vie politique, votes principaux, propositions, lettres et discours* (Toulouse, 1876), p. 35.

[60] A. N., Assemblée nationale, C 2866, *Commission de décentralisation*, Procès-verbaux, séance du 12 mai 1871.

[61] *Journal officiel*, vol. 32, p. 147.

[62] Gabriel de Belcastel, *A mes electeurs*, p. 200.

of domicile, figuring that a prolonged residence requirement would disenfranchise the more unstable elements of the population. Some even wanted to restrict the electorate in communal elections to those "born in the commune." In this way, Amédée Lefèvre-Pontalis explained, every male could vote "some place, except vagabonds and nomad workers."[63] Some approached the problem from the viewpoint of candidate eligibility. Comte Raudot, for example, sponsored a measure that would have made cabaret owners ineligible for the office of mayor.[64] Neither the *cens* nor universal suffrage would have accomplished the social objectives at which these measures aimed. The property qualification disenfranchised people whom legitimists considered reliable because of their social function and enfranchised others who were not for the same reason. It was not a sociological but uniquely a materialistic standard and hence distasteful to them. The same was true of universal suffrage because it threw subversives together with "responsible" social groups indiscriminantly.

This concern with sociological factors led to the application of quite different standards according to the electoral situation. Whereas the deputies strongly opposed universal suffrage for elections to municipal councils, they were not too upset about it when elections to the general councils were in question. Objections to universal suffrage in the municipalities, of course, reflected their deep distrust of the cities. It is true that most of the communes were hardly more than villages, and it might have been possible to eliminate universal suffrage in the larger communes while leaving it in the smaller—had they wanted as much.[65] But legitimists really lacked

[63] A. N., Assemblée nationale, C 2866, *Commission de décentralisation,* Procès-verbaux, séance du 19 mai 1871.

[64] *Ibid.*, séance du 6 fev. 1874.

[65] The Census of 1866 shows the preponderance of rural communes.

No. of Communes	No. of Inhabitants
16,674	0-500
15,976	501-1,500
2,972	1,501-2,500
955	2,501-3,500
796	3,501-10,000
130	10,001-30,000
12	30,001-40,000
10	40,001-50,000
6	50,001-60,000
17	60,000 +

confidence in the electorate of the larger villages, and besides the adoption of any such plan for the municipal electorate would not have been feasible because of its obvious discrimination. These problems, however, did not exist for elections to the general councils. During the Second Empire each canton had elected one councillor. If each canton had been allotted representation by population, urban cantons would have received more councillors but this had not been the case. As a result, although ostensibly elected by universal suffrage, it was violated, since councillors from sparsely populated rural cantons dominated the general councils. Relatively sure of the peasantry supporting traditional social authorities, most legitimists were prepared, if somewhat reluctantly, to give general councils elected by universal suffrage extensive powers in the departments. But only a small minority was willing to grant similarly elected municipal councils much authority. They preferred to subject municipal councils either to the control of the prefect or to the general councils unless a "safe" electorate could be found. This is why Armand Fresneau and others fought so hard for a property qualification in municipal elections. It was not ideal but its adoption would permit the legitimists to proceed with their task of decentralization.

Of their projected institutional reforms those in education probably gave legitimists least reason for hesitation. Since their goal was to place education under the control of the Church and the lay notables, they had to design a system which would keep the institutions out of radical hands. Part of the reform sought to promote the growth of private Church-run schools. They wanted the state to stop its program of primary education for young girls and return this instruction, such as it was, to the Church. In secondary and higher education, they demanded that "private institutions [be given] the right to deliver diplomas and confer degrees."[66] Inasmuch as the Church was not a democratic institution, there was no reason for misgivings about its assuming such control. The other part of the reform pertained to the *Université* itself. Legitimists advocated repeal of the modification Napoleon III had made in the Superior Council of Public Instruction and the academic councils. Once again the councils were to be elective instead of appointive, but, as previously, the elective principle posed little difficulty. None of the legitimists contemplated elections by uni-

[66] A. N., Assemblée nationale, C 3129, *Commission de la liberté de l'enseignement supérieure.* The quote is taken from an amendment Ferdinand Boyer made to the committee's bill.

versal suffrage. Rather, they intended for bishops, magistrates, general councillors, and other selected and selective groups to send representatives to these councils. No trouble could arise from enhancing the powers of councils so chosen over the *Université*. This does not mean that a complete accord existed among the legitimists about education. There was much uneasiness and conflicting opinion concerning the selection of *instituteurs*. During the Empire they had been appointed by the prefects, and many legitimists suggested that the municipal councils assume the task. Since this could have alarming consequences if anticlerical radicals controlled municipal councils, there was considerable doubt whether the prefect should lose this power—unless the composition of the municipal councils could be assured by a proper electoral law. Legitimists, moreover, disagreed rather sharply about the *Université*'s role in education. Some preferred removing the state from the education business altogether, that is, turning education over to the Church exclusively. But most felt that they could accomplish more practically their objectives by permitting Church schools to compete on an equal footing with the *Université*, while bringing it under the sway of ecclesiastical and lay notables. This disagreement, however, in no way signified that legitimists were ready to abandon fundamental reforms in education as they had in the case of the army. Although they might disagree about the extent of change, they all concurred that the *Université*'s control over education had to be curtailed and that the institution itself needed basic structural reforms.

Thus legitimists renounced many of the reform ideas that they had developed about French institutions during their years of political obscurity. It was not just that they had changed their minds. It went much deeper than that, for their minds had themselves undergone something of a transformation. Few people are ever the same at any moment of their existence because their innermost consciousness is being affected by life's experiences. In the relative tranquillity of the Second Empire, remote from the practical cares and responsibilities of the centers of power, the legitimists had viewed the institutions of France with different eyes from those subsequently educated by the events of 1870–1871 and the perplexities faced by the legislator. Events had confirmed their faith in the principle of legitimacy. Indeed, for some the feeling that France suffered from an orgy of egoism led them to join, for

206

the first time, in an effort to restore "moral order" through the medium of legitimate monarchy. At the same time, however, they quite paradoxically came to appreciate the importance of state power as an aid to social stability. Some had sensed as much before 1870, but now the sentiment possessed them as never before. The majority, therefore, renounced any intention of dismantling a military structure that they had previously condemned for having, because of its methods of recruitment and training, disastrous social effects. Nor were they interested in abolishing the prefectural system that had been the specific target of earlier criticism. On closer analysis drafting institutional reforms of great scope had proved extremely difficult. In the rush of events and the thick of legislative debates, the dividing line between a "good" and a "bad" legislative provision seldom appeared as clear as once thought, for its effects could be desirable in certain respects and undesirable in others and, in any event, the consequences envisioned were highly speculative and therefore questionable.

Still these men did not turn away entirely from the reforms so long sought. If they refused to countenance the elimination of the prefectural system, they wanted much of the prefect's administrative and judicial functions handed over to the notables. In particular, the prefectural councils were to be suppressed and their judicial functions assumed by regular courts. Moreover they wanted a standing committee (of four to seven members) created by the general councils in each department to assume the budgetary, tax, and other administrative jurisdictions heretofore handled by the prefectural councils. In certain situations, they felt the general councils, acting collectively, should usurp the functions of the national executive. During the war and the Commune the notables had stood by helplessly, while the regime in Paris was seemingly at the mercy of the revolutionary "mobs." They had also watched Gambetta, who was put into office by the revolution, take over the ministry of the interior and, using the authority of his position, dissolve the general councils in order to get rid of the only official organs that could have served as a center of conservative opposition to his Republican policies. The legitimists wanted to prevent a repetition of such events or even worse by giving the general councils the legal right to establish a national government on their own initiative whenever they decided the central government could not function due to war or rebellion, and several cosponsored a legislative proposal to that effect.[67] And, with proper guarantees, they all believed that the state's role in education and the executive's interference in the magistracy could be significantly changed without hampering the state's ability to track down subversives, crush strikes, or quell insurrections.

In the National Assembly, legitimists favored legislation that was bound to arouse vehement opposition. Marxists and other non-idealists often interpreted legislative struggles in terms of private economic group interests, and this sort of conflict frequently transpired. Winegrowers, regardless of political affiliations, united to protect their fiscal and economic interests; sugar-beet growers, textile manufacturers, and economic groups of various political persuasions did the same. But legislation is also the vehicle through which ideas are made concrete. These ideas often mask economic interests, but they also express ideological preconceptions so that the clash of wills over legislation is equally a clash of ideologies. From this point of view, there was no chance that the Gambetta-led republican Left would accept legitimist-backed measures. Superficially both seemed to agree about the necessity of some reforms. The republican Left approved of decentralization that would occur in a democratic way, the exact opposite of the position held by the legitimists. The leftists, moreover, concurred with those legitimists who approved of universal military training but again for totally different reasons. They wanted a democratic army in which the urbanites would hold a prominent place and the officer corps would be open to talented men regardless of social origins. They wanted a militia. The Gambetta republicans' support for another measure dear to legitimists, freedom of association, was predicated on the assumption that the social elements (Jacobin clubs, labor unions, masonic societies, etc.) which legitimists despised would prosper under freedom's regime. On other issues the nature of their antagonism emerged more clearly. Although it did not identify with the *Communards*, the Left opposed most of the measures that the frightened conservatives sponsored after the Civil War. They fought efforts to fetter freedom of speech, press, and assembly

[67] They were La Rochefoucauld-Bisaccia, Vétillart, Bridieu, and Cumont. See A. N., Assemblée nationale, Propositions des lois, No. 158. *Proposition de loi relative à la convocation des conseils généraux dans des circonstances exceptionnelles.* Annexe aux procès-verbaux de la séance du 21 avril 1871.

or limit the democratic process as embodied in universal suffrage because these democratic freedoms were not only the theoretical basis of republicanism but also practically the most effective weapons that republicans could use to combat the organization of society under the principles of the "moral order." Still, inasmuch as the republican Left was a small minority, the success of legitimist-favored legislation depended, as in the case of Chambord's restoration, on the attitude of the deputies in the Center and the Right-Center. Objections were not raised to the immediate and direct suppression of the "revolutionaires." Almost all the conservatives supported the law outlawing the International, which was easily enacted, and similar antisubversive measures. This had been the purpose of their electoral fusion in 1871. But legislation to shape the socioeconomic order so that a "moral order" could prevail was another matter precisely because it involved ideological preoccupations. It was noted in Chapter Four that the legitimists could not be separated from most of the Catholic conservatives sitting in the Right-Center by social attitudes. These men were just as eager as the legitimists to promote legislation that would help restore the "moral order," but the Voltaireans in the Center led by Thiers were another story. Because they accepted a middle-class democracy within the framework of a strong state, which could crush social revolution, they tended to oppose decentralization and support, if cautiously, greater popular representation. Because they admired the Enlightenment, they were wary of efforts to re-Catholicize education, even though they felt that religion was the "opiate of the masses." The Center was not large, but legislation could not be passed without the support of some of its members. Still, not being a rigid bloc, the voting behavior of its members varied according to specific issues.

Within this legislative context there was hardly any doubt about the fate of the reforms over which the legitimists were themselves divided. Many conservative republican and Orleanist landlords supported the proposals for poor relief and agricultural credit in rural areas and often for social reasons quite similar to those advanced by legitimists. The republican Marcel Barthe, for example, speaking on behalf of a bill setting up credit facilities for landowners, used arguments that could have come from the lips of any of its legitimist supporters. "The ruined *propriétaire*," he stated, "whose domain has been expropriated, the worker who does not receive enough profit from the application of his intelligence and strength, leave their villages and go to the cities to swell the ranks of the uprooted who are a continual element of agitation and disorder."[68] But most of the Center and Right-Center deputies joined the majority of the legitimists in opposing these measures. Apparently the motives behind this opposition were mixed. Like the legitimists the Catholics in the Right-Center seemed to fear that the state would interfere in the social relations between landlord and peasant if it assumed these functions. Social factors, however, probably weighed less than fiscal ones in the centrists' calculations. The state's entry into these new areas of jurisdiction simply violated their laissez-faire ideology, and, since the deputies were particularly economy minded, they objected to any additional expenses that would burden a treasury already charged with the costs of paying for a lost war. With such overwhelming opposition, these bills never even came to a vote on the Assembly floor.

Neither the army's regional reform nor the reform of the magistracy fared much better. Although they were at loggerheads over the army's organizational structure and social composition both legitimist proponents of regional military training and radical republican advocates of a militia supported universal military training in the Assembly. They were joined, moreover, by many Right-Center deputies, like General Trochu, who shared the legitimists' concern with the social effects of the *armée de caserne*, who felt the German menace could only be met by numbers, and who adopted the regional system of training as the optimum solution to both the military and the social problem. However, the majority of the Right-Center and the Center allied with most of the legitimists against universal training. *Pro forma*, all the deputies in the Center and Right-Center approved of a statement of principle which asserted that every Frenchman owed military service, but this was meaningless. The real test between proponents of a mass-recruited-regionally-trained army and a barracks-trained-professional army came over length of service. The former wanted "all Frenchmen who [had] not been declared unfit for military service [to] serve in the active army for three years" and then pass into the ready reserve; the latter were interested in at least five years' military service that could not have been required of all Frenchmen because of the economic and social costs and, if adopted, would automati-

[68] *Journal officiel*, vol. 15, p. 378.

cally have led to a professional army.[69] Most of the deputies who opposed universal military training, including the legitimists, tried to salve their conscience by requiring all Frenchmen who did not serve for five years to serve for six months, but this stipulation did not affect the army's organization. Its core would be the five-year draftee. When the vote came, most of the Right, Right-Center and the Center united against a minority of legitimists, Orleanists and left-wing republicans to defeat three-year service, 455 to 227.[70] The law that this victorious coalition passed divided the annual draft into two contingents, one (the largest) to serve six months, the other for five years, and in a subsequent law on army organization the regional system was set aside for an army in which each unit was recruited nationally not regionally and trained in urban located barracks. Hence the old *armée de caserne* was retained. With fear of the social revolution making legislative bedfellows out of legitimists, Orleanists, and conservative republicans, the regional army could only come to grief.

The conjuncture of legislative forces that checked reform of the magistracy was somewhat different. The seventy-five legitimists who opposed any reform were a minority, and, although the Center, under Thiers' urging, also opposed reforms, most of the deputies wanted to abolish executive control over the judiciary. However, dissension arose among the reformers about the method of selection and promotion that would replace the old system. For the most part, the Right-Center like the legitimist Right, not wanting competitive examinations or "lawyers, clubs, and cabarets" to select the judiciary, opted for a plan that would permit the bench itself to choose magistrates and supervise their promotion.[71] But the republicans, convinced that a self-recruiting magistracy would produce, in Emmanuel Arago's words, "an order, a class, a caste," rejected the conservative scheme.[72] Only a small group of radicals sought democratic elections, but most republicans, including moderates in the Left-Center, preferring a system in which the bar predominated, clearly favored a change in the magistracy's

---

[69] *Ibid.*, vol. 12, p. 217. For a discussion of this law see Neal Brogden, "French Military Reform after the Defeat of 1870–1871," Diss., University of California at Los Angeles.

[70] *Journal officiel*, vol. 12, p. 217.

[71] Dehesdin, *Etude sur la recrutement et l'avancement des magistrats*, p. 73.

[72] *Ibid.*

social composition. If the seventy-five legitimists had supported the conservative plan, it might have passed, but with their support the status quo deputies in the Center and the republicans combined to defeat the conservatives. The conservatives, on the other hand, with the support of the standpatters, easily defeated the republicans. All efforts at compromise failed. After months of labor the Assembly produced no law and the antireform minority triumphed.

If division among legitimists helped defeat these measures, their inability to solve problems connected with freedom of association and municipal government forced them to withdraw their support of legislation, thereby contributing to the defeat of reforms that they had almost unanimously desired. All the conservatives shared the legitimists' misgivings about labor unions and radical political associations. The centrists, therefore, were quite content to let the government regulate associational life. Right-Center deputies, however, were like the legitimists anxious to extend freedom of association to "inoffensive and useful" social groups. However, no law on association ever came to vote in the Assembly since the Right and Right-Center could never overcome their fears of radicalism sufficiently to promote more liberal legislation. In fact, freedom of speech as well as association suffered in this Assembly. As noted, legitimists quickly rallied to a regime of repression against political and social "subversives." Alone they would have been incapable of passing restrictive laws, but they were joined by members of the Right-Center and Center in this search for internal security. The republican minority fought hard but the conservatives generally prevailed. The law on the press that the conservatives passed in 1875 reaffirmed the principle of crimes of opinion, that is, the propagation of antisocial doctrine and incitement to riot. It gave the minister of justice an advantage in prosecuting the press by removing certain offenses—notably "crimes of defamation, outrages, and public injury against any person and all constituted bodies"—from courts where they could be tried by jury, and by giving them to correctional tribunals where they would be tried by magistrates.[73] To buttress further the government's authority, the law granted public prosecutors the right to bring charges against persons who defamed civil servants whether or not a formal complaint had been lodged by the injured party. Moreover the law specifically maintained martial law in the depart-

[73] *Annales de l'Assemblée nationale de 1871*, vol. 44, p. 241.

ments of Seine, Seine-et-Oise, Rhône, and Bouches-du-Rhône, i.e., in the major population centers. When the republicans tried to eliminate the state of siege provision, they lost, 360 to 316; the legitimists voted with the majority.[74] Legitimists, however, were not satisfied with these restrictions. They also wanted the prefects to be able, as they had during the Empire, to forbid the circulation of newspapers on the streets. Republicans managed with votes from the Center to strike down the Right and Right-Center backed measure 337 to 332.[75] Ironically, legitimists contributed to the republican success, for three of them voted with the majority, but this fact alone illustrates their long retreat from freedom of speech and association.

Frustration of municipal government reform stemmed from the Assembly's inability to solve the problem of the electorate's composition. During the debate on municipal councils, Louis Blanc— that *bête noire* of the conservatives—exclaimed, "municipal autonomy, that is true autonomy."[76] Since the republican Left confidently expected to control these councils, their theoretical pronouncements were made in the comfortable context of a favorable political reality. Again, however, the centrists were content to keep the municipality under strict executive tutelage, although they were willing to permit democratic elections of relatively powerless municipal councils. The bulk of the Right-Center, on the other hand, approved of greater autonomy, but, like the legitimists, they based their support on an effective restriction of the municipal electorate. Despite persistent efforts to mold a "safe" electorate, the rightists failed. The multiple voting schemes of which so many legitimists approved seemed too clumsy for implementation and never received widespread support in the Committee of Decentralization (except by legitimists) or the Assembly. Conservatives also ended by abandoning the property qualification because, as the legitimist Lefèvre-Pontalis opined, "present day ideas force us not to ask it."[77] The conservatives pinned their hopes on age and strict residence requirements, but the republicans, with the help of the Cen-

---

[74] *Ibid.*, p. 266.

[75] *Ibid.*, vol. 42, p. 240. The amendment read: "Administrative authority can no longer decree the interdiction of the sale and distribution on the public streets of a specific newspaper."

[76] *Ibid.*, vol. 15, p. 360.

[77] A. N., Assemblée nationale, C 2866, *Commission de décentralisation*, procès-verbaux, séance du 12 mai 1871.

ter, blocked these efforts, and universal manhood suffrage emerged unscathed. In their initial enthusiasm, fervent decentralizationists enacted a law in 1872 that gave municipal councils the right to elect mayors.[78] Inasmuch as a municipal electoral law had not been passed, many conservatives, including half the legitimists, voted against the bill, but the others approved "under the reservation," La Bassétière later explained, "expressed by myself and other members, that the communal electorate be considerably modified."[79] When this modification did not materialize, the legitimists and Orleanists reversed themselves and voted for a law enacted in 1875 that returned the appointment of mayors to the minister of the interior. That partisan of decentralization Armand Fresneau explained, if we make "good" municipal councils we can give them

> . . . all sorts of jurisdiction including the election of mayors; if not, not. At present the communes even have cabaret owners for mayors; and the communal fortune is no longer protected. The Caesar system was better than the present one, and if we cannot change it [then we must allow] the choice of mayors by [central] authority.[80]

Fear of communal democracy prompted these conservatives, legitimists and Orleanists alike, not just to renounce decentralization on the communal level but to unite with the prostatists in the Center to reinforce governmental control.

Reforms that legitimists supported without fear of democratization experienced various legislative fates. Some were not enacted. This happened in the case of the bill granting *liberté de tester*. It is not clear what exactly took place. The bill was hardly discussed in the Committee on Decentralization and never debated in the Assembly. This is strange considering that legitimists and many nonlegitimists in the Right-Center had considered its passage vital to the reconstruction of the social order. Republicans and Bonapartists attacked the measure in the name of the egalitarian achievements of the Revolution, but their opposition could not have buried the bill. Obviously, its former supporters in the Right abandoned it. Because of their silence on the matter, one can only speculate about the reasons for their inaction. One possible explanation is

[78] *Journal officiel*, vol. 2, p. 353. The bill passed 279–269.

[79] A. N., Assemblée nationale, C 2866, *Commission de décentralisation*, séance du 5 mars 1872.

[80] *Ibid.*, séance du 2 fev. 1872.

that the reformers realized how unpopular their inheritance bill would be among a peasantry who were strongly attached to the revolutionary inheritance system. There was no reason to irritate the peasantry over a bill, the passage of which was doubtful because of republican, Bonapartist, and centrist opposition. It is also possible that many concluded that ownership of land kept the peasants in the countryside, and the individual peasant *propriétaire*, whatever his shortcomings from the legitimist viewpoint, was in Meaux's words a greater "guarantee for the socal order" than the peasant emigrant in the cities.[81] Whatever the cause the project was removed from the Assembly's agenda. Special legislation favoring the creation of a ministry of agriculture, an agricultural school at Versailles, and an extension of the *fermes-écoles* program also failed. The results are surprising because a large coalition of *propriétaires* of various political persuasions seemed to desire ardently their adoption. They even organized the *Réunion libre des agriculteurs de l'Assemblée nationale* for the purpose of steering such legislation through the Assembly.[82] But the measures in question were never even seriously debated. They simply disappeared in the legislative windmill. As a result the reasons for their demise are again difficult to ascertain. Apparently they were victims of economy moves. Hard-pressed to balance budgets swollen by the costs of the war and sensitive to taxes, the legitimists and others might have reluctantly discarded the projects because they would have added significant financial burdens to the treasury. The only part of the legitimist proagriculture economic program adopted was a tax on stocks and bonds. Adolphe Thiers and his followers in the Center fought the bill, but a coalition of anticorporate-business leftists, Right-Center *propriétaires*, and legitimists pushed the tax through.

In two institutional reforms, departmental government and education, the legitimists could count the Assembly's action as a qualified success. The same constellation of legislative forces was at play in departmental as in municipal government reform: the left-wing republicans sought democratic decentralization, centrists and Bonapartists central control, and the Right-Center and legitimists non-democratic decentralization. On the crucial question of the de-

[81] Vicomte de Meaux, *Les conclusions de l'Enquête agricole*, p. 9.

[82] In the first meeting of the group legitimists numbered fifty-eight. They were important, but about forty members of the Left-Center and forty from the Right-Center also joined.

partment's electorate, the radical Naquet proposed proportional representation for each canton. That, the Right and Center easily defeated. The republicans, with aid from the Center, however, managed to frustrate conservative attempts to limit the electorate by multiple voting, property qualifications, or age and strict domicile requirements. But these results did not overly discourage the nondemocratic decentralizationists. They were reasonably confident, even with universal suffrage, that the notables would continue to dominate the general councils since the rural cantons outnumbered the urban. Besides, the conservatives were reassured when the Assembly adopted a provision that forbade payment of salaries to general councillors.[83] Where in a similar situation the nondemocratic decentralizationists forgot about communal autonomy, they proceeded energetically to draft legislation granting the general councils greater authority in departmental government. The law of August 10, 1871, gave general councils a decisive voice in departmental affairs. They had final say in matters concerning departmental buildings and lands, departmental roads, institutions of public charity, and all projects financed out of the department's funds. The prefect remained the department's chief executive, but the councils received power to watch him in order to see that he carried out its wishes. To this end the law required the prefect to prepare the budget but the council to vote it article by article. It also required the prefect to present his accounts to the general council at its April session, so that it could scrutinize them in detail before voting the budget. Between sessions the general council could survey the prefect's daily administration through newly created departmental commissions. Elected by the general council, the departmental commission examined the prefect's accounts monthly, reviewed his budget proposals before the general council met, and reported thereon to the general council when it assembled. In 1872, moreover, the Assembly enacted a law, over left-wing republican opposition, which authorized the rurally based general councils, in case the National Assembly could not meet, to form a provisional Assembly invested with full sovereignty, thereby satisfying one of the legitimists' chief demands.

From the standpoint of the purest legitimist decentralizationists, these reforms were completely inadequate, for the prefectural system was left intact. They were, however, a minority since most legitimists never intended to get rid of the prefects. Still the reforms

[83] *Annales de l'Assemblée nationale*, vol. 4, p. 368.

did not meet majority demands. If they accepted the prefects, they wanted to suppress the prefectural councils and hand over the day-to-day administration to the departmental commission. The Committee on Decentralization actually voted for their elimination, but this aroused the ire of the ardent statist president of the Republic.[84] Thiers, who often threatened to resign and leave the shaky conservatives in the lurch when his will was thwarted, managed to cow the legitimist and Right-Center-dominated committee and the Assembly into submission, and the prefect's councils were kept. Most legitimists also thought that the law of August 10 gave the prefects powers that should have gone to the general councils. They claimed, for example, that the councils should distribute any financial aid (*fonds de secours*) which the minister of the interior allotted to a department, for they had unpleasant memories of how the imperial prefects had used such funds as political bribes.[85] But when the Committee on Decentralization reported a bill with this provision included, Thiers, arguing that the general councils would be distributing money taken from the national treasury, raised sufficient votes (333 to 303) to win his point. (Twenty legitimists assured his victory when they voted with the government.)[86] This dispute illustrates the legitimists' basic complaint about the reform. The prefect was not just the department's executive, he represented the central government in the department and as such claimed to uphold national interests. If in his judgment the general council's actions encroached on "political" questions or national affairs, the law permitted him to silence the general councils. Legitimists believed that this power in reality gave him too much influence in the department because it was easy for him to declare most problems of national instead of departmental concern and remove them from the councillors' competence. To most legitimists, therefore, the legislation on the general councils fell short of expectations, but it did move toward their ideal of decentralized government. The left-wing republicans agreed. The party of order, the radical deputy Tolain complained after the vote on the law of August 10, "thinks that it has found a way by the law on departmental organization to assure its preponderance. This po-

---

[84] See the objections to the suppression of the prefectural councils raised before the Committee on Decentralization by the government ministers of interior, finance, and public works. A. N., Assemblée nationale, C 2866, *Commission de décentralisation*, séance du 7 juin 1872.

[85] *Journal officiel*, vol. 4, p. 564.   [86] *Ibid.*

litical preoccupation, whatever one says, seems to me to have completely dominated the law."[87]

Since left-wing republicans were the avowed enemies of clericalism, legitimists' hopes in education rested once more on the Center. Nothing, of course, could have been done without the Catholic Right-Center votes, but the Right-Center and Right combined needed votes in the Center for a majority. The Center's attitude toward Catholic education varied somewhat. There were devout Catholics like Henri Wallon, deputy from Nord, author of the famous Wallon amendment which broke the back of the monarchists by setting up the republican executive, who appreciated Catholic education out of religious conviction and free thinkers like Thiers who approached it as utilitarians. Because of their number and influence, the support of the utilitarians was crucial. They were prepared, provided that the state system was not compromised, to admit Catholic education in order to promote social stability by reinforcing religious belief among the people. Catholic legislation fared accordingly. In primary and secondary education, the Catholics suffered a clear setback. Jules Simon, Thiers' minister of public instruction, introduced a bill on primary education that embodied republican principles of free obligatory education in state schools and was unacceptable to Catholic conservatives. The Committee of Primary Instruction, presided over by Bishop Dupanloup, totally overhauled Simon's bill and reported a counterproject based on the Falloux law to the Chamber. This bill encountered the hostility of Thiers' government and became a victim of a legislative stalemate. The Committee of Primary Instruction refused to write a bill that was acceptable to the government, and the government rallied enough votes in the Center to defeat any project initiated by the committee. Consequently the Assembly passed no comprehensive reform legislation on primary and secondary education. In higher education, on the other hand, the Assembly passed a law in 1875 that permitted any private school, with three faculties, to call itself a university. But, on the important question of degree-granting privileges, the Center was not willing to give private institutions the rights of the state's. The law, a compromise, permitted students in private universities to have the option of taking their examination before a state jury or before a mixed jury, half the members of which could be drawn from state and the other half from private faculties. In 1873, moreover, the As-

[87] *Annales de l'Assemblée nationale*, vol. 14, p. 387.

sembly adopted another major piece of legislation affecting education that, in the spirit of the Falloux law, increased the non-
academic representation on the councils of public instruction and
once more made membership elective. Generals, industrialists,
merchants, and large landlords joined ecclesiastics, magistrates,
and general councillors, who were also landlords, that the Falloux
law had placed on the councils, to give the notables a greater voice
in educational policy.[88]

Legitimists were sorely disappointed with these results. Aside
from an obvious displeasure with the legislative deadlock over the
primary education bill, they were unhappy with the law on higher
education because it failed to give private universities the right
to confer degrees. The Nîmes lawyer Ferdinand Boyer had amended
the bill in order to allow private universities "concurrently with
the state . . . the right to deliver diplomas and to confer degrees,"
but the amendment had been defeated in committee.[89] If Legitimists had to placate supporters of state education by abandoning
parity between private and state faculties, still they had reason for
some satisfaction with the law. For the first time since the Revolution, Catholic universities had the right to exist and the authority,
if partial, to issue diplomas. The reformed academic councils in
which the "social authorities" now found themselves solidly entrenched weakened the control of academics over education. Even
the legislative stalemate in primary education had its positive side,
for, if the Catholics had failed, they had also stopped the republican attempt to expand the state system. Secondary education,
moreover, continued to operate under the regime set up by the Falloux law that, if not perfect, had fostered a rapid growth of en-
rollment in Catholic *collèges* accompanied by a net decrease in
students attending the state schools.[90]

Of all the major reforms, however, only that affecting child
labor gave complete satisfaction. In *La croix, les lys, et la peine
des hommes*, royalist Xavier Vallat praised the humane sentiments

[88] Hébert et Carnec, *La Loi Falloux*, p. 231.

[89] A. N., Assemblée nationale, C 3129, *Commission de la liberté de l'enseignement supérieur.* The quotation is taken from the Boyer amendment.

[90] Statistics of increased Catholic participation in primary and secondary
education are given in Hébert et Carnec, *La Loi Falloux*, p. 216. They
show that parochial schools (primary) grew from a total of 7,570 (796,917
students) in 1843 to 17,206 (1,610,674) in 1863 and that secondary Catholic schools gained nearly eleven thousand students between 1850 and 1854
compared with a net loss of two thousand in the state schools.

219

of the legitimist deputies of 1871—sentiments, he maintains, which stood in stark contrast to those exhibited by the parties of "material interests" in the Assembly's Center.[91] One cannot deny perhaps their sincere feeling for human suffering, but it must not be forgotten that their social conceptions shaped their humanitarian outlook. In the case of child labor, legitimists had been concerned with the physical welfare of the child not his education for social advancement. This was a republican idea. Therefore they favored a less stringent law than other deputies who were preoccupied with education. It is true that one of the more liberal amendments to the child labor bill, which would have forbidden any work before age twelve, was presented by a legitimist, Vétillart. But only nine legitimists voted for Vétillart's measure that failed 380 to 211.[92] The bulk of the amendment's support came from the Left. Moreover, if voting behavior is a proper yardstick for judgment, it would appear that most of the Center deputies were no less "humane" than the rightists because the bill that eventually passed with the overwhelming support of the legitimists also received the votes of most of the Center, especially the Catholic Right-Center. The law, which ended the worst abuses of child labor in France, forbade work up to age ten, limited the working day for those between ages ten and thirteen (ten and fourteen for girls) to six hours "divided by a rest period," and forbade night work for girls. As far as legitimists were concerned, the law had been supported partly to render elemental justice to the terribly wronged and as proof that the "directing classes" were meeting their social responsibilities. From the vantage point of the workers, however, it is doubtful if this gesture aroused much gratitude. Besides, the law regulated large factories and most Frenchmen worked in small shops. To the extent that legitimists expected the bill to promote harmony within the social order, therefore, it, despite the fact that they got the bill they wanted, certainly failed to achieve this objective.

Thus the legislative effort to establish the institutional and social framework in which the restoration of the "moral order" could occur foundered. After four years legitimists found themselves not only unable to restore the monarchy but also engaged in a last ditch losing battle in the Assembly to prevent the establishment

[91] Xavier Vallat, *La croix, les lys, et la peine des hommes* (Paris, 1960), pp. 165–173.
[92] *Journal officiel*, vol. 15, p. 413.

of definitive republican institutions. There is no need to describe
the familiar story of the struggle over the constitutional laws of
1875. It is sufficient to say that the Center, with the support of
some deputies in the Right-Center, rallied to a conservative Republic. It was conservative because the Center wrote an undemo-
cratic constitution. Although they allowed the "people" a voice
when they created the popularly elected Chamber of Deputies, they
silenced it with an upper house (the Senate) dominated by the
rural notables and an executive (the President) elected for seven
years by a Parliament that, they thought, would be conservative
in character. It was a Republic because these laws provided the
institutional basis for the regime that had been proclaimed on the
fourth of September. Legitimists stood by helplessly while the
Assembly enacted the constitution. The only thing they could do
was to try to make the new institutions as conservative as possible.
Thus they had worked to set the voting age for the Chamber of
Deputies electorate at twenty-five only to see the republicans prevail again. Legitimists were less upset with the electorate for the
Senate that was based on an indirect suffrage weighted in favor of
rural areas, and relatively satisfied, from the point of view of order,
to see the monarchist Marshal MacMahon in the presidency. But
there was no joy, only despair born out of the knowledge that they
had to face an unknown future, for, its work completed, the National Assembly, which had been their platform, passed into history.

When reviewing the legislative performance of legitimists in the
National Assembly, it is worth asking what caused the failures.
Often, of course, they resulted from sheer lack of numbers. If the
legitimists had possessed sufficient strength, they would have been
able not only to have defeated the republican laws but also to have
restored the monarchy, although it is uncertain how long a monarchy installed by the Assembly would have lasted. With sufficient
votes, they could have passed educational reforms that would
have at least given the Church schools parity with those of the
state. Greater representation, moreover, would have permitted
them, after fixing the municipal electorate, to have written a comprehensive law on municipal government allowing considerable
municipal autonomy, and the reform of the magistracy that most
of them envisioned could have succeeded with enough votes to
make the magistracy self-recruiting. However, the deep divisions
that appeared in their ranks and the hesitancy with which they

221

approached so many of their own reforms indicate that their program failed for much more complicated reasons than insufficient numbers.

The rising tide of democracy combined with a fear of popular insurrection had thwarted their attempt to organize a regionally trained army in place of the city-trained barracks army. Indeed, legitimists had been hard put to find any large groups in French society in which they could place their trust in the program of decentralization. Even if they found them, moreover, they had difficulties devising legislation that would give them local control. The case of the municipal councils' electorate, where legitimists discovered that the idea of limiting the vote to property holders was so unpopular in a nation accustomed to universal suffrage that it could not be seriously entertained, is a good example. An even better one is the untenable situation that arose when they thought of dividing Lyons into a cluster of little communal governments dominated by the propertied classes. The idea emerged as an alternative either to the prefect's running the city or divesting authority in a single communal administration. The legitimists disliked the bureaucratic smell of the first and they dreaded the revolutionary possibilities of the second, for, if the radicals could capture city hall by a *coup d'état*, and it was located in the poor section of the city, they could paralyze city government. Aside from the objections to the oligarchical character of their counter-project, it also ran into a technical roadblock that the legitimists simply could not overcome: the complicated needs of an urban area—finance, street systems, sewage, public welfare, police—required the presence of a central coordinating authority. Lyons could not be transformed into many little "villages," so the legitimists ended by accepting the prefect's jurisdiction.[93]

Proposals promoting prosperity in the countryside in order to stop the rural exodus had also posed all sorts of problems. Those that would have enlisted state aid would have increased the influence of the bureaucracy at the expense of the local notables, thereby canceling any social advantages that might have accrued if the policy had worked. Efforts to foster this economic well-being by private initiative ran afoul of their fears that freedom of association would release the energies of the "subversives." As it turned out, improvement in agriculture could not be seriously entertained

[93] A. N., Assemblée nationale, C 2866, *Commission de décentralisation*, séance du 11 fév. 1873.

without running the risk of subversion, for the avenues along which new economic ideas penetrated the village—press, education, railroad—were the same for the penetration of "subversive" sentiments. An illiterate peasantry would remain submerged in economic and social routine; a literate one might develop radical political ideas without the benefit of improved agriculture, but against the political background of the time, it would probably not imbibe new economic ideas without changing its political outlook.[94] Nor could the legitimists rely on society spontaneously to organize the population working in industry as they envisioned. Too few industrialists and workers understood or appreciated their corporate conceptions.

In sum, all the votes in the National Assembly could not change social realities. The legitimist legislation had been designed to use society for its own "regeneration," but French society in the third quarter of the nineteenth century was too "demoralized" to be utilized for their purposes. Many of the legitimists came to realize this, and they fell back on the state as an instrument to preserve not only order but also the social order itself. This policy contradicted their social philosophy, but it was necessary since their own solutions proved unworkable. The National Assembly did not represent public opinion in France because it was not a microcosm of French society. It did not represent legitimist France either, but it stood as a fortress against most of the nation, a fortress in which the legitimists had a considerable place. When it disappeared the legitimists were forced to leave its shelter and go out once again into society and find their political way, unprotected from the forces that along with those in the Assembly, had made shambles of their reformation.

[94] This does not mean that economically backward areas could not have a peasantry imbued with a mentality of equality or that a breakdown in the mentality of submission to the upper classes necessarily brings agricultural innovations. It means that the avenues for the penetration of new economic ideas into an area where the peasantry is submissive—press, speech, railroads—were the same for the penetration of egalitarian ideas during the Third Republic.

Chapter Six

THE ELECTORAL DEFEAT OF 1876

In *La fin des notables* Daniel Halévy selected January 9, 1879, the date of the second senatorial electoral contest provided for by the Constitution of 1875, as the moment that marked the final passage from the old France to the new.[1] Then the republicans, after having captured a majority of the municipal councils, which chose most of the senatorial electors, won control of the Senate. With the municipalities, the Senate, and the Chamber of Deputies in republican hands, the last refuge of the "moral order" remained the person of Marshal MacMahon, but less than a month after the senatorial elections the Marshal resigned rather than continue in impotent isolation and the parliament elected the moderate republican, Jules Grévy, President of the Republic. Eight years after their triumph, therefore, almost all the notables who had graced the Right in the National Assembly were removed from the central stage of French political life, and none more than the loyal supporters of the old monarchy.

Yet, if 1879 marked the final passage, it had not been an abrupt one. Eighteen seventy-nine was the culmination of a process that had begun much earlier, one in which the elections of 1876 played a pivotal part and which had really begun well before 1876. In 1871 Baron Chaurand noted that his election to the National Assembly had cost 200 francs.[2] In January 1872 Charles Chesnelong, who had been returned in a by-election, informed his wife (January 26, 1872) that his election had cost 6,000 francs.[3] This thirtyfold cost differential illustrates the vast transformation that occurred in electoral politics in these months. Baron Chaurand had not campaigned and had only bought a few ballots. Chesnelong had campaigned, rented halls, bought electoral circulars and ballots, posted bills, and paid the electoral agents who did his bidding. Whereas in February 1871 politics had been momentarily

---

[1] Daniel Halévy, *La fin des notables* (Paris, 1930), p. 9.
[2] "Agenda," *Chaurand MSS.*
[3] Ltr., Chesnelong to his wife, Jan. 27, 1872, *Chesnelong MSS.*

confined to building a coalition among the notables, thereafter, it entailed the increasingly expensive procedure of wooing votes in the electoral market place. There had been campaigning before, particularly at the end of the Empire, but with the freedom ushered in by the Republic, it proceeded at an intensity never previously experienced. Chesnelong had been successful under these conditions, but his victory counted among only a half dozen registered by legitimists in the numerous by-elections between 1871 and 1875.[4] Nor had the Orleanists fared better. The real victors had been the defeated of February 8. Just five months after their loss, the republicans took 99 out of 114 seats in the special by-elections of June 2, 1871 and many of these went to the Gambetta republicans.[5] Thereafter they continued to win, so that by the end of 1875, republicans had acquired more than 150 additional seats in the Chamber. Gambetta rose once again to national prominence, and, with his support and that of his colleagues, the republican constitution won its narrow victory in the National Assembly. At the same time universal suffrage permitted Bonapartists to reemerge from the political wilderness to which they had been consigned by the debacle of 1870. Their successes never equaled those of the republicans; nonetheless they affirmed that Bonapartists had once again become a major force in French politics. Still these had been by-elections. Although they weakened the royalists, they did not deprive those sitting in the National Assembly of their mandates. The elections of 1876, on the other hand, were much more significant because they were general elections that determined who controlled the legislature and through it the executive of the new regime. In the senatorial contest the conservatives won, but the republicans gained a sizeable majority in the democratically elected Chamber of Deputies. The results of 1876, moreover, set the stage for the famous *seize mai* crisis of the following year. Faced with the hostility of the Chamber of Deputies, Marshal MacMahon, prompted by Prime Minister Duc de Broglie and supported by the conservative majority in the Senate, attempted to remake the Chamber of Deputies in a conservative fashion. Although the government used every instrument of electoral pressure at its command to insure a conservative triumph, it failed. The republican victory of 1877

[4] Jacques Gouault, *Comment la France est devenue républicaine* (Paris, 1954). Gouault carefully traces the progress of both republicans and Bonapartists in the by-elections.

[5] Gouault, *Comment la France est devenue républicaine*, p. 116.

broke the conservative's back; the *seize mai* crisis led directly to the denouement of 1879. Yet there would have been no *seize mai* crisis had the republicans lost the Chamber of Deputies in 1876. Indeed the elections of 1877 were largely a rerun of the earlier election, and the outcome only verified the previous decision. The real test had come for social conservatives immediately after the dissolution of the National Assembly.

Since the results of the elections of 1876 are well known there is no need, in a study about legitimists, to discuss them as a whole. However, it is important to look closely at these elections because they end the specific history of the legitimist deputies of 1871 and determine the political fate of legitimism in general. Although in 1848 legitimists had not done particularly well in the elections to the Constituent Assembly, a year later they came into the Legislative Assembly in impressive numbers. Universal suffrage under the "tutelage" of the imperial bureaucracy had not favored them either, but in 1871 they had triumphed. After 1876, however, there was no subsequent victory for the legitimists as there had been after defeats in the past. These elections, therefore, formed the historical arena in which the outcome of the socio-political process that destroyed what remained of the legitimist notables' power became manifest, and they reveal once again their principal sociopolitical preoccupation.

Before dealing with the elections proper it is important, because some historical confusion surrounds the question, to discuss the legitimist attitude toward the contests. Probably the greatest source of difficulty in clarifying this attitude has arisen because of the practice of what is called the *politique du pire*. *Politique du pire* is an act whereby an extreme group unites with its political opposite in order to defeat moderates, thereby, however, hurting its cause more in the long run by shortsightedly helping its most implacable enemies at the expense of those who are much closer to it in political philosophy and social outlook. Two famous incidents of *politique du pire* were discussed in an earlier chapter in connection with the problem of identifying the legitimist deputies and they require further comment in this electoral context.[6] The first happened in May 1874 when the *Chevau-légers* brought down the Broglie government, which they suspected of drafting an Orleanist constitution. The second occurred in December 1875 during the election of lifetime members to the new Senate when legitimists helped

[6] See pp. 37–40.

elect the republican list. These two events are significant because they illustrate the intense hatred of the legitimists toward the Orleanists whom they blamed for having robbed them and France of the monarchy. But the fact that legitimists indulged in such political behavior raises some serious questions about their concern with preserving the social hierarchy. How could legitimists engage in maneuvers that could only work to the advantage of republicans? Could it be that they were blind to the consequences of their actions?

It has been stressed throughout this study not only that the social conceptions of the Right and much of the Right-Center were similar but also that the extreme and moderate Right did not differ in this respect. The legislative behavior of the *Chevau-légers* during the struggle for social-economic reform proves this contention. Although divisions occurred among legitimists, they did not reflect any split between the *Chevau-légers* and the moderate Right. Members of both groups were supporters and opponents of the regionally trained army, of the Napoleonic magistracy, of greater freedom of association for trade unions, of a more liberal child labor law, of extensive decentralization. Moreover, if these differences cannot be used to distinguish the extreme from the moderate Right, they cannot in truth be cited as the basis of any fundamental disagreement about society since they were tactical disagreements about the best way to defend a social order in which all believed. For this reason an attack on the conservative coalition in power would be all the more detestable. Granted the dissidents thought that the restoration of the monarchy was essential to the preservation of the social order and hated the Orleanists for blocking it. However, if punishing the Orleanists for their perfidy in no way advanced the monarchical cause but politically weakened the social groups upon which a defense of the social order and even an eventual restoration of the monarchy depended, it was indefensible. Moreover, if the legitimists or an important group of them engaged in such activity, it would have constituted a radical switch in behavior from that of the men who, in February 1871, forgot dynastic convictions in order to build the victorious conservative coalition that they later would have so foolishly destroyed. But the question is only posed. What is the answer?

The answer was given to some extent earlier when analyzing the two examples of *politique du pire*. Fifty-two *Chevau-légers* abandoned the Right and brought down Broglie's government, and they were roundly condemned by legitimists as well as Orleanists for their action. But it is debatable just how significantly their act weakened the social order. Their efforts to stop Broglie's government from introducing constitutional laws only succeeded temporarily because the laws were later taken up and passed. Some argue that these *Chevau-légers* actually hastened the passage of the republican constitution because they sent disgusted Orleanists scurrying after a conservative republic. But this is a moot point since it is not at all certain that the Broglie government was not headed in that direction in the first place. In any event the damage done to conservatives was not that great since the National Assembly still existed after their vote, and any government that came into existence was responsible to it.

The accusation that the *Chevau-légers* undermined the social order in the affair of the lifetime senators is much more serious. The leader of the renegades, Ernest de La Rochette, was himself conscious of the implications of his actions. He claimed that, in voting for the republicans at the expense of the Orleanists, his group had not weakened the social order. "I affirm," he noted, "that the Left-Center is as socially conservative as the Right-Center, and that, in the Senate, they [the Left-Center] will be with our friends in the struggle against the allurements, unhappily too much to be feared, of the Revolution."[7] This was undoubtedly true in the sense that the moderate republicans elected would always cooperate with the Right to crush an insurrection. But it was not true in the sense that these republicans shared the Right-Center's conception of the "moral order." Besides, the Right-Center was not the only victim of the La Rochette group's politics. Legitimists carried on the rightist lists were defeated along with the deputies in the Right-Center. Indeed, on the eve of the crucial struggle for control of the Senate and the Chamber of Deputies, these legitimists had heedlessly given the initial advantage to the republicans, and in helping to consolidate the Republic, their action in the long run worked to the advantage of the radicals.

But how extensive was this revolt? Historians usually point out that the *Chevau-légers* or the extreme Right made the agreement that upset the Right's calculations, and one distinguished historian, Alfred Cobban, has even stated that "The legitimists so hated the Orleanists that they joined with the republicans to exclude them

---

[7] *La République libérale*, Jan. 1, 1876.

from the Senate. . . ."[8] A close scrutiny of the incident, however, shows that only eleven members of the extreme Right participated in the revolt and they can neither be considered the legitimists nor the extreme Right. Indeed most legitimists, including those in the extreme Right, although they might have understood the motives of the renegades, condemned their action on social grounds. This was the case when the *Réunion des Chevau-légers* expelled the La Rochette group, proclaiming that they ". . . formally rejected any idea of an alliance with those groups in the Assembly in which are found the most decided adversaries of the legitimate monarchy, the avowed enemies of the Church and the Christian social order."[9] The reception that the dissidents received from the legitimist deputies also was echoed in legitimist and Catholic circles throughout the country. At the height of the incident (when the vote was being taken in the Chamber) one of Baron Chaurand's political friends, the editor of a small legitimist newspaper in Rhône (*L'Echo de Fourvière*) wrote about his defection: "I have never questioned the purity of your intentions, but each day, on reading the anxiously awaited dispatches, I receive the most painful impression on seeing the letter g [*gauche*] beside your name. . . . For myself I cannot admit that one could vote for the declared enemies of religion and social order, whatever the reason."[10] A few days later, another friend reported the sharp reaction that his act aroused among his erstwhile supporters.

It will be a long time before you are forgiven. Later, I hope, people will understand your motives, but I fear it will not happen until very late. I regret it especially right now because the scandal of this affair makes it almost impossible for you to be a candidate for a seat in the Chamber of Deputies. If the elections took place much later, it is not sure whether you could run but I must tell you that today the clergy itself is hostile to you.[11]

What these men said in private others expressed in public. There is no need to cite the attitude of the moderate legitimist press on this score, which was everywhere hostile, but it is instructive to

[8] Alfred Cobban, *A History of Modern France, 1799–1945* (London, 1961), vol. II, p. 216.

[9] See the *Procès-verbal de la réunion des Chevaulégers, en date du 15 decembre 1875.*

[10] Ltr., Dec. 20, 1875, *Chaurand MSS.*

[11] Ltr., author unknown to Baron Chaurand, Dec. 24, 1875, *ibid.*

note that the intransigent legitimist press shared these sentiments. The staunch legitimist *Le Pas-de-Calais*, for example, lamented that La Rochette, who died a few days after this event, "had been able to err in the last act of his public life."[12] Another, *Le Messager de l'Allier*, went out of its way to dissociate the extreme Right from the La Rochette group. "Of 200 rightist deputies, of whom approximately 70 were on the extreme Right," it wrote, only "10 or 11 made the agreement which routed the Right-Center."[13] An occasional voice arose publicly in their defense. *L'Espérance du peuple*, which the La Rochette family owned in Nantes, tried to justify their action, but they were drowned in the general indignation that swept the legitimist community.

The point about both of these incidents is that they do not appreciably contradict the idea that the preservation of social order held a preeminent place in legitimist thinking. Because of this, moreover, they serve as a bridge to understanding the attitude that these royalists assumed toward the elections in 1876, but only a bridge since in themselves they offer insufficient evidence about the opinion of such a large and diverse community as that of the legitimists. A really thorough knowledge of this sentiment would require detailed regional if not local studies of the legitimist notables and their clientele during the elections, which are beyond the scope of this investigation. But one fairly accessible guide, the press, is of particular help. By 1876 the royalist press had developed markedly in the provinces. These newspapers could not have survived without important financial backing from the local notables and their very existence, therefore, permitted them to shape as well as reflect public opinion. Inasmuch as they published the *professions de foi* of candidates, discussed local as well as national issues, and advised their readers for whom to vote, they present the historian with a reasonably comprehensive picture of legitimist electoral attitudes in every region of France.

Not surprisingly the principal issue in the legitimist press was socioreligious. Often newspapers accused the republicans of attacking property. *L'Indépendance bretonne*, for example, stated that they advocated a "tax on wealth" that amounted to no less than "legal theft"; *L'Espérance du peuple* denounced them for promoting a graduated income tax, and *Le Publicateur* maintained that republicans wanted ". . . the state to control private prop-

[12] *Le Pas-de-Calais*, Jan. 21, 1876.
[13] *Le Messager de l'Allier*, Feb. 5, 1876.

230

erty."[14] Defense of property, however, received less emphasis than that of religion, probably because it was slightly absurd to accuse the tight-fisted bourgeois republicans, even anticlerical republicans, of such attitudes considering that they were the guardians of property rights. But they uniformly and repeatedly proclaimed, as did Albert de Mun in Brittany, that the fundamental issue was the preservation of the Catholic religion, and frequently they enlisted the support of the clergy, as did *Le Courrier du Lot*, which published a letter from a country priest who attacked a nonroyalist for his lack of devotion to "the cause of order and religion."[15] Republicans were frequently accused of being the natural enemy of the faith. *La Gazette de Nîmes* wrote: "It is absolutely impossible to be a true Catholic and a republican at the same time. . . . The Catholic republican will always be the 'Trojan horse' of radicalism."[16] Almost as often newspapers assailed the republicans as enemies of the family and posed themselves as its guardians. Thus property, religion, and the family composed the electoral liturgy of the royalist press, and as such it reflected their continuing and urgent concern with the mutually reinforcing complex of material and sociopsychological factors which were, in their opinion, the pillars of the social order.

But the fact that legitimist newspapers everywhere stressed these socioeconomic issues is not effective proof of their primacy in the election. What was needed, as in 1871, was a willingness to sacrifice royalist convictions in the interests of conservative solidarity, and here the picture is more complicated. In July 1875 the royalist Emile Keller, who had voted against all the constitutional laws, remarked in the National Assembly that "for his part he accepted the terrain of the constitution as the basis for defending all Christian and conservative forces and principles," and a few days later (July 19) he wrote his wife: "[o]ne must admit that we have a Republic and not wish, like doctrinaires, to dance indefinitely on a tight rope."[17] No doubt Keller was sincere in his pragmatism. He was

[14] *L'Indépendance bretonne*, Feb. 26, 1876; *L'Espérance du peuple*, Feb. 15, 1876; *Le Publicateur*, Feb. 20, 1876. For legitimists' attacks against the "republican" income tax also see *Le Conservateur de Lot, L'Union franc-comtoise, La Gazette de Languedoc*, and *La Gazette de Nîmes*.

[15] Feb. 12, 1876. For the Comte de Mun, see *L'Indépendant de l'Ouest*, Feb. 18, 1876.

[16] Feb. 20, 1876.

[17] Both quotations are given in Gustave Gautherot, *Emile Keller (1828–1909). Un demi-siècle de défense nationale et religieuse* (Paris, 1922), p. 26.

among the first of an increasing number of legitimists who, as it became an incontrovertible and permanent fact of political life, resigned themselves to operating within the republican framework. Acceptance of the Republic, however, did not mean that Keller had been converted to republicanism, unless it is robbed of any social and ideological content. He was just as adamantly an ultramontane Catholic, just as firmly attached to a hierarchical conception of a "moral order," and he would have welcomed the monarchy had its restoration been a possibility. Keller's attitude, moreover, was premature among legitimists. He had been converted to legitimism after 1870 and could abandon more easily, than legitimists of long standing, what to him was clearly a lost cause in order to concentrate on socioreligious problems. Yet if psychologically unprepared to abandon royalism, legitimists who had struggled to bring about a social-conservative fusion were not about to reverse themselves in an electoral situation. The moderate legitimists, therefore, deemphasized dynastic rivalries. Indeed in republican strongholds on occasion they declared an "allegiance" to a Republic. This happened in Ardennes, for example, where Gaston de Béthune addressed the senatorial electors in the perhaps purposely ambiguous terms: "I said in 1871 that I would loyally support a Republic that would insure France order, work, and prosperity. Today I will still support this Republic as loyally as before."[18] Even in royalist areas like the West moderate legitimists willingly ran as constitutional-conservatives. They argued, like Bernard-Dutreil and Gaulthier de Vaucenay in the Mayenne, that the best guarantee for a successful defense "of order and all the great religious and social principles (without which government is impossible)" was to identify with the constitution and Marshal MacMahon.[19] Such declarations served their purposes well because they permitted them to avoid accepting the Republic while evading the pitfall of an outright royalist declaration which could frustrate efforts to form a broad social conservative fusion.[20]

But if the moderate legitimists characteristically made these concessions, what of the intransigents who had consciously distinguished themselves from the moderates in terms of purity of

[18] *Le Nord-Est*, Jan. 26, 1876.

[19] *Le Journal de Château-Gontier*, Jan. 23, 1876.

[20] The constitutional laws explicitly stated that the constitution would be open for revision at a future date and thus royalists could claim to support the constitution with the intention of changing it.

royalist convictions? The press shows that the bitterness which the extreme Right had felt toward the Orleanists and moderate legitimists in the National Assembly spilled over into the elections. Some newspapers preferred to wage- a vendetta against the "traitors" in the Right and Right-Center rather than unite against the republicans. In Gard, for example, the royalist newspaper *L'Extrême-Droite* refused to support Louis-Numa Baragnon because, while a cabinet minister, he defended Marshal MacMahon against the attacks of the ultras; in Puy-de-Dôme, *La Gazette d'Auvergne* denounced Charles de Lacombe's senatorial candidacy for similar reasons, and in Allier, *Le Messager de l'Allier* refused to accept the candidacy of Eugène de Montlaur because of his supposedly "lukewarm royalist attitude."[21] Some intransigent legitimists in Morbihan would not support the fusionist legitimist Audren de Kerdrel for the Senate, and in Ille-et-Vilaine, they ran a candidate of their own against the moderate Rightist La Borderie.[22] But, although numerous examples of this sort exist, their importance should not be magnified. Ultra attacks on candidates did not mean that they refused to cooperate with nonlegitimists but only that they had a grudge against a specific man. Thus *L'Espérance du peuple*, which had applauded La Rochette's vote against the Orleanist deputies, bowed to the exigencies of coalition politics in 1876. It backed an electoral fusion in the department of Loire-Inférieure because, as it remarked of one of "its" candidates, "his political ideas are not ours but he is a good merchant and a good Catholic while his opponent is a freethinker."[23] Numerous incidents of former *Chevau-légers* cooperating with liberal monarchists in the interests of conservative fusion, moreover, are cited in the press. La Rochefoucauld-Bisaccia, for example, refrained from running for the Senate in Sarthe because he felt the coalition's appeal would be enhanced if a liberal monarchist were nominated in his place. La Bassétière's withdrawal from the senatorial race in Vendée was similarly motivated and he threw his support to a Catholic (Vandier) who had voted for the constitutional laws.[24] If prepared

[21] See the attack on Baragnon in the Feb. 13 issue of *L'Extrême-droite*. *La Gazette d'Auvergne,* Jan. 29, 1876. *Le Messager de l'Allier,* Jan. 15, 1876.

[22] On La Borderie's feud see *La Gazette de Bretagne,* Feb. 9, 1876. On Audren de Kerdrel, see *Le Journal de Rennes.*

[23] Feb. 12, 1876.

[24] For La Rochefoucauld-Bisaccia, see his letter published in *L'Union de la Sarthe,* Jan. 30, 1876. For La Bassétière, see *L'Indépendant de l'Ouest,*

to support nonlegitimists, these *Chevau-légers* usually clearly stated their own royalist convictions, but on occasion even they avoided the subject of regime either by ignoring constitutional questions altogether, as did Quinsonas in Isère, or by letting themselves be credited, as did Abbadie de Barrau in Gers, with "accepting the constitution of February 25, 1875, subject to revisions authorized by this law."[25] On the other hand, there are examples of *Chevau-légers*, who persisted in playing the *politique du pire*, being politically ostracized. Baron Chaurand, as his correspondent predicted, was so unpopular in Ardèche that he could not run for the Senate or the Chamber of Deputies; Félix du Temple, another of the La Rochette group, disappeared into Morbihan during the elections without the slightest political ripple, so completely ignored was he by the royalists. The intransigents were so effectively isolated in most departments that, as one unhappy ultra newspaper in Eure-et-Loir admitted, they were "politically alien to the commencing electoral contest, not having counted for anything in the selection of candidates."[26] A survey of the press discloses, therefore, that local legitimist groups who had sympathized with the *Chevau-légers* were not much less prepared than the moderates to wreck conservative chances by fighting with other Catholic social conservatives during the elections.

If legitimists sought to place social conservative solidarity above dynastic questions, the success of this policy depended on finding nonlegitimist notables who would cooperate with them. In 1871 the propertied classes had coalesced into an antiwar propeace party, but in the interim the situation had drastically changed. The war had ended, the foreign indemnity been paid, the country freed from foreign occupation, the Commune crushed, and the revolutionary Left effectively silenced. By 1875 no war and no threat of insurrection existed and conservative fusion on the basis of fear of the red specter was impossible. Legitimists of course believed that insurrections were only manifestations of a mentality of insubordination, but this idea was something quite different as an appeal to

---

Feb. 15, 1876. In Hérault the ultra-legitimist Rodez-Benavent not only ran on a coalition list for the Senate but signed a pledge that he would, if elected, resign unless all the candidates on the fusion were elected. In this way he warned all legitimists to vote for the fusionists and not to ignore the Orleanists on the list. See *L'Union nationale*, Jan. 22, 1876.

[25] *Le Conservateur et le Gers réunis*, Jan. 20, 1876.

[26] Feb. 6, 1876.

counterrevolutionary unity from that which sprang from actual chaos. It meant that a revolutionary mentality consisted of any questioning of traditional values and authority, and, translated into social terms, it signified respect for the notables who had been running France since 1815. The legitimists needed to find electoral allies who shared this sentiment, and their search was complicated by the fact that they had to seek them not only among the men with whom they had run in 1871 but among the regenerated Bonapartist party.

What would be the response of their *co-listiers* of 1871 to a new call for defense of the social order? The answer to this question lay in the transformation that had occurred in the republican party since its defeat. Chastened by this experience and fearful that the Assembly might restore the monarchy, the radicals had learned to speak the language of moderation. This was the secret to their victories in the 1871 by-elections and the stance which they adopted in the general elections of 1876. In effect a new republican party, under the leadership of Adolphe Thiers, emerged. To the former radicals, it promised an orderly progression toward the democratic Republic, to moderates it offered peace and order under a constitution that set aside the perils of radicalism. The republican press constantly reiterated the conservative basis of this new unity. "All conservatives, all men of order," *Le Drapeau national* proclaimed, "must rally to a liberal and conservative Republic."[27] "To vote for moderate Republicans," *L'Impartial lorientais* wrote, "is to vote for order, security, and stability."[28] Even Gambetta donned the conservative mantle. "Is there a conflict over questions of property, of conscience, of public order, of family?" he asked.

> Not one of these necessary principles has been questioned. . . . One is a conservative when one wants a society without privileges such as the Civil Code organized. . . . One is a conservative when he wants the institution of the family as it was formed after the abolition of *majorat, substitutions*, and primogeniture.[29]

In their attacks on the legitimists, they stressed the dangers of a reactionary upheaval. *L'Indépendant des Basses-Pyrénées*, for example, warned the peasants that the followers of Henri V planned

[27] Feb. 20, 1876.   [28] Feb. 20, 1876.
[29] Quoted in *La Revue de l'Yonne*, Jan. 27, 1876.

to restore feudalism.[30] *L'Indicateur* (Vendée) cautioned the voters that the return of Henri V would mean new privileges similar to those that existed before 1789, the elimination of which would require another revolution.[31] A conjunction of international events enabled republicans to label their opponents as men of disorder and warmongers. The elections coincided with Bismarck's *Kulturkampf* and a civil war in Spain caused by the Carlist pretender's attempt to seize the throne. French royalists sided with the Spanish Carlists, and French Catholics supported the Church against Bismarck. Catholics were also up in arms against the new Italian kingdom for keeping the Pope a "prisoner" in the Vatican. Republicans charged, therefore, that a Catholic-royalist electoral victory would mean war with Spain, Germany, and Italy plus a constitutional crisis at home and the possibility of civil war. An imperialist victory, they alleged, would bring a renewal of the Bonapartist conflict with Prussia.

Republicans who had participated in the peace coalition of 1871 easily broke with their former electoral allies and entered this republican coalition, and they were accompanied by former Orleanists like the cognac distiller Charles Martell about whom a local newspaper *Le Journal de Château-Gontier* wrote during the election: "Previously a constitutional monarchist, he became a conservative republican because, for him, the Republic is the only possible government today."[32] To these men the emergence of a middle-class democracy, which defended property, was acceptable if not ardently desired. But the bulk of the Right-Center did not agree. They accepted the constitution of 1875 as the framework of government, but they did not want to share power with the anticlerical, egalitarian republicans. These were the same men who had worked with the legitimist deputies in the Assembly to protect the moral order, and they carried this cooperation over into the elections. For them it was not just a question of order but of preserving property, the family, and religion as the basis of the social order. Thus the electoral coalition of 1871 dissolved, not at the point that separated the Right-Center from the legitimists but where the moderate republicans and a number of republican converts from the Left and Right-Center decided to throw in their lot with the Republic of Monsieur Thiers. Men who had been elected to the National Assembly on the same lists were in opposite camps in 1876 and some-

[30] Feb. 16, 1876.   [31] Feb. 20, 1876.   [32] Jan. 23, 1876.

times directly opposed each other in an election. This happened in Doubs, Ardèche, Nièvre, Saône-et-Loire, Seine-Inférieure, Ardennes, Loire-Inférieure, and Eure-et-Loir in senatorial elections and even in a few contests for seats in the Chamber of Deputies where the smallness of the electoral district, which was also a single-member constituency, decreased the possibility of direct confrontations. The loss of the Center and part of the Right-Center sensibly reduced the scope of the conservative electoral fusion, but it still contained most of the Orleanists, the moderate legitimists, and the *Chevau-légers.*

The extent to which Bonapartists entered into this monarchist coalition varied according to the complicated character of Bonapartism itself. The Second Empire had been run by an authoritarian-bureaucratic elite in its own interest and in that of rich landlords, merchants, and industrialists. Consequently, the domination of the notables economically and socially had been perpetuated but only by radical means. In effect, Bonapartists subscribed to the doctrine of *appel au peuple,* "the most subversive and most revolutionary," *L'Espérance du peuple* observed, "of modern times."[33] Like the radicals the Bonapartists sought to root their power in the masses, and they frequently adopted a revolutionary point of view. "With the white flag," the editor of the Bonapartist newspaper *L'Appel au peuple* warned the peasants in Gers, "you have the return of the old privileges; you have the suppression of universal suffrage; you will go back to the epoch when the very rich and very noble alone had the right to participate in public affairs, in a word, had alone the right to vote."[34] But the simple juxtaposition of radical means to conservative ends does not do justice to the complexities of Bonapartism. The appeal to the masses placed it in its relations with the community on quite a different footing than that of either legitimism or Orleanism. Whereas the monarchists expected the masses to respect their social superiors, some Bonapartists at least were back-slapping ward politicians who had acquired an intimate knowledge of the people. Their positive reaction to social mobility based on talent or merit clearly distinguished them from the rank conscious oligarchic outlook fashionable among the monarchists. Yet it is just as clear that many Bonapartists were close to their monarchist colleagues in political behavior and social attitudes since they stressed the importance of

[33] Jan. 8, 1876.   [34] Feb. 20, 1876.

237

family, religion, and property as the foundation of society and the political process as one of passive respect toward the social authorities. These differences plus the tactical practicalities of local politics produced an electoral situation of considerable confusion in respect to Bonapartist and monarchist electoral cooperation.

In some departments the Bonapartists, legitimists, and liberal monarchists fused their efforts. For example, in Gironde the conservatives worked out an agreement whereby no monarchist or Bonapartist would oppose each other in an electoral district and all would support the lone conservative candidate selected. The Bonapartist *Le Journal de Bordeaux* campaigned almost as hard for the two non-Bonapartists running for the Chamber of Deputies in the department as it did for the Bonapartists. Of one, the *Chevau-léger* Carayon-Latour, it wrote: "Between a revolutionary candidate and the honorable M. de Carayon-Latour, in whom the great traditions of honor, principle, of patriotism and faith are incarnate, hesitation is not possible. Bonapartists who do not vote for him will perform an act of indiscipline and of detestable politics."[35] The principal legitimist newspaper in the department *La Guienne* reciprocated by supporting the Bonapartists in districts where they were the conservative candidates, explaining its action to its readers with the pragmatic observation, "We are not naive enough to play the republican game by fighting Bonapartists."[36] The press gave the same excuse in Rhône, Isère, Somme, Vienne, and Deux-Sèvres, where similar fusionist arrangements were made. The Bonapartist *Le Journal de la Vienne et des Deux-Sèvres* emphasized the social conservative character of both legitimism and Bonapartism; the legitimist *La Décentralisation* (Rhône) justified its support of the Bonapartist Terne by asserting that he was less an intransigent Bonapartist than a good Catholic; the royalist *L'Echo de la Somme* gave the same reason for backing the Bonapartist Baron de Fourment; and *Le Courrier des Alpes* explained the fusion with the comment that Orleanists, legitimists and Bonapartists might be politically divided but "all, at least, are in favor of stopping not only social revolution but premature reform."[37] The tendency to fuse these efforts was pronounced where Republicans were strongest but the existence of fusions in a traditionally monarchist department like Deux-Sèvres and a Bonapartist stronghold like Gironde proves that these were not acts of desperation.

In other departments, by contrast, Bonapartists and monarchists

[35] Feb. 17, 1876.   [36] Feb. 15, 1876.   [37] Jan. 18, 1876.

were irreconcilable enemies. Sometimes they attacked each other in the most scurrilous personal invective. The royalist newspaper *Le Conservateur et le Gers réunis*, for example, which accused the Cassagnacs, a well-known and fervent Bonapartist family, of preaching "the people's rights to wealth which is pure socialism," inveighed against "these two men, father and son, who presume to subject the department of Gers to their doctrines, their complots, and their low intrigues."[38] In their newspaper *L'Appel au peuple*, the Cassagnacs responded in kind. In these instances the press reactions illustrate the monarchists' revulsion against Bonapartist mass action politics. *Le Courrier des campagnes* (Morbihan) criticized the Bonapartist Cadoret for cheap demagogic tricks like distributing photographs of the Prince Imperial to widows and children.[39] *Le Conservateur et le Gers réunis* attacked a Bonapartist, who was obviously setting up drinks at the local bars, for making "popularity a question of the cabaret and universal suffrage a drinking machine."[40] In Maine-et-Loire the legitimist *Le Journal de Maine-et-Loire* characterized the campaign of Janvier de la Motte, son of a popular Imperial prefect, as "a Homeric combat conducted by the apostle of campaigning by tipplers, tips, cabarets, photographs and other electoral concoctions."[41]

The Bonapartist factor in 1876, therefore, could hinder or aid monarchist electoral chances. For conservatives interested in defeating republicans, Bonapartist help could be a blessing, even when this aid was accepted less than enthusiastically. Thus in Nièvre the legitimist newspaper *Le Conservateur de la Nièvre* could disclaim any cooperation with Bonapartists but could benefit from the Bonapartist fusionist ticket which listed a legitimist among their candidates. As a republican newspaper noted after their defeat, "no doubt the Bonapartists had the skill to take M. de Bouillé for a candidate but M. de Bouillé had the skill or the talent of letting himself be taken."[42] Even when reluctant, then, Bonapartist and monarchist communities could work together against a common foe. Incidents of noncooperation, although they occurred, were rare. Usually they kept their integrity vis-à-vis each other in the first electoral campaign only to form a united front against Republicans in case of run-off elections. Since run-offs occurred frequently, they

---

[38] The first quotation is from the Feb. 17 issue and the second from the Jan. 22 issue.

[39] Feb. 20, 1876.   [40] Feb. 12, 1876.   [41] Feb. 14, 1876.

[42] *La République*, Feb. 3, 1876.

were very useful to each other. Nevertheless too great a gulf existed between Bonapartists and monarchists for effective electoral fusion. Every gain in Bonapartist strength hurt republicans, but it did not help the monarchists, especially in departments located in the Southwest where the Bonapartist notables wiped out the monarchists as the dominant conservative party. The legitimist-Orleanist electoral fusion, therefore, was the core of the conservative coalition. It was, however, when compared with the peace coalition of 1871, weakened by defections to the Left and menaced as well as aided by revived Bonapartism.

Although senatorial elections took place before those to the Chamber of Deputies, the results of the latter will be dealt with first because they are more significant. In 1871 elections were conducted by *scrutin de liste*. Conservatives did not like list-balloting because they believed it lent itself to ideological issues whereas they preferred local issues and the prestige of the candidate in the community to weigh most heavily in elections. Therefore, if they failed to limit suffrage, the conservatives in the Assembly did manage to arrange elections to the Chamber of Deputies in single-member constituencies, and the Legitimists had voted with the majority on the issue. Although they had no illusions about winning in the cities, they had not lost confidence in the peasantry. This confidence was relative, of course, since legitimists realized that they were doomed unless they could stop or reverse the social process that was dissolving the social order in the countryside. Their legislative reforms had failed but in the short run most expected the loyalty of the rural masses to resist "demagoguery," hoping in the meantime that something would occur that might save them. Yet there was plenty of evidence that this confidence in the peasantry had been misplaced even in the short run. In 1870 a national telegraph and railroad network existed. After that date the press, using wire services and reprints from Parisian newspapers, flourished in the provinces; indeed this proliferation of local and departmental newspapers coincided with the founding of the Republic. With the accelerated circulation of men and ideas that these developments permitted, the dynamics of social interaction of which the Legitimists had been so aware led to a more rapid politicization of the rural masses than they had anticipated.

The process of politicization had begun to bear fruit in the by-elections. Like the monarchists, the republicans realized that the elections would be decided in the countryside. Big city and rural

240

republicans, therefore, carried out a concerted campaign to bring the maximum electoral persuasion to bear on the peasantry. Electoral agents flooded rural areas with newspapers, pamphlets, photographs of republican leaders, posters, ballots, and other forms of campaign literature. Nationally prominent republicans toured electoral districts reassuring the electorate in towns and villages about the stability of the Republic and the great hope it held for a better life for all Frenchmen. Candidates systematically worked their districts, addressed crowds in every hamlet, organized local electoral committees to see to it that efforts did not lessen after they pushed on to other meetings, and returned repeatedly to make sure that these efforts had not failed. These were the techniques that republicans had used so successfully in the by-elections and which they now intensified on a national scale.

Legitimists, who had protested against the evil influences of the city, reacted vehemently to the infiltration of the republicans into what they considered to be their domain. "We understand from various sources," *Le Journal de Maine-et-Loire* commented "that shameful agents of certain radical committees are scouring our countryside and deceiving our peasants."[43] Do not listen, *L'Abeille de la Creuse* warned the peasantry, to "the traveling salesmen for the Republic which the urban committees send you."[44] The sheer energy republicans expended impressed the monarchists so much that, on occasion, they could not, even while condemning them, avoid expressing their admiration. "He has worked without respite and without truce," the ultralegitimist *La Vraie France* noted about one republican candidate in the Nord,

> with an indefatigable ardor, to which his adversaries must render justice. He has unceasingly followed the same path, knocking on every door, speaking, writing, agitating, forcing all the district to take notice of him, canvassing it (the district) over and over again, and organizing it, canton by canton, commune by commune, with the hand of a master.[45]

But this very praise posed the problem. Legitimists could not just lament republican activity (or eulogize it), they had to call on their own resources to counteract it.

At the beginning of the campaign, Louis Monjaret de Kerjégu wrote an article, which was published in many conservative news-

[43] Feb. 17, 1876.   [44] Jan. 26, 1876.   [45] Feb. 23, 1876.

241

papers, calling on all landlords to take a direct interest in the elections.

> It is urgent for the *propriétaire* to return and live on his properties in order to counteract the fatal influences which assault the country worker from every side. . . . Leave everything to place yourself by the side of your tenants for the purpose of enlightening, supporting and directing them during the six weeks' electoral period.[46]

With his appeal the legitimist was not breaking precedent, for he was relying on the traditional pressures of the social hierarchy to keep the peasants in line. But under the circumstances, the presence of the notable in the village would be inadequate to the task. The notables were temperamentally incapable of acting like the republican candidates or their clientele in a universal suffrage situation. They could try to counter the ideological content of republicanism with appeals to the sanctity of the family, property, and the Church. However, they could not reach the voters from the lofty place they held in society. They found the process of charming, coaxing, or even bribing them personally distasteful. They could not meet the voters on their own ground: the cabaret. Indeed some of the legitimists never realized the necessity of so doing. In Eure-et-Loir, for example, one royalist candidate proclaimed that the "mayors, *curés*, school teachers (and others) had received his electoral circulars. To do more would constitute an impertinence. God will execute his will regardless of the bartering and hawking."[47] Neither the candidates nor the supporters drawn from their social milieu, therefore, proved able to cope with the challenge of universal suffrage even when living on their properties, and it is by no means certain that all of them heeded Monjaret de Kerjégu's advice and returned to their estates.

It is an admission of their basic helplessness, then, that the monarchists had to rely on others to do their electioneering. One of the most influential if traditional resources was the clergy. Opinion within the Church was not uniform about the elections. Some clerics clearly did not think that the republican Catholic was the "Trojan horse" of radicalism; some were themselves obviously republicans. Others who were uneasy about the possible detrimental consequences that a republican, especially a radical republican

[46] *L'Impartial du Finistère*, Jan. 14, 1876.
[47] *Le Journal de Chartres*, Feb. 20, 1876.

victory, would have on the Church, nonetheless feared the repercussions of getting directly involved in partisan politics. This was true of many bishops who restricted their electoral remarks officially to rather vague statements about the need to elect "good Christians." But, unofficially, members of the hierarchy generally sided with the monarchist coalition and occasionally boldly asserted their right to intervene vigorously in electoral affairs. *L'Echo religieux*, a semiofficial spokesman for the clergy in the Southwest, stated:

> The priest is a citizen; therefore he has a right to be occupied with politics like any other citizen. Does it bother you, good people of our countryside, if your *curé* gives you good advice? Does not your *curé* have as much right to speak to you of elections as, for example, *Messieurs* the mayors, *Messieurs* the school teachers, *Messieurs* whomever, or *Messieurs* the cabaret owners?[48]

Usually, when the *curé* intervened, his entry was not trumpeted in the monarchist press since undue clerical pressure could be cited as sufficient grounds to annul an election (unfair electoral practices). Most public references to the clergy's involvement did not appear, therefore, in monarchist newspapers, but the republican press often protested about unwarranted clerical pressure on the voters. Moreover affidavits appended to the official electoral results registered widespread complaint by republican candidates or republican voters against the clergy.[49] These sources must be treated circumspectly because of their obvious bias, but they do clearly suggest that the clergy worked energetically on behalf of monarchist candidates. They passed out their electoral literature to the voters, made partisan electoral appeals from the pulpit, and often distributed the conservative candidate's ballots to the congregation whom they led directly from mass (elections were held on Sunday) to the polls. The lower clergy engaged in the kind of grass roots electioneering that the notables could not do themselves.

The second group on which the legitimist-Orleanist coalition depended was state officials. The election law gave the government a great deal of repressive muscle because it expressly forbid the propagation of ideas that undermined respect for the constitution,

[48] Quoted in *Le Mémorial des Pyrénées*, Feb. 12, 1876.
[49] The election results, with appended protests, are deposited in A. N., C 3459 A 12 to C 3473 A 26, *Elections—1876*.

the social order, and public authority. Moreover, the law required every publishing firm "before publication, to deposit a copy of all electoral literature with the secretary general of the prefecture," and on its distribution, to see that all such literature carried the costly official stamp of approval.[50] This provision permitted prefectural agents to examine electoral publications brought to them for possible subversive content. Since no freedom of association existed, prefectural agents could also closely survey electoral meetings, for legally, each meeting had to receive prior approval and take place in the presence of a police official who, if he judged that it deviated from its stated purpose or engaged in sedition, could bring it summarily to an end. The government had the same powers to meddle in elections that had existed under the Second Empire, but the question was how determined the government was to use these powers and in what specific way. The legitimists expressed an ardent desire to see the government throw its weight behind the conservatives. Their attitude confirms the tendency, which had been marked throughout the history of the National Assembly, to forget about decentralization. Whether they admitted it in theory, they had abandoned attacks on the state for a close cooperation between state, Church, and the traditional social authorities against the forces of secular democracy. However, the government was not in the hands of the legitimists. The cabinet that presided over the elections was composed primarily of deputies drawn from the Center and the Right-Center of the National Assembly, and the attitude of these men would determine how vigorous the state's support would be.

The cabinet was united in its resolve to thwart the electoral agitation of the radical Left. Minister of Interior Buffet instructed his prefects to keep a close watch on electioneering and to apply the full letter of the law to radical agitators. The radicals, in order to escape the government's muzzle, frequently broke the law by distributing electoral propaganda without the prefectural approval that they knew would not be forthcoming. Whenever the prefectural authorities discovered unlawful radical electoral activities, the *Garde des Sceaux*, Dufaure, prosecuted the offenders. The correspondence between Dufaure and his *procureurs généraux* is filled with references to a wide variety of legal actions taken against violators of the press law. At Bourges, the *procureur général* hauled

[50] Ltr., minister of the interior to the prefect, Feb. 2, 1876, A. D. (Nord), M 37-1, *Elections—1876*.

a colporteur into court for peddling the radical newspaper *Le Peuple* without prior authorization from "the administrative authorities."[51] Dufaure instructed the *procureur général* in Angers to bring charges against all colporteurs not registered with the *parquet* who disseminated radical propaganda.[52] In Brives, the *procureur général* attempted to find and prosecute a worker who was accused of waving a "seditious emblem" (the red flag).[53] These actions, which legitimists applauded, show the vitality, if faded, of the fear of the red specter which had brought the conservatives together in 1871.

However, such fears had no currency in the struggle between "respectable" republicans, including the subdued Gambetta, and the monarchists. When a supposed threat of revolution was not the issue, the cabinet divided over the proper attitude its officials should assume. Buffet openly sided with the candidates of the legitimist-Orleanist coalition and frequently with the Bonapartists; Minister of Finance Léon Say and Jules Dufaure, who favored a conservative Republic, counseled their subordinates to remain neutral in most contests. This split sometimes set bureaucrats working at cross purposes. Buffet's prefect in the Jura, for example, asked Dufaure's *procureur général* to prosecute a group of republicans for having said that monarchists could not govern a republic, but the *procureur général* refused to bring charges, explaining that, contrary to the prefect's contention, such republican attacks on the monarchists in no way amounted to a violation of the constitution of 1875.[54] Legitimists severely criticized the government for its lack of unity. The royalist newspaper *La Décentralisation*, for instance, demanded that Dufaure and Say leave the cabinet and that Buffet (even though they hated him for voting in favor of the constitutional laws!) be allowed a free hand. "[The] unity of action reestablished in Paris would bring in its train a unity of action for conservatives throughout the nation."[55] Because this unity never occurred, legitimists kept carping about the government's ineptitude. Writing three days after the elections to the

---

[51] Report, *Procureur général* (Aix) to the *Garde des Sceaux*, A. N., BB[30] 490[1], and, Report, *Procureur général* (Bourges) to the *Garde des Sceaux*, A. N., BB[30] 490[2], *Election fraude—1876*. These reports are classed by Courts of Appeal.

[52] *Ibid.* (Court of Appeal, Angers).

[53] *Ibid.* (Court of Appeal, Limoges).

[54] *Ibid.*, BB[30] 490[3] (Court of Appeal, Chambéry).

[55] Jan. 11, 1876.

Chamber of Deputies, the legitimist *L'Union du Sud-Ouest* summed up the grievance: "It is under the influence of radicalism that the elections have taken place. The government has dazzled only by its weakness, its nullity, and its impotence."[56]

But legitimist disappointment must not be taken too seriously. In the major population centers where martial law was still operative the commanding generals openly intervened in the elections, using the authority granted under the state of siege to forbid republican electoral meetings. More importantly, the partisan outlook of some ministers, especially the powerful minister of the interior, moved hundreds of officials to work for monarchists. Sometimes the actions of the civil servants were of doubtful legality, as when the prefect's men tore down the anti-imperialist placards of republicans in Nièvre, even though they had been legally posted.[57] In fact, administrative officials engaged in outright blackmail to pressure voters into supporting conservative candidates. In Ariège a group of electors complained that they could not be inscribed on flood relief rolls unless they first picked up their ballots at the mayor's office. "If [we] did not, [we] did not get the money."[58] But the administration employed more subtle techniques in aiding the conservatives. In Ardèche the monarchist newspaper *Le Bas-Vivrais* announced, "as a result of the intervention of M. Broët (a candidate), M. Wallon, Minister of Public Instruction, has given our commune (Largentières) 2,000 francs for the purpose of repairing its church."[59] The same newspaper published a letter from the minister of public works to the deputy Tailhand in which the minister noted that he had given, as a result of Tailhand's solicitation, "an initial credit of 10,000 francs which will permit an immediate start on the improvements of national route 104."[60]

The electoral law of 1875 expressly forbade "agents of public or municipal authority" to take part in elections, but the government interpreted this restriction in such a way as to make it ineffectual. The *procureur général* in Caen, for example, claimed that "of right, the law was not intended to cover mayors and adjuncts [because they were] magistrates of an administrative order, [not]

---

[56] Feb. 23, 1876.

[57] Report, *Procureur général* (Bourges) to the *Garde des Sceaux*, A. N., BB³⁰ 490².

[58] A. N., C 3459, *Elections—1876*, Ariège. The reference is to letters of protest attached to the results.

[59] Jan. 12, 1876.   [60] *Le Bas-Vivrais*, Jan. 15, 1876.

agents of public or municipal authority."[61] This meant that any official in the prefectural or municipal administration could endorse candidates and they freely did so. In Sarthe, "at the annual meeting for the selection of army recruits [*tirage au sort*]," the subprefect of Auberge presented La Rochefoucauld-Bisaccia to the mayors as his candidate for the deputation and in the same department the Marquis de Juigné, who was also a candidate for the Chamber, received the enthusiastic support of the mayors in his district of La Flèche.[62] In Vendée a subprefect recommended the candidacy of La Bassétière to the mayors in the district of Sables, and in Savoie republicans complained that the mayors officially supported conservative candidates. The *Garde des Sceaux* and the minister of finance might have been neutral, but their officials were less vital factors in the electoral equation than the men at the minister of the interior's command who often used their considerable resources to pressure the voters into casting their lot for the candidates of moral order.

Anybody who has followed the returns, say, of an American presidential election on election night cannot help but be struck by the immense grandeur and even mystery present when democracy speaks. Analysts who have been busy predicting what would happen often congratulate themselves on the clarity of their analysis, but all too frequently they discover how wrong their pre-electoral analysis had been, and with the results in hand, they forget immediately most of what they had previously said in order to show by the skill of their electoral post mortem how the results could not have been any different from what they were. Historians have the advantage over prognosticators because they know the electoral results that they set out to explain, but even this task is not easy. After all, when the historian asks why men voted the way they did, he is really asking the most difficult kind of question since to answer it he needs to have detailed knowledge of the psychological state of masses of people and the complex conditioning factors which shaped their mentality. To obtain such knowledge in any absolute sense is impossible because of our inability to penetrate into the conscious or subconscious mind of the faceless numbers of electoral participants.

Yet a concerted effort has been made by sociologists to see

[61] Report, *Procureur général* (Caen) to the *Garde des Sceaux*, A. N., BB[30] 490[3].

[62] *L'Union de la Sarthe*, Feb. 5 and 8, 1876.

causal patterns behind the voting behavior of the French electorate. Regional studies have been made, departments and cantons scrutinized. These studies have been concerned much less with explaining the psychological effect of environment on group mentality than with showing that a kind of mentality was associated with a particular environment. For example, rather than show how the religious experience created a particular type of person who voted a certain way, they relate how religiously devout populations voted in a fairly predictable manner. Moreover, these electoral studies are incomplete in that some electorates have been examined in detail, others more superficially, and still others ignored. No complete sociology of the French electorate exists for any period, and none has been attempted specifically for the elections of 1876. To describe the effects that the electoral campaign had on the voters in that year, to go into the various districts where legitimists ran and point out precisely how and why the electorate responded to the leadership of the traditional authorities (whether lay notables, clerics, state officials, or all three) or the peculiar patterns of grass roots republican and Bonapartist electoral agitation, is beyond this study. Indeed to do so, in the present state of electoral scholarship, is beyond the capacity of any scholar. But the subject need not be left there. The legitimists were interested in the very sociological process, the results of which came now directly to bear on the electorate. With the knowledge gained from the legitimists themselves, comments made by contemporaries, and insights acquired from French electoral sociology, a general explanation of the results can be given as they pertain to the legitimists. The analysis will neither be precise nor original but to ignore it on that account would be to detach this study of legitimist electoral defeat from the social process which is its chief concern.

Nothing illustrates the general sense of alienation that legitimists felt in urban areas more than their electoral fate there in 1876. They had so little support in the cities that they did not run, and elections there consisted of battles between republicans of more or less moderate persuasion. There were exceptions. In the Midi where the Catholic Church had a strong following among the working and middle classes in many cities, the royalists profited. In Nîmes the *Chevau-léger* Ferdinand Boyer was elected; in Alais, the monarchist Valons.[63] Moreover, in the industrial town Le Creusot,

[63] All the election results are deposited in A. N., C 3459 A 12 to C 3473 A 26. They are arranged alphabetically by department. Since all electoral

Schneider's chief engineer, a monarchist-conservative, easily defeated a republican opponent while the peasants in the surrounding countryside voted republican. These results complicate the usual interpretation of urban electoral sociology. The victory in Le Creusot does not present too much of a problem since this industrial town was somewhat of a closed society where the voters were economically dependent on one company and still (although this would soon change) behaved somewhat like industrial serfs. Moreover, for the less respectful industrial workers, economic intimidation on the part of the company, which controlled the town's livelihood, could be efficacious. However, in southern cities and in Belfort, where Emile Keller was elected, the economic and social structure was diverse and no single notable dominated the scene. The notables, therefore, could not rely on the population's economic dependence or on a paternalistic relation with their workers (with the possible exception of Alais where the workers in Benoist d'Azy's ironworks made up an important segment of the district's electorate) or their isolation from outside influences in the elections; their success can be attributed uniquely to the Church. But this in itself is no satisfactory explanation, for sociologists have commented about the dechristianization of urban population because of its mobility. Historical reasons have been given for the persistence of Catholic-royalist sentiment among the citizenry of certain cities, but no adequate explanation exists for its persistence in some cities and disappearance in others. Still dechristianization and anticlericalism were the rule in urban France. The voters did not fill the churches on Sundays nor follow the lead of the clergy. Nor did they pay any attention to the state officials who, in any case, did not have the wherewithal to force electoral compliance. The urban electorate did not listen to these groups, and the monarchists, as they themselves knew, were unable to check republican propaganda.

The rural areas, however, presented a more diverse pattern of voter responses. In the southeastern departments, the departments located in the Rhône-Saône valley, the Center, the Southwest, and the Midi, the peasantry was generally immune to royalist-Catholic electioneering. Several explanations for this have been advanced. One, cited by electoral sociologists, is the system of land tenure

---

results come from this source the reference will not be repeated for other results cited in the text.

that had eliminated the large landlord as the dominant socioeconomic force in the countryside. It is true that in many electoral districts (in the Southeast, the Rhône-Saône valley, and the Center, for example) the peasants owned most of the land and acted with the independence that this economic self-sufficiency permitted. But there were departments, like Cher, where the large landlords predominated, and the peasantry refused to vote for them. Although not to be discounted, land tenure appears less important a factor in voter attitudes than religion. The regions mentioned were dechristianized and this fact had serious repercussions for the monarchists because clerical support was ineffectual. Indeed, as Philibert de La Guiche was informed by an electoral agent, the clergy's work on his behalf hurt more than helped his chances among the fiercely anticlerical peasantry of Charolles (Saône-et-Loire).[64] The focal point of peasant social life was not the Church but the cabaret, that syndrome of radicalism which legitimists had recognized and underscored. There was little the notables could do, therefore, to counteract the radical electoral agitation in the countryside. Indeed, socially speaking, the advantage was all to the republicans because their sources of communications had been prepared by habits of life. The clearest example of this happened in Creuse, where the masons of Paris, who were among the most politically conscious workers in the capital, traveled back and forth to the peasant communities from which so many of them originally came, politically educating the department's peasantry. Radical Parisian newspapers were brought into Creuse. The local republican newspapers published appeals drafted in Paris by the masons and signed by name to the peasants back home. One of their number, Martin Nadaud, who had been elected from Creuse in 1848, ran again in 1876 and the peasantry duly sent him as their representative to the Chamber of Deputies.[65] The experience in Creuse was not unique.

[64] Ltr., Magnin to La Guiche, Feb. 6, 1876, *La Guiche MSS*, dossier 12335, Lettres diverses, Elections, M-Z. In an effort to win support where it counted La Guiche sent his electoral circulars to all the cabaret owners in his district but without any success since it was difficult for him to find any who would support him. La Guiche, then, knew well the power groups in his district. And he did not hesitate to deceive the voters. One agent remarked, "We are obligated to tell the peasants that you are not a legitimist, otherwise they will not vote for you." *Ibid.* But this deception failed.

[65] See the *L'Echo de la Creuse*, Jan. 29, 1876, which published a letter, signed by a group of Parisian workers, that urged all the people back home to elect Martin Nadaud to the Chamber of Deputies.

Emigrant peasant workers moved from other departments to the radical centers in Marseilles and Lyons as well as Paris and psychologically prepared the peasantry for the republican appeal when it came. Some even worked as unofficial electoral agents during the campaign. The ease with which they could meet with each other in the cabaret lightened the tasks of electioneering among a peasantry that was effectively sealed off from any countervailing influences which the monarchists might have attempted to exert.

The monarchists could not even rely on the state's support in many localities. Minor state officials like the postmen were peasants themselves and often responded to community opinion rather than the wishes of officialdom. One monarchist (La Guiche again) was warned that he should take special care when he forwarded his ballots to an electoral agent because the local postman could not be trusted to deliver them.[66] Another complained that the postman delivering his ballots stopped for a drink in the local cabaret and, while there, his ballots mysteriously disappeared and the candidate had no time to reorder and distribute new ones before election day.[67] There were instances, moreover, where important officials refused to cooperate with ministers. In Gers a conservative, the moderate legitimist Rességuier, claimed official candidacy. "We have seen letters coming from a minister and other officials close to the chief of state," *Le Conservateur et le Gers réunis* boasted, "all of which express very favorable opinions toward M. de Rességuier and formulate the most energetic desire to see him soon retake his place in the national representation."[68] But pressure from Paris was fruitless against the Bonapartist sentiment of local administrators. The prefect soon discovered his limitations when "more than ten mayors and adjuncts threatened to resign" rather than follow a prefectural order which prohibited their attendance at electoral meetings sponsored by the Bonapartists, and the prefect, not the mayors, backed down.[69]

Under these conditions the legitimist-Orleanist coalition had no chance. In the southeastern departments and the Rhône-Saône

[66] Ltr., Perret to La Guiche, n. d. (Probably written in Feb. 1876), *La Guiche MSS*, dossier 12335, Lettres diverses, Elections, M-Z.

[67] Report, *Procureur général* (Limoges) to the *Garde des Sceaux*, A. N., BB³⁰ 490¹. The *procureur* who reported the incident had the postman fired but went on to comment that the civil servants too frequently serve radical political interests in the Corrèze.

[68] Feb. 12, 1876.

[69] *L'Appel au peuple*, Feb. 9, 1876.

valley, where monarchists had done poorly even in 1871, republicans simply overwhelmed their opponents. Legitimists themselves thought so little of their prospects in many districts that they let moderate and radical republicans dispute the seats. In the few districts they contested, moreover, royalists were soundly thrashed. Quinsonas lost 4,518 to 7,994 in Isère; La Guiche 5,334 to 8,384 in Saône-et-Loire; and Saint-Victor succumbed 12,526 to 3,690 in Rhône. Not one of the legitimists of 1871, in fact not one legitimist, was returned to the Chamber of Deputies from these two regions. In the Center, where the conservative peace lists had won in 1871, the legitimists fared no better. Amédée Lefèvre-Pontalis lost 3,907 to 10,510 in Eure-et-Loir; the Marquis de Sers 4,919 to 9,907 in Loir-et-Cher; Comte Raudot 3,207 to 11,193 in the Yonne; and Saincthorent 501 to 5,641 in Creuse. Again none of the legitimists elected in 1871 was sent to the Chamber of Deputies. Nor was the defeat restricted to their number, for the electoral experience of their Orleanist allies was quite similar. Only two Bonapartist successes in Nièvre kept the republicans from taking every district. As Benoist d'Azy had noted about the *nivernais* peasantry earlier, "[our] peasants are rather attached to the Napoleonic dynasty because they have become convinced that it is all for them and against us."[70] The Bonapartist victories, therefore, signified no less a repudiation of the monarchists and their clientele than the republicans.

In the Southwest Bonapartist strength in the countryside more than counterbalanced republican strength in the cities. The electoral contests there were strictly republican-Bonapartist affairs, with the latter garnering most of the seats. As *Le Republicain du Lot* remarked, "thanks to the *images d'Epinal*, to a few songs of Béranger and to the war stories of old militarists, the Bonapartist fetish dominates the countryside. The peasants see in Napoléon I . . . the demolisher of the Old Regime and the greater legislator who has given them their land."[71] The monarchist defeat in this region (where the Orleanist-Legitimist fusion had won a complete victory in 1871) was catastrophic. In many districts their outlook was so dim that they did not present candidates, and where they confronted Bonapartists and republicans, they invariably ran a poor third. In Gers, Rességuier received 1,897 votes to the republican's

---

[70] Ltr., Denys Benoist d'Azy to Charles Benoist d'Azy, Sept. 8, 1870, *Benoist d'Azy MSS.*
[71] Mar. 5, 1876.

3,059 and the Bonapartist's 5,007; Gontaut-Biron got 3,576, his republican opponent 5,846, and the Bonapartist 10,463; in Lot-et-Garonne, Cazenove de Pradine received 1,583 votes to a Bonapartist's 7,315 and a republican's 10,452; and in Landes, a legitimist in the district of St-Sever obtained 2,793 votes, his republican opponent 5,679, and a Bonapartist 10,013. Not even the popularity of the Bonapartists, moreover, could save the royalists. The *Chevau-léger* Carayon-Latour in Gironde and the moderate legitimist Edmond Ernoul in Vienne, who received strong Bonapartist endorsements, ran very well but lost.[72] The Bonapartists saw the burden of an alliance with the legitimists. "Our rural population," the Bonapartist newspaper *Le Courrier du Lot* commented about the defeat suffered by a legitimist it had supported,

> see a flag behind this candidate which, rightly or wrongly, they do not want at any price, and they have preferred to throw themselves into the arms of the republicans rather than march under the ferula of people too well known for their ultra-royalist opinions. . . . This fear is unreasonable, I know, but unfortunately it exists, and the conservative party must keep it in mind.[73]

History, religion, and property systems, on the other hand, combined in other regions of France to make the monarchist-conservative electoral practices much more effective. The devout western peasantry, subjected to an upper-class, which owned a major part of the land, reacted with customary deference to the wishes of the clergy and the lay notables. Indeed in the West, as the republican newspaper *La Phare de la Loire* sadly observed, "a too numerous section of the bourgeoisie obeyed the commands of the nobility and the clergy."[74] During the Second Empire, when the force of the imperial bureaucracy had been used against them, notables like Durfort de Civrac in Maine-et-Loire, La Rochejaquelein in Deux-Sèvres, and Henri de Champagny in Morbihan had commanded the votes of the peasantry in elections to the general councils. Now with the administration and the clergy actively supporting them in district after electoral district, the conservatives did very well. Legitimists in particular reaped the benefits of centuries of peasant subservience. Durfort de Civrac in Maine-et-Loire, Huon de

---

[72] Carayon-Latour lost (4th District Bordeaux) 9,311 to 10,917. Ernoul lost in Poitiers, 5,568 to 5,992.

[73] Feb. 21, 1876.   [74] Feb. 1, 1876.

Penanster and Largentaye in Côtes-du-Nord, and Louis Monjaret de Kerjégu in Finistère were elected without opposition. Biliais, Juigné, and La Rochette (the brother of the deputy of 1871) in Loire-Inférieure; Rohan-Cabot, Bodan, and Perrien in Morbihan; Bourgeois, La Bassétière, and Baudry d'Osson in Vendée; Provost de Launay and Bélizal in Côtes-du-Nord; Maillé in Maine-et-Loire; Gonidec in Ille-et-Vilaine; and Perrochel in Sarthe won comparatively easy victories. With the churches full, the peasantry isolated in its economic dependence on the landlord, the vehicles of republican electioneering—the migrant worker, the cabaret owner, and the school teacher—could not sufficiently penetrate the physical and psychological barriers that defended the social hierarchy in these rural districts.

Nowhere did the legitimist ascendancy over the peasantry rival that shown in these western districts, but there were regions where the rural populations remained relatively loyal in 1876. In much of the Central Massif the large *propriétaire* managed to keep his "social authority" over a poor isolated Catholic peasantry. Although the legitimist notables had seldom felt secure enough to defy the imperial administration during the Empire, the prefects, in contrast to those in the Center, the Southwest, and the Rhône-Saône valley departments, had been quite willing to accept these legitimists as "official candidates," especially for elections to the general councils, because of their obvious influence in the rural cantons. With the backing of the clergy, the landlords, and the prefects, candidates of the "moral order" retained enough support among the rural population to run a strong race in many districts. The constitutional monarchists Joseph de Chambrun in Lozère and Barascud in Aveyron were so well-entrenched in their districts that they were unopposed. The moderate legitimist Valady in Aveyron and Florentin Malartre in Haute-Loire defeated their republican opponents. Royalists who lost, moreover, occasionally ran well. In Aveyron, for example, the Vicomte de Bonald (District of Millau) lost to his republican opponent 8,139 to 6,632, and in Gard (District of Uzès) Louis-Numa Baragnon lost 11,234 to 7,920. Compared with the disasters in departments like Creuse or Saône-et-Loire, these were respectable showings.

In the commercially, industrially, and agriculturally rich departments of the North (Nord, Pas-de-Calais, Somme, and Oise) the patterns of peasant loyalty that had made the legitimist notables such formidable opponents during the Second Empire continued in 1876. In 1870 La Grange, Kolb-Bernard, and Rotours in Nord, Partz-de-Pressy in Pas-de-Calais, and Blin de Bourdon in Somme held seats in the general councils. In fact, Kolb-Bernard and the liberal monarchist Plichon had been elected to the *Corps législatif* against administrative opposition. In these rural districts, the strength of these men depended on the support of the clergy that often had immense influence over the population. In 1859 the prefect of Nord, reporting on the electoral chances of Kolb-Bernard, noted that "[he] does not have a great deal of personal ascendancy in the region and his influence comes more from the ideals he represents than the friends he has. The clergy which has a greater influence in his district than the others is very devoted to his candidacy and will support him energetically."[75] Plichon had been so powerful that he beat the prefect's "official candidate" 7,750 to 2,716 in an election held in 1863.[76] In commenting on Plichon's extraordinary influence, one official remarked that "even the civil servants had secretly cooperated towards his triumph."[77] Thus, when the local population respected the clergy and the notables, the prefect could no more control his own officials than he could when very different social circumstances gave republicans and Bonapartists such a hold over the population in a rural district. In 1876 Plichon and the moderate legitimist Rotours in Nord and the moderate legitimist Blin de Bourdon in Somme ran unopposed in their districts; the legitimist Jules Leurent and the liberal monarchist Jules Brame in Nord and the *Chevau-léger* Partz-de-Pressy in Pas-de-Calais handily defeated their republican foes. Seats monarchists lost, moreover, were usually hotly contested. The *Chevau-léger* La Grange lost 5,103 to 5,791 in Nord; the Catholic monarchist Descat 4,633 to 4,854 in Nord; the Catholic monarchist Clercq 9,529 to 9,882 in Pas-de-Calais; and the moderate legitimist Labitte 10,191 to 10,642 in Oise. Although rarer than in the North, legitimist notables received the same sort of support from the peasants in some districts in the eastern and northeastern departments. Voters in three rural districts in Haute-Saône and in one district in Meuse elected moderate legitimists, and those in two districts in Haute-Marne and in one in Vosges gave them sufficient

[75] *Mémoire* (author unknown) for the Prefect, A. D. (Nord), M 30/27 *Elections—1869.*

[76] Ltr., subprefect (Hazébrouck) to the *Conseiller d'Etat*, n. d., A. D. (Nord), M 30/27 *Elections.*

[77] Ltr., Wormhoudt to unknown, May 29, 1863, *ibid.*

support to make a good showing in losing contests (7,038 to 8,613 in Vosges; 9,753 to 10,356 and 11,125 to 12,123 in Haute-Marne).

In Seine-Inférieure, Manche, Eure, and Orne the monarchist-conservative electoral performance resembled that in the North except that the victors were Orleanists and Bonapartists. Indeed, the electoral strength of the party of moral order here and in the North, the Northeast, the East, and the Central Massif was not limited to the districts in which the legitimists won or ran well. There were many candidates who called themselves conservative republicans, like Dewsy who ran with legitimist backing in the first district of Arras in the Pas-de-Calais (The legitimist newspaper *Le Pas-de-Calais* noted that, although Deusy did not share their political convictions, on religious grounds he was "as conservative as our friends could desire.")[78] Goos (District of Dunkerque), Massiet de Brest (District of Hazebrouck), Gailly and Philippoteau in Ardennes, Destremx, Rouverure, and Seignebos in Ardèche (who had run with the Legitimists in 1871) as well as the eight Bonapartists elected with legitimist support from the four northern departments (Nord, Pas-de-Calais, Somme, and Oise). Their electoral base was scarcely different from that of the Catholic royalists. The clergy and the prefectural administration worked for them against more radical republicans. The ascendancy they established in their districts reveals the same symbiosis of socio-religious factors at play among the peasantry that made it respect the social hierarchy where legitimists ran. Conversely the defeat of legitimist notables in the Midi did not bring the consolation that nonlegitimist Catholic conservatives had succeeded where they failed. Although the Catholic-royalist landlords constituted a powerful group among the social authorities in these southern departments, they did not live among a peasantry that respected the social hierarchy. The Catholic notable, whether legitimist or nonlegitimist, had ceased to be an effective electoral force in the Midi because the peasantry no longer listened to the clergy. Falling under the sway of the cabaret and the egalitarian lower middle-class groups, they voted for Gambetta republicans.

Even though the results in the elections to the Chamber of Deputies demonstrate that the peasantry still respected the social hierarchy in many rural districts, they really affirm the degree to which the peasantry, in spite of the pressure of clergy, landlord,

[78] Feb. 16, 1876.

and the state, had rejected the notables' call for a defense of the social order. Sometimes the notables lost because of internal dissension as, for example, in Loire-Inférieure where a republican picked up a seat because the Bonapartist refused to withdraw in a runoff election. But such failures were exceedingly rare. Cooperation in runoff elections happened more frequently. In Deux-Sèvres the Marquis de La Rochejaquelein won because his Bonapartist opponent supported him in a runoff election; in Loiret, the *Chevau-léger* Aboville asked his supporters to vote for the Bonapartist Jahan; in Sarthe, La Rochefoucauld-Bisaccia benefited from the backing of the Bonapartist in his district, and a Bonapartist (Haentjens) from the endorsement of a legitimist in his. Failure could not be attributed, then, to split votes. Rather, the peasantry responded to the radical republican and Bonapartist appeals eating away at the islands of royalist strength even in areas where it had been especially prominent. Falloux, who stressed the influence of the cabaret owner in Segré (Maine-et-Loire) during the Second Empire saw the Bonapartist Janvier de La Motte, that "apostle of candidacy by tipplers, tips, [and] cabarets," elected in his district; a Bonapartist almost beat Albert de Mun in Morbihan and republicans made creditable showings in other western rural districts. In the village clash between republicans and monarchists in the East, the Northeast, Normandy, and the Central Massif, the republicans carried most of the seats. Coupled with the places gained in their sweep of the Rhône-Saône valley, the Center, and the Midi, republicans commanded an impressive majority of over three hundred deputies in the new Chamber. Seventy-five Bonapartists had also been elected, but only eighty of the candidates of the legitimist-Orleanist coalition (among whom fifty were legitimists) had survived the perils of universal suffrage. The slight hope that they had that the peasantry would keep sufficiently true to traditional notables to give them a victory over the urban republicans remained unrealized.[79]

Republicans and Bonapartists had employed the same dynamic electoral techniques in the senatorial campaign that succeeded in the subsequent elections to the Chamber of Deputies. The royalist *Le Conservateur de Saône-et-Loire* described this process immediately after the vote:

[79] See the map on page 258 for a geographical breakdown of legitimist representation in the Chamber of Deputies.

MAP 3. Legitimist Representation in the
Chamber of Deputies, 1876

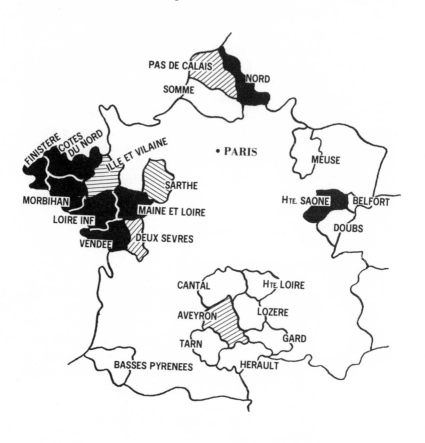

1 □   2 ▨   3 OR MORE ■

Our opponents have not failed to distribute brochures, departmental and Parisian newspapers, electoral manifestoes, ballots, etc., in profusion. One special Republican electoral organ was sent from Paris, without charge, to mayors, municipal councillors, and communal delegates. But that was not enough. The senatorial electors were visited one by one. Emissaries worked regions assigned to them on foot. The Republican candidates have shown themselves to their electors; they have visited them individually; they have spoken to them. This is what the radicals have done and what we have not done. The conservatives err in keeping apart. They think, after meeting in a closed committee where they have scrupulously examined the possible candidates that they have sufficiently worked for their cause. At the risk of displeasing them, let us say that they have done nothing. Let them imitate their foe.[80]

The conservative candidates relied on the clergy and administration to do their bidding and sometimes quite effectively. As the *L'Avenir du Morbihan* complained immediately after the elections, "the members of the rural municipal councils need a great and very rare firmness of character in order for them to preserve their independence when they find themselves badgered by the presbytery, the administration, and the large landlords living alongside them."[81] The senatorial elections had been quite different from those to the Chamber because of the composition of the electorate. The senatorial electorate consisted of (1) the deputies to the National Assembly, (2) general councillors, (3) district councillors, and (4) one delegate elected by each municipal council from the electors of the commune. Since delegates chosen by the municipal councils were by far the more numerous, they decided the elections, and since municipal councils were elected by universal suffrage, ultimately they were subject to the democratic process. But the municipal councils that selected the electors in 1876 had taken office prior to the campaign when local instead of national political questions had determined elections. The communal electorate had voted more conservatively in the municipal elections than they did in the elections to the Chamber of Deputies. Therefore the electors whom the municipal councils chose and with whom the republicans, Bonapartists, and monarchists had to deal were more conservative than their constituencies.

[80] Feb. 3, 1876.   [81] Feb. 2, 1876.

Consequently, the senatorial electoral results differed from those to the Chamber. Republicans did win, especially in the Southeast, the Rhône-Saône valley, and the Center where the village republicans had already wrested the municipal councils from the monarchists. Sometimes, too, republicans benefited from conservative factionalism as, for example, in Ardèche when the "error of several misguided" legitimists deprived the Orleanist Broët of a seat.[82] But the royalists more than compensated for these losses because of the fight between republicans and Bonapartists. In Haute-Garonne, for example, the legitimists ran behind republicans and Bonapartists on the first ballot only to win a seat (Belcastel) because republicans voted for them on the second. Generally the conservative alliance did not break down. In many departments, conservative solidarity produced an easy first ballot victory. In Morbihan, despite the intransigent legitimist revolt against Audren de Kerdrel, he and the *Chevau-léger* La Monneraye were elected together by a broad royalist coalition of voters. In Ille-et-Vilaine and Vendée, a solid conservative front produced similar results, and a closely knit Bonapartist-monarchist coalition triumphed in Lot-et-Garonne and Nièvre. In departments, where a conservative split necessitated a second ballot, the Bonapartists and monarchists usually cooperated. Despite the intransigent legitimists' protests, the *Chevau-léger* Féligonde withdrew in Puy-de-Dôme rather than split the vote, and the electors rallied behind the Orleanist Barantes and the Bonapartist Mèze, both of whom were elected. In Lot-et-Garonne, a Bonapartist-monarchist agreement brought the election of the Bonapartist Noubel and the monarchist Bastard. In Somme the Bonapartists withdrew in favor of the stronger monarchist candidates. And so it went until the monarchists and Bonapartists registered a victory that more than offset the numerical advantage that the republicans had obtained in the lifetime Senate. Bonapartists weighed more heavily in the conservative victory than in 1871, but among the conservative majority in the new Senate sat forty-five avowed legitimists plus many moderates who were more discreet about their dynastic opinions.

But of the two elections, the one to the Chamber of Deputies had greater consequences. When the aggressive republican majority, which the voters sent to the Chamber, revoked the right of Catholic universities to grant degrees, attacked the budget of the Ministry of Religion, demanded civil burials, forced the government to pro-

[82] *Le Bas-Vivrais*, Feb. 2, 1876.

hibit the circulation of a bishops' petition asking for all-out French support of papal independence from the Italian government, and demanded an end to administrative control of the press, they showed that they intended to dismantle what was left of the institutional apparatus which the Catholic royalists considered essential for the preservation of the social hierarchy. Moreover, short of a *coup d'état*, the badgered conservatives had to rely on the electorate that had defeated them to repudiate the republican majority. This is what Marshal MacMahon and the Duc de Broglie, with the support of the conservative community, attempted to do during the *seize mai* crisis. "The struggle is between order and disorder," Marshal MacMahon proclaimed. Again a conservative electoral coalition appeared on social and religious grounds; once more the republicans united during the electoral campaign. In 1877 the government resolved to use all its agents to insure a conservative triumph. Official candidates were proclaimed, and MacMahon himself intervened on behalf of the candidates of "moral order." There were no neutrals in the government as in 1876, but it made little difference. The issues were the same, the avenues along which the Republicans reached the electorate were still open, and the results only verified the decision reached in 1876. These same avenues, moreover, were used to bring the municipal councils increasingly under control of the village republicans, thereby, after altering the senatorial electorate in a republican sense, producing the republican victory in the senatorial elections of 1879.

Legitimist notables continued to receive the support of the peasantry in some electoral districts. In the North Partz-de-Pressy represented the district of St. Pol (Pas-de-Calais) for the first two decades of the Third Republic; Blin de Bourdon (Somme) sat in the Chamber of Deputies from 1876 to 1893, and Eugène des Rotours represented a rural constituency in Nord for a comparable period. In the West even more legitimists found a safe electoral refuge among the peasantry, but the republicans swept around these strongholds in their conquest of the countryside. The legitimist notable found himself a stranger among peasants who no longer submitted to the symbols of the "moral order." When the Comte de Chambord died in 1883, he was sincerely mourned by the faithful in France, but his death caused scarcely a stir in a population for whom neither he nor the social principles he represented had much meaning.

Chapter Seven

CONCLUSION

George Lichtheim wrote in a work on Marxism that after 1848 "belief in the possibility of stating valid principles binding upon all was gradually abandoned."[1] This development did not mean that the goal of finding the "truth" was renounced, but only that the possibility of anybody having "it" within his grasp was highly unlikely. Truth became an ideal to be pursued by free men competing in the open market place of ideas. This was the liberal conception of life, one that made toleration, except for toleration of the intolerant, into a dogma because of the relative validity of any set of ideas or system of ethics, each of which depends on the political, social, and economic interests that are defended or on the general state of knowledge that mankind has attained at a particular moment in history. The legitimists of 1871 had not abandoned the "possibility of stating valid principles binding upon all." They believed that these principles were not the progressive fruits of human reason but divinely inspired timeless verities. The fruits of human reason, in their opinion, had produced the principal evils of modern times, evils outlined so trenchantly in Pius IX's Syllabus of Errors— "the code," Emile Keller proclaimed, "not only of religious but of political and social common sense and truth."[2] The restoration of the legitimate monarchy was part of the legitimist effort to suppress the modern tendency to let truth sink into a quagmire of subjectivity in favor of reestablishing traditional beliefs valid and binding upon all.

Both the belief in valid principles binding upon all and the principles to which they actually adhered set legitimists apart from most of their compatriots. Indeed a chief preoccupation of this study has been the extent to which legitimists could be considered anachronisms. Various examples of their lack of comprehension

---

[1] George Lichtheim, *Marxism, An Historical and Critical Study* (New York, 1961), p. 33.

[2] G. Gautherot, *Emile Keller (1828–1909). Un demi-siècle de défense nationale et religieuse* (Paris, 1922), p. 9.

and of their understanding of their times have been given. Benoist d'Azy's shock on hearing that his workers did not vote for their foremen, and Franclieu's distress on discovering that his peasants would ignore what influence he might wish to exercise on them illustrate the former, and much of the discussion of the sociology of moral order the latter. The subject, however, is quite complicated, not just because contradictory examples can be given but because of the theoretical difficulties involved in determining what makes people historical anachronisms. Three points of reference have been used here to measure the degree to which legitimists moved against or followed the grain of contemporary social developments; (1) their relationship to the growth of the state; (2) their relationship to the process of industrialization; and (3) the extent to which they represented or mirrored the ideas of outmoded social groups reminiscent of the Old Regime. None of these points of reference is mutually exclusive, but each is, nonetheless, analytically distinct, and has offered a fairly comprehensive basis for judging legitimist performance and mentality.

Max Weber noted, when introducing his conception of the growing rationality of modern society, that one essential characteristic of our time, as opposed to previous eras, is the development of the centralized state bureaucracy. The legitimists tended to believe in the old proprietary state in which state positions were considered the personal property of families if not social groups. As a result, they argued that appointment and promotion to state positions be based more on family origins than technical expertise. They denigrated the idea that mere knowledge or ability was the best criteria for assuming positions of authority. By rejecting the people's right to rise to top state offices according to individual talent, the legitimists limited the state's ability to recruit administrators to a small proportion of the population, thereby denying the principle of efficiency, Weber spoke about, in favor of social criteria. Such conclusions are warranted from the discussion of legitimists' attitudes toward the position of justice of the peace in the community, the selection and promotion of regular judges, the powers of the members of academic councils in regulating education, the widespread jurisdiction of the prefects in public and private life, and a number of other subjects handled primarily in Chapters Four and Five both of which point to the conclusion that they favored giving power to the local social authorities at the expense of the technically trained professional state administrator.

Nonetheless the legitimists' attitude toward the growth of state functions had a positive as well as a negative side. There is nothing to indicate that they had any idea of restoring the pre-Revolutionary proprietary state. Nobody suggested, for example, that positions in government, the magistracy, or the administration should be bought and owned by private citizens and passed on to their posterity. Nor did they believe that the state could function by completely ignoring the principles of efficiency. Educational qualifications were considered insufficient for appointment to state functions, but they never denied the necessity for proper instruction, especially where the position required technical expertise. Thus legitimists were quite willing to let candidates for the magistracy take examinations to determine their technical knowledge as long as appointment was not made solely on the scores achieved. Many legitimists, moreover, had moved a long way toward accepting the idea of the state functioning as a social engineer. They might have wanted the Church's role expanded in education but relied on the state in partnership with the Church to set pedagogical standards (for example, the expansion of technical training in agriculture). If ready to curtail state services in urban areas, many were favorably disposed to expanding them in the countryside. The idea that state programs be used for promoting social mobility was anathema to them, but a better use of the state to prepare people for their function in society was acceptable. They had no quarrel with the peasants being trained to be good farmers, the landlords intelligent agronomists, the iron workers skilled craftsmen, the engineers superb roadbuilders, etc. Indeed this group of legitimists felt that proper state action might strengthen the social order rather than dissolve it. Besides, it must not be forgotten that legitimists abandoned decentralization in favor of a strong state capable of maintaining order. They may have disliked an army of civil servants, but they were ready to create an efficient police—plenty of them in order to suppress subversion.

Numerous examples have been given, moreover, to show that the legitimists' reaction to industrialization was mixed. Legitimists were not economic men. They did not think that the "end of life [was] life itself," certainly not in a material sense. They gave priority to social rather than economic matters. Thus, their widespread criticism of liquid securities and urbanization coupled with a general praise of rural life sprang from social considerations. No matter how economically productive the city might be, they could not

264

accept it as socially desirable. Moreover, legitimists can be accused of hampering growth and rationalization of productive techniques by depriving the economy of the talent needed because of their objection to social mobility. On the other hand, their active participation in agriculture, their concern, both from the point of view of personal and social interest with improving rural economic productive techniques and farm income, their activity in many professions, occupations and businesses which were creating large-scale industry shows that legitimists were not insensitive to economic development. Even their social attitudes proved adaptable to industrialization. Among the reform proposals outlined in Chapter Five were some designed to introduce moral order into the large-scale industrial community and others that would have fostered technical training for individuals since legitimists did not see the social order being destroyed if peasants, craftsmen, or manufacturers were skilled and capable practitioners of their calling.

The degree to which legitimists represented outmoded groups reminiscent of the Old Regime is also open to question. Half of the legitimist deputies descended from the old aristocracy and the remainder from an old Catholic oligarchy. The deputies tended to live in their own social milieu, especially in the countryside where the aristocrats often treated the bourgeois *société* with haughty disdain. This seems to indicate that the old feud between the aristocracy and bourgeoisie had been projected into their times. Nonetheless the evidence given in Chapters Three, Four, and Five shows the serious limitations of trying to identify the legitimists even partially with the old aristocracy. Sometime ago Professor Andrew Lossky, an expert on the Old Regime, concluded, after reading this manuscript, that the aristocrats described here had a singularly bourgeois cast of mind. Lossky's remark appears particularly perceptive because it illuminates the point that the aristocrats, no matter how hard they tried, could not escape the reality of their world, and the most important aspect of this reality was that the aristocracy no longer existed as a viable social group in post-Revolutionary France. The legitimists of aristocratic extraction were forced to acknowledge this when they fished around for social categories with which to identify a social hierarchy. Nothing in their sociology of moral order indicates that they thought of the nineteenth century social elite in terms of the old aristocracy; nothing in their electoral behavior shows any penchant to identify the notables with nobles. When the legitimists of noble extraction demanded respect for religion, family, and property, they expressed ideas that were not only perfectly acceptable to legitimist bourgeois notables but were in essence theirs. Even the desire to protect a landlord class does not belie this contention because the landlords cannot be identified with the old nobility. The nobles' inability to make themselves an exclusive elite was in itself a recognition of the social results of the Revolution and the grounds for their fusion with legitimists of bourgeois origins.

Thus the legitimist belief in valid principles binding upon all seems to involve a distinction between form and content. All the legitimists conceived of the form of human relations in terms of a hierarchically organized society in which a man's place in the social scale was predetermined. That they thought about society this way did not make them exceptional. Some people have always believed in this kind of social ethic. (Even today in America one can hear talk about "people coming from good families" or "people keeping their place," as if men were marked by their origins for a certain role in life and that following that role is morally right.) It is not, therefore, so much the form of the legitimist social ethic as its specific socioeconomic content that offers the key to determining the historical basis of legitimism in mid-nineteenth-century France and this content was hardly rigid vis-à-vis the past. Although there was a certain tension between aristocrats and bourgeois, the legitimists were much less interested in perpetuating any conflict between these groups than in protecting the position of the nineteenth-century notables from the threat of mass democracy. They did not let the social groups of the Old Regime predetermine those of the early Third Republic. In this respect their society had evolved. Nor did they picture the social hierarchy solely in terms of the newer or older social creations of economic development. The independent-minded peasant *propriétaire* and the agricultural day laborer whom they disliked were not products of industrialization; they would be hard pressed to survive economically in a highly developed market economy. The radicalized Paris that they detested was composed of small workshops, shops, and cabarets characteristic of a preindustrial mode of economic activity. The legitimists foresaw greater possibilities in maintaining social order in a new industrial establishment located in the countryside or small town than in the artisanal quarters of the big cities. Their social ethics did not correspond to the groups fostering or hindering economic change. Legitimists were willing to accept a newer social content that could

266

be shaped to the social form they admired. This accounts for their preoccupation with corporate organization of industry, a preoccupation that is similar to that of the twentieth-century Right.

What was true of the legitimists, moreover, was true of many of their opponents. Liberals, of course, denounced a conception of society in which a man's place was predetermined. But the liberal ideology was scarcely adaptable to the process of rationalization of human endeavors. Liberals (and radicals too) are not famous for modeling their conception of administration on the efficiency principle. They were skilled politicians; they could win elections and turn the notables out of office, but they were no less susceptible than legitimists to letting social instead of technical criteria be the operative principle in state administration. Radical republicans, for example, wanted to subject bureaucratic positions to democratic elections, a proposal that was hardly calculated to enhance efficiency. Indeed, the history of the Third Republic under radical control is hardly a testimony to the growth of rationality in state administration. Liberalism, moreover, was neither economically progressive nor regressive. Farmers in Normandy could be quite advanced economically and liberal politically, but as Laurence Wylie in *Village in the Vaucluse* illustrates, no group of peasants was more backward economically and radicalized politically and socially than those in southeastern France. Indeed, a revolutionary peasantry, as twentieth-century history shows, can appear in an economy sunk in economic routine as readily as in one undergoing innovation. Although industrialists could be and were liberals, often middle-class liberals, with their individualistic philosophy, were enemies of large-scale industrial enterprise and hence the defenders, no less than many of their legitimist colleagues, of the industrial techniques of preindustrial France.

Moreover, compared to legitimists, the republican, Orleanist, or Bonapartist record in education was hardly impressive, from either a democratic or technocratic point of view. The great declaration of the Rights of Man and the Citizen had stated that "all citizens . . . are equally admissible to all public dignities, offices and employments, according to their capacity, and with no other distinction than that of their virtues and talents." The educational system that Napoleon established and which Orleanists and republicans helped perpetuate was clearly designed to create an *élite dirigeante* that would monopolize all public employments. Inasmuch as the baccalaureate was restricted in practice to the bourgeoisie and since a baccalaureate was a prerequisite for entry into the university and professional schools and degrees from these institutions were necessary for success in public or private employments, only the middle and upper classes were "admissible to all public dignities, offices and employments," declarations of equal opportunity notwithstanding. Even the famous republican educational achievement of the 1880s, free, secular, obligatory, primary instruction, did not change matters since pupils from the primary schools could not advance into the *collège* or *lycée* in order to get the coveted baccalaureate. They continued to recruit students from separate, narrow, class-based preparatory schools, requiring payment of fee. Bonapartist, Orleanist, and republican emphasis on secular education, furthermore, had little to do with preparing the *élite dirigeante* for the industrial world. The system of education Napoleon founded stressed the classics, with some science tacked on as an afterthought. It imparted a general culture to its students. Some nineteenth-century reformers, like Victor Duruy, tried to improve the level of technical education, but they were opposed effectively. The only significant change in secondary education before World War I happened when students were permitted an option between a classical or modern language curriculum, scarcely a reform promoting technical knowledge. Legitimists were themselves severe critics of the technical deffiencies of the post-Revolutionary educational system. They were not, of course, technocrats themselves but neither were, with few exceptions, their opponents. On the eve of World War I, a generation after the republicans had come to power, technical instruction in France remained in an alarmingly retarded state.[3]

In Chapter Three the hypothesis was advanced that the separation of the Industrial and the French Revolutions offers a good analytical tool for understanding the place the legitimists and their opponents held in their society. The fact that both could be receptive to modern economic ideas and processes or oppose them seems to verify this point. However, it still needs to be asked to what extent the contemporary socioeconomic developments in France produced social results that could be adapted to the legitimist conception of society. Had France been, as general Ducrot

[3] For a good résumé of the deficiencies of nineteenth-century French education see "Introduction" in John E. Talbott, *The Politics of Educational Reform in France, 1918–1940* (Princeton, New Jersey, Princeton University Press).

remarked, a "hierarchical society" like Prussia on the eve of industrialization, she would have suffered serious dislocations during subsequent economic growth, but she would have incorporated much of the social ethic of the old hierarchical society into the new industrial state. But France was not Prussia precisely because she had experienced the Revolution, and the Revolution had produced a rural and urban society, with very different political and social habits from those across the Rhine. "An industrial society" was neither the historical object or subject of the French Revolution but the fact that the social order had been liberalized before intensive industrialization began made the social effects of industrialization (especially through the communication arts) so much more disturbing from the legitimists' point of view.

Legitimists' complaints about the effects of industrialization, therefore, were really complaints about industrialization taking place in a liberalized society. Consequently, technically speaking, it might be possible to argue that their distress is only about liberalization not industrialization since the one is possible without the other and this was really the basis of their fight with the moderate republicans and Orleanists. Some evidence was produced in Chapter Four to support such an idea. It was noted that Germany and Japan, societies that industrialized without liberalizing, have retained much of the social ethic of what legitimists called moral order. Evidence was produced to show how the legitimists themselves tried to work out corporate conceptions for the socioreligious organization of industrial towns and how these conceptions were probably more adaptable to the complex social conditions of modern industrial society than older laissez-faire conceptions. Still this attempt to make legitimists no less modern than their opponents, when it comes to industrialization, must not be construed to mean that they were not anachronisms in their society. France had been profoundly affected by the Revolution. This great event had touched all aspects of French life including the economic process itself. When the legitimists turned on the Revolution, on the liberal presumption, they knew what they were doing. They even knew the sociological dynamics through which revolutionary ideas spread. But as the failure of their reform programs and their electoral defeat indicates, they were helpless to do anything about it. They might have been enlightened about economic change or state growth in terms of their own social conceptions but the fact that these conceptions proved to be inoperative in most of France

269

and that economic and social change was being fostered by men under a system opposed to their own, made them outsiders.

Moreover, they were not outsiders just because they rejected the liberal presumption. The need to apply absolute ideas to each individual situation a person encounters, the need for a world view, a set of ideas binding on all, is not anachronistic in itself. The liberal presumption, with its ideals of relativism and pluralism has been construed (if erroneously) to be valueless for the individual in real life situations because it leaves him without a critical basis for living. A conception of moral order, then, seems to be necessary, for individuals in society have to make choices. For any society to exist relative values are insufficient; it must have a set of common values. The legitimist attack on the relativists, therefore, has great appeal to men and it arouses sentiments of assent among people today who are deeply concerned with the disappearance of civilized standards. What made the legitimists anachronisms in their society was not so much that they believed in a moral order but the specific moral order in which they believed.

APPENDIX

Legitimist deputies who belonged to the *Réunion des Chevau-légers* and/or the *Réunion Colbert* and those who belonged to the *Réunion Colbert* and/or the *Réunion Centre-Droite* are identified with the following code:

C/L   Member of the *Chevau-légers.*
C/L, C   Member of both the *Chevau-légers* and *Colbert.*
C   Member of *Colbert.*
C/D, C   Member of *Centre-Droite* and *Colbert.*
C/D,   Member of *Centre-Droite.*

Sometimes legitimists did not join the *Chevau-légers, Colbert,* or the *Centre-Droite.* The deputies who have no affiliation given after their names either fall into this category or they did not figure on the membership lists that were found. There were a few minor *réunions* at Versailles which, for purposes of clarity, have been ignored. Knowing the deputies who joined them does not help determine who was a royalist. The same is true of one large group, the *Réunion des Réservoirs.* Deputies in the extreme Right, the Right, and Right-Center belonged to this *Réunion.* Thus, affiliation with *Réservoirs* reveals nothing about the deputy's particular brand of monarchism.

Deputy	Affiliation	Department Represented
Abbadie de Barrau, Bernard d'	C/L, C	Gers
Aboville, Auguste d'	C/L	Loiret
Andelarre, Jules d'	C/D, C	Haute-Saône
Arfeuilleres, Achille d'	C	Corrèze
Auberjon, Louis d'		Haute-Garonne
Aubry, Maurice		Vosges
Audren de Kerdrel, Vincent d'	C	Morbihan
Aurelle de Paladines, Louis d'	C	Allier
Auxais, Jules d'	C	Manche

271

Deputy	Affiliation	Department Represented
Aymé de la Chevrelière, Emile	C/D, C	Deux-Sèvres
Bagneux, Louis de	C/L	Seine-Inférieure
Balleroy, Pierre de		Calvados
Baragnon, Louis-Numa	C	Gard
Baucarne-Leroux, Louis	C/D	Nord
Beauvillé, Félix de	C	Somme
Belcastel, Gabriel de	C/L	Haute-Garonne
Benoist d'Azy, Denys	C	Nièvre
Bermond, Charles de	C/D, C	Tarn
Bernard-Dutreil, Jules	C	Sarthe
Besson, Paul		Jura
Béthune, Gaston de	C/L, C	Ardennes
Beurges, Henri de	C	Haute-Marne
Bidard, Théophile	C/D	Ille-et-Vilaine
Blin de Bourdon, Robert	C	Somme
Bodan, Charles du	C/L	Morbihan
Bois-Boissel, Hyacinthe de	C/L	Côtes-du-Nord
Boisse, Adolphe	C/L	Aveyron
Bonald, Victor de		Aveyron
Bouché, Jean		Morbihan
Bouillé, Charles de	C/L	Nièvre
Bouillier de Branche, Augustin	C	Mayenne
Bourgeois, Paul	C/L, C	Vendée
Boyer, Ferdinand	C/L	Gard
Brettes-Thurin, François de	C/L	Haute-Garonne
Bridieu, François de		Indre-et-Loire
Brunet, Jean		Seine
Busson-Duvivier, Ernest		Sarthe
Byras, Charles de	C	Pas-de-Calais
Callet, Pierre	C/D	Loire
Carayon-Latour, Joseph de	C/L	Gironde
Carron, Emile	C	Ille-et-Vilaine
Cazenove de Pradine, Edouard de	C/L	Lot-et-Garonne
Chamaillard, Charles de	C	Finistère
Champagny, Henri de	C/L	Côtes-du-Nord

Deputy	Affiliation	Department Represented
Charette de la Gontrie, Charles de	C/L	Bouches-du-Rhône
Chatelin, Alexandre	C/D, C	Maine-et-Loire
Chaurand, Jean	C/L	Ardèche
Chesnelong, Charles	C	Basses-Pyrénées
Cintré, Armand de	C/L	Ille-et-Vilaine
Colombet, Bernard de	C/L	Lozère
Combier, Charles	C/L	Ardèche
Cornulier-Lucinière, Albert de	C/L	Loire-Inférieure
Costa de Beauregard, Charles	C/L, C	Savoie
Courbet-Poulard, Alexandre	C/D	Somme
Crussol d'Uzès, Emmanuel de	C	Gard
Cumont, Arthur de	C/D, C	Maine-et-Loire
Dahirel, François	C/L	Morbihan
Dampierre, Roger de	C	Landes
Daussel, Philippe	C	Dordogne
Delavau, Henri	C/D, C	Maine-et-Loire
Delpit, Martial	C/D, C	Dordogne
Delsol, Jean	C/D	Aveyron
Dépasse, Emile	C/D	Côtes-du-Nord
Depeyre, Octave	C	Haute-Garonne
Dezanneau, Théobald	C/L	Loire-Inférieure
Diesbach, Eugène de	C/L	Pas-de-Calais
Dompierre d'Hornoy, Albert de	C	Somme
Douay, Antoine	C	Pas-de-Calais
Douhet, Guillaume de	C/L	Puy-de-Dôme
Ducrot, Auguste	C/D, C	Nièvre
Dufaur, Xavier	C	Basses-Pyrénées
Dumarnay, Augustin	C/D, C	Finistère
Dumon, Jean-Baptiste	C/L	Gers
Dupin, Félix	C	Hérault
Durfort de Civrac, Louis de		Maine-et-Loire
Ernoul, Edmond	C	Vienne
Féligonde, Pierre de	C/L, C	Puy-de-Dôme

Deputy	Affiliation	Department Represented
Fleuriot de la Fleurière	C/L, C	Loire-Inférieure
Fontaine, Joseph de	C/L	Vendée
Forsanz, Paul de	C/L	Finistère
Foucaud, Ludovic de		Côtes-du-Nord
Fournier, Henri	C	Cher
Franclieu, Charles de	C/L	Haute-Pyrénées
Fresneau, Armand	C/L	Morbihan
Gasselin de Fresnay, André	C/D, C	Sarthe
Gaulthier de Vaucenay, Victor		Mayenne
Gavardie, Henri de	C	Landes
Gillon, Paulin	C/L	Meuse
Giraud, Louis	C/D, C	Vendée
Gontaut-Biron, Elie de	C	Basses-Pyrénées
Gouvello, Charles de	C/L	Morbihan
Grange, Humbert	C/L	Savoie
Grasset, Henri de	C/L	Hérault
Hespel, Octave de	C/D, C	Nord
Huon de Penanster, Charles	C/D, C	Côtes-du-Nord
Jaffré, Jean	C/L	Morbihan
Jamme, Henri	C/D, C	Tarn
Journu, Jean		Gironde
Juigné, Charles de	C/L, C	Loire-Inférieure
Jullien, Alexandre	C	Loire
Keller, Emile		Belfort
Kéridec, Hippolyte de	C/L	Morbihan
Kergariou, Henri de	C/L	Ille-et-Vilaine
Kergorlay, Louis de	C	Oise
Kermenguy, Emile de	C/L	Finistère
Kersauson de Pennendreff, V. de		Finistère
Kolb-Bernard, Charles	C/L	Nord
La Bassétière, Edouard de	C/L	Vendée
Labitte, Auguste		Oise

Deputy	Affiliation	Department Represented
La Borderie, Louis de	C/D, C	Ille-et-Vilaine
La Bouillerie, Joseph de	C/L	Maine-et-Loire
La Grange, Alexis de	C/L, C	Nord
La Guiche, Philibert de	C	Saône-et-Loire
Lallié, Alfred	C/D, C	Loire-Inférieure
La Monneraye, Charles de	C/L	Morbihan
La Pervanchère, Richard de	C	Loire-Inférieure
Larcy, Roger de	C	Gard
Largentaye, Charles de	C/L, C	Côtes-du-Nord
La Roche-Aymon, François de	C/L	Creuse
La Rochefoucauld-Bisaccia, Charles de	C/L	Sarthe
La Rochejaquelein, Gaston de	C/L	Deux-Sèvres
La Rochethulon, Stanislas de	C	Vienne
La Rochette, Charles de	C/L	Loire-Inférieure
Lassus, Marc de	C	Haute-Garonne
Laurenceau, Adolphe	C/D	Vienne
Le Chatelain, Ernest	C	Mayenne
Lefèvre-Pontalis, Amédée	C/L, C	Eure-et-Loir
Legge, Henri de	C/L, C	Finistère
Le Lasseux, Ernest	C/D	Mayenne
Lespinasse, Raymond	C	Tarn-et-Garonne
Lestourgie, Auguste de		Corrèze
Leurent, Jules	C/D	Nord
Limairac, Jules de	C/L	Tarn-et-Garonne
Lorgeril, Louis de	C/L	Côtes-du-Nord
Lucien-Brun	C/L	Ain
Lur-Saluces, Amédée de	C/L	Gironde
Maillé, Louis de	C	Maine-et-Loire
Malartre, Florentin	C	Haute-Loire
Marchand, Jacques	C/D	Charente
Marhallac, Félix du	C/L	Finistère
Martin, Charles	C/D, C	Nièvre
Martin d'Auray, Joseph	C/L, C	Morbihan
Maurice, Nicolas		Nord
Mayaud, Paul		Maine-et-Loire
Meaux, Alfred de	C	Loire

Deputy	Affiliation	Department Represented
Melun, Louis de	C	Nord
Merveilleux de Vignaux	C/D, C	Vienne
Monjaret de Kerjégu, François	C	Finistère
Monjaret de Kerjégu, Louis	C	Côtes-du-Nord
Monnet, Alfred	C/L	Deux-Sèvres
Monteil, Pierre		Dordogne
Montgolfier, Pierre de		Loire
Montlaur, Eugène de	C	Allier
Mortemart, Roger de	C	Rhône
Nouaillan, Joseph de	C	Ariège
Pajot, Jules	C/L	Nord
Paris, Auguste	C/D, C	Pas-de-Calais
Partz de Pressy, Adolphe de	C/L	Pas-de-Calais
Pioger, Frédéric de	C/L	Morbihan
Ploeuc, Sebastian de	C/L, C	Seine
Pontoi-Pontcarré, Paul de	C	Eure-et-Loir
Princeteau, Charles	C	Gironde
Puiberneau, Henri de		Vendée
Puvis de Chavannes, François		Saône-et-Loire
Quinsonas, Adolphe de	C/L	Isère
Raudot, Claude	C	Yonne
Rességuier, Albert de	C	Gers
Riant, Léon		Allier
Rincquesen, Louis de		Pas-de-Calais
Rodez-Benavent, Théophile de	C/L	Hérault
Rocquemaurel de St. Cernin	C	Ariège
Rotours, Eugène de		Nord
Sacase, Jean	C/D	Haute-Garonne
Saincthorent, Jean de	C/L, C	Creuse
Saintenac, Henri de	C/L	Ariège
Saint-Pierre, Louis de	C	Manche
Saint-Malo, Joseph de	C/L	Pas-de-Calais

Deputy	Affiliation	Department Represented
Saint-Victor, Louis de	C/L	Rhône
Saisy, Hervé de	C/L	Côtes-du-Nord
Savignhac, Amédée de		Morbihan
Sers, Henri de	C	Loir-et-Cher
Soury-Lavergne, Pierre	C/L	Haute-Vienne
Staplande, Louis de	C/L, C	Nord
Sugny, Joseph de	C	Loire
Tailhand, Adrien	C	Ardèche
Tarteron, Ernest de	C/L, C	Gard
Temple de la Crois, Félix du	C/L	Ille-et-Vilaine
Théry, Antoine	C/L	Nord
Tréveneuc, Fernand de		Finistère
Tréveneuc, Henri de		Côtes-du-Nord
Tréville, Herman de	C/L	Aude
Valady, Henri de		Aveyron
Vauguyon, Stanislas de		Mayenne
Vaulchier, Charles de	C/L, C	Doubs
Ventavon, Louis de	C	Hautes-Alpes
Vétillart, Michel	C/D, C	Sarthe
Vidal, Saturnin	C	Ariège
Vilfeu, Edouard	C/D, C	Mayenne
Vimal-Dessaignes, Pierre	C/L	Puy-de-Dôme
Vinols de Montfleury, Jules de	C/L	Haute-Loire
Vogüé, Léonce de	C	Cher

BIBLIOGRAPHY

Public Archives

Archives nationales, Paris. Series: BB^{30} 490^1 to 490^4 (election frauds, 1876), F^{ic} III (Elections, prefects' reports and correspondence with the minister of the interior); F^7 12431–12444 (general police, royalist intrigues, 1875–1908; I have consulted box F^7 12431); F^7 12477–12486 (general police, clerical intrigues, 1872–1908; I have consulted box F^7 12478); F^{19} 5610 (general police, reports and notes on the attitude of the clergy and particularly the bishops, 1872–1906); F^{19} 5617 (elections, attitude of the clergy, 1876–1886); C 2802 (National Assembly of 1871, agriculture, committee hearings and legislative proposals concerning agricultural reforms); C 2806 to C 2809 (National Assembly of 1871, military reform, committee and subcommittee hearings and legislative proposals concerning the recruitment and the reorganization of the army and navy); C 2839 (National Assembly of 1871, legislative proposals concerning the press); C 2841 (National Assembly of 1871, diverse documents, committee hearings and legislative proposals concerning public and medical assistance in the countryside, the International, and *associations syndicales*); C 2857 (National Assembly of 1871, committee hearings on legislative proposals to repeal the law on coalitions); C 2866 (National Assembly of 1871, committee and subcommittee hearings on decentralization); C 2873 (National Assembly of 1871, child labor, committee hearings and legislative proposals concerning child labor in factories); C 2878 (National Assembly of 1871, parliamentary investigation into the origins of the Commune, public testimony); C 3024 (National Assembly of 1871, parliamentary investigation into working class conditions, public testimony, correspondence 1872–1873, miscellaneous documents 1872–1873); C 3025 (National Assembly of 1871, parliamentary investigation into working class conditions, subcommittee hearings); C 3026 (National

278

Assembly of 1871, parliamentary investigation into working class conditions, committee and subcommittee hearings); C 3129 (National Assembly of 1871, education, committee hearings and legislative proposals concerning primary and higher education); C 3459 A 12 to C 3473 A 26 (elections of 1876, reports of election results).

Archives départementales. Ariège: 2 M 41[1] (correspondence, prefects to the minister of the interior), Zf 290 (elections); Gard: 2 M 70 (elections); Haute-Garonne 4 M 86 (report on political parties in 1866 by subprefect of Muret and addressed to the prefect), 2 M 41 (legislative elections, 1871–1876); Hérault: 2 M⁷ 27 (election of Feb. 8, 1871), 2 M⁸ 11 (election, general council, 1852), 2 M⁸ 45 (election, general council, 1870), 19 M 44 (elections), M 4 (political and administrative reports, 1869–1874), E 190 (Grasset MSS); Ille-et-Vilaine: 3 Me 18 (legislative elections, 1871), 3 Me 19 (legislative elections, 1876–1879), 8 Mf 7 (subprefects' reports, 1859–1876); Maine-et-Loire: 20 M 48–51 (general police); Nord: M 6/9 (general police), M 26/16 (elections, 1838), M 28/4:8 (elections), M 30/5:7 (elections, 1852), M 30/25 and M 30/26 (elections, 1869), M 30/9 (elections, 1859), M 30/27 (elections, 1863), M 30/29 (elections, 1867), M 37/1 (elections, 1876), M 39/2 (political police), M 121/31 (distinctions); Saône-et-Loire: M 258 (elections, Feb. 8, 1871); Basses-Pyrénées: Chesnelong MSS (letters, Charles Chesnelong to his family 1868–1876, and letters, Kolb-Bernard, Maurice Aubry and Olivier de Sugny to Charles Chesnelong 1870–1876); Vienne: 3 M 6/31 to 34 (information on the deputies from the Vienne, 1873); Haute-Vienne: M 162 (elections).

PRIVATE ARCHIVES

Archives of M. le Vicomte Benoist d'Azy (Château du Vieil Azy, St-Benin d'Azy, Nièvre). I have consulted the following: Correspondance des Baron, Baronne Charles avec leur famille (classed by year, 1866–1876); and Azy: Correspondance et Divers, Comte Denys et Baron Charles (I) (no classification). I have also seen the document: Succession du Cte. Benoist d'Azy, Denys.

279

Archives of M. le Baron Chaurand (Château de Chanel, Paysac, Ardèche). Letters written to Baron Chaurand, 1870–1876 (no classification), scrapbook, newspaper clippings, and agenda, 1870–1871.

Archives of M. le Marquis Costa de Beauregard (Château de Beauregard, Chens-sur-Léman, Haute-Savoie). Manuscript biography of Costa de Beauregard written by his wife, Emilie de Quinsonas, and newspaper clippings in a scrapbook concerning the life of Costa de Beauregard.

Archives of Mme. la Comtesse de Fraguier (Sarthe). Titres et documents pour servir de preuves à l'histoire de la maison de Bastard. XIXᵉ siècle. Branches de Guienne. I have consulted Tome 32: Titres et documents concernant Octave, Comte de Bastard d'Estang.

Archives of M. Léon Fresneau ("Le Hamonay," Bourg-des-Comptes, Ille-et-Vilaine). Résumé in manuscript of Armand Fresneau's father's career (unsigned and not dated). Draft of letter (n. d.) written by Armand Fresneau to the Orleanist Pretender after the death of the Comte de Chambord in which Fresneau discusses monarchist organization in France and particularly in Morbihan. Twenty-six newspaper articles (by Armand Fresneau) clipped from various newspapers.

Archives of Jean d'Iribarne (Boulogne-sur-Seine, Seine). Last will and testament of Charles Chesnelong. M. d'Iribarne also possesses the famous letter, addressed to Charles Chesnelong, in which the Comte de Chambord refused, October 1873, to abandon the white flag.

Archives of M. le Marquis de La Guiche (Château de Chaumont, St. Bonnet de Joux, Saône-et-Loire). The La Guiche manuscripts have been organized by a professional archivist. I have consulted the following which concern the deputy Philibert de La Guiche: Dossier 21, No. 473, 473³ᵃ, and 473⁵ᵃ, Autographes mélangés. No. 12291, 1ᵉ Dossier: Prélats et ecclésiastiques. No. 12292, Dossier: Personnages politiques et littéraires. No. 12334 A-L, Dossier: Mis. Philibert de La Guiche, Lettres diverses, élections. No. 12335 M-Z, Dossier: Mis. Philibert de La Guiche, Lettres diverses, élections. No. 12338, Mis. Philibert de La Guiche, documents divers sur les élections. No. 12339, Mis. Philibert de La Guiche, Divers, *Le Journal de Mâcon*, Champvans. Partage des successions confondues de Monsieur le Marquis et Madame la Marquise de La Guiche.

Archives of M. le Marquis de Lordat (Château de la Tour, St-Chaptes, Gard). The Lordat archives have been organized by a professional archivist. I have consulted the following which concern the deputy Roger de Larcy. Dossier: Famille de Larcy; Biens de la famille de Larcy; Prairie d'Alais; Documents, requêtes, etc., concernant divers autres biens. Dossier: Familles Soubert de Larcy et de Roux-Larcy—Biens. Dossier: Lettres envoyées aux membres de sa famille par Baron Roger de Larcy. Dossier V: Larcy, lettres reçues A-D, E-O. Dossier Vᵃ: Larcy (Roger de Soubert, Baron de) Notes et papiers divers. Mémoires incomplets du Baron de Larcy suivis des lettres de l'Abbé Sauvage, son secrétaire. Larcy (Roger Bon. de), la vie politique (1830–1870). Dossier VIᵃ: Famille Roux-Larcy. Ernest Baron de. Documents personnels, vie politique et lettres envoyées. Roux-Larcy, Valentine de, lettres envoyées.

Archives of M. Armand Malartre ("Les Vignes," Dunières, Haute-Loire). Letters from Florentin Malartre to his wife, 1870–1876. The Malartre manuscripts are not catalogued.

Archives of M. Xavier Soury-Lavergne (family home, Rochechouart, Haute-Vienne). Letters from Pierre Soury-Lavergne to his wife, 1871–1876.

Archives of M. le Comte de Sugny (Paris). Visites au Comte de Chambord, 1872–1883. A résumé (typewritten) of Comte de Sugny's visits to the pretender, written after each visit.

Archives of M. Guy Viennet (family home, Béziers, Hérault). Letters, Louis Viennet to members of his family and from members of his family, 1871–1876.

These private archives have never been consulted. They have been locked in rooms and attics awaiting the historians' curiosity. And yet, they are not only of great value for studying the deputies of 1871. Four archives warrant special comment:

1. Armand Malartre archives. Florentin Malartre wrote to his wife, who was an invalid, almost daily when he was in Versailles. In these well-written letters, which sometimes run several pages in length, he describes not only political but social events (balls, receptions, etc.) and with great skill.

2. La Guiche archives. Although these archives contain few letters written by the deputy, they are filled with letters he received from people of national and local importance. This correspondence is especially valuable for studying the electoral history of Saône-et-Loire.

3. Benoist d'Azy archives. Denys Benoist d'Azy's political career spanned half a century. The archival holdings touch on much of the period. Because he was also an important financier-industrialist, the archives contain a great deal of information about early industrialization in France, especially in the metallurgical industries of Gard and Nièvre.

4. Lordat archives. Roger de Larcy was active in politics for fifty years. He was minister of public works in one of Thiers' cabinets. The documents in the Lordat archives cover, if incompletely, much of this period.

Published Documents

Aubry, Maurice. *Discours prononcé par . . . , représentant du peuple (Vosges) dans la discussion du projet de loi relatif au délit d'usure.* Séance du 27 juin 1850. Paris: Typographie Panckouchke, 1850.

France. Annales parlementaires. *Annales de l'Assemblée nationale,* 48 vols.

France. Assemblée nationale. *Documents parlementaires.* Annexes au procès-verbaux des séances. Projets et propositions de loi. Exposés des motifs et rapports.

France. Corps législatif. *Enquête parlementaire sur le régime économique.* Déposition de Maurice Aubry, membre de la Chambre de Commerce de Paris. Séance du 8 juin 1870. Paris: Imprimerie et Librairie du Journal officiel, 1870.

France. Ministère de l'agriculture, du commerce, et des travaux publics. *Enquête agricole.* 38 vols. Paris: Imprimerie impériale, 1867–1872. This publication contains 37 volumes and a volume of tables. It is divided into four series: 1ᵉ série, Documents généraux, décrets, rapports. Séances de la commission supérieure. 1869–1870. 4 vols.; 2ᵉ série, Enquêtes départementales, 28 vols. The departmental investigations were conducted by regional committees which investigated conditions in several departments. Metropolitan France was divided into 28 regions (circonscriptions); 3ᵉ série, Dépositions orales reçues par la commission supérieure; 4ᵉ série, Documents recueillis à l'étranger, 3 vols.

Meaux, Vicomte de. *Discours prononcé par . . . .* Loi sur les associations. Extrait du Journal officiel de 6 mars 1872. Paris: Imprimerie et Librairie du Journal officiel, 1872.

Melun, Comte de. *Rapport fait au nom de la commission chargée d'étudier la situation des classes ouvrières en France. Situation matérielle et économique des ouvriers par* . . . . Paris: Chaix et Cie., 1875.

Princeteau, C. J. *Discours à la séance du 25 avril 1872.* Extrait du Journal officiel du 26 avril 1872. Paris, 1872.

PROVINCIAL NEWSPAPERS

The following newspapers were consulted for the two electoral periods, January–February 1871 and January–March 1876. They often contain biographical features as well as electoral news and are invaluable for electoral studies. The newspapers dealing with the elections of 1876 are deposited in the Versailles Annex of the Bibliothèque nationale. Only a few of the issues covering the 1871 elections can be found in Versailles. Those found were in municipal libraries, departmental archives, or private archives. The election (1871 and/or 1876) for which the newspaper was read is given after the newspaper's name. If consulted in the provinces, the place where the newspaper is located is also cited. Abbreviations: B. M., Bibliothèque municipale; A. D., Archives départementales; P. A., Private archives.

Ain
Le Courrier de l'Ain, 1871 (B. M., Brou), 1876.
Allier
Le Mémorial de l'Allier, 1876.
Le Messager de l'Allier, 1876.
La Semaine de Cusset et du Vichy, 1876.
Hautes-Alpes
L'Appel au peuple des Hautes-Alpes, 1876.
La Constitution du 25 février, 1876.
La Durance, 1876.
L'Indépendant des Alpes, 1876.
Ardèche
Le Bas-Vivrais, 1876.
L'Echo de l'Ardèche. 1876.
Le Journal d'Annonay, 1871 (P. A., Malartre), 1876.
La République libérale, 1876.
Ardennes
Le Courrier des Ardennes, 1876.

Le Moniteur ardennais, 1876.

Le Nord-Est, journal républicain des Ardennes, 1876.

Ariège

L'Ariégeois, 1876.

Le Progrès de l'Ariège, 1876.

Aude

Le Courrier de l'Aude, 1876.

Le Courrier de Narbonne, 1876.

Le Républicain de Narbonne, 1876.

L'Union de l'Aude, 1876.

Aveyron

L'Aveyronnais, 1876.

Le Courrier de l'Aveyron, 1876.

Le Journal de l'Aveyron, 1876.

Le Peuple, 1876.

Le Républicain de l'Aveyron, 1876.

Calvados

Le Bonhomme normand, 1876.

L'Echo honfleurais, 1876.

L'Indicateur de Bayeux, 1876.

Le Journal de Caen, 1876.

L'Ordre et la liberté, 1876.

Cher

Le Courrier du Berry, 1876.

L'Echo du Cher, 1871.

Le Journal de Sancerre, 1871, 1876.

Le Journal du Cher, 1876.

L'Union républicaine, 1876.

Corrèze

Le Corrézien, 1876.

Le Journal de la Corrèze, 1876.

La République, 1871, 1876.

Côtes-du-Nord

L'Armorique, 1876.

L'Indépendance bretonne, 1876.

Le Journal de Lannion, 1871.

Le Moniteur des Côtes-du-Nord, 1876.

La Presse bretonne, 1871.

Le Progrès des Côtes-du-Nord, 1876.

Le Propagateur des Côtes-du-Nord, 1876.

Le Publicateur des Côtes-du-Nord, 1871.

Creuse
L'Abeille de la Creuse, 1876.
Le Courrier de la Creuse, 1876.
La Creuse républicaine, 1876.
L'Echo de la Creuse, 1876.

Dordogne
La Dordogne, Gazette des campagnes, 1871 (A. D., Dordogne).
L'Echo de la Dordogne et de Vésone, 1871 (A. D., Dordogne), 1876.
Le Journal de Bergerac et de la Dordogne, 1876.
Le Périgord, journal de la Dordogne, 1871 (A. D., Dordogne), 1876.
Le Progrès de Bergerac et de la Dordogne, 1876.

Doubs
Le Courrier franc-comtois, 1876.
La Démocratie franc-comtoise, 1876.
Le Journal de Pontarlier, 1876.
L'Union franc-comtoise, 1876.

Eure-et-Loir
L'Echo dunois, 1876.
Le Journal de Chartres, 1871 (A. D., Eure-et-Loir), 1876.
L'Union agricole, 1871 (A. D., Eure-et-Loir), 1876.

Finistère
Le Finistère, 1876.
L'Impartial du Finistère, 1876.
Le Morlaisien, 1876.
L'Océan, 1876.

Gard
Le Drapeau national, 1876.
L'Echo des Cévennes, 1876.
L'Extrême-Droite, 1876.
La Gazette de Nîmes, 1871 (A. D., Gard), 1876.
Le Midi, 1876.
L'Opinion du Midi, 1871 (A. D., Gard).

Haute-Garonne
La Gazette de Languedoc, 1876.
Le Journal de Saint-Gaudens, 1876.
Le Journal de Toulouse, 1871 (B. M., Toulouse).
Le Progrès libéral, 1871 (B. M., Toulouse).

Gers
L'Appel au peuple, 1876.

285

L'Avenir, 1871, 1876.

Le Conservateur et le Gers réunis, 1876.

Le Conservateur, 1871.

Gironde

Le Courrier de la Gironde, 1876.

La Guienne, 1876.

Le Journal de Bordeaux, 1876.

La Victoire de la démocratie, 1876.

Hérault

Le Conservateur du Midi, 1876.

L'Echo de Lodève, 1876.

La Liberté, 1871 (B. M., Montpellier).

Le Messager du Midi, 1871 (B. M., Montpellier), 1876.

La République, 1876.

L'Union nationale, 1876.

Ille-et-Vilaine

L'Avenir de Rennes, 1876.

La Gazette de Bretagne, 1876.

Le Journal de Rennes, 1871 (A. D., Ille-et-Vilaine), 1876.

Le Journal de Redon, 1871 (A. D., Ille-et-Vilaine).

Le Journal de Saint-Malo, 1876.

Indre-et-Loire

L'Indépendant d'Indre-et-Loire, 1876.

Le Journal d'Indre-et-Loire, 1871, 1876.

Le Messager d'Indre-et-Loire, 1876.

Le Républicain d'Indre-et-Loire, 1871.

L'Union libérale, 1871, 1876.

Isère

Le Courrier de l'Isère, 1876.

L'Impartial dauphinois, 1876.

Le Journal de Vienne et de l'Isère, 1876.

L'Unité française, le messager dauphinois, 1876.

Jura

L'Avenir du Jura, 1876.

Le Courrier du Jura, 1876.

Le Journal du Jura et de la Franche-Comté, 1876.

Le Salinois, 1876.

La Sentinelle du Jura, 1876.

Loir-et-Cher

L'Echo de Loir-et-Cher, 1876.

L'Indépendant, 1876.
Le Journal de Loir-et-Cher, 1876.
Loire
Le Journal de Montbrison, 1876.
Le Mémorial de la Loire, 1871 (P. A., Malartre), 1876.
Le Républicain de la Loire et de la Haute-Loire, 1876.
Le Stephanois, 1876.
Haute-Loire
L'Indépendant de Brioude, 1871 (P. A., Malartre).
La Haute-Loire, 1871 (P. A., Malartre).
Loire-Inférieure
L'Espérance du peuple, 1876.
La Gazette de l'Ouest, 1871 (A. D., Loire-Atlantique).
Le Journal de Chateaubriand, 1876.
Le Phare de la Loire, 1871 (A. D., Loire-Atlantique), 1876.
L'Union bretonne, 1871 (A. D., Loire-Atlantique), 1876.
L'Union démocratique, 1871 (A. D., Loire-Atlantique).
Loiret
Les Amis de l'ordre du Loiret, 1871, 1876.
L'Avenir du Loiret, 1876.
Le Courrier du Loiret, 1871, 1876.
L'Indépendant de Gien, 1876.
Le Journal du Loiret, 1876.
Lot
Le Conservateur du Lot, 1876.
Le Courrier du Lot, 1871, 1876.
Le Gourdonnais, 1871.
Le Journal du Lot, 1876.
Le Mémorial de Figeac, 1876.
Le Réformateur, 1876.
Le Républicain du Lot, 1876.
Lot-et-Garonne
Je Journal de Lot-et-Garonne, 1876.
Le Progrès, 1876.
Le Réveil du Lot-et-Garonne, 1876.
L'Union du Sud-Ouest, 1876.
Lozère
L'Echo des montagnes, 1871.
Le Propagateur de Florac, 1871.

287

Maine-et-Loire

Le Journal de Maine-et-Loire, 1871 (A. D., Maine-et-Loire).

Le Patriote, 1871 (A. D., Maine-et-Loire).

Manche

L'Avranchin, 1876.

L'Echo régional de la Normandie et la Bretagne, 1876.

Le Journal de Granville, 1876.

Haute-Marne

L'Echo de la Haute-Marne, 1876.

La Haute-Marne, 1876.

La Presse langroise, 1876.

L'Union de la Haute-Marne, 1876.

Mayenne

L'Ami des campagnes, 1876.

L'Echo de la Mayenne, 1876.

L'Indépendant de l'Ouest, 1876.

Le Journal du Château-Gontier, 1876.

L'Ordre, 1876.

Meuse

Le Courrier de Verdun, 1876.

L'Echo de l'Est, 1876.

L'Indépendant de Montmédy, 1876.

La Meuse, 1876.

Morbihan

L'Avenir du Morbihan, 1876.

Le Courrier de Bretagne, 1876.

Le Courrier des campagnes, 1876.

Le Journal du Morbihan, 1876.

Nièvre

Le Conservateur de la Nièvre, 1876.

Le Journal de la Nièvre, 1876.

Le Nivernais, 1876.

La République, 1876.

Nord

Le Courrier populaire du Nord de la France, 1876.

L'Echo du Nord, 1876.

Le Propagateur du Nord et du Pas-de-Calais, 1876.

La Vraie France, 1876.

Oise

L'Echo de l'Oise, 1876.

Le Journal de l'Oise, 1876.

Le Moniteur de l'Oise, 1876.

Le Semeur de l'Oise, 1876.

Pas-de-Calais

L'Avenir d'Arras et du Pas-de-Calais, 1876.

L'Avenir de Saint-Pierre, 1876.

Le Courrier de Pas-de-Calais, 1876.

Le Mémorial artésien, 1876.

Le Pas-de-Calais, 1876.

Puy-de-Dôme

Le Conservateur du Puy-de-Dôme, 1876.

La Gazette d'Auvergne, 1876.

Le Moniteur du Dimanche, 1876.

Le Moniteur de Puy-de-Dôme, 1876.

Le Riom-Journal, 1876.

Basses-Pyrénées

L'Avenir de Pyrénées et de Landes, 1876.

L'Echo des Pyrénées, 1876.

La Gazette des Pyrénées, 1876.

L'Indépendant des Basses-Pyrénées, 1876.

Le Mémorial des Pyrénées, 1871 (A. D., Basses-Pyrénées),
1876.

Haute-Pyrénées

L'Abeille des Pyrénées, 1876.

L'Ere nouvelle, 1876.

L'Observateur, 1876.

Rhône

Le Courrier de Lyon, 1876.

La Décentralisation, 1876.

L'Echo de Fourvière, 1876.

Le Salut public, 1871 (P. A., Malartre), 1876.

Haute-Saône

L'Avenir de la Haute-Saône, 1876.

L'Indépendant de la Haute-Saône, 1876.

Le Journal de la Haute-Saône, 1876.

Saône-et-Loire

Le Conservateur de Saône-et-Loire, 1876.

Le Courrier de Saône-et-Loire, 1876.

L'Echo de Saône-et-Loire, 1876.

L'Echo du Charollais, 1876.

Le Journal de Saône-et-Loire, 1871 (A. D., Saône-et-Loire),
1876.

Sarthe
  L'Avenir, 1876.
  La Chronique de l'Ouest, 1871 (A. D., Sarthe), 1876.
  Le Journal du Mans, 1876.
  La Sarthe, 1871 (A. D., Sarthe), 1876.
  L'Union de la Sarthe, 1871 (A. D., Sarthe), 1876.
Savoie
  Le Bons sens de la Savoie, 1876.
  Le Courrier des Alpes, 1876.
  Le Patriote savoisien, 1876.
Seine
  Le Figaro, 1876.
  Le Français, 1876.
  La Gazette de France, 1876.
  Le Temps, 1876.
  L'Union, 1876.
  L'Univers, 1876.
Seine-Inférieure
  La Gazette de Normandie, 1876.
  Le Journal de Rouen, 1876.
  Le Havre, 1876.
  Le Nouvelliste de Rouen, 1876.
Deux-Sèvres
  Le Mémorial des Deux-Sèvres, 1876.
  Le Poitou, 1876.
  La Revue de l'Ouest, 1876.
  La Sèvre, 1876.
Somme
  L'Echo de la Somme, 1871, 1876.
  Le Journal d'Amiens, 1876.
  Le Journal de Péronne et de la Somme, 1876.
  Le Propagateur picard, 1876.
Tarn
  L'Echo du Tarn, 1876.
  Le Journal du Tarn, 1876.
  Le Patriote albigeois, 1876.
  Le Tarn, 1876.
Tarn-et-Garonne
  Le Courrier de Tarn-et-Garonne, 1876.
  Le Républicain de Tarn-et-Garonne, 1876.

Vendée
  L'Avenir de la Vendée, 1876.
  La Gazette vendéenne, 1876.
  L'Indicateur, 1876.
  Le Libéral de la Vendée, 1876.
  Le Publicateur de la Vendée, 1876.
  Le Publicateur, journal de la Vendée, 1871 (B. M., Roche-sur-
    Yon), 1876.
Vienne
  L'Avenir de la Vienne, 1876.
  Le Dimanche, 1876.
  Le Journal de la Vienne, 1871 (A. D., Vienne), 1876.
  Le Journal de l'Ouest, 1876.
Haute-Vienne
  Le Courrier du Centre, 1871 (B. M., Limoges), 1876.
Vosges
  L'Abeille des Vosges, 1876.
  La Gazette vosgienne, 1876.
  L'Impartial des Vosges, 1876.
  Le Journal de Remiremont, 1876.
  Le Vosgien, 1876.
Yonne
  La Bourgogne, 1876.
  La Constitution, 1876.
  Le Nouvelliste de l'Yonne, 1876.
  La Revue de l'Yonne, 1876.
  L'Yonne, 1876.

BOOKS, MEMOIRS, ARTICLES, AND PAMPHLETS
WRITTEN BY THE LEGITIMIST DEPUTIES

Only the publications that have been most useful in preparing this study are cited. Other works written by the legitimist deputies can be found in the Bibliothèque nationale. Consult the general catalogue.

Books and Memoirs

Aubry, Maurice. *Théorie et pratique ou union de l'économie politique avec la morale.* Paris: Guillaumin et Cie., 1851.
Belcastel, Gabriel de. *A mes électeurs. Cinq ans de vie politique, votes principaux, propositions, lettres et discours.* Toulouse: Imprimerie de M. M. Douladoure, 1876.

Chesnelong, Charles. *Les derniers jours de l'Empire et le gouverne-ment de M. Thiers. Mémoires publiés par son petit-fils.* Paris: Librairie Académique Perrin, 1932.

————. *Un témoignage sur un point d'histoire. La campagne monarchique d'octobre 1873.* Paris: Librairie Plon, 1895.

Diesbach de Belleroche, Comte Eugène de. *Souvenirs et mémoires du* ————. *Ancien député à l'Assemblée nationale de 1871. De 1817 à 1905.* Namur: Imprimerie Dupagne-Counet et fils, 1911. Edition exclusivement réservée à la famille de Diesbach de Belleroche.

Franclieu, Mis. de. *Les libre-échangistes ne sont pas des écono-mistes—législation des céréales.* Paris: Librairie de l'agricul-ture, 1868.

Fresneau, Armand. *Une nation au pillage.* Paris: Librairie Cleriot, Henri Gautier, successeur, 1888.

Gavardie, E. de. *Etudes sur les vraies doctrines sociales et poli-tiques.* Pau: Imprimerie et Lithographie Véronèse, 1862.

Gouvello, Amédée de. *Vues sur la réorganisation de la France.* Vannes: Imprimerie de L. Galles, 1871.

Lacombe, Charles de. *Journal politique de Charles de Lacombe député à l'Assemblée nationale.* 2 vols. Paris: Alphonse Picard et fils, 1907–1908.

Lefèvre-Pontalis, Amédée. *L'Assemblée nationale et M. Thiers. Premier partie: les essais de constitution.* Paris: Jules Gervais, 1879.

Lucien-Brun. *Introduction à l'étude du droit.* 2ᵉ édition. Paris: Librairie Victor Lecoffre, 1887.

Meaux, Vicomte de. *Souvenirs politiques: 1871–1877.* Paris, 1905.

Montlaur, E. de. *L'ordre social.* Moulins: Imprimerie et Librairie de L. Thibaud, 1849.

Valades, P. B. des. *Martial Delpit, député à l'Assemblée na-tionale, journal et correspondance.* Paris: Maison Didot, 1898.

Vinols de Montfleury, Baron de. *Mémoires politiques d'un membre de l'Assemblée nationale constituante de 1871.* Le Puy: Im-primerie de J. M. Freyclier, 1882.

Articles

Belcastel, Gabriel de. "Les principes de 89. Discours prononcé le 13 octobre 1887 au congrès des jurisconsultes catholiques à Montpellier." *Revue catholique des institutions et du droit,* XXX (1888), 487–592.

Benoist d'Azy, Denys. "Désastre des mines de Lalle." *L'Almanach illustré de l'ouvrier pour l'année 1863*, 1862, pp. 69–80.

Fresneau, Armand. "Itinéraire de la République à la Légitimité." *Revue trimestrielle*, no. 2 (15 avril 1880), 278–310.

————. "La crise des subsistances." *Revue trimestrielle*, no. 3 (15 juillet 1880), 497–534.

————. "Six ans de bons sens et d'honnêteté dans le gouvernement économique de la France." *Revue trimestrielle*, 2e année, no. 1 (15 janvier 1881), 35–68.

————. "Les spectres," *Revue trimestrielle*, no. 1 (15 janvier 1880), 106–136.

————. "Le suffrage universel," *Revue trimestrielle*, 2e année, no. 2 (15 avril 1881), 344–373.

Kergorlay, Comte de. "Allocution de M. le comte de Kergorlay, président." *Société internationale des études pratiques d'économie sociale*, IV (1873), 21–27.

Kolb-Bernard, Charles. "La révolution et M. Thiers." *Le Contemporain: Revue d'économie chrétienne*, 3e série, VI (novembre 1873), 193–229.

————. "Le Septennat." *Le Contemporain: Revue d'économie chrétienne*, 3e série, VII (mai 1874), 769-780.

Pamphlets

Aubry, Maurice. *Les écoles d'enseignement primaire supérieur, d'enseignement secondaire spécial ou d'enseignement professionnel du point du vue commercial.* Paris: Imprimerie Ve Ethiou-Perou & A. Klein, 1878.

————. *Le travail des femmes dans les ateliers, manufactures et magasins.* Nancy: Typographie de N. Collin, 1875.

Baragnon, Louis-Numa. *Documents pour mes collègues de l'Assemblée.* Paris: A. Wittersheim et Cie., 1874.

————. *Les écoles populaires et le droit des pères de famille.* Paris: Librairie de la société-bibliographique, 1879.

Bidard, Théophile. *De la liberté d'enseignement. Du droit de conférer les grades.* Rennes: Imprimerie Catel, 1876.

Bourgeois, Dr. Paul. *A Monsieur le Comte de Chambord.* Nantes: Imprimerie Bourgeois, 1879.

————. *Versailles, le 28 mars 1871.* Versailles: Imprimerie de Crète, 1871.

Chaurand, Baron. *De l'enseignement de l'agriculture.* Paris: Imprimerie de C. Lahure, 1867.

Chesnelong, Charles. *La conversion au Sénat*. Paris: Imprimerie F. Lève, 1883.

―――. *La situation financière de la France en 1883*. Paris: Imprimerie F. Lève, 1882.

Cumont, Arthur de. *Les incurables*. 2ᵉ édition. Angers: Imprimerie Lachese et Dolbeau, 1883.

Delpit, Martial. *Les questions du jour. Lettre aux électeurs de la Dordogne*. Périgueux: Imprimerie Dupont, 1848.

Franclieu, Mis. de. *Rapport au roi sur le vote universel honnêtement pratiqué*. Tarbes: Imprimerie A. J. Lescamele, 1874.

―――. *Rapport sur les propositions de M. Dejernon*. Tarbes: Th. Talmon, Imprimeur de la Préfecture, 1869.

Fresneau, Armand. *L'atelier français en 1879*. Paris: E. Dentu, 1879.

―――. *La planche de salut*. Paris: Cornon, Libraire-éditeur, comptoir des imprimeurs unis, 1851.

―――. *Kermandis, du 1 avril au 15 août 1868. Rapport adressé à M. le Cte de Segur d'Agusseau. Comment on peut quintupler le revenu d'une ferme bretonne*. Versailles: Imprimerie de Brunox, 1868.

―――. *Le roi*. Paris: T. Olmer, 1877.

Gouvello, Amédée de. *Colonies agricoles pour les enfants trouvés et abandonnés*. Blois: Imprimerie Lesesne, 1862.

―――. *Société des agriculteurs de France. Rapports de* ―――. *Fermes-écoles*. Paris: Imprimerie de A. Laine, 1869.

―――. *La dépopulation des campagnes. Les asiles ruraux et les orphelinats agricoles*. Paris: Blériot, Libraire-éditeurs, 1869.

Keller, Emile. *Le budget d'un catholique*. Besançon: Paul Jacquin, 1891.

―――. *Dix années de déficit de 1859 à 1869*. Paris: Librairie Poussielque frères, 1869.

Lacombe, Charles de. *M. Berryer et la situation présente*. Paris: Librairie Didier et Cie. et Librairie de Ch. Douniol et Cie., 1874.

Lefèvre-Pontalis, Amédée. *L'Assemblée nationale et M. Thiers. Première Partie. Les essais de constitutions*. Paris: Jules Gervais, Libraire-éditeur, 1879.

Le Lasseux, Ernest. *Enquête parlementaire—questionnaire agriculture*. Comices agricoles du canton de Grez-en-Bouère. Château-Gontier: Bézier, imprimeur, n. d.

―――. *Comices agricoles de Laval. Rapport de la commission chargée par les comices agricoles de Laval de signaler au gou-*

vernement les entraves apportées aux progrès de l'agriculture par suite de la coalition générale des mines de la Sarthe et de la Mayenne. Laval: Imprimerie de H. Godbert, 1853.

Lucien-Brun. *La politique des expédients et la politique des principes.* Paris: Librairie de la société-bibliographique, 1881.

————. *Discours prononcé dans la discussion générale sur les projets de lois relatifs à l'organisation des pouvoirs publics.* Paris: Fechoz, Libraire-éditeur, 1875.

————. *L'union de la paix sociale.* Tours: Alfred Mame et fils, Libraires-éditeurs, 1872.

Meaux, Vicomte de. *L'Assemblée nationale en 1872.* Paris: Charles Douniol et Cie., 1872.

————. *Les conclusions de l'Enquête agricole.* Paris: Charles Douniol, Libraire-éditeur, 1869.

Monjaret de Kerjégu, F. de. *Brest et les transatlantiques.* Brest: Imprimerie de J. B. Lefournier ainé, 1875.

Monjaret de Kerjégu, Louis de. *Quelques réflexions à propos de l'Enquête parlementaire agricole.* Brest: J. B. et A. Lefournier, 1870.

————. *Les souffrances de l'agriculture.* Brest: Imprimerie de J. B. Lefournier ainé, 1866.

————. *Les souffrances de l'agriculture.* II. *Propriété obligée.* Brest: Imprimerie de J. B. Lefournier ainé, 1866.

Mun, Cte. Albert de, Chesnelong, et Belcastel, Gabriel de. *L'aurore du salut de la France dans les trois oeuvres des cercles catholiques d'ouvriers des comités catholiques et du voeu national au Sacré-Coeur.* Trois discours. Perpignan: Aymerick. Imprimeur-libraire, n. d.

Pervanchère, Richard de la. *L'agriculture en Bretagne.* Nantes: Imprimerie du commerce, 1867.

Princeteau, C. J. Conseil général de la Gironde. Séance du 12 septembre 1849. *Rapport fait au nom de la commission de décentralisation.* Bordeaux: Imprimerie d'Emile Crugy, 1850.

Raudot, Claude. *L'administration locale en France et en Angleterre.* Paris: Charles Douniol, Libraire-éditeur, 1863.

————. *De l'agriculture en France.* Paris: Charles Douniol, Libraire-éditeur, 1857.

BIOGRAPHICAL WORKS

"Andelarre, Jules Jaquot." *Polybiblion: Revue bibliographique universelle, nécrologie.* 2ᵉ série, IX (January–June, 1879).

"Anselin-Paul Pasquier, Marquis de Franclieu." *Polybiblion: Revue bibliographique universelle, nécrologie.* 2ᵉ série, VI (July–December, 1877).

Ariège pittoresque, Revue hebdomadaire. Illustrée. 3ᵉ année, no. 98 (April 30, 1914).

Audiat, Louis. "Le Marquis Elie de Dampierre, 1813–1896." *Extrait de La Revue de Saintonge et d'Aunis, Bulletin de la Société des Archives historiques de la Saintonge et de l'Aunis,* March 1, 1896.

Baunard, Mgr. "Kolb-Bernard." *Reliques d'histoire: Notices et portraits.* Paris: Libraire Ch. Pousselgue, 1899, pp. 238–387.

Beaune, Henri. *Lucien Brun. Notice biographique.* Paris: Librairie Victor Lecoffre, 1901.

Beraud, Edmond. *Le Dernier des La Rochejaquelein.* Paris: Librairie H. Oudin, 1898.

Bertry, L., Abbé. *Vie de Léon de Jouvenel.* Député de la Corrèze (1811–1886). Paris: Imprimerie Chastrusse, Praudel et Cie., 1931.

Biré, Edmond, *Biographies contemporaines. XIXᵉ siècle.* Lyon-Paris: Librairie Emmanuel Vitte, 1905.

Edouard de Cazenove de Pradine (1838–1896). Paris: de Saye et fils, 1897.

"Célébration solennelle du centenaire d'Alfred Lallié." *Bulletin de la Société archéologique et historique de Nantes et de la Loire-Inférieure,* LXI (1931), 5–70.

"M. Claude-Marie Raudot," *Polybiblion: Revue bibliographique universelle, nécrologie.* 2ᵉ série, IX (January–June), 456.

Clerc, A. V. *Nos députés à l'Assemblée nationale, leur biographies et leurs votes, documents historiques sur la législature de 1871–1872.* Paris: A. le Chevalier, 1872.

Clere, Jules. *Biographie des députés. Avec leurs principaux votes.* Paris: Garnier Frères, Libraires-éditeurs, 1875.

Combes de Patris, B. *Des Gardes français à la Convention:* Valady (1766–1793). Paris: E. de Boccard, 1930.

Cornulier-Lucinière, Ernest de. *Généalogie historique de la maison de Cornulier. Autrefois de Cornille en Bretagne.* Orléans: H. Herluison, Libraire-éditeur, 1889.

Les Députés par groupes parlementaires. Paris: Librairie des Publications législatives, 1873.

Devigne, Paul. *Charette et les zouaves pontificaux. Les grands hommes de l'église au XIXᵉ siècle.* Paris: Librairie P. J. Beduchaud-éditeur, 1913.

Dictionnaire biographique et album. Gard. Paris: Néauber et Cie., éditeurs, 1905.

Dictionnaire biographique de la Loire-Inférieure. Paris: Henri Jouve, Imprimeur-éditeur, 1895.

Dictionnaire biographique illustré d'Eure-et-Loir. Paris: Flammarion, 1911.

Dictionnaire biographique illustré. Ille-et-Vilaine. Dictionnaires biographiques illustrés départementaux. Paris: Flammarion, 2ᵉ édition, 1909.

Didierjean, le père. *Elèves des jésuites. Souvenirs des collèges de la Compagnie de Jésus en France, 1850–1880.* Première série. Tome premier. Paris: V. Palme, 1882.

Dutemple, Edmond. *Guide impartial des électeurs. Biographie et travaux des représentants à l'Assemblée nationale.* Paris: Lachaud et Burdin, éditeurs, 1874.

Douchy, M. "Notice biographique de M. le comte de Melun," *Annales de la Société historique et archéologique de Château-Thierry*, 1888, pp. 69–75.

Etoc-Demazy, F. "Notice sur M. M. F. Vétillart." *Bulletin de la société royale d'agriculture, sciences et arts du Mans*, II (1837), 202–207.

Gautherot, Gustave. *Emile Keller (1828–1909). Un demi-siècle de défense nationale et religieuse.* Paris: Plon-Nourrit et Cie., 1922.

Généalogie de la famille Bernard. Lille, 1924.

Le Gouriérec, Th. *Les candidats députés de la Loire-Inférieure. Silhouettes et Portraits.* Nantes: Imprimerie administrative de Paul Plédian, 1876.

Guérin, Jean et Bernard. *Des hommes et des activités autour d'un demi-siècle.* Bordeaux: Editions B. E. B., 1957.

Hauterive, Borel d'. *Annuaire de la noblesse de France et des maisons souveraines de l'Europe.* Paris: Borel d'Hauterive, 1849–1891.

Kerviler, René *et al. Répertoire général de bio-bibliographie bretonne.* Livre premier. *Les Bretons.* 17 vols. (Aa-Guerpin). Rennes: J. Plihon et L. Hervé, 1886-1908.

Kirwan, D. de. *Charles Chesnelong. Son rôle sous le Second Empire et les régimes qui ont suivi.* Paris: Sueur-Charrecey, Librairie-éditeur, 1909.

Labourasse, H. M. *Félix Gillon.* Nancy: A. Crépin-Leblond, 1898.

Laveille, Mgr. *Chesnelong, sa vie, son action catholique et parlementaire (1820–1899)*. Paris: P. Lethielleux, Libraire-éditeur, 1912.

Maillard, E. *Nantes et le département au XIXᵉ siècle. Littérateurs, savants, musiciens, et hommes distingués*. Nantes: Librairie Vier, 1891.

Le Comte Florentin Malartre. Le Puy: Imprimerie de l'Avenir de la Haute-Loire, 1913.

Marcey, M. de. *Charles Chesnelong son histoire et celle de son temps*. Paris: Librairie Emmanuel Vitte, 1908.

Merveilleux du Vignaux, Charles. *Un peu d'histoire à propos d'un nom. Ernoul*. La Chappelle et Montligeon: Imprimerie de Notre-Dame de Montligeon, 1900.

"Notice sur le comte Anatole de Melun," *Société de Saint-Vincent de Paul*. Lille: Imprimerie de J. Lefort, 1888.

"Notice sur les membres de l'Institut des provinces: M. le marquis de Montlaur de l'Allier," *Annuaire de l'Institut des provinces*. 2ᵉ série, XIV (1862), 571–573.

Rabbé, *et al. Biographie universelle et portative des contemporains*. Paris: Chez l'éditeur, 1836.

Raymond-Cahussac, Charles de. "Notice sur M. Gabriel de Belcastel, membre résident de la société d'agriculture de la Haute-Garonne." *Journal d'agriculture pratique de la Haute-Garonne*, LXXXVI (juin 1890).

Ribeyre, Félix. *La Biographie des représentants*. Angers: Au bureau de la publication, 1872.

Robert, A. *et al. Dictionnaire des parlementaires français*. 5 vols. Paris: Bourloton, 1890 ff.

Le Marquis de La Roche-Aymon. Hommage et souvenirs. Moulins: Imprimerie Etienne Auclaire, 1892.

Saint-Allais, N. Viton de. *Nobiliaire universel de France ou recueil général des généalogies historiques des maisons nobles de ce royaume*. Paris: Au bureau du nobiliaire universel de France, 1814–1843.

Gabriel de Saint-Victor. Lyon: Imprimerie X. Jevain, n. d.

Salliard, Etienne. *Les Laurenceau Vouillé au siècle dernier*. Poitiers: Société des antiquaires de l'Ouest, 1950.

Salmon, Charles A. *M. Paulin Gillon (1796–1878)*. Bar-le-duc: Imprimerie Contaut-Laguerre, 1881.

Spoll, E. A. *Nos représentants et leurs votes*. Paris: E. Polo, éditeur, 1873.

Vapereau, Gustave. *Dictionnaire universel des contemporains.* Paris: Librairie de L. Hachette, 1880.

Secondary Works

Books

Anderson, Eugene N. and Pauline R. *Political Institutions and Social Change in Continental Europe in the Nineteenth Century.* Berkeley and Los Angeles: University of California Press, 1968.

Audiffret-Pasquier, Duc d'. *La maison de France et l'Assemblée nationale, Souvenirs, 1871–1883.* Paris: Librairie Plon, 1938.

Augé-Laribé, Michel. *La politique agricole de la France de 1860 à 1940.* Paris: Presses universitaires de France, 1950.

———. *La révolution agricole.* Paris: Editions Albin Michel, 1955.

Barber, Elinor G. *The Bourgeoisie in Eighteenth Century France.* Princeton, N. J.: Princeton University Press, 1955.

Beau de Loménie, Emmanuel. *Les dynasties bourgeoises et la fête impériale.* Paris: Sequana, 1942.

———. *Les responsabilités des dynasties bourgeoises.* Tome I., *de Bonaparte à Mac-Mahon.* Paris: Les Editions Denoël, 1943.

———. *La restauration manquée. L'Affaire du drapeau blanc.* Paris: Editeurs des Portiques, 1932.

Belleval, le Marquis de. *Souvenirs de ma jeunesse.* Paris: Librairie historique des Provinces, Emile Lechevalier, 1895.

Bertier de Sauvigny, Gabriel de. *La restauration.* Paris: Flammarion, 1955.

Bloch, Marc. *Les caractères originaux de l'histoire rurale française.* 2ᵉ edition. Paris: Armand Colin, 1960.

Bodan, Charles du. *Discours prononcés de 1838 à 1858. Précédés d'une lettre à ses fils.* Corbeil: Imprimerie de Crète et fils, 1868.

Bodley, John Edward Courtenay. *France.* London: Macmillan, and Co., Ltd., 1899.

Boudet, Jacques (Director of Publication). *Le monde des affaires en France de 1830 à nos jours.* Paris: Société d'éditions de dictionnaires et encyclopédies, 1952.

Brabant, Herbert F. *The Beginning of the Third Republic. A History of the National Assembly (February–September, 1871).* New York: Macmillan, 1940.

Brimo, A. *Méthode de la Géo-sociologie électorale.* Paris: Inst. Et. Pol., 1968.

Brogden, Neal Haun. "French Military Reform after the defeat of 1870–71." Diss., University of California at Los Angeles, 1961.

Brown, Marvin L. Jr., *The Comte de Chambord, The Third Republic's Uncompromising King.* Durham, North Carolina: Duke University Press, 1967.

Bury, J. P. T. *Gambetta and the National Defense: A Republican Dictatorship in France.* London: Longmans, Green and Co., 1936.

Chambers, J. D. and Mingay, G. E. *The Agricultural Revolution, 1750–1880.* London: B. T. Batsford Ltd., 1968.

Clément-Simon, Gve. *La Comtesse de Valon. Apollonie de Rochelambert. Souvenirs de sa vie, ses amis, ses correspondantes.* Paris: Plon, Nourrit et Cie., 1909.

Clinchamps, Philippe du Puy de. *Le Royalisme.* Paris: Presses Universitaires de France, 1967.

Cobban, Alfred. *A History of Modern France, 1799–1945.* Vol. II. London: Penguin Books, 1961.

————. *The Social Interpretation of the French Revolution.* Cambridge: Cambridge University Press, 1964.

Collins, Irene. *The Government and the Newspaper Press in France, 1814–1881.* London: Oxford University Press, 1959.

Croce, Benedetto. *History of Europe in the Nineteenth Century.* New York: Harcourt, Brace & World, Inc., 1963.

Dehesdin, Maurice. *Etude sur le recrutement et l'avancement des magistrats.* Thèse pour le doctorat. Paris: Librairie nouvelle de droit et de jurisprudence, Arthur Rousseau, éditeur, 1908.

Desjoyeux, Claude-Noël. *La fusion monarchique, 1848–1873.* Paris: Plon, Nourrit, et Cie., 1913.

Doudeauville, Duc de. *Une politique française au dix-neuvième siècle.* Paris: Libraire ancienne Honoré Champion, 1927.

Dreux-Brézé, Marquis Henri-Scipion-Charles de. *Notes et souvenirs pour servir à l'histoire du parti royaliste, 1872–1883.* Paris: Imprimerie de J. Dumoulin, 1902.

Drouillet, Paul, Jean et Henri. *Histoire de Saint-Benin d'Azy.* Paris: Edition de la "Revue de Centre," 1937.

Drumont, Edouard. *La fin d'un monde. Etude psychologique et sociale.* Paris: Nouvelle librairie parisienne, Albert Savine, éditeur, 1899.

Dubreuil, Léon. *La vente des biens nationaux dans le département des Côtes-du-Nord (1790–1830).* Paris: Honoré Champion, éditeur, 1912.

Duroselle, J. B. *Les débuts du catholicisme social en France.* Paris: Presses Universitaires de France, 1951.

Duveau, Georges. *Les instituteurs.* Paris: Editions du Seuil, 1961.

———. *La vie ouvrière en France sous le Second Empire.* 5ᵉ edition. Paris: Gallimard, 1946.

Falloux, Alfred F. P., Cte de. *Mémoires d'un royaliste.* 2 vols. Paris: Perrin et Cie., 1888.

Favre, Jules. *Gouvernement de la Défense Nationale.* Paris: Plon Imprimeur-éditeur, 1871.

Friedmann, Georges, ed. *Villes et campagnes: Civilisation urbaine et civilisation rurale en France, deuxième semaine sociologique organisée par le Centre des Etudes Sociologiques du Centre National de la Recherche Scientifique.* Paris: Armand Colin, 1953.

Girardet, Raoul. *La société militaire dans la France contemporaine (1815–1939).* Paris: Plon, 1953.

Girard, Louis, ed. *Les élections de 1869,* Vol. XXI of Bibliothèque de la Révolution de 1848. Paris: Librairie Marcel Rivière et Cie., 1960.

Godechot, Jacques. *Les institutions de la France sous la Révolution et l'Empire.* Paris: Presses Universitaires de France, 1951.

Gouault, Jacques. *Comment la France est devenue républicaine.* Les élections générales et partielles à l'Assemblée nationale, 1870–1875. Paris: Librairie Armand Colin, 1954.

Halévy, Daniel. *La fin des notables.* Paris: Bernard Grasset, 1930.

———. *La république des ducs.* Paris: Bernard Grasset, 1938.

Hanotaux, Gabriel. *Histoire de la fondation de la Troisième République. Le Gouvernement de M. Thiers, 1870–1873. L'echec de la monarchie et la fondation de la république, 1873–1876.* 2 vols. Paris: Librairie Plon, 1925–1926.

Hébert, M. and Carnec, A. *La Loi Falloux et la liberté d'enseignement.* La Rochelle: Editions Rupella, 1953.

Hoffmann, Stanley *et al. In Search of France.* Cambridge, Mass.: Harvard University Press, 1965.

Hommage de Gazette de France à la mémoire du roi. Paris: Gazette de France, 1883.

Kent, Sherman. *Electoral Procedure Under Louis Philippe.* New Haven: Yale University Press, 1937.

La Gorce, Pierre de. *Histoire de la Seconde république française.* Paris: Librairie Plon, 1887.

Le Bras, Gabriel. *Etudes de sociologie religieuse.* Tome I. *Sociologie de la pratique religieuse dans les campagnes françaises.*

Tome II. *De la Morphologie à la typologie.* Paris: Presses Universitaires de France, 1955–1956.

Leenhardt, Albert. *Vieux hôtels montpelliérains.* Bellegarde: Imprimerie Sadag, 1935.

Le Play, Frédéric. *La réforme sociale en France.* 6ᵉ édition. 4 vols. Tours: Alfred Mame et fils, 1878.

Lhomme, Jean. *La grande bourgeoisie au pouvoir (1830–1880). Essai sur l'histoire sociale de la France.* Paris: Presses Universitaires de France, 1960.

L'Huillier, Fernard. *La lutte ouvrière à la fin du Second Empire.* Paris: Armand Colin, 1957.

Lichtheim, George. *Marxism, An Historical and Critical Study.* New York: Praeger, 1961.

Loth, Arthur. *L'echec de la restauration monarchique en 1873.* Paris: Perrin, 1910.

Lorwin, Val R. *The French Labor Movement.* Cambridge, Mass.: Harvard University Press, 1954.

Marx, Karl. *The Eighteenth Brumaire of Louis Bonaparte.* Moscow: Co-operative Publishing Society of Foreign Workers in the U.S.S.R., 1934.

Mason, Edward S. *The Paris Commune.* New York: Macmillan, 1930.

Monteilhet, J. *Les institutions militaires de la France (1814–1932).* 2ᵉ édition. Paris: Librairie Felix Alcan, 1932.

Montreuil, Jean. *Histoire du mouvement ouvrier en France des origines à nos jours.* Paris: Aubier, 1946.

Nakane, Chie. *Japanese Society.* London: Weidenfeld & Nicholson, 1970.

Niepce, Léopold. *La magistrature lyonnaise, 1771 à 1883.* Paris: Larose et Farcel, éditeurs, 1885.

Olivesi, Antoine. *La commune de 1871 à Marseille et ses origines.* Paris: Marcel Rivière et Cie., 1950.

Osgood, Samuel M. *French Royalism under the Third and Fourth Republics.* The Hague: Martinus Nijhoff, 1960.

Payne, Howard C. *The Police State of Louis Napoleon Bonaparte, 1851–1860.* Seattle, Wash.: University of Washington Press, 1966.

Pierre-Henry. *Histoire des préfets. Cent cinquante ans d'administration provinciale, 1800–1950.* Paris: Nouvelles éditions latines, 1950.

Ponsot, Pierre. *Les grèves de 1870 et la Commune de 1871 au Creusot*. Paris: Editions sociales, 1957.

Pradel de Lamase, Paul, Cte. de. *Légitimisme et papauté. La dernière presse légitimiste—le ralliement*. Souvenirs publiés et annotés par Martial de Pradel de Lamase. Paris: Mercure de France, 1942.

Proudhon, P. J. *General Idea of the Revolution in the Nineteenth Century*. Translated by John Beverly Robinson. London: Freedom Press, 1923.

Rémond, René. *La droite en France de 1815 à nos jours*. Paris: Aubier, 1954.

Robinet de Cléry. *Les deux fusions (1800–1873)*. Paris: Librairie Félix Guven, 1908.

Rousselet, Marcel. *La magistrature sous la monarchie de juillet*. Thèse principale pour le doctorat ès lettres. Paris: Librairie du Recueil Sirey, 1937.

Siegfried, André. *Tableau politique de la France de l'Ouest sous la troisième république*. Paris: A. Colin, 1913.

Smith, Henry Nash. *Virgin Land. The American West as Symbol and Myth*. Cambridge, Mass.: Harvard University Press, 1950.

Stendhal. *Lucien Leuwen*. 2 vols. Monaco: Editions du Rocher, 1945.

Thiers, Adolphe. *Mémoires of M. Thiers 1870–1873*. Translated by F. M. Atkinson. London: George Allen & Unwin, Ltd., 1915.

Thuillier, André. *Emile Martin*. Nevers: Chambre de Commerce et d'Industrie de Nevers et de la Nièvre, 1968.

Thuillier, Guy. *Georges Dufaud et les débuts du grand capitalisme dans la métallurgie en Nivernais au XIXe siècle*. Paris: S.E.V.P.E.N., 1959.

Tudesq, André-Jean. *Les grands notables en France*. 2 vols. Paris: Presses Universitaires de France, 1964.

Vallat, Xavier. *La croix, les lys, et la peine des hommes*. Paris: Editions des quatre fils Symon, 1960.

Varagnac, André. *Civilisation traditionnelle et genre de vie*. Paris: Editions Albin Michel, 1948.

Véran, G. *Les habiles. Appel à la raison publique*. Angers: Imprimerie-librairie Germain et Grassin, 1883.

Vitu, Auguste. *Guide financier, répertoire général des valeurs financières et industrielle cotées sur les bourses françaises et sur les principaux marchés de l'Europe, de l'Amérique, et des Indes*. Paris: L. Hachette, 1864.

Weber, Max. *From Max Weber: Essays in Sociology*. London: Oxford University Press, 1946.

Wehler, Hans-Ulrich, ed. *Moderne deutsche Sozialgeschichte*. Cologne: Kiepenheuer & Witsch, 1968.

Weill, Georges. *Histoire du parti républicain en France de 1814 à 1870*. Paris: Ancienne Librairie Germer Baillière et Cie., Felix Alcan, éditeur, 1900.

Zeldin, Theodore, *The Political System of Napoleon III*. London: Macmillan Co., Ltd., 1958.

Articles

Baratier, J. "Note sur la loi des associations." *Revue catholique des institutions et du droit*, II (1874), 195–196.

Bayaud, Pierre. "Pierre-Louis Tourasse, propagandiste républicain (1876–1881)." *Ministère de l'Education nationale. Comité des travaux historiques, Actes*, 1959, pp. 139–159.

Beaujouan, Guy and Lebée, Edmond. "La fondation du Crédit Industriel et Commercial." *Histoire des enterprises*, no. 6 (novembre 1960), 5–40.

Becarud, Jean. "La noblesse dans les chambres, 1815–1848." *Revue internationale d'histoire politique et constitutionelle, nouvelle série*, no. 11 (1953), 189–205.

Bouvier, Jean. "Aux origines du Crédit Lyonnais: Le Milieu économique et financier lyonnais au début des années 1860." *Histoire des enterprises*, no. 6 (novembre 1960), 41–77.

Calan, Comte de. "Le recrutement régional des partis politiques de 1789 à 1914. Un pays de gauche: La Champagne." *Revue des sciences politiques*, XXXVII (janvier à juin 1917), 243–264.

———. "Le recrutement régional des partis politiques de 1789 à 1914. Un pays de droite conservatrice: La Guyenne." *Revue des sciences politiques*, XXXVII (15 octobre 1917), 206–294.

Chaulnes, Gabriel de. "Etude d'économie sociale: La Femme de l'ouvrier." *Revue catholique des institutions et du droit*, II (1874), 100–103.

"Les Coalitions—procès-verbaux des séances des 5 et 23 avril 1872 de la Société d'économie charitable." *Le Contemporain —Revue d'économie chrétienne*, III (août 1872), 899–916.

"Conférence de M. Lahaussois—organisation de l'armée française," *Société internationale des études pratiques d'économie sociale*, IV (1875), 281–312, 313–352.

Crozat, J. "De la révolution dans la loi ou du retour de la barberie." *Revue catholique des institutions et du droit*, II (1874), 180–188.

Delaunay, Paul. "L'esprit public dans le département de la Sarthe pendant et après la guerre de 1870–1871." *Revue historique et archéologique du Maine*, XXIX (1949), 136–147.

Derruau-Boniol, S. "Le département de la Creuse, structure sociale et évolution politique." *Revue française de science politique*, VII (1957), 38–66.

Desportes, F. "L'enquête sur les classes laborieuses," *Le Contemporain—Revue d'économie chrétienne*, XXX, 3ᵉ série, III (avril 1872), 64–91.

Everat, Ed. "Examen sommaire de la nouvelle loi sur l'enseignement supérieur," *Revue catholique des institutions et du droit*, V (1875), 321–334.

"Examen de la situation morale et matérielle des ouvriers à Paris." *Société internationale des études pratiques d'économie sociale*, Séance du 9 mars 1872, IV (1850), 154–183.

Germiny, Cte. de. "La question des corporations ouvrières." *Revue catholique des institutions et du droit*, VI (1875), 34–53.

Hervé-Bazin. "Les trois écoles en économie politique," *Revue trimestrielle*, IV (15 octobre 1880), 835–864.

Hormel, M. "Comment les comités catholiques peuvent aider aux oeuvres catholiques de la famille ouvrière." *Revue des institutions et du droit*, IV (1874), 332–337.

Journal de l'agriculture. Nos. 102–350 (1871–1875). The *Journal de l'agriculture* published the *procès-verbaux* of the *Réunion libre des agriculteurs de l'Assemblée nationale*.

Kernaeret, Jude de. "La corporation des ouvriers chrétiens." *Revue catholique des institutions et du droit*, VI (1875), 80–83.

———. "La libéralisme." *Revue catholique des institutions et du droit*, II (1874). 197–207.

"Liste générale de membres de la société d'économie sociale." *Société internationale des études pratiques d'économie sociale*, IV (1875), 883–894.

Locke, Robert R. "A New Look at Conservative Preparations for the French Elections of 1871." *French Historical Studies*, V:3 (Spring 1968), 351–358.

———. "Drouillard, Benoist, et Cie." *Revue d'histoire de la sidérurgie*, VIII, no. 4 (1967), 277–299.

Melun, Vte. de. "Application de la mutualité à l'assistance dans les campagnes." *Le Contemporain—Revue d'économie chrétienne,* 3ᵉ série, VI (octobre 1873), 5–19.

———. "Supplément aux oeuvres et institutions religieuses et charitables de Paris." *Le Contemporain—Revue d'économie chrétienne,* 3ᵉ série, I (juillet-septembre 1870–1871), 123–124.

"Les migrants temporaires et la propagation des idées revolutionnaires en France au XIXᵉ siècle." *1848: Revue des révolutions contemporaines,* no. 188 (mai 1951), 6–18.

Perier, Enn. "L'Internationale." *Revue catholique des institutions et du droit,* I (1873), 124–134.

———. "La suppression des Conseils de préfecture serait-elle utile?" *Revue catholique des institutions et du droit,* II (1874), 360–370.

"Question de l'assistance publique dans les campagnes." *Le Contemporain—Revue d'économie chrétienne,* 3ᵉ série, V (mai 1873), 328–342.

"Question du service obligatoire." *Le Contemporain—Revue d'économie chrétienne,* 3ᵉ série, III (juin 1872), 499–524.

"Réflexions sur les lois projetées." *Revue catholique des institutions et du droit,* II (1874), 80–94.

"Revue des travaux de l'Assemblée nationale." *Revue catholique des institutions et du droit,* I (1873), 589–600, 655–665; II (1874), 59–68, 119–132, 157–161.

"Session de 1869: Liste générale des membres de la société d'économie sociale au 1ᵉʳ décembre 1869." *Société internationale des études pratiques d'économie sociale,* III (1872), 228–240.

"Société d'économie charitable—Enquête sur les associations syndicales. Séances des 5, 8 et 29 mars 1873." *Le Contemporain—Revue d'économie chrétienne,* 3ᵉ série, V (juillet 1873), 677–690; (août 1873), 880–894.

"Le suffrage universel, exposition de divers systèmes." *Revue catholique des institutions et du droit,* II (1874), 204–215.

Thuillier, Guy. "Pour une histoire bancaire régionale. En nivernais de 1800 à 1880," *Annales, économies, sociétés, civilisations,* Xᵉ année (octobre-decembre 1955), 494–512.

Touzaud, Daniel. "Les professions libérales et les abus de l'enseignement du droit," *La réforme sociale, organe de l'école de la paix sociale,* 3ᵉ année, VI (decembre 1883), 529–535.

Pamphlets

Boudon-Lashermes, A. *Les origines de l'industrie de la dentelle et de la soie en Vélay et en Forez.* Le Puy-en-Velay: Editions de la Terre Villave et Brivadoise, 1930.

Chambord, le Cte. de. *Lettre de M. le Comte de Chambord sur les ouvriers, 20 avril 1865.* Montpellier: Typographie de Pierre Grollier, 1871.

Eyssautier, L. A. *Réforme de la magistrature et de la procédure.* Lyons: Imprimerie J. Rossier, 1871.

Genique, Gaston. *L'election de l'Assemblée législative en 1849. Essai d'une répartition géographique des partis politiques en France.* Paris: F. Riedec et Cie., 1921.

Jouin, Henri. *L'Assemblée nationale et les ouvriers.* Angers: Imprimerie de Laene frères, 1872.

————. *Le livre et l'ouvrier.* Paris: E. Lachaud, Libraire-éditeur, 1873.

Picot, Georges. *La magistrature et la démocratie. Une épuration radicale.* Paris: Librairie nouvelle, 1884.

Schram, Stuart R. *Traditions religieuses et réalitées politiques dans le département du Gard.* Alençon: Imprimerie Corbière et Jugain, 1953.

INDEX

Abbadie de Barrau, Bernard d', 57, 61n, 234
L'Abeille de la Creuse, 241
Aboville, Auguste d', 124, 172n, 257: opinions on dechristianization in the countryside, 172; education and peasantry, 163; landlord absenteeism and bureaucracy, 161
absenteeism, 161, 241–242
Aciers de la Marine, 115
Adam, Edmond, 130
agribusiness, 110–111, 122–123, 126
agricultural education, 168, 215
agricultural reforms, 194
Agricultural Society of France, 125
Ancel, Jules, 130
Anjou, peasantry in, 153
L'Appel au peuple, 239
appel au peuple, 174: legitimists view of, 237
Arago, Emmanuel, 211
Argout, Vicomte d', 79
aristocracy, 58, 62, 63: and legitimists, 56ff, 70ff; and liberalism, 71; life style of, 63
aristocrats: contempt for bourgeois, 265
armée de caserne, 162, 198–199, 200, 210, 211
army: socially harmful aspects of, 160–162, 163; reform of, 198–200, 210–211
army reserve, 160, 161
associations syndicales, 194, 195
Assurances Maritimes, 130, 131
Assurances Maritimes du Havre, 130
Aubry, Maurice, 68n, 75, 146: as industrial pioneer, 115, 117, 120;

business career of, 77, 114–115, 131, 132; opinions on Orleanists, 34; paternalism, 188; putting-out-system, 186
Audiffret-Pasquier, Duc d', 71, 129
Audren de Kerdrel, Vincent d', 64, 233, 260: opinion on army reform, 199
Augé-Laribé, Michel, 123
Aurelle de Paladines, Louis d', 61, 87
L'Avenir du Morbihan, 259
Avignon-Marseilles, 109

Bagneux, Louis de, 88n
Bakuninites, 12
Balzac, Honoré de, 180
Banque d'Emission et de Placement, 130
Banque de France, 79
Baragnon, Louis-Numa, 90, 233, 254: electioneering in 1870, 22; opinion on religion and moral order, 143
Barthe, Marcel, 209
Barante, Prosper de, 24n, 130, 260
Barascud, Antoine, 254
Bastard, Octave de, 260
Bastard, Vicomte de, 32
Le Bas-Vivrais, 246
Batbie, Anselm, 128
Baucarne-Leroux, Louis, 101, 125
Baudry d'Osson, 254
Bazaine, Marshal, 14
Beau de Lomenie, Emmanuel, 42, 203
Belcastel, Gabriel de, 31, 57, 79, 125, 260: opinions on decadence, 151; legitimism, 35; suffrage, 203

311

Library of Congress Cataloging in Publication Data

Locke, Robert R.   1932-
   French legitimists and the politics of moral order in the
early Third Republic.

   Bibliography: p.
   1. France—Politics and government—1870-1940.
2. Right and left (Political science)   I. Title.
DC340.L6   320.9'44'081   73-17404
ISBN 0-691-05215-8